EMOTIONAL DEVELOPMENT AND EMOTIONAL INTELLIGENCE

EMOTIONAL DEVELOPMENT AND EMOTIONAL INTELLIGENCE

Educational Implications

EDITED BY

PETER SALOVEY

AND

DAVID J. SLUYTER

BasicBooks
A Division of HarperCollins*Publishers*

Library of Congress Cataloging-in-Publication Data

Emotional development and emotional intelligence : educational implications / edited by Peter Salovey, David J. Sluyter ; with a foreword by Daniel Goleman. —1st ed.
    p. cm.
Includes bibliographical references and index.
ISBN 0-465-09587-9
1. Emotions and cognition. 2. Emotions in children. 3. Emotional maturity. 4. Child development. 5. Affective education.
I. Salovey, Peter. II. Sluyter, David J.
LB1073.E46   1997
370.153—dc21   96-45053
                                          CIP

97 98 99 00 ❖/RRD 9 8 7 6 5 4 3 2

CONTENTS

PART II: SOCIAL AND EMOTIONAL COMPETENCIES

PART III: APPLICATIONS

CONTRIBUTORS

Chapter

Authors	**Educators**

Foreword
Daniel Goleman
30 South Street
Williamsburg, MA 01096

1.	John D. Mayer Department of Psychology Conant Hall University of New Hampshire Durham, NH 03824	Karol DeFalco Social Development Department New Haven Public Schools 480 Sherman Parkway New Haven, CT 06511
	Peter Salovey Department of Psychology Yale University P.O. Box 208205 New Haven, CT 06520–8205	
2.	Carolyn Saarni Department of Counseling Sonoma State University 220 Nichols Hall Rohnert Park, CA 94928	Marianne Novak Houston Vicksburg Middle School 348 East Prairie Vicksburg, MI 49097
3.	Thomas Hatch Harvard Project Zero Longfellow Hall, Appian Way Cambridge, MA 02138	Linda Lantieri RCCP National Center 163 Third Avenue #103 New York, NY 10003
4.	Mark T. Greenberg Jennie L. Snell Department of Psychology, NI–25 University of Washington 146 North Canal St., Suite 111 Seattle, WA 98103	Jo-An Vargo Redwood Day School 3245 Sheffield Avenue Oakland, CA 94602

Chapter

Authors	Educators

5. Nancy Eisenberg
    Department of Psychology
    Arizona State University
    Box 871104
    Tempe, AZ 85287–1104

    Richard A. Fabes
    Family Resources and
        Human Development
    Arizona State University
    Box 872502
    Tempe, AZ 85287–2502

    Sandra Losoya
    Department of Psychology
    Arizona State University
    Box 871104
    Tempe, AZ 85287–1104

Rebecca Nellum-Williams
Sanders Corner Elementary
    School
43100 Ashburn Farm Parkway
Ashburn, VA 20147

6. Eliot M. Brenner
    Lakeside Counseling Center
    9008 Indianapolis Blvd.
    Highland, IN 46322

    Peter Salovey
    Department of Psychology
    Yale University
    P.O. Box 208205
    New Haven, CT 06520–8205

Patricia Moore Harbour
712 Staunton Ave. NW
Roanoke, VA 24016

Jill Stewart
Kellogg Community College
Grahl Center
125 Seeley Street
Coldwater, MI 49036

7. Steven R. Asher
    Department of Educational
        Psychology
    University of Illinois at
        Urbana-Champaign
    1310 S. Sixth Street
    Champaign, Il 61820

    Amanda J. Rose
    Department of Psychology
    University of Illinois
        at Urbana-Champaign
    603 East Daniel Street
    Champaign, IL 61820

Robert (Chip) Wood
Northeast Foundation
    for Children
71 Montague City Road
Greenfield, MA 01301

Chapter

Authors

Educators

8. Jeannette Haviland-Jones
   Department of Psychology
   Tillett Hall—Livingston Campus
   Rutgers University
   New Brunswick, NJ 08903

   Marianne Novak Houston
   Vicksburg Middle School
   348 East Prairie
   Vicksburg, MI 49097

   Janet L. Gebelt
   Center for Social and Community
      Development
   Building 4161 Section 200
   Livingston Campus
   Rutgers University
   Piscataway, NJ 08855

   Janice C. Stapley
   Department of Psychology
   Monmouth University
   Long Branch, NJ 07764

9. Joseph E. Zins
   University of Cincinnati
   339 Teachers College
   Cincinnati, OH 45221

   Mickey Kavanagh
   Social Development Department
   New Haven Public Schools
   480 Sherman Parkway
   New Haven, CT 06511

   Lawrence F. Travis III
   Division of Criminal Justice
   University of Cincinnati
   P.O. Box 210389
   Cincinnati, OH 45221–0389

   Penny A. Freppon
   The Literacy Program
   Division of Teacher Education
   College of Education
   University of Cincinnati
   P.O.Box 210002
   Cincinnati, OH 45221–0002

A Note from the Editors

IN RECENT YEARS, innovative private and public schools have developed programs in what has been termed variously *emotional literacy, emotional intelligence, social development,* or *social competence.* These classes teach children about their feelings, how to manage them, and how to get along with each other. The curricula vary considerably in content and may be either didactic or experiential, focusing on self-understanding, conflict resolution, social problem solving, decision making, or the emotions themselves. Many of these programs have achieved national prominence; the few that have been evaluated scientifically show promising results.

Until recently, there has been little contact between educators developing programs dealing with emotions and investigators, principally developmental, personality, and social psychologists studying human emotions, their neurological underpinnings, and emotional development. Under the auspices of the Fetzer Institute in Kalamazoo, Michigan, and The Collaborative for the Advancement of Social and Emotional Learning, originally located at the Yale Child Study Center in New Haven, Connecticut, groups of educators and researchers have come together over the past several years to discuss this fascinating application of our understanding of human emotion. The motivation for this volume came from these discussions: Could a book be created that presented cutting-edge research on emotions and emotional development in a manner useful to educators, not just those developing programs but to anyone else who needs to understand the unfolding of emotions throughout childhood? In response to this challenge, we present this volume in which researchers describe the scientific basis for our knowledge about emotion, with each chapter followed by a short commentary from an educator who elaborates on how these advances can be used in practical applications with children.

We thank, first, the Fetzer Institute, which provided the funding to bring together groups of scientists and educators interested in the emotions at a beautiful setting fostering mutual understanding and a cooperative spirit.

A Note from the Editors*A Note from the Editors*

Some of these conferences were deftly organized by Daniel Goleman, who graciously provided a foreword to this volume. Peter Salovey also acknowledges the support of the American Cancer Society, the Andrew W. Mellon Foundation, and the National Science Foundation, which facilitated the preparation of this volume. We are grateful as well for the administrative support of Janet Zullo and Roberta Mouheb and for the enthusiasm and encouragement of our editors at Basic Books, Jo Ann Miller, Eric Wright, Juliana Nocker, and Michael Wilde.

Peter Salovey
New Haven, CT

David J. Sluyter
Kalamazoo, MI

March 1997

Emotional Intelligence in Context

DANIEL GOLEMAN

SO OFTEN IN THE EARLY STAGES of social innovations individual pioneers labor alone, not realizing that their creative work is part of a larger fabric. This volume represents the fruition of several such separate lines of development, both in theory and in practice, that have only recently come together in a rich convergence. The fields woven together here are as diverse as neuroscience and child development, intelligence theory and practical pedagogy. Their cross-pollination in this volume offers fresh answers to the perennial question, What do children need to learn in order to flourish in life?

One set of answers to that question has as its background the urgent mission of stemming the rising tide of perils children increasingly face in their adolescent years and beyond: substance abuse, violence, unwanted pregnancy, dropout, teen smoking, depression, and the like. Over the last decade an important new strategy in primary prevention has emerged that uses the schools to help children better master the social and emotional competencies that can inoculate them against these dangers. As is so often the case in educational innovation, the origins of this approach were at first a bit haphazard, taking the form of ad hoc programming for schools, typically focused on targeting a specific hazard, such as preventing drug abuse or violence. Some worked and others did not; a few even made things worse.

A consortium sponsored by the W. T. Grant Foundation did a methodical survey of this landscape and distilled the active ingredients that seemed crucial to the success of those programs that worked.[1] Among the hallmarks of the better programs—apart from elements like integrating the lessons into the culture and curricula of schools, and teaching them in a developmentally appropriate way over a sustained number of years—were inculcating a list of key skills. These include emotional and social competencies like self-awareness of and managing feelings, impulse control, empathy and perspective-taking, cooperation, and settling disputes. These are among the abilities that help children resist the pulls toward dangers like substance abuse, pregnancy, and violence.

In the last 5 to 10 years, school-based programs that seek to inculcate these competencies have begun to spread across the country. Some call it an "emotional literacy" movement, but the programs go under a variety of names: "social development," "life skills," "self-science," "social competency," and "resolving conflict creatively" among them. The Collaborative for Social and Emotional Learning, begun at the Yale Child Studies Center, in New Haven, Connecticut, has served to help school districts find quality programming in this area. The Nueva School in Hillsborough, California, was the first to start such a program, and New Haven was the first city to implement such a program in public schools districtwide. Now, as I write, more than 700 school districts across America have expressed an interest in implementing the emotional literacy approach, including cities like Milwaukee, Los Angeles, San Antonio, and San Juan, Puerto Rico.

This practical approach has found its organizing framework in a completely separate line of development that was purely theoretical: the recognition that there are kinds of intelligence other than the purely cognitive. With a long, though fitful, history in theories of intelligence, this notion gained steam in 1983 with Howard Gardner's influential model of multiple intelligence, which added to the standard academic spectrum of analytic reasoning, verbal abilities, and the like some unorthodox varieties, including musical and movement, and two "personal" intelligences—intrapersonal and interpersonal.[2] The nature of social intelligence and its development in children has been explored by Gardner's associate, Thomas Hatch.

But Gardner's description of the personal intelligences was sparse in detailing the role of the emotions. The seminal theory that connects the emotions to intelligence was put forward by Yale psychologist Peter Salovey, coeditor of this volume, and his colleague John D. Mayer, now at the University of New Hampshire. Their model is an elegant summation

---

[1] W. T. Grant Consortium on the School-based Promotion of Social Competence. (1992). Drug and alcohol prevention curricula. In J. David Hawkins et al., *Communities that care*. San Francisco: Jossey-Bass.

[2] Howard Gardner. (1993). *Multiple intelligences: The theory in practice*. New York: Basic Books.

of what it means to be intelligent about one's emotional life and relationships. As a theoretical framework, it has had an electrifying effect, for example, among many who are dedicated to primary prevention and the emotional literacy movement, offering a guiding principle for emotional and social competencies that on-the-ground experience had shown was of critical importance.

The concept of emotional intelligence has also proven itself a catalyst to the thinking and planning of educators, foundation officers, and policy makers. It offers a unified way of looking at what had been seen as only loosely related efforts in primary prevention. For example, under this banner, policy makers in one state are seeking to use school-based programs to unify primary prevention efforts in crime, mental health, public health, even with the unemployed—all efforts that had previously been fragmented. The emotional intelligence competencies are to a greater or lesser extent at cause in problems in all these areas, and to the degree that these skills can be bolstered, they offer a way to lower the risk of problems like family violence or chronic unemployability. Business, too, is seeing practical value in the emotional intelligence idea, which offers a way to think about a key range of skills that make people not just employable but that distinguish highly effective performers from mediocre ones.

A third major strand comes from research on child development, a field like others in psychology that has been relatively late in coming to a systematic consideration of the role of emotions. The most influential early developmental psychologists, like Piaget, focused on cognitive development, setting that field's early research agenda. But in recent years child development research has expanded its scope to study the unfolding of children's social and emotional lives. The result has been a new understanding of what, for example, makes a child socially adept or better able to regulate emotional distress. This new strata of scientific understanding can be of immense help in informing the practical efforts of the emotional literacy movement.

Neuroscience feeds still another stream of growing knowledge about the development of emotional and social competence. The brain is the last organ of the body to become fully mature anatomically, continuing to grow and shape itself throughout childhood into adolescence. In this continued anatomical development the circuits that regulate emotional competence appear to be among the last parts of the brain to reach full maturity. The brain is remarkably plastic, shaping itself through repeated experiences that strengthen one set of neural circuitry rather than another. These facts of neuroanatomy suggest that childhood offers a remarkable window of opportunity to give children the repeated experiences that will help them develop healthy emotional habits—for self-awareness and self-regulation, for empathy and social skill.

All of these fields have had rich harvests. But this is the first volume to attempt an integration that will help those who labor at the front lines of education, trying to help children master these essential life skills. Too often researchers in the academy yield findings that are shared only within their own field but would be of extreme interest to teachers. This volume represents a concerted effort to build bridges between those fields, as well as between theory and practice. As a harbinger of a new alliance between research and teaching this book offers an integration of lasting significance—and hope—for the future.

PART I

General Principles

CHAPTER 1

What Is Emotional Intelligence?

JOHN D. MAYER AND
PETER SALOVEY

INTRODUCTION

A FOURTH-GRADE BOY was shivering on a school playground when a teacher asked him if he owned a warmer coat. He replied he did not (and his friend agreed). That afternoon, the teacher and the school nurse called the boy's home and offered to buy him a new coat. The boy's mother was delighted, and so the next morning, they outfitted the boy. Two boys noticed the child's new coat at recess and accused him of stealing it. When the boy denied it, the accusers launched such a venomous attack that none of the other children dared to defend the boy. Teachers and staff arrived and began to break up the confrontation. One of the accusers yelled "suck eggs" at the school nurse. "You suck eggs!" she replied. The teacher who had bought the coat was disturbed that her gift had caused such pain. The school nurse wondered how she could have said "suck eggs" to a child. The teacher whose class contained the troublemakers wondered how her boys could have acted that way. The staff members discussed what had happened and tried to determine what to do next.[1]

Reasoning about this situation requires sophisticated problem solving: What social rules were followed or broken? What perceptions were logical or illogical? Does community support exist for disciplining the children?

3

How can such problems be avoided in the future? Implicit in each of these questions is also the need for information about feelings. Why were the accusers so angry? What can be done about the nurse's guilt? A feeling-blind response to the situation is possible: An administrator could declare that henceforth teachers should not give gifts to students. Such a response radically de-emphasizes feelings, however, in that it punishes those who care and would embarrass the boy who received the coat. Alternative courses of action deal better with the feelings intrinsic to this situation. Reasoning that takes emotions into account is part of what we have referred to as *emotional intelligence*.

The concept of emotional intelligence has recently received considerable attention in various books, magazines, and journals.[2] Each new discussion of the concept, however, seems to employ a different definition or make a different claim for its importance. This interest has prompted us to clarify further the concept of emotional intelligence. In the remainder of this chapter we discuss: the general scope and origin of emotional intelligence; the development of the concept of emotional intelligence; a revised definition and conceptualization of emotional intelligence; the assessment of emotional intelligence; and applications of emotional intelligence in the schools and beyond.

THE GENERAL SCOPE AND ORIGIN OF EMOTIONAL INTELLIGENCE

Understanding the concept of emotional intelligence requires exploring its two component terms, *intelligence* and *emotion*. Since the eighteenth century, psychologists have recognized an influential three-part division of the mind into cognition (or thought), affect (including emotion), and motivation (or conation).[3] The cognitive sphere includes such functions as human memory, reasoning, judgment, and abstract thought. Intelligence is typically used by psychologists (and those who came before) to characterize how well the cognitive sphere functions. That is, intelligence pertains to abilities such as the "power to combine and separate" concepts, to judge and to reason, and to engage in abstract thought.[4,5]

Emotions belong to the second, so-called affective sphere of mental functioning, which includes the emotions themselves, moods, evaluations, and other feeling states, including fatigue or energy. Definitions of *emotional intelligence* should in some way connect emotions with intelligence if the meanings of the two terms are to be preserved. Recall that motivation is a third sphere of personality. It refers to biological urges or learned goal-seeking behavior. To the extent that it is involved in emotional intelligence, it should be thought of as secondary.

Not everything that connects cognition to emotion, however, is emotional intelligence. Over the past 15 years or so, a great deal of study has been devoted to the mutual interaction of feelings and thought. This general area of research is called *cognition and affect.* Emotion is known to alter thinking in many ways—but not necessarily in ways that would make a person smarter. For example, research indicates that moods generally bias people's thoughts: People in good moods think they are healthier than others, that the economy is improving, and that Paris is a better example of a city than Calcutta. People in bad moods tend to think they are sicker than others, that the economy is getting worse, and that Calcutta exemplifies the present-day urban condition fairly accurately.[6] This mood-biasing effect, termed mood-congruent judgment, occurs when "an affective match between a person's moods and ideas increases the judged merit, broadly defined, of those ideas."[7] Note that with mood-congruent judgment, mood and cognition interact without anyone being more or less smart. The field of cognition and affect also includes studies of emotional self-control, such as when a person buries her anger. Note that this doesn't necessarily improve the quality of the person's emotions or intelligence. It may be smart to be angry at times.

Emotional intelligence, as opposed to more general research, should in some way refer to heightened emotional or mental abilities. Although this criterion seems straightforward, some definitions of emotional intelligence don't really adhere to it. For example, one popular definition of emotional intelligence says it involves "self-control, zeal and persistence, and the ability to motivate oneself."[8] This definition focuses on motivational characteristics such as zeal and persistence rather than on emotion. The concept of a motivational intelligence has been proposed to incorporate such alternative definitions.[9]

A slightly abbreviated version of the definition of emotional intelligence that we prefer is: "the ability to perceive emotions, to access and generate emotions so as to assist thought, to understand emotions and emotional knowledge, and to reflectively regulate emotions so as to promote emotional and intellectual growth." This definition combines the ideas that emotion makes thinking more intelligent and that one thinks intelligently about emotions. Both connect intelligence and emotion.

THE DEVELOPMENT OF THE CONCEPT OF EMOTIONAL INTELLIGENCE

Initial Work Relating Emotional Intelligence to Intelligence

The logic for identifying an intelligence within psychology is: (a) to define it, (b) to develop a means for measuring it, (c) to document its partial or complete independence from known intelligences, and (d) to demonstrate that it predicts some real-world criteria. Very simply, one might define a "vocabulary" intelligence, measure it with a vocabulary test, show that vocabulary intelligence is different from previously discovered intelligences, and demonstrate that it predicts success at, say, studying literature.

Each of these four steps is necessary. Because a great deal of research on intelligences exists, one of the most important steps in this series involves demonstrating that a new intelligence is different from those already known. Knowledge of vocabulary, for example, is typically indistinguishable from the already established verbal intelligence (to be discussed shortly).

Two intelligences are said to be the same if they are highly correlated with one another. A high correlation between two variables means that the two tend to rise and fall together. For example, the lengths of a person's right arm and left arm are highly correlated: some people have long right and left arms; some people have short right and left arms; and greatly dissimilar arms in the same person are unusual. Similarly, two intelligences are correlated if the intelligence levels correspond within each person: that is, both intelligences are high in person A, low in person B, medium in person C, and so forth. A complete lack of correlation would mean that one intelligence would tell you nothing about the level of the other. Most intelligences are moderately correlated with one another. That is, in a given individual, the intelligences will tend to operate at levels that are closer together than one would expect by chance. The correlation among intelligences is only moderate, as opposed to high (as in the arm length example), which allows for a moderate amount of difference among intelligences in the same person. This agrees with everyday experience, because we know people who are good at some mental tasks but less good at others.[10]

If two intelligences correlate highly then they are considered to represent the same intelligence. For example, vocabulary size and reading ability closely coincide in most people and as a consequence are usually considered part of one broader intelligence (in this case, *verbal-propositional* intelligence). Analogously, rather than discuss a person's right arm length and left arm length, one could refer simply to arm length. Ideally, a new intelligence should be low-to-moderately correlated with earlier intelligences. A low–moderate correlation (as opposed to a high one) means that the new intelligence is distinct from old ones and will tell you something new about a person; if it correlated too highly with the original intelligence, one might be overfishing the same water. At the same time, a low-to-moderate correlation is preferable to a nonexistent correlation; no correlation at all could suggest the new "intelligence" is so different that it is not an intelligence at all.

The idea of testing whether intelligences correlate (move up and down together) is the standard way of determining whether an intelligence exists; this method has been employed throughout the century.[11] A few alternative methods for establishing intelligence have been employed, and it is worth mentioning these before returning to the more influential correlational approach. Some people have tried to establish the existence of intelligence primarily through theoretical analysis. J. P. Guilford and R. Hoepfner proposed that 120 intelligences existed, on the basis that there were roughly that number of combinations of basic mental processes. For example, they considered "memory for single words" as one such intelligence because it combined processes of memory, word recognition, and analyses of single units (i.e., words)—each of which they considered to be a discrete process. This potentially useful model lost favor because it was difficult to test with the correlational method (one problem was there were just too many intelligences to track).[12] More recently, Howard Gardner developed his elegant theory of multiple intelligences, including linguistic, musical, bodily kinesthetic, and personal intelligences (one of which resembles emotional intelligence). Gardner argues that his intelligences exist on the basis of their cultural significance and their correspondence to human brain structures. He avoids the correlational approach: Although he admits its utility for studying observed, expressed abilities, he notes that it provides only an indirect measure of internal brain processes. This is true, but so little is known about brain structure that Gardner's own conception has only modest support beyond its original formulation.[13]

The exceptions of Guilford, Gardner, and some others aside, the twentieth century has relied on the correlational approach to identifying intelligences.[14] In fact, researchers have developed measures for as many intelligences as they could imagine, and there has been a free-for-all examination of different intelligences and their interrelations throughout the century. In the 1930s, Thurstone suggested the existence of about a dozen intelligences, including verbal comprehension, word fluency, associative memory, and perceptual speed.[15] Later in the century, the Educational Testing Service published a reference kit that measured dozens of cognitive intelligences.[16] Careful examination of the intelligences suggests that although there is an overall moderate correlation among them, some intelligences are more independent of one another than others. One empirically supportable idea earlier in the century was that the intelligences seemed to divide into two or three subgroups. The first of these is a verbal-propositional intelligence, which includes measures of vocabulary, verbal fluency, and the ability to perceive similarities and to think logically. The second of these is a spatial-performance intelligence, which includes abilities of assembling objects and recognizing and constructing designs and patterns. The third, more controversial intelligence, social intelligence, is concerned with people's skills in relating to one another.

Historically, there were serious difficulties in developing the concept of social intelligence because it seemed so highly correlated with the first two intelligences as to be indistinguishable from them. That is, people's reasoning about social situations rises and falls so closely with their verbal-propositional and spatial-performance skills that the justification for treating social reasoning as a separate intelligence seemed uncertain. So, there appeared to be little need for studying this third, more purely social, variety of intelligence.[17] The major midcentury intelligence test, Wechsler's intelligence scales, measured only the verbal-propositional and spatial-performance portions of general intelligence. Although both the verbal and performance measures included social reasoning, social intelligence was not measured as a distinct entity.

At the outset of our work, we thought that it might make sense to exchange emotional for social intelligence in this proposed triumvirate of intelligences. Emotional intelligence would combine a group of skills that were more distinct from both verbal-propositional and spatial-performance intelligence than social intelligence had been and at the same time would still be close enough to the concept of an intelligence to belong to the triad. We therefore expected emotional reasoning to be correlated with but distinct from other intelligences; the evidence to date supports this position (as we will describe in the section on measuring emotional intelligence).

One final issue was important to defining emotional intelligence: It had to be distinguished from traits and talents. Traits can be defined as characteristic or preferred ways of behaving (e.g., extroversion, shyness); talents as nonintellectual abilities (e.g., skill at sports). Certain recently proposed intelligences seemed more like valued traits or talents than legitimate intelligences. Scarr has written:

> There are many human virtues that are not sufficiently rewarded in our society, such as goodness in human relationships. . . . To call them intelligence does not do justice either to theories of intelligence or to the personality traits and special talents that lie beyond the consensual definition of intelligence.[18]

We editorialized in the journal *Intelligence* that emotional intelligence could be considered an actual intelligence as opposed to, say, a highly valued social trait.[19] Scarr's "goodness in human relationships" might indeed be composed of the traits of sociability, trustworthiness, and warmth. But in addition there might exist actual abilities, such as knowing what another person is feeling, that may involve considerable thinking and consequently could be considered an intelligence. In this way, we distinguished a mental skill that could legitimately be called emotional intelligence (e.g., being able to figure out one's own and others' emotions) from preferred ways of behaving (e.g., being sociable or warm).

Initial Work Relating Emotional Intelligence to the Emotions

The conceptual development of emotional intelligence required relating it not only to intelligence research but also to research on emotion. We began with the observation that emotion and intelligence have often been seen as adversaries, with emotions viewed as an intrinsically irrational and disruptive force.[20] For example, the idea that the mind is "hijacked" by intense emotional experiences—although true in some instances—emphasizes how emotions disrupt thought. In many instances, however, extreme emotional reactions promote intelligence by interrupting ongoing processing and directing attention toward what may be important. In this sense they prioritize cognition.[21] We view emotions of all sorts as potentially contributing to thought rather than disorganizing it.

Our concept of emotional intelligence is primarily focused on the complex, potentially intelligent tapestry of emotional reasoning in everyday life. For most healthy individuals, we assume that emotions convey knowledge about a person's relationships with the world.[22] For example, fear indicates that the person is facing a relatively powerful or uncontrollable threat. Happiness typically indicates one's harmonious relations with others, and anger often reflects a feeling of injustice. According to this view, there are certain generalities and laws of emotions. These general rules and laws can be employed in recognizing and reasoning with feelings. For example, certain universals of emotional expression exist and people should be able to recognize them.[23] Emotional reasoning therefore extends into questions about relationships. For example, an insulted person might feel anger, or if the person was insecure and nonassertive, might feel shame, humiliation—or repressed anger. Recognizing these reactions requires some form of intelligence.

What we are getting at is that emotional intelligence requires at least some "right" answers as to feelings. Of course, some questions about emotions don't have right answers. For example, the question "What is the best emotional response to shouting?" has no answer. If one's parents plainly loved each other but often shouted at one another, then one may grow up comfortable with shouting. If one's parents first yelled at one another on the day they decided to get a divorce, one may be uncomfortable with it. To the first person, shouting reflects frustration in the context of a loving relationship. To the second person, shouting represents adult hatreds. So, no right response exists. An answer to the question can be given, however, if more information is provided (e.g., if we know something about the person's individual learning history). We also recognize the need to consider culture and subculture. For example, individuals in warmer climates are described and describe themselves as more emotionally demonstrative than those in colder climates.[24]

Examining more complex manifestations of emotional intelligence (beyond that of the simple identification of emotion) often requires understanding the individual's own cultural framework. Only by knowing the person's standards can certain "emotional reactions and models . . . be assessed according to their logical consistency, and hence, their intelligence."[25]

A REVISED DEFINITION AND CONCEPTUALIZATION OF EMOTIONAL INTELLIGENCE

In our earlier work we defined emotional intelligence according to the abilities involved in it. One of our first definitions of emotional intelligence was "the ability to monitor one's own and others' feelings and emotions, to discriminate among them, and to use this information to guide one's thinking and action."[26] But this and other earlier definitions now seem vague in places and impoverished in the sense that they talk only about perceiving and regulating emotion, and omit thinking about feelings. A revision that corrects these problems is as follows:

> Emotional intelligence involves the ability to perceive accurately, appraise, and express emotion; the ability to access and/or generate feelings when they facilitate thought; the ability to understand emotion and emotional knowledge; and the ability to regulate emotions to promote emotional and intellectual growth.

We have diagrammed these skills in Figure 1.1. The four branches of the diagram are arranged from more basic psychological processes to higher, more psychologically integrated processes. For example, the lowest level branch concerns the (relatively) simple abilities of perceiving and expressing emotion. In contrast, the highest level branch concerns the conscious, reflective regulation of emotion. Each branch has four representative abilities on it (in boxes). Abilities that emerge relatively early in development are to the left of a given branch; later developing abilities to the right. Because the developmentally early skills (to the left) are usually poorly integrated with one another, they most clearly illustrate the distinctions among branches. Later developing abilities (to the right) emerge within a more integrated adult personality and are consequently less distinct. Each ability applies to emotions internally and in others except where otherwise noted. People high in emotional intelligence are expected to progress more quickly through the abilities designated and to master more of them. In the following discussion we will examine each branch in turn, including the boxed abilities from left to right, referring to them as Boxes 1 through 4, respectively.

Perception, Appraisal, and Expression of Emotion

Figure 1.1's lowest branch concerns the accuracy with which individuals can identify emotions and emotional content. Infants and young children learn to identify their own and other's emotional states and to differentiate among those states. The infant distinguishes emotional facial expressions early on and responds to the parent's expressions. As she grows she will more accurately identify her own muscular and bodily sensations and social surroundings (Branch 1, Box 1). A mature individual can carefully monitor internal feelings. If we ask a grown person who

FIGURE 1.1

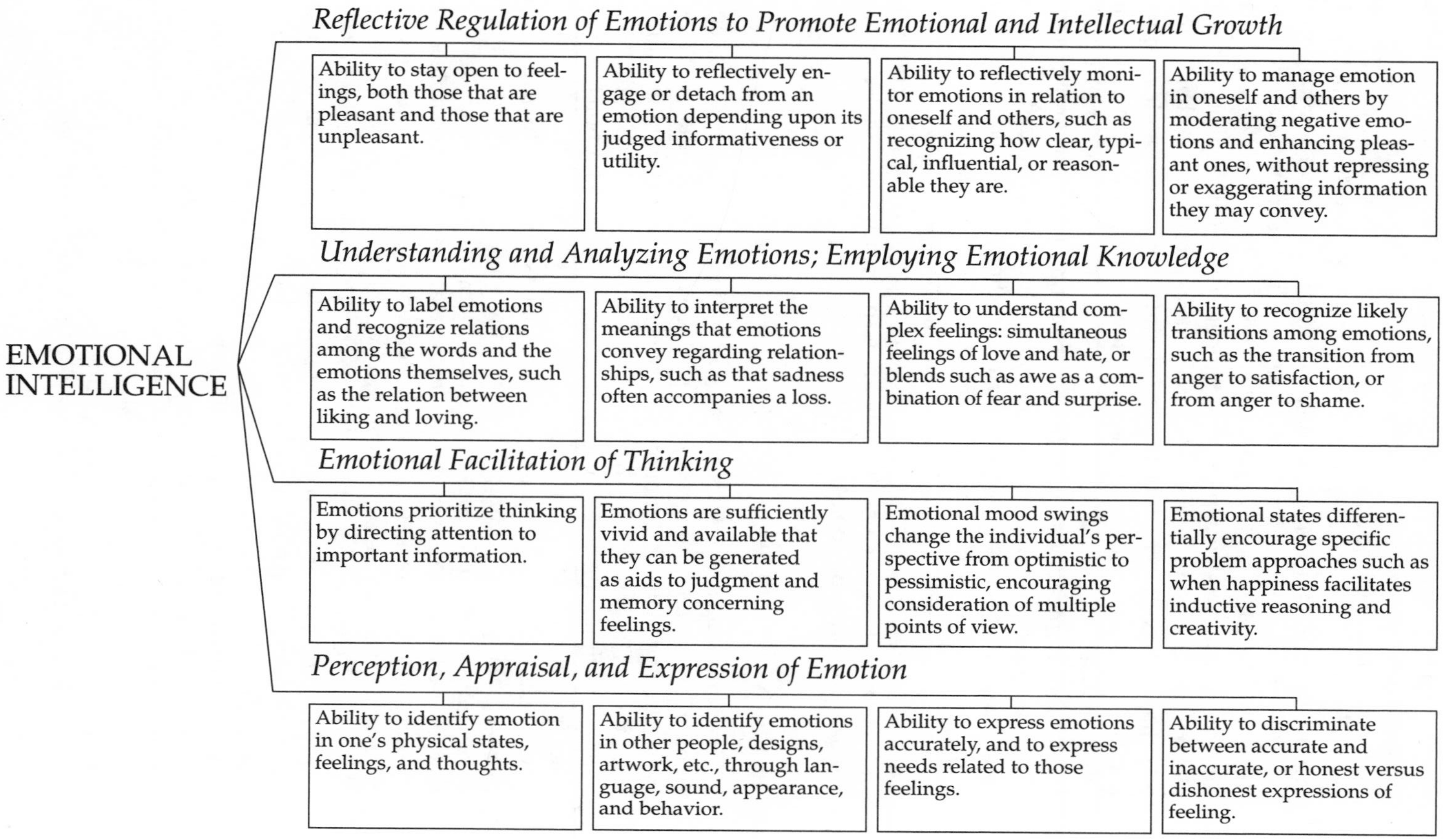

EMOTIONAL INTELLIGENCE

Reflective Regulation of Emotions to Promote Emotional and Intellectual Growth

- Ability to stay open to feelings, both those that are pleasant and those that are unpleasant.
- Ability to reflectively engage or detach from an emotion depending upon its judged informativeness or utility.
- Ability to reflectively monitor emotions in relation to oneself and others, such as recognizing how clear, typical, influential, or reasonable they are.
- Ability to manage emotion in oneself and others by moderating negative emotions and enhancing pleasant ones, without repressing or exaggerating information they may convey.

Understanding and Analyzing Emotions; Employing Emotional Knowledge

- Ability to label emotions and recognize relations among the words and the emotions themselves, such as the relation between liking and loving.
- Ability to interpret the meanings that emotions convey regarding relationships, such as that sadness often accompanies a loss.
- Ability to understand complex feelings: simultaneous feelings of love and hate, or blends such as awe as a combination of fear and surprise.
- Ability to recognize likely transitions among emotions, such as the transition from anger to satisfaction, or from anger to shame.

Emotional Facilitation of Thinking

- Emotions prioritize thinking by directing attention to important information.
- Emotions are sufficiently vivid and available that they can be generated as aids to judgment and memory concerning feelings.
- Emotional mood swings change the individual's perspective from optimistic to pessimistic, encouraging consideration of multiple points of view.
- Emotional states differentially encourage specific problem approaches such as when happiness facilitates inductive reasoning and creativity.

Perception, Appraisal, and Expression of Emotion

- Ability to identify emotion in one's physical states, feelings, and thoughts.
- Ability to identify emotions in other people, designs, artwork, etc., through language, sound, appearance, and behavior.
- Ability to express emotions accurately, and to express needs related to those feelings.
- Ability to discriminate between accurate and inaccurate, or honest versus dishonest expressions of feeling.

is staying up late how she feels, she might respond that she is partly full of energy, partly fatigued, and anxious about whether or not her thinking is still clear.

Feelings can be recognized not only in oneself but in other people and in other objects. As a child grows that child imaginatively attributes feelings to animate and inanimate objects. This imaginative thinking may help the child generalize from himself to others. For instance, he may connect times when he is personally anxious and has a constricted posture to physical constriction observed in pets, other children, objects, and pictures, enabling him to recognize anxious expressions in other people and things (Box 2). Suitably developed and abstracted, the developing person begins to evaluate emotion wherever it might be expressed—in other people, in architecture, in artworks, and so on.[27] So, when we see Munch's well-known painting *The Scream* (of a cartoonish figure howling), not only do we immediately recognize the face of anxiety but how right it is that in the painting's background, the world is dissolving into nothingness at the same time. The individual is also able to express feelings accurately and to express needs surrounding those feelings (Box 3). Because emotionally intelligent individuals know about the expression and manifestation of emotion, they are also sensitive to its false or manipulative expression (Box 4).

Emotion's Facilitation of Thinking

The next branch up, "Emotional Facilitation of Thinking," concerns emotion acting on intelligence; it describes emotional events that assist intellectual processing. Emotion serves as an alerting system essentially from birth. The infant cries when it needs milk, warmth, or other care, and laughs in response to smiles and other pleasures. Emotions thus operate from the start to signal important changes in the person and in the environment. As the person matures, emotions begin to shape and improve thinking by directing a person's attention to important changes. For example, a child worries about his homework while watching TV. A teacher becomes concerned about a lesson that needs to be completed for the next day. The teacher, with his better developed thinking, moves on to complete the task before his concern overtakes his enjoyment (Box 1).

A second contribution of emotion to thinking is to generate emotions "on demand" so that they can be better understood. When asked "How does the character in a story feel," or when deciding how another person feels, children may generate the feelings within themselves so as to put themselves in the other's place.[28] This permits an immediate, real-time inspection of the feeling and its characteristics. In the growing person, the ability to generate feelings assists with planning. The individual can anticipate how entering a new school, taking a new job, or encountering a social criticism might feel. Anticipating such feelings can help a person decide whether to take a job or make a criticism. There exists, in other words, an "emotional theater of the mind," or more technically, a processing arena in which emotions may be generated, felt, manipulated, and examined so as to be better understood. The more accurately and realistically such an emotional theater operates, the more it can help the individual choose alternative life courses (Box 2).[29]

The remaining two abilities of Branch 2 are examples of a larger set of emotional contributions to more sophisticated, efficient thoughts. Emotionality may help people consider multiple perspectives. Recall that mood-congruent judgment involves good moods leading to optimistic thought; bad moods, to pessimistic thought. A sad high school senior may feel inadequate and consequently apply to a lot of colleges with easy admissions standards. Then, as her mood improves, she might apply to more selective colleges. This individual's shifting moods led her to consider more possibilities, which will be an advantage in conditions of uncertainty (Box 3). Close relatives of manic-depressives are likely to have more mood swings than others, assisting them to change perspective often. This may explain why such relatives are rated as exhibiting higher creativity in both their occupational and nonoccupational activities.[30] The final ability on this branch recognizes that different kinds of work and different forms of reasoning (e.g., deductive versus inductive) may be facilitated by different kinds of moods (Box 4).[31]

Understanding and Analyzing Emotions; Employing Emotional Knowledge

The third branch up of Figure 1.1 concerns the ability to understand emotions and to use emotional knowledge. Soon after the child recognizes emotions he begins to label them and perceive relations among those labels. For example, many emotions form sets along continua of intensity. The child begins to recognize similarities and differences between liking and loving, annoyance and anger, and so on (Box 1).[32] The child is simultaneously learning what each feeling means in terms of relationships. Parents teach children about emotional reasoning by linking emotions to situations. For example, they teach the connection between sadness and loss by helping a child recognize she is sad because her best friend won't spend time with her anymore. A formal philosophy of feelings has developed over the centuries. For example, Spinoza defined shame as "pain accompanied by the idea of some action of our own, which we believe to be blamed by others."[33] Some consensus exists as to these meanings, with anger frequently viewed as arising from the perception of injustice, sadness arising from loss, fear from threat, and so forth.[34] Emotional knowledge begins in childhood and grows throughout life, with increased understanding of these emotional meanings (Box 2).

The growing person also begins to recognize the existence of complex, contradictory emotions in certain circumstances. The child learns that it is possible to feel both love and hate toward the same person.[35] Probably also at this level of development, blends (or combinations) of emotions are acknowledged. For example, awe is sometimes viewed as a combination of fear and surprise; hope as a combination of faith and optimism (Box 3).[36] Emotions tend to occur in patterned chains: Anger may intensify to rage, be expressed, and then transform to satisfaction or guilt, depending upon the circumstance. The person goes on to reason about sequences of emotion: An individual who feels unlovable might reject another's care for fear of later rejection. Reasoning about the progression of feelings in interpersonal relationships is central to emotional intelligence (Box 4).

Reflective Regulation of Emotions to Promote Emotional and Intellectual Growth

The highest branch of Figure 1.1 concerns the conscious regulation of emotions to enhance emotional and intellectual growth. Emotional reactions must be tolerated—even welcomed—when they occur, somewhat independently of how pleasant or unpleasant they are. Only if a person attends to feelings can something be learned about them. For that reason, this highest level branch begins with openness to feelings (Box 1).

As the child grows, her parents teach her not to express certain feelings: to smile in public even if feeling sad, to go to her room if angry. Gradually, the child internalizes these divisions between feeling and acting: The child begins to learn that emotions can be separated from behavior.[37] Parents teach rudimentary emotion control strategies ("Count to 10 when you are angry"). As a consequence, the child learns to engage and disengage from emotion at appropriate times. Rage against another or against an injustice may be useful in reasoning about the situation, but probably less so when the feeling is at its climax. At those times the emotionally mature individual will know to draw back and discuss matters with more cool-headed confidants. Later, the emotional insight and energy provided by such experiences may be applied to the reasoning process, and may both motivate it and provide a means by which to, for example, elicit others' anger in opposition to the injustice (Box 2). As the individual matures, there also emerges a consistently reflective or meta-experience of mood and emotion. These feelings involve experiences of mood such as "I don't fully understand the way I'm feeling," or "This feeling is influencing how I'm thinking."[38] Such thoughts are conscious reflections on emotional responses, as opposed to simple perceptions of feelings. The meta-experience of mood seems divisible into two parts: meta-evaluation and meta-regulation. The evaluations include how much attention one pays to one's mood, and how clear, typical, acceptable, and influential one's mood is (Box 3). The regulation concerns whether the individual is trying to improve a bad mood, dampen a good one, or leave the mood alone. The meta-experiences of mood appear to be related to important phenomena, such as how long one dwells on traumatic experiences. The laws of meta-experiences are not as of yet well understood, but new measures have been developed to assess both their ongoing dynamics and dispositional qualities. One quality that seems important is that emotions are understood without exaggerating or minimizing their importance (Box 4).

Emotional Intelligence, Emotional Achievement, and Emotional Competencies

Up to now we have been discussing a concept of emotional intelligence that is reflected in a set of abilities. Consideration of emotional intelligence raises the issue of whether there exists emotional achievement and emotional competence, just as, say, academic intelligence can be compared to academic achievement and academic competence.[39] In the sphere of academic intelligence, intelligence is the aptitude, achievement represents what one has accomplished, and competency indicates that one's achievement meets a particular standard. Analogous to such concepts, emotional intelligence represents the core aptitude or ability to reason with emotions. Emotional achievement represents the learning a person has attained about emotion or emotion-related information, and emotional competence exists when one has reached a required level of achievement. All things being equal, a person's emotional intelligence determines her emotional achievement. But things are rarely equal, and the family in which one grew up, the lessons about emotions one was taught, the life events one has undergone—all influence how much one has achieved in learning about emotions.

Many educational psychologists prefer speaking in terms of competencies rather than intelligences, and the idea of emotional competencies has already been introduced by Saarni.[40] It focuses on the knowledge and skills the individual can attain in order to function adequately across situations rather than on the more difficult to assess and, in some ways educationally less relevant, issue of emotional intelligence. Some advocates of competency testing view it as a safeguard against the misuse of haphazardly administered group intelligence tests.[41] It is plainly more focused on the educational process than on psychological aptitude. From at least a theoretical standpoint, it makes sense to develop the ideas of emotional intelligence, emotional achievement, and emotional competencies together.

At least part of the excitement with which the concept of emotional intelligence has been greeted, we think, has been the definite implication that we understand emotions well enough to speak in terms of specific emotional abilities and competencies at those abilities. Without the concept of emotional intelligence, teaching about emotion must be geared toward the institutionally sanctioned requirement of behaving "well" or "nicely." Emotional intelligence provides a more flexible (if less easily defined) criterion for emotional competence: One increases one's emotional abilities to an agreed-upon level. Emotional intelligence is a good goal for a democratic culture. It does not dictate the outcome of a person's emotional behavior but rather encourages a process of personal investigation that can occur in the context of the person's own politics, ethnicity, religion, and other characteristics.

THE ASSESSMENT OF EMOTIONAL INTELLIGENCE

Now that we have described emotional intelligence, it is worth considering the evidence that it exists. As noted at the outset, understanding the form emotional intelligence takes will require demonstrating that the abilities included under the term "emotional intelligence" are meaningfully different from general intelligence and yet related enough to it to qualify as an intelligence. The media depiction of a monolithic EQ is without question premature. The determination of whether emotional intelligence is, say, one true intelligence, multiple skills unrelated to general intelligence, or something in between will depend upon its measurement and assessment.

The Measurement of Emotional Intelligence

Earlier we reviewed a great deal of psychological literature that suggests that some of the abilities on the branches of Figure 1.1 can be measured.[42] When we turn to studies that actually speak to the existence of emotional intelligence, only a small minority of the studies directly inform us of its existence or nonexistence. This small number of studies must meet three criteria. First, an ability of the type described in Figure 1.1 must be measured. Note that this excludes a great number of important personal qualities, such as optimism and motivation, which do not specifically involve emotional contributions to intelligence or intellectual understanding of emotion.[43] A second criterion is that the studies directly measure an ability rather than a person's self-description of how emotionally intelligent he or she is. Self-descriptions of intelligence can be of some research value but are not dependable enough to demonstrate that the concept exists. In the realm of academic intelligence, every instructor is familiar with the bright student who believes she isn't very smart and the not-so-smart student who believes she is much smarter than she is. Asking people to solve a problem produces a more valid sample of behavior for study. The third criterion is that such studies should connect multiple abilities from Figure 1.1 to one another, or one or more emotionally intelligent abilities to an important criterion.

Only a few studies meet the aforementioned criteria. In one study with Maria DiPaolo,[44] we found evidence supporting the idea that there is a basic skill that accounts for individual differences in recognizing (consensual) emotion not only in faces but in abstract designs and even in colors. That is, skills at decoding faces, designs, and colors were either generally high, medium, or low in a given individual. Moreover, people higher in these skills also obtained higher scores on a scale of self-reported empathy, a skill also envisioned as part of emotional intelligence. These findings argue for the existence of emotional intelligence as described in the first branch of the diagram (perception of emotion), in that they point to a unity of emotional recognition in faces, colors, or designs. Mayer and Geher further found that emotional perception of characters in situations correlates with SAT scores (a measure of intelligence), with empathy, and with emotional openness (from the highest, "regulatory" branch). At the time this chapter went to press, these findings were replicated and extended using a new scale that measures skills from all four branches of Figure 1.1.[45]

Important additional information concerning the third, "understanding emotions," branch comes from work by Averill and Nunley on emotional creativity.[46] In one of their tasks, participants are asked to write a brief description of a situation in which they might feel three emotions together (e.g., joy, relief, and distress). As our conceptualization of emotional intelligence (or theirs of emotional creativity) would predict, success at this task appears related to but independent of general intelligence. These few studies suggest that many of the abilities in Figure 1.1 intercorrelate with one another and are partly independent of general intelligence. Development of tasks requires caution because serious theoretical and empirical issues must be considered. These include, most pressingly, "How do we find the right answer to a test item in emotional intelligence?"—especially as those answers become more sophisticated. A more detailed discussion of this issue can be found in the article by Mayer and Geher (1996).

What Emotional Intelligence Predicts

Given that emotional intelligence has been studied so little, not much is known about what it predicts. Psychologists recognize that general intelligence predicts some aspects of success—defined as academic achievement and occupational status. General intelligence is often said to account for between 10% and 20% of such success, leaving about 80% to 90% of it to be explained by other factors.[47] So there is certainly room for emotional intelligence to predict a portion of such achievement. Generally speaking, a single personality factor explains only a small portion of life outcomes, so even a 10% contribution of emotional intelligence would be considered very large indeed. Some observers believe they have identified such contributions in the workplace. For example, some have argued that emotional intelligence contributed to success among engineers at Bell Laboratories, in particular their ability to network effectively.[48] In the Bell Labs study "networking" meant that engineers found answers from one another by bartering with information. This meant:

> first becoming a technical expert in a particularly sought-after area, then letting people know of your expertise, then making yourself available to others. Once an engineer has developed his or her bargaining chips, it's possible to gain access to the rest of this knowledge network.[49]

Such bartering seems to us to depend more on understanding the unwritten demands of the job than on emotional intelligence.[50] Although the bartering might involve emotional intelligence, we just do not know because no measures were taken of it. We do believe that emotional intelligence can contribute to success, at least when success is defined broadly.

More emotionally intelligent individuals might succeed at making their workers feel better, at communicating in interesting ways, and at designing projects that involve infusing products with feelings and aesthetics. Emotional intelligence may make the difference between constructing the Brooklyn Bridge, with its renowned beauty, and the more mundane Fifty-ninth Street Bridge.[51]

As more research is carried out, we can better evaluate what emotional intelligence contributes to achievement. In the meantime, the potential gains from teaching emotional intelligence will need to be considered with caution. It is to those applications we turn next.

APPLICATIONS OF EMOTIONAL INTELLIGENCE IN THE SCHOOLS AND BEYOND

Emotional intelligence as described here is expected to be involved in the home, in school, in work, and other settings. In many of these settings, emotional problems frequently are solved well. The story that opened this chapter, about the boy who was given a coat, was resolved with emotional intelligence. At the end of the fight some of the teachers and staff were already saying something like, "There are often fights between middle-class and poorer children in this school. Perhaps it was good that all this is out in the open because now it can be dealt with." The school principal called in the boys who started the fight, talked to them, and had them write letters of apology to the boy who received the coat. The principal chose to have them write letters of apology, he said, because it required them to think about what happened for a while. He also decided to devote a staff development day to what had happened so that the teachers could further understand what was going on in the school. The boy with the new coat wrote a letter of thanks to the teacher and the nurse. When the teacher received it, she said, "I understand it created some problems for you." The boy replied, "Oh, it's okay, they apologized . . . and I really like the coat." This doesn't totally take care of the problem, of course, but then, human problems are complex.

Acquiring Emotional Intelligence

If one wanted to improve emotional skills, how would that be done? Most skills can be improved through education, and it is likely this will hold true for at least some of the skills related to emotional intelligence. Emotional skills begin in the home with good parent-child interaction. Parents help children identify and label their emotions, to respect their feelings, and to begin to connect them to social situations. This process may succeed to a greater or lesser degree in each home. We have come to realize over the course of our study that individuals operate from different emotional starting places. These can be considered their emotional knowledge base.[52] The opportunities for learning emotional skills are not always equal. Parents may suffer from psychological limitations so severe that they are unable to initiate an emotional-cognitive learning process. A child may learn incorrect lessons about emotions: Parents may avoid feelings, or a parent may deny he is angry even while behaving with hostility. As a consequence, children sometimes develop disorders in which they become far removed from their feelings or misunderstand them. Sometimes a psychotherapist will be necessary to correct the problem. Psychotherapists are trained in empathic listening, reflection of feeling, and searching for lost emotions that need to be constructed, recovered, or acted on in better ways. For example, a therapist may see a client who is consistently taken advantage of, exploited, and yet denies any anger. The therapist may inquire as to whether anger is there and help the individual to channel it productively for the purposes of self-protection and placing limits on others' inappropriate behavior. It is also possible for some remedial learning to take place in the schools. Some of the most important learning takes place in the informal relationships between child and teacher; teachers often serve in the role of an important and potentially wise adult model. Another place where emotionally intelligent skills are taught is in the standard curriculum—a point to which we turn next.

The Incorporation of Emotional Intelligence in the Standard Curriculum

Particularly useful, we believe, is the natural emotional teaching that comes with many of the liberal arts and with various value systems as well. In school reading lessons that involve engaging stories, children begin to learn about feelings of characters. Story characters have an inescapable tendency to become happy, afraid, jealous, and so forth, and children can observe both what makes those characters feel as they do and also how the characters cope in response to the feelings. This learning proceeds throughout the educational system, and as stories become more complex, so does emotional learning. The ways in which the feelings of characters motivate their actions, which in turn moves forward the plot, is a lesson in emotional perception for young adults as much as it is in plot construction. In fact, one cannot evaluate a plot without asking "What does this character, with his history and personal style, feel in this situation," and then, "How reasonable is it that someone feeling this way would act as the character does?" Literature is probably the first home of the emotional intelligences. But so, too, are art programs, music, and theater.

Nor is the importance of values to be overlooked, as these determine in part the person's more conscious knowledge of the emotions. Values are often discussed and taught in such liberal arts subjects as history, citizenship, and (more often in private schools) religion. From these we learn about the value systems within which emotional responsivity occurs. Different styles of emotionality exist within different systems. One prevalent Western tradition esteems individual life, democracy, equality among individuals, and education, while it abhors destruction of life and property, discrimination, and ignorance. Such values define expected emotional responses. Cultural and/or religious observances further define expected emotions. The Jewish holiday of Yom Kippur requires those who worship to traverse cycles of repentance for sins during the year. The repentance begins with a critical self-appraisal with accompanying regret, guilt, and shame. Next, the person takes action to remedy those mistakes that can be repaired. After sincere repentance, there will follow solemnity, calmness, relief, and perhaps joyousness.[53] Making available these resources does not always work. The student may not read much, art courses may be curtailed, the student may reject religious, ethical, or national value systems. In such cases, should the school system step in directly with programs focused on emotional competencies?[54]

We think it is worth exploring this issue. Keep in mind that courses directly focused on the topic should be approached cautiously, as there is little scientific guidance about how they should be designed. To discuss the "correct" response(s) to a complex social event seems to stretch our knowledge. We cannot be sure we know all the right answers. But some discussion of such issues seems reasonable.

Educational Programs Directly Concerning Emotional Intelligence

Emotions have been taught in the schools before the concept of emotional intelligence was developed. We are impressed with the inventive ways in which some instructors have arranged affective curricula, but we also have concerns about them. In some schools and some programs where such materials are carefully worked out and the staff is well trained, a unique and potentially valuable program is undoubtedly being implemented. Just the same, as we examine details of some programs, we are at times uncomfortable. For example, programs that seem to adopt an "emotions are good" philosophy untempered by the fact that emotions exist in the context of other personal characteristics and interpersonal relationships are troubling to us.

Presumably, those students who need emotional education most desperately have come from households in which emotional communication is skewed in some way or another. These individuals already employ maladaptive emotional responses. We are not sure such severely damaged children profit from, say, being required to share their emotions in a class discussion, or whether they will be overwhelmed by it, or feel coerced.

Another concern is that individuals from different subcultures approach emotions differently. Although most share Western values, some will have been taught to "let it all hang out," whereas others may take a more "stoical" view. Some may emphasize a Christian attitude of turning the other cheek when confronted, so as to emphasize peace; others may emphasize a more Jewish attitude of employing anger to expose injustice and hence repair the world. (These are simplifications that cannot do justice to the more complete religious teachings.) In some instances, individuals may be members of discriminated-against groups and the target of such serious but covert hatred as to feel unable to participate in exercises that assume a degree of interpersonal trust.

A more promising starting point is exemplified by some conflict resolution programs we have seen. For example, Linda Lantieri, who runs the Resolving Conflicts Creatively Program in the New York City public school system, argues that conflict resolution is based on learning the skills of an emotionally intelligent person. Her program teaches how to identify the feelings of your adversary, your own feelings, and the feelings of others involved.[55] Violence reduction is an important and central goal in schools, where its threat is so salient as to greatly interfere with learning and concentration. It is more concrete and easier to agree upon implementing a conflict resolution curriculum (from our perspective) than a program devoted to increasing emotional intelligence (should such be possible) per se. The more focused goals of such a program also prevent it from being misinterpreted as teaching the "right" (or "best") way to feel.

Teaching basic social skills, or even basic socioemotional skills, if you prefer, is different from teaching an intelligence. Most beginning cooks who carefully follow a recipe can produce a good-tasting meal without necessarily knowing about all the ingredients. Similarly, any student enrolled in these programs can learn the social recipes without necessarily learning emotional intelligence. In our experience, many such school-based programs seem focused on these basic recipes, and this is to their credit. It makes assessing their outcomes relatively easy, and it avoids difficult issues like whether emotional intelligence can be assessed or taught, and by which cultural or multicultural criterion it will be evaluated. Might these programs teach a bit of emotional intelligence? Perhaps; just as gaining experience around the kitchen might help someone begin to develop as a chef. But whether or not it occurs doesn't matter. If the program reduces maladaptive interpersonal distress, we are happy about it.

CONCLUSION

Emotional intelligence is the ability to perceive emotions, to access and generate emotions so as to assist thought, to understand emotions and emotional meanings, and to reflectively regulate emotions so as to promote both better emotion and thought. It is our belief that the adaptive use of emotion-laden information is a significant aspect of what is meant by anyone's definition of intelligence, yet it is not studied systematically by investigators of intelligence nor included in traditional school curricula. As we have argued, using the emotions as one basis for thinking, and thinking with emotions themselves, may be related to important social competencies and adaptive behavior. Presently, we are at the beginning of the learning curve about emotional intelligence; the coming years should bring exciting research that contributes to our understanding of the concept.

GLOSSARY

Achievement—The level at which a person has learned to perform a particular skill.

Affect—One of three traditional spheres of mental activity (along with motivation and cognition), involving emotions, moods, and other associated feeling states such as liveliness and tiredness.

Cognition—One of three traditional spheres of mental activity (along with motivation and affect), involving learning, thought, judgment, memory, and other forms of thinking.

Competence—The condition of meeting a standard of achievement.

Conation—see Motivation.

Correlation—A statistical measure of the degree to which two variables are related. Correlation coefficients typically take on values from 1.0 to –1.0. A correlation of 1.0 means that variables rise and fall together with an exact correspondence. When variables are said "to be correlated," it more often means they rise and fall together according to a loose pattern; this pattern is represented by a number between 0.0 and 1.0, where a higher value close to 1.0 indicates a stronger association. Negative correlations involve movements of the variables in opposite directions (i.e., one rises as the other falls) and are represented by numbers between 0.0 and –1.0.

Emotion—Short-term feeling states including happiness, anger, or fear, that mix varying amounts of pleasantness-unpleasantness and arousal-calm, among other sensations.

Emotional Intelligence—This intelligence involves the ability to perceive accurately, appraise, and express emotion; the ability to access and/or generate feelings when they facilitate thought; the ability to understand emotion and emotional knowledge; and the ability to reflectively regulate emotions in ways that promote emotional and intellectual growth.

Intelligence—Traditionally, a characterization of how well the cognitive sphere operates, e.g., how quickly someone can learn, how well they can judge and think, and so on.

Meta-Experience (or **Meta-Mood Experience**)—A reflective thought or feeling about an emotion or mood, such as "I don't like this feeling."

Motivation (or **Conation**)—One of three traditional spheres of mental activity (along with affect and cognition) that concerns both basic urges such as hunger and thirst, and more complex goal-directed activities such as the pursuit of friendship, achievement, or power.

Talent (and **Nonintellectual Talent**)—A talent is any human skill or ability. A nonintellectual talent is an ability that does not involve (or only minimally involves) human cognition or intelligence, such as the ability to walk long distances, to eat hot peppers, etc.

Trait—Any fairly consistent behavior or set of behaviors an individual tends to exhibit such as enjoying being with people, being conscientious, or trying new things.

NOTES

References

Anastasi, A. (1967). Psychology, psychologists, and psychological testing. *American Psychologist, 26*, 1036–1037.

Anastasi, A. (1988). *Psychological testing.* New York: Macmillan.

Arnheim, R. (1954/1974). *Art and visual perception: A psychology of the creative eye* (new version). Berkeley, CA: University of California Press.

Averill, J. R., & Nunley, E. P. (1992). *Voyages of the heart: Living an emotionally creative life.* New York: Free Press.

Bower, G. H. (1981). Mood and memory. *American Psychologist, 36*, 129–148.

Buck, R. (1984). *The communication of emotion.* New York: Guilford.

Clynes, M. (1977). *Sentics: The touch of emotions*. Garden City, NY: Doubleday.

Cronbach, L. J. (1960). *Essentials of psychological testing* (2nd ed.). New York: Harper and Row.

Detterman, D. K. (1982). Does "g" exist? *Intelligence, 6*, 99–108.

Ekman, P. (1985). *Telling lies: Clues to deceit in the marketplace, politics, and marriage*. New York: Norton.

Ekman, P., Friesen, W. V., O'Sullivan, M., Chan, A., Diacoyanni-Tarlatzis, I., Heider, K., Krause, R., LeCompte, W. A., Pitcairn, T., Ricci-Bitti, P. E., Scherer, K., Tomita, M., & Tzavaras, A. (1987). Universals and cultural differences in the judgments of facial expressions of emotion. *Journal of Personality and Social Psychology, 53*, 712–717.

Ekstrom, R. B., French, J. W., Harman, H. H., & Dermen, D. (1976). *Manual for kit of factor-referenced cognitive tests* (3rd ed.). Princeton, NJ: Educational Testing Service.

Emmons, R. A., & Colby, P. M. (1995). Emotional conflict and well-being: Relation to perceived availability, daily utilization, and observer reports of social support. *Journal of Personality and Social Psychology, 68*, 947–959.

Forgas, J. P. (1995). Mood and judgment: The Affect Infusion Model (AIM). *Psychological Bulletin, 117*, 39–66.

Frijda, N. H. (1988). The laws of emotion. *American Psychologist, 43*, 349–358.

Gardner, H. (1983). *Frames of mind: The theory of multiple intelligences*. New York: Basic Books.

Gardner, H. (1993). *Frames of mind: The theory of multiple intelligences* (10th Anniversary Edition). New York: Basic Books.

Gardner, H. (1995). Cracking open the IQ box. In S. Fraser (Ed.), *The bell curve wars* (pp. 23–35). New York: Basic Books.

Gerrig, R. J. (1993). *Experiencing narrative worlds: On the psychological activities of reading*. New Haven, CT: Yale University Press.

Gibbs, N. (1995, October 2). The EQ factor. *Time*, pp. 60–68.

Goleman, D. (1995a, September 10). Ideas and trends: The decline of the nice-guy quotient. *New York Times* (Sunday Week in Review), p. 6.

Goleman, D. (1995b). *Emotional intelligence*. New York: Bantam Books.

Guilford, J. P., & Hoepfner, R. (1971). *The analysis of intelligence*. New York: McGraw Hill.

Hilgard, E. R. (1980). The trilogy of mind: Cognition, affection, and conation. *Journal of the History of the Behavioral Sciences, 16*, 107–117.

Isen, A. M., Shalker, T. E., Clark, M., & Karp, L. (1978). Affect, accessibility of material in memory, and behavior: A cognitive loop? *Journal of Personality and Social Psychology, 36*, 1–12.

Kelley, R., & Caplan, J. (1993). How Bell Labs creates star performers. *Harvard Business Review, 71*, 128–139.

Lazarus, R. S. (1991). *Emotion and adaptation*. New York: Oxford University Press.

Mandler, G. (1984). *Mind and body: Psychology of emotion and stress*. New York: Norton.

Mayer, J. D. (1986). How mood influences cognition. In N. E. Sharkey (Ed.), *Advances in cognitive science* (Vol. 1). Chichester, England: Ellis Horwood.

Mayer, J. D. (1995). A framework for the classification of personality components. *Journal of Personality, 63,* 819–877.

Mayer, J. D., & Gaschke, Y. N. (1988). The experience and meta-experience of mood. *Journal of Personality and Social Psychology, 55,* 102–111.

Mayer, J. D., Gaschke, Y., Braverman, D. L., & Evans, T. (1992). Mood-congruent judgment is a general effect. *Journal of Personality and Social Psychology, 63,* 119–132.

Mayer, J. D., & Geher, G. (1996). Emotional intelligence and the identification of emotion. *Intelligence, 22,* 89–113.

Mayer, J. D. & Hanson, E. (1995). Mood-congruent judgment over time. *Personality and Social Psychology Bulletin, 21,* 237–244.

Mayer, J. D., & Mitchell, D. C. (in press). Intelligence as a subsystem of personality: From Spearman's *g* to contemporary models of hot-processing. In W. Tomic & J. Kingma (Eds.), *Reflections on the concept of intelligence.* Greenwich, CT: JAI Press.

Mayer, J. D., & Salovey, P. (1988). Personality moderates the interaction of mood and cognition. In K. Fiedler and J. Forgas (Eds.), *Affect, cognition and social behavior: New evidence and integrative attempts* (pp. 87–99). Toronto: C. J. Hogrefe.

Mayer, J. D., & Salovey, P. (1993). The intelligence of emotional intelligence. *Intelligence, 17,* 433–442.

Mayer, J. D., & Salovey, P. (1995). Emotional intelligence and the construction and regulation of feelings. *Applied and Preventive Psychology, 4,* 197–208.

Mayer, J. D., & Stevens, A. (1994). An emerging understanding of the reflective (meta-) experience of mood. *Journal of Research in Personality, 28,* 351–373.

Mayer, J. D., Caruso, D., & Salovey, P. (1997). A test of emotional intelligence. Manuscript in preparation.

Mayer, J. D., DiPaolo, M. T., & Salovey, P. (1990). Perceiving affective content in ambiguous visual stimuli: A component of emotional intelligence. *Journal of Personality Assessment, 54,* 772–781.

Mayer, J. D., Salovey P., & Caruso, D. (in press). *Emotional IQ test* [CD-ROM version]. Needham, MA: Virtual Knowledge.

Mendelssohn, M. (1755/1971). *Moses Mendelssohn: Gesammelte Schriften Jubilaum Sausgabe* (Band 1: *Schriften zur Philosophie und Asthetik*). Stuttgart: Friedrich Frommann Verlag (Gunther Holzboog). (Original work published 1755)

Miller, A. (1990). *The drama of the gifted child* (R. Ward, Trans.). New York: Basic Books.

Mischel, W., Shoda, Y., & Peake, P. K. (1988). The nature of adolescent competencies predicted by preschool delay of gratification. *Journal of Personality and Social Psychology, 54,* 687–696.

Mitchell, D., & Mayer, J. D. (1997). *Empathy and the identification of emotion.* Manuscript.

Nannis, E. D. (1988). Cognitive-developmental differences in emotional understanding. In E. D. Nannis & P. A. Cowan (Eds.), *Developmental psychopathology and its treatment: New directions for child development* (Vol. 39, pp. 31–49). San Francisco: Jossey-Bass.

Neisser, U., Boodoo, G., Bouchard, T. J., Boykin, A. W., Brody, N., Ceci, S. J., Halpern, D. F., Loehlin, J. C., Perloff, R., Sternberg, R. J., & Urbina, S. (1996). Intelligence: Knowns and unknowns. *American Psychologist, 51,* 77–101.

Palfai, T. P., & Salovey, P. (1993). The influence of depressed and elated mood on deductive and inductive reasoning. *Imagination, Cognition, and Personality, 13,* 57–71.

Peli, P. (1984). *Soloveitchik on repentance.* New York: Paulist Press.

Pennebaker, J. W., Rimé, B., & Blankenship, V. E. (1996). Stereotypes of emotional expressiveness of Northerners and Southerners: A cross-cultural test of Montesquieu's hypothesis. *Journal of Personality and Social Psychology, 70,* 272–280.

Piaget, J., & Inhelder, B. (1969). *The psychology of the child.* New York: Basic Books.

Plutchik, R. (1984). Emotions: A general psychoevolutionary theory. In K. R. Scherer and P. Ekman (Eds.), *Approaches to emotion* (pp. 197–219). Hillsdale, NJ: Erlbaum.

Richards, R., Kinney, D. K., Lunde, I., Benet, M., & Merzel, A. P. C. (1988). Creativity in manic-depressives, cyclothymes, their normal relatives, and control subjects. *Journal of Abnormal Psychology, 89,* 286–290.

Roseman, I. J. (1984). Cognitive determinants of emotion: A structural theory. *Review of Personality and Social Psychology, 5,* 11–36.

Saarni, C. (1988). Emotional competence: How emotions and relationships become integrated. In R. A. Thompson (Ed.), *Nebraska symposium on motivation* (Vol. 36, pp. 115–182). Lincoln: University of Nebraska Press.

Salovey, P., & Birnbaum, D. (1989). Influence of mood on health-related cognitions. *Journal of Personality and Social Psychology, 57,* 539–551.

Salovey, P. & Mayer, J. D. (1990). Emotional intelligence. *Imagination, Cognition, and Personality, 9,* 185–211.

Salovey, P., Hsee, C., & Mayer, J. D. (1993). Emotional intelligence and the self-regulation of affect. In D. M. Wegner and J. W. Pennebaker (Eds.), *Handbook of mental control* (pp. 258–277). Englewood Cliffs, NJ: Prentice-Hall.

Salovey, P., Mayer, J. D., Goldman, S., Turvey, C., & Palfai, T. (1995). Emotional attention, clarity, and repair: Exploring emotional intelligence using the Trait Meta-Mood Scale. In J. W. Pennebaker (Ed.), *Emotion, disclosure, and health* (pp. 125–154). Washington, D.C.: American Psychological Association.

Sattler, J. M. (1982). Assessment of children's intelligence and special abilities (2nd ed.). Boston: Allyn and Bacon.

Scarr, S. (1989). Protecting general intelligence: Constructs and consequences for interventions. In R. L. Linn (Ed.), *Intelligence: Measurement, theory, and public policy.* Urbana, IL: University of Illinois Press.

Schaffer, L. F., Gilmer, B., & Schoen, M. (1940). *Psychology.* New York: Harper & Brothers.

Scherer, K. R. (1993). Studying the emotion-antecedent appraisal process: An expert system approach. *Cognition and Emotion, 7,* 325–355.

Shoda, Y., Mischel, W., & Peake, P. K. (1990). Predicting adolescent cognitive and self-regulatory competencies from preschool delay of gratification: Identifying diagnostic conditions. *Developmental Psychology, 26,* 978–986.

Smith, C. A., & Ellsworth, P. C. (1985). Patterns of cognitive appraisal in emotion. *Journal of Personality and Social Psychology, 48,* 813–838.

Spearman, C. (1927). *The abilities of man: Their nature and measurement.* New York: Macmillan.

Spinoza, B. (1984) Ethics (Part III): On the origin and nature of the emotions. In C. Calhoun & R. C. Solomon (Eds.), *What is emotion?* Oxford: Oxford University Press. (Original work published 1675)

Sternberg, R. J. (1988). *The triarchic mind: A new theory of human intelligence.* New York: Penguin.

Sternberg, R. J. (1994). Commentary: Reforming school reform: Comments on "Multiple intelligences: The theory in practice." *Teachers College Record, 95,* 561–569.

Sundberg, N. D., Snowden, L. R., & Reynolds, W. M. (1978). Toward assessment of personal competence and incompetence in life situations. *Annual Review of Psychology, 29,* 179–221.

Thorndike, R. L., & Stein, S. (1937). An evaluation of the attempts to measure social intelligence. *Psychological Bulletin, 34,* 275–284.

Thurstone, L. L. (1938). *Primary mental abilities.* Chicago: University of Chicago Press.

Tice, D., & Baumeister, R. F. (1993). Controlling anger: Self-induced emotion change. In D. M. Wegner & J. W. Pennebaker (Eds.), *Handbook of mental control* (pp. 393–409). Englewood Cliffs, NJ: Prentice-Hall.

Wagner, R. K., & Sternberg, R. J. (1985). Practical intelligence in real-world pursuits: The role of tacit knowledge. *Journal of Personality and Social Psychology, 50,* 737–743.

Walsh, W. B., & Betz, N. E. (1995). *Tests and assessment* (3rd ed.). Englewood Cliffs, NJ: Prentice-Hall.

Wechsler, D. (1958). *The measurement and appraisal of adult intelligence* (4th ed.). Baltimore, MD: Williams & Wilkins.

Young, P. T. (1936). *Motivation of behavior.* New York: John Wiley & Sons.

Young, P. T. (1943). *Emotion in man and animal: Its nature and relation to attitude and motive.* New York: John Wiley & Sons.

1. This is a true story in which a few details have been changed to protect the privacy of those involved. Similarly, the aftermath reported later in the chapter is what occurred.
2. Discussion of the concept has occurred in academic research settings (Emmons & Colby, 1995), in popular news magazines such as *Time* (Gibbs, 1995), and in a popular book (Goleman, 1995b).
3. This three-part division is basic to the modern enterprise of psychology. Historical reviews can be found in Hilgard (1980) and Mayer (1995); the origins of the system date from Mendelssohn (1755/1971).
4. Wechsler (1958), for example, defined intelligence as related not only to cognition but to general adaptation as well. In Mayer and Salovey (1995), we have examined the distinction between adaptation and intelligence. Although adaptation is plainly involved in intelligence, it is in-

sufficient by itself to characterize intelligence. Many organisms, such as ants, are well adapted without necessarily being highly intelligent in the sense employed here.

5. "The power to combine and separate" was suggested by the philosopher Thomas Aquinas, 1225–1274 (cited in Walsh & Betz, 1995); the importance of reasoning and judgment was evident in the early Binet tests (see Sattler, 1982); Spearman (1927) emphasized the importance of abstract reasoning.

6. A number of research laboratories have examined mood-congruent judgment. A few key publications include: Bower (1981); Forgas (1995); Isen, Shalker, Clark, and Karp (1978); Mayer and Salovey (1988); Mayer, Gaschke, Braverman, and Evans (1992); Salovey and Birnbaum (1989).

7. Mayer et al. (1992, p. 129).

8. This brief definition forms one of the several definitions employed by Goleman (1995b, p. xii). A second definition is similar to ours; a third definition says that emotional intelligence is "character" (1995b, p. 285).

9. Motivational intelligences are discussed briefly in the introduction to Mayer and Geher (1996). The view that intelligences might be divided into cognitive, affective, and motivational sets rather than the social (and intrapersonal) intelligences, most recently popularized by Gardner, has been studied under different names by earlier researchers.

10. When psychologists speak about intelligence they are keeping in mind the full range of the variable, from its lowest manifestations in the severely retarded, where most individuals possess very few skills, to the level of the extremely gifted, where individuals can do many things with at least some skill. (For example, Einstein played the violin in a chamber group, although always a bit stiffly.)

11. Some psychologists were interested in further interpreting this cohesion among the various intelligences (i.e., that they rose and fell together). For example, Spearman (1927) believed that their movement together occurred because they drew on a common mental resource that, if possessed in quantity, helped a person excel, and if possessed in poverty, limited a person's abilities. This general common resource, termed g for general intelligence, could be estimated for a person according to various mathematical models that were developed for that purpose. Although there exists consensus that all the intelligences are empirically interrelated (i.e., rise and fall together across individuals), the g model of intelligence was more controversial. Alternative explanations for this collective rise and fall of abilities exist (see, e.g., Detterman, 1982). Whether one believed in g, or not, the mathematical models developed with it provided an accurate and convenient means for keeping track of the degree to which the intelligences cohered.

12. One of us recalls this critique of Guilford and Hoepfner's (1971) model: If everyone in the field of personality testing joined in, it could still take 100 years to establish so many intelligences. Although it attracted some attention in the 1970s, interest in the theory dropped off. In fact, we could find no coverage of their model in several contemporary volumes on psychological testing.

13. Gardner's theory (1983, 1993) is beautifully described and intuitively compelling. Although he recognizes that all intelligences intercorrelate

(Gardner, 1993, p. xx), he wonders whether this may be an accident of the experimental methods employed (Gardner, 1993, p. xi). Other theorists join him in maintaining a skepticism concerning the obtained correlations among intelligences (e.g., Detterman, 1982). Still, it leaves no way to test the theory of multiple intelligences, and the theory is regarded by many experts in the field (including ourselves) as appealing but lacking in empirical support as of now (Sternberg, 1994).

14. Another plausible exception is Sternberg's (1988) triarchic theory of intelligence. Sternberg does sometimes employ the correlational method, however. The centrality of correlational methods is supported by a recent task force summary of the status of intelligence research, reported in the *American Psychologist* (Neisser et al., 1996, p. 78).

15. Thurstone (1938).

16. Ekstrom, French, Harman, and Dermer (1976).

17. Thorndike and Stein (1937) contributed some of the empirical findings; Cronbach (1960) presented an influential review arguing that further examination of social intelligence was unwise.

18. Scarr (1989, p. 78).

19. Mayer and Salovey (1993).

20. For example, Schaffer, Gilmer, and Schoen (1940, pp. xii, 521); Young (1936, pp. 457–458; 1943, p. 263).

21. George Mandler (1984) first popularized this idea as a component of human information processing.

22. Many philosophers and psychologists have said this before us; our reasoning is presented in Mayer and Salovey (1995).

23. See Frijda (1988), for the lawfulness of emotions; also, see Ekman, Friesen, O'Sullivan, Chan et al. (1987).

24. The original hypothesis concerning this dates to Montesquieu; the modern test was conducted by Pennebaker, Rimé, and Blankenship (1996).

25. Mayer and Salovey (1995, p. 197).

26. For example, Salovey and Mayer (1990, p. 189).

27. For example, Arnheim (1954/1974); Clynes (1977).

28. For example, Piaget and Inhelder (1969, pp. 120–122) consider interpersonal perspective taking as emerging partially within the concrete-operations stage. See also Gerrig (1993).

29. The *arena* is a memory location within which symbols are manipulated by one or more intelligences (Mayer & Mitchell, in press). In emotional intelligence, the individual would generate a feeling—sadness, for instance—on command so as to think about its facets, meanings, and associated thoughts. Having the emotions in this processing arena can presumably reduce the requirements on memory for processing.

30. A more elaborate description of how mood swings affect the college planning process is outlined in Mayer (1986); relevant evidence for mood-congruent judgment over time is in Mayer and Hanson (1995); information about the first-degree relatives of manic-depressives can be found in Richards, Kinney, Lunde, Benet, and Merzel (1988).

31. Palfai and Salovey (1993) present evidence that specific moods enhance specific forms of mental processing.

32. Plutchik (1984).

33. Spinoza (1984, p. 83).

34. For recent reviews of these ideas, see Lazarus (1991); Plutchik (1984); Roseman (1984); Scherer (1993); Smith and Ellsworth (1985).

35. Nannis (1988) considers full understanding of multiple feelings as requiring fairly sophisticated thoughts—that is, arising late in development.

36. Plutchik (1984).

37. The parent's ability to suppress feelings in the child is described in Alice Miller's (1990) book, *The Drama of the Gifted Child*. Miller emphasizes, in terms somewhat different from the argument here, that some children will deny negative feelings in themselves altogether as a consequence of parental disapproval.

38. Nannis (1988) refers to introspection and levels of consciousness concerning emotion as occurring very late in development. The original discussion of meta-experience can be found in Mayer and Gaschke (1988). The concept is developed more recently in both Mayer and Stevens (1994) and Salovey, Mayer, Goldman, Turvey, and Palfai (1995). Some actual approaches to mood regulation are examined by Tice and Baumeister (1993).

39. Anastasi (1988) presents a good introduction to these concepts.

40. Saarni (1988), this volume.

41. Anastasi (1988, p. 264); additional discussion can be found in Anastasi (1967) and Sundberg, Snowden, and Reynolds (1978).

42. See in particular Salovey and Mayer (1990); Salovey, Hsee, and Mayer (1993).

43. Research on delay of gratification, an example of which is the popularly reported "marshmallow test" (see Gibbs, 1995), is fascinating. We view it, however, as more closely related to motivation than emotion. The studies in question are by Mischel, Shoda, and Peake (1988) and Shoda, Mischel, and Peake (1990).

44. Mayer, DiPaolo, and Salovey (1990).

45. A replication and extension of the Mayer and Geher work using a new scale based on the Figure 1.1 model is reported in Mayer, Caruso, and Salovey (1997). The new scale is a computer-based testing instrument (Mayer, Salovey, & Caruso, in press). The Mayer and Geher (1996) article illustrates many of the complexities that will arise in measuring emotional intelligence and that tend to be swept aside in the present wave of enthusiasm for the concept. Several criteria were used for the "correct" answer as to what a character was feeling in a story. One criterion involved the character him or herself who was in the particular situation (real situations were used). A second criterion was the overall consensus of the participants in the study as to what the person was feeling. These two criteria behaved differently in the study. Interestingly, however, they both supported the existence of an actual emotional intelligence. Another replication and extension of the work is described in Mitchell and Mayer (1997).

46. Averill and Nunley (1992).

47. Howard Gardner (1995, pp. 26–27) has suggested this range, which seems consistent with the current literature.

48. This was the central illustration employed in the *New York Times* coverage of the topic, and appeared in *Time* and a popular book as well

(Gibbs, 1995; Goleman, 1995a, 1995b). The original study was reported by Kelley and Caplan (1993) in the *Harvard Business Review*.

49. Kelley and Caplan, 1993 (p. 132).
50. Incidentally, "tacit intelligence" refers to the ability to recognize the implicit demands of a job. It has been studied in some depth by Wagner and Sternberg (1985).
51. We do recognize, however, that the Fifty-ninth Street Bridge has inspired its own musical lore, notably, "The 59th Street Bridge Song (Feelin' Groovy)," by Paul Simon of the musical group Simon and Garfunkel.
52. See Mayer and Salovey (1995) for a more extensive discussion of the emotional knowledge base.
53. Peli (1984).
54. It does not seem, to our ear, appropriate usage to talk about teaching an intelligence. The definition of an ability is that it is a capacity rather than a topic to be taught. To teach intelligence sounds to us like exercising a person's sports ability. One exercises muscles to build strength; similarly, one teaches emotional skills to build emotional intelligence.
55. This program is described in Goleman (1995b).

AUTHORS' NOTE

The authors gratefully acknowledge the support of the Fetzer Institute, which sponsored several conferences on emotional literacy that we attended. Many of the conferees, including the other authors and commentators of this volume, made valuable suggestions that improved this chapter. Other educators, psychologists, and like-minded individuals contributed their comments as well. We are especially indebted to David Caruso, Kevin M. Carlsmith, Deborah Davis, Karol DeFalco, Deborah Hirsch, Dan Smith, and Chip Wood. Kevin M. Carlsmith also helped design and construct Figure 1.1.

Correspondence regarding this chapter may be addressed to John (Jack) D. Mayer, Department of Psychology, University of New Hampshire, 10 Library Way, Durham, NH 03824.

EDUCATOR'S COMMENTARY

KAROL DEFALCO

FEW WOULD DISAGREE that the purpose of schools is to promote academic skills and knowledge and to take students from one level to the next. However, that's difficult to accomplish if the student is absent; if the student is suspended or expelled; if the student is dropping out of school; if the student is dealing with a death; if the student believes that life is something that happens to him and he has no control over it. Although some students dealing with these issues are in our classrooms and doing fine, many are absent. Others are in our classrooms in body but not mind. Their minds are dealing with the above stressors of home, of community, of peers, of life. Although these young people are in our classrooms, their thoughts are on these social/emotional issues. They're often not paying attention, have low concentration, participate little, neglect the assignments, act out. For these kids, the parts of speech and the addition of mixed numbers are not high priorities. When standardized tests do not show improvement, school districts traditionally have responded by increasing the amount of time spent in class, choosing a new textbook, reassigning teachers, and reevaluating assessment tools. Each of these responses can provide benefits. However, they do not speak to the needs of students who are skipping school or are being suspended. They do not address the needs of those students who are in school in body only. Nor do they meet the needs of the students mentioned at the opening of this chapter: the boys who accused a fourth-grader of stealing the new coat he was wearing. In that vignette, it is easy to surmise that, after returning from recess, there was more than one student in that class who was not focused on academics. The victim of the tirade, the bullies, and the students who had witnessed the venomous attack may all be dealing with that social/emotional event rather than attending to the lesson. The young people in this account need skills not usually considered part of a school's core curriculum: impulse control, stress management, empathy, dealing with an accusation, and problem solving. To get these students to their next academic levels, we must meet them where they are and give them skills and resources to cope with stressors so that they will then be better able to attend to academics. Without these social/emotional skills, the stressors take over and prevent our students from living up to their academic potential. So, in addition to teaching emotional competencies for their own sake, we teach them in order to impact academics.

Let's talk about emotional competency programs. Some say that emotional competency programs teach "the best way to feel, the correct way to act." I am not an advocate of these values-based programs in public schools. I support curricula that teach social skills as part of a comprehensive, sequential program. Just as there are many math skills, there are many social skills, including:

impulse control
anger management
empathy
recognizing similarities and differences among people
complimenting
self-monitoring
communication
evaluating risks
positive self-talk
problem solving
decision making
goal setting
resisting peer pressure

Some educators implement emotional competency lessons in response to a problem in the cafeteria, hallway, gym, or on the playground (as in the opening story), and although there is a role for this type of intervention, I prefer a program that comes from a prevention point of view: one offered to all students—not just "problem kids"—to reduce the occurrence of antisocial or at-risk behaviors, one offered to all students so that when the stressors of life confront them, they will be able to cope. After all, which student will not have to resist impulses at some point in her life? Which student will not have to evaluate risks? Which student will not be in a situation needing anger management skills? Emotional competency programs for all!

How should social/emotional skills be taught? Well, think about the way other skills are taught. A math teacher might present the material, model the skills by doing an example on the board, give students a chance to practice, require students to apply the skill to a project, and reward the student for doing a good job—present, model, practice, apply, reward. Also, math skills are taught sequentially as part of a comprehensive K–12 program. They are taught every day to every child, every grade, every year.

Yet when social skills are taught, they are often introduced in a hit-or-miss fashion after a problem has occurred rather than as part of a planned program. Sometimes hundreds of students are called to the auditorium for a program that is supposed to address social competencies. After the program, the students return to their classrooms and adults hope that the 45-minute presentation will make a difference in student attitudes or behaviors. Would a 45-minute auditorium program be an appropriate way to teach math? Hardly. Neither does it work for social skills. Social skills should be taught in the same way as academic skills: sequentially, as part of a comprehensive program, to every child, every day, every year, using a present/model/practice/apply/reward format.

In New Haven, where I am a middle school teacher, there is a comprehensive K–12 Social Development Program. The curriculum includes social/emotional competencies for each grade. In kindergarten through grade 3, students work on self-awareness, relationships, and decision making. Fourth- and fifth-graders are focused on empathy training, impulse control, and anger management. In middle schools, students learn a problem-solving process using stress management, problem identification, goal setting, solution generating, consequential thinking, and planning. They also learn peer pressure resistance skills. Among other skills, high-schoolers learn decision making, which includes the consideration of others' points of view and recognizing risks/opportunities.

The boys involved in the stolen coat accusation were called to the office, talked to by the principal, and assigned letters of apology. The boy who received the new coat wrote a thank-you letter. These are all appropriate gestures. Are they enough? Have the bullies learned empathy skills? Have they learned to accept others? Have they learned to accurately express emotion? Has the victim learned stress management skills or problem-solving skills? Does he have the necessary skills to cope with similar situations as they arise in his life? Talking about emotions is a start. Talking about story characters' feelings is a start. Building competencies is the goal.

As Mayer and Salovey point out, "We are at the beginning of the learning curve about emotional intelligence; the coming years should bring exciting research that contributes to our understanding of the concept." May I add: It will contribute to the way we work with kids.

CHAPTER 2

Emotional Competence and Self-Regulation in Childhood

CAROLYN SAARNI

A PERSONAL PREAMBLE

Psychologists do not talk much about wisdom, *yet here I am, a psychologist having proposed yet another Western culturally biased construct, emotional competence, and nowhere in the essay that follows do I address wisdom. I cannot imagine wisdom without emotional competence, but can one be emotionally competent and yet not have wisdom? I think so, and that is where development comes in: We mature and acquire the skills of emotional competence, which are anchored in the cultural context in which we live. But for us to become* wise, *we need first to become emotionally competent; second, to live our life fully; and third, to cultivate discernment in the ways of the heart—that is, we must examine and learn about human character, with the breadth that comes from embracing cultures different from our own and with the depth that comes from relishing our personal relationships. The title of this volume hints at the possibility of wisdom in our commitment to education: One title that was considered,* Teaching from the Heart, *suggests a wise teacher who recognizes that learning always involves feelings and that those*

Portions of this chapter have been adapted from C. Saarni (in press), *Developing emotional competence*. New York: Guilford.

feelings are experienced as much by the teacher as by those who are taught. I hope that after reading my essay, readers will recognize skills of emotional competence both in themselves as well as in their students, and we will continue together to seek wisdom.

INTRODUCTION

I begin this essay with a vignette that illustrates two constructs: emotional competence and self-regulation. It also illustrates a context that can potentially lead to maladaptive behavior, but such a context can be tempered by protective factors.

Six-year-old Samuel lived in a two-room apartment with his Mom and little sister Jessie in a run-down part of the city. Gang activity, pimping, drug dealing, and their associated violence were part of their lives. Once their television screen had been blasted by a stray bullet; now Mom kept the shades drawn day and night. Then some bad news hit hard: Mom found out that she was being laid off her day job, and the only immediate option she had was to work a night shift in a downtown hotel. Frantically, she tried to arrange nighttime child care for the two children so that she could continue working. With time running out, Mom's last option was to persuade the older woman down the hall to sleep in their apartment on the nights she had to work; the woman, Mary, ambivalently agreed to try it for a couple of weeks. Little did Mom or the children know that Mary's adult son was a drug addict and had regularly terrorized his mother for money to support his addiction.

Mary's son, Fred, quickly found out where she was spending the night and managed to get her to open the apartment door. He pushed his way in and started to stuff various objects into a large garbage bag to take with him. Mary struck him from behind with a lamp, and he whirled around to beat her. Samuel awakened upon hearing the screaming, and terror struck him that it was his mother being hurt. He felt Jessie shaking next to him and told her to hide in the closet. He then recognized that it was Mary who was screaming. He knew from his Mom's "emergency drills" that he was supposed to call 911 for help, but the phone was in the other room! He made sure that Jessie was in the closet, and then talking softly aloud to himself, he tried to figure out what he should do. If he could get the lights out, then the bad man couldn't see. He knew the switch was just outside his door, and he slowly eased open the door and flicked off the switch. The bad man started to shout and curse; Mary was moaning and crying. Samuel heard the front door slam, and he peeked out into the dark room. Fortunately, his eyes had already accommodated to relative darkness, and he saw that the man was gone. He double-bolted the front door and crept to the phone and punched in 911.

The police were very impressed that a little 6-year-old boy had "kept his cool" and knew what to do in an emergency. He had also told the police where to call his Mom, and he told them he would not let anybody in unless they used the code word his Mom had taught him, and he wasn't about to give them the code word. En route, the police had called Mom at work to get the code word, and, of course, she rushed home at once. Mary was taken away by the paramedics in an ambulance, and Jessie clung to Mom. While the police officer interviewed Samuel, he kept one hand in his mother's hand. The next day a newspaper reporter interviewed him for the evening news on TV. She asked him how he had managed not to get scared. Samuel responded, "I was scared, but I knew bad guys can't see in the dark."[1]

Samuel's emotional competence and self-regulation were evident in his ability to manage his fear in support of effective problem solving, even when faced with a crisis. When we are highly emotionally aroused by negative affect, we often cannot process information as well; however, that is exactly what we need to be able to do in order to solve problems, especially when we are dealing with an extraordinarily challenging situation. In a crisis such as Samuel endured, our overwhelming goal is to flee danger, but if there is no ready exit, we need to be able to take stock of what we do have control over and try to use that knowledge to cope with the risky or threatening situation. Samuel spoke aloud to himself as a strategy to reduce his terror and thus think more purposefully. He acted prosocially by protecting his sister and hiding her in the closet. His belief that "bad guys can't see in the dark" might not be completely realistic, but it was adequate for undertaking action that he did have some control over: He knew the light switch was right outside his door. Once he achieved some degree of success with his plan for switching out the light, he was able to sustain his problem-solving focus long enough to lock the door and then follow through with his mother's "emergency drill." (Parenthetically, when parents rehearse with their children what to do in an emergency, they are also providing their children with a self-regulating strategy.)

We can infer that young Samuel's self-concept had a good foundation within his family and that perhaps he would also qualify as one of the resilient or invulnerable children so richly described by Murphy and Moriarty in their longitudinal study.[2] Among the protective factors noted by Masten, Best, and Garmezy[3] that help children cope with chronic adversity, little Samuel appeared to have good problem-solving skills, a positive relationship with family members, and very likely a sense of competence or efficacy. I trust the reader now has an intuitive sense of what emotional competence and self-regulation might entail. A more specific discussion of these constructs follows.

Emotional Competence

Emotional competence is defined as *the demonstration of self-efficacy in emotion-eliciting social transactions.*[4] This is a deceptively concise definition that belies the complexity of emotional competence, for we must also understand what is meant by self-efficacy and why emotion-eliciting social interaction is so central to a definition of emotionally competent functioning. The definition of self-efficacy used here is that the individual has the capacity and skills to achieve a desired outcome.[5] When the notion of self-efficacy is then applied to emotion-eliciting social transactions, we are talking about how people can respond emotionally, yet simultaneously and strategically apply their knowledge about emotions and their emotional expressiveness to relationships with others. In this way they can both negotiate their way through interpersonal exchanges and regulate their emotional experiences.

Competence

To some extent, the notions of competence and efficacy are redundant, for the notion of competence has been defined as the capacity or ability to engage in transactions with a variable and challenging social-physical environment, resulting in growth and mastery for the individual.[6] With the term *emotional competence,* we can begin to articulate what are the *emotion-related* capacities and abilities people need to engage with the changing environment such that they emerge as more differentiated, better adapted, effective, and confident.

Emotional competence presumes emotional development, but within any given age group some children or youths or adults function more emotionally competently than others. They demonstrate emotion-related capabilities that are more adaptive to the specific context in which they find themselves. I will frequently refer to these emotion-related capacities and abilities as skills to emphasize the effective functioning implicit in the notion of emotional competence. In the latter part of this essay I will review what the specific skills and capabilities of emotional competence are.

Social Meaning of Emotions

I also assume that our emotional responses are contextually anchored in social meaning, that is, we have learned cultural messages about the meaning of social transactions, relationships, and even our self-definitions. Emotional competence is inseparable from cultural context. Our biological evolution has endowed us to be emotional, but our embeddedness in relationships with others provides the diversity in emotional experience, the challenges to emotional coping, and the immensely rich ways in which we communicate our emotional experience to others. Thus, our relationships influence our emotions, and our emotions reciprocally influence our relationships.

Moral Character

Lastly, emotional competence is integrated with such concepts as sympathy, self-control, fairness, and a sense of reciprocity. These concepts are closely related to Aristotle's virtues[7] and what the contemporary philosopher Wilson views as moral sense or moral character.[8] One could possess the "skills" of emotional competence in a narrowly defined way and yet conceivably be a moral chameleon or even a sociopath. Granted, this is unlikely, particularly if one demonstrates the emotionally competent skill or capacity for being empathically responsive to others' feelings. However, I take the position that having emotional "skills" divorced from a moral sense does not constitute a genuine emotional competence. Emotional competence entails "doing the right thing."

Self-Regulation

The definition of self-regulation used here overlaps considerably with Block and Block's ego control construct.[9] I view self-regulation as the ability to manage one's actions, thoughts, and feelings in adaptive and flexible ways across a variety of contexts, whether social or physical. Optimal self-regulation contributes to a sense of well-being, a sense of self-efficacy or confidence, and a sense of connectedness to others. However, optimal self-regulation does not mean that one is always happy, involved only in conflict-free relationships, and never experiences self-doubt. In short, one is optimally self-regulating when one has a rich and varied emotional life that is shared with others and when one meets the inevitable challenges of living with a broad repertoire of effective coping strategies.

As children mature, their self-regulating capacity reflects their growing cognitive complexity, exposure to diverse experiences, opportunities to learn new ways of coping with distressing circumstances, and the degree to which they receive appropriate supportive guidance for dealing with life's challenges (e.g., in the preceding vignette Samuel's mother provided guidance to him by teaching him emergency strategies). The younger the child, the more likely she will turn to her caregivers to help her regulate herself at times of stress.[10] The school-age child is more likely to begin to look to peers for support, and, indeed, the comparison of oneself with others that starts in earnest in middle childhood can provide a great many challenges to a previously confident child.

These self/other comparisons in middle childhood mean that children begin to evaluate their talents, aptitudes, appearance, material goods, and families relative to others. Despite the common occurrence of positive bias in self-appraisals,[11] evaluating oneself relative to others can contribute to feelings of inadequacy, failure, futility, or humiliation. These experiences require self-consciousness, and the emotions of shame, envy, and anxiety are further elaborated when compared with their earlier manifestation in the preschool period.[12] It is in the elaboration of these self-conscious emotional experiences that we can see children trying to cope with the experience of a vulnerable self by altering the expression of these emotions, particularly if that appears to be one of the few factors under their control.[13]

A resilient self-regulation is also manifested in a higher threshold for tolerance of negative emotions, including aversive self-conscious emotions, but this does not mean such a child or youth is merely stoic. Instead, such resilient individuals are aware of their feelings and strategically opt for genuine or modified expression of them relative to the relationship context in which the feelings are experienced (e.g., vulnerable emotions such as sadness or anxiety are more likely to be genuinely expressed in close relationships).[14] The self-regulating individual uses her emotional responses as cues both for action and for coping effectively within relationships. The conceptual boundaries between self-regulation and emotion-regulation begin to blur when we talk about tolerance for negative emotions in interpersonal encounters, for in most cases we are combining how to deal with an aversive emotional experience with how to cope with a taxing situation. The reader is referred to Brenner and Salovey's essay in this volume and to Thompson's excellent essay for a full discussion of how emotion regulation includes both temperamental influences and "emotion dynamics" such as intensity, timing, modulation, and range. His definition of emotion regulation is included here for the reader: "Emotion regulation consists of the extrinsic and intrinsic processes responsible for monitoring, evaluating, and modifying emotional reactions, especially their intensive and temporal features, to accomplish one's goals."[15]

THE SELF-SYSTEM AND EMOTIONAL EXPERIENCE

The perspective taken in this essay is that our emotional experience is integrated with our *self-system*. Without a self capable of reflecting on itself, we would have feelings but not know that it was ourselves experiencing them. We would not be able to use emotion-descriptive language to communicate our feelings across time and space to others, nor would we be able to use our own emotional experience as a guide in understanding others' feelings. And, significantly, we would be very limited in figuring out how to respond to others in a planful, intentional way. In Western societies we assume that people have a relatively explicit belief in a self-concept, but we should keep in mind in the subsequent discussion that non-Western societies may be more likely to anchor the individual in a kinship system or view individuals as "defined" by the roles or social categories they occupy, such as gender, age group, or caste.

Subjective and Objective Selves

The notion that the self is a duality is an old one and was well articulated by Cooley[16] and James.[17] They proposed a typology of the self that was composed of both subjective and objective selves. The subjective self is without awareness of itself; it processes experience. The subjective self has also been referred to as the existential self, or the "I" in the English language. The subjective self possesses a practical knowledge, which is most evident in our habitual routines and in our intentional behavior. Developmental psychologists studying infants believe that the foundation of a subjective self emerges in intentional behavior. More specifically, when an infant learns to control some sequence of action or some interesting event, she learns a contingent relationship between an action stemming from her own body action and an outcome that she desires. This begins very early in infancy and suggests a simple discrimination of self versus not-self.[18] When infants are given the opportunity to develop contingent play routines or contingent interactions with caregivers, they do so with relish and endless enthusiasm (e.g., playing peekaboo).

The objective self is that aspect of the self that does include self-awareness. The objective self has also been referred to as the categorical self, the self concept, and the social self; it is the "me" in English language. The objective self has been aptly termed the categorical self because we describe ourselves according to categories with lexical concepts. When we announce to another, "I consider myself to be sensitive to others' feelings," we are verbally ranking ourselves as high in the category of sensitivity. Obviously the objective self requires self-awareness: "I" look at "me" and categorize what is seen. Thus people may describe themselves according to personality traits, likes and dislikes, or simply list the social roles they occupy, for example, student, spouse, artist, scientist, and so forth. The categories applied to the self by the self may be accurate or inaccurate, specific or global, positive or negative, clear or vague, but they are meaningful to the self and contribute significantly to whether we experience low or high self-esteem.[19]

In a sense, we possess a subjective self from an early age: Infants act on the world, have emotional states, and respond to social and physical stimuli. It is not until we develop the capacity to *reflect* on ourselves that we begin to develop objective self-awareness. The sociologists Cooley and Mead both emphasized that our relationships with others are pivotal to how we come to describe ourselves—and thus develop a self-concept.[20] Others give us feedback: For example, parents tell their children, "You are a good girl" or "You are a brat," and perhaps later with their adolescents, "I can't believe how selfish you are!" As children come to be able to appreciate the perspective of another, they can begin to reflect upon their feelings and behavior as viewed through the psychological lenses of others.[21]

With increasing maturity, older children and adolescents can selectively choose whether to concur with others' views of themselves or not. Indeed, a common conflict experienced by many North American adolescents is whether to go along with their parents' expectations for themselves or whether to pursue those activities preferred by their friends but not by their parents. I suspect that adaptive resolutions of such conflicts require self-reflection and goal striving, which take into account one's *moral disposition* and sense of emotional self-efficacy. Interestingly, social psychologists have determined that those individuals who rely excessively on others' evaluations of themselves rather than on their own self-reflections are more prone to experience low self-esteem. As a result, they also experience more frequently mood swings and negative emotions.[22] In sum, their sense of well-being is fragile.

Neisser's Ecological, Extended, and Evaluative Selves

Another approach to the self-system that is also very useful for understanding how emotions and "selfhood" are intertwined was proposed by Neisser.[23] His typology of the self reflects his interest in cognition, perception, and the acquisition of skillfulness as a general way to examine the adaptiveness of humans to their variable environments.

Ecological Self

His notion of the ecological self is premised on how we perceive our environment in terms of what it affords us as opportunities for interaction. He gives us an example: Ceilings afford flies an opportunity to walk on them; they do not for humans. For a young infant, a rattle with a narrow midsection affords an opportunity to grasp it; handing that same baby a tennis ball would not. Thus, the individual interacts with an environment that is bidirectional: What happens is a joint function of what we can do with the environment and what the environment provides us as an accessible structure (i.e., its *affordances*).[24]

The ecological self is much like a subjective self in that the emphasis is on the individual engaged in transactions with those features of the environment that permit or afford interaction. This is equivalent to what was referred to earlier as practical knowledge demonstrated by individuals as they pursue their daily routines. We do not have to think about what our legs are doing as we pedal our bicycle; we just "know" how to do it. But what would we do if some crazed inventor presented us with a so-called bicycle that had square wheels? Such an object would not "afford" us a means of transportation.

The ecological self is also significant for the development of emotional competence because of its emphasis on the self *in relationship to an environment*. Obviously that environment includes other people, which means that the social environment can also be looked at as presenting an array of *affordances* or opportunities for interaction to the individual. This gets very interesting in a room full of people (e.g., a classroom of children) who are from a variety of cultures, many of whom may not speak much English. What are the affordances for social interaction in such a setting when the individuals may differ greatly in their assumptions of how social relations are defined? This is indeed a challenge faced daily by our teachers in culturally diverse communities.

The Extended Self

Neisser's concept of a self extended in time is intended to address the fact that we are not only in a relationship to a present environment but are also concerned with the past and the future. The extended self permits us to imagine the possible, not just the actual. The preschooler's imaginary play is an early example of an extended self. For example, the young child might imagine herself in positions of power, strength, and authority and temporarily disregard her relative powerlessness and dependency as she acts out the behavior of "Kimberly, the Pink Power-Ranger" or "Jean, of the X-Men" (these being the current favorites of one of my 5-year-old informants).

Expectations are especially powerful influences on which opportunities we seek out (or avoid) in our social and physical environments. Such expectations can be based on past experience of ourselves in some transaction or on communications from others or observations of others as to what to expect. The extended self also facilitates the development of schemas and scripts: We have a readiness for how to respond to a new environment based on some of its similarities to what we have learned as interaction strategies in former environments. Children demonstrate the influence of expectations acquired in previous interactions on their behavior in similar, but novel situations. As an illustration, consider 6-year-old Kelly's experience:

> Debra, Kelly's Mom, had been divorced since Kelly was 2. She had dated several men and had lived with a couple of them, but the relationships ended after a year. Now she was involved with Mac, and they were moving into an apartment together with Kelly.
>
> Debra's previous partner, Bill, had been emotionally abusive and had often threatened to or indeed broken Kelly's toys when he perceived her as somehow not complying with his wishes. Now in the new apartment with Mac, Kelly became panic-stricken about the whereabouts of her toys and struggled to keep them hidden from Mac. Mac was puzzled, and after buying her a box of Lego blocks, he offered to help build something with her. Kelly burst out crying and said, "You'll break it, won't you!" Debra witnessed the exchange and realized what was happening. She explained to Mac what Kelly's experience had been with Bill, and together they sought to try to reassure Kelly and pointed out to her on subsequent occasions how different Mac was from Bill.

This illustration also shows the extended self as having anticipations about how to cope with some emotionally challenging situation. The degree to which one has had efficacious experiences in similar earlier situations will influence the sense of self-agency or self-confidence one brings to bear upon the new situation. In contrast, if preceding similar situations had tended to end poorly, as they did for Kelly, then one is less likely to feel self-confident in approaching the new situation. Alternative responses may also include false bravado, and avoidant behavior is an especially common response to such anxiety-laden challenges.

The Evaluative Self

With this feature of the self Neisser highlights the feelings people attach to their interactions with the physical and social environments: We like or dislike parties, we are provoked or dejected by social injustices, we are entertained or scared witless by movies like *Pulp Fiction*. The evaluative self is a goal-directed self, and as a consequence, our environmental interactions are motivated toward some outcomes and away from others. As Neisser aptly phrases it, "The ecological self does not have a motivational dimension. Babies know what they want, but they do not know who wants it."[25] When the evaluative self develops, as it commonly does between 2 and 3 years of age,[26] then the toddler *knows* how she feels. She is able to use language to communicate her feelings, to self-refer to her own experience. She also becomes conscious of others' feelings about her, and in conjunction with her self-extended-in-time, she can begin to maneuver her interactions with others so as to attain certain advantages or avoid disadvantages.

Neisser's model of the tripartite self helps us to look at emotional experience within the individual as it unfolds (a) in a physical and social environment (the ecological self), (b) relative to a temporal framework (the extended self), and (c) in response to the standards and values of the family and societal context (the evaluative self). In sum, the concepts of the ecological, extended, and evaluative self permit us to look at functional interactions between individuals and their social and physical environments. This triple concept of self also gives us a conceptual tool to look at how individual differences may manifest themselves in why Person A feels self-efficacious in a particular social situation while Person B feels overwhelmed in seemingly the same social situation. The point to be made here is that the ostensibly similar social situation is not experienced *transactionally* as uniform. The social situation becomes a dynamic experience and functionally varies according to how Person A's multifaceted self engages in it as opposed to how Person B's multifaceted self engages in it. Emotional competence then becomes linked to how a particular multifaceted self experiences self-efficacy in particular transactions. This implies some degree of inconsistency or variability in emotional competence. We may demonstrate emotional competence in 99 different interactions, but in the 100th we may encounter that situation we are not prepared for or do not have the skills to cope with, and we experience a sense of diminishment, stress, or inadequacy. We may also find that we would rather deceive ourselves about our negative experience altogether than deal directly with our emotional incompetence.[27]

ATTACHMENT AND SELF-REGULATION

The degree to which emotional experience is integrated adaptively with self-regulatory processes may derive from our experience of our early attachment relationships. Attachment reflects a complex social interaction involving the dynamic interplay between caretakers and infants. This process may well reflect cross-generational transmission of innate and learned behaviors, and some researchers hypothesize that the quality of attachment in early life influences later emotional "style."[28] A healthy attachment lends itself to the expression of and experimentation with a greater repertoire of emotional behaviors, whereas insecure or avoidant attachment results in rigid and constrictive responses. I will briefly summarize the recent argument put forth by Cassidy[29] as to how attachment and emotional "style" may be connected.

Drawing upon work by Bowlby[30] and Main,[31] Cassidy describes how the infant is biologically disposed to maintain proximity to the caregiver and thus learns to tailor its responses to the caregiver in light of her or his responses to it; that is, the infant can make use of reciprocal feedback in adjusting its strategies for facilitating closeness with the caregiver. To illustrate, after a brief separation, securely attached infants respond to reunion with their caregivers with warmth, relief, and responsiveness upon her return (mothers always seem to be the caregivers in this sort of research). They do not show the wariness, avoidance, or resistance that characterizes infants who do not enjoy secure attachments (i.e., infants who are insecurely or anxiously attached). Mothers of securely attached infants apparently reliably demonstrate sensitive responses to their infants' emotional signals, and thus their presence is a "safe haven" from which the infant can venture forth to explore the environment. That environment can, of course, produce taxing or difficult situations that require the infant or toddler to cope with it, and using Mom as an ally and support base for when things get tough is an excellent coping strategy.

Cassidy goes on to say that for the securely attached infant negative emotions such as anger and fear come to be associated with maternal sympathetic assistance, and that these negative feelings are associated neither with any sort of invalidation of the young child nor with denial of the negative feelings. What this does for emotional regulation is to enable the young child to tolerate aversive emotion temporarily so that she can begin to make sense of the frustrating or conflictual situation that faces her and figure out a response.

If securely attached infants can use their caregivers as "safe havens" from which to venture forth to explore the physical and social environment, it is also likely that such caregivers provide a sense of stability such that the child can also explore a range of emotions. For example, hanging on to Mom or Dad makes scary things tolerable and eventually "fun" (e.g., fireworks displays, amusement park rides). The caregiver's empathic sharing of emotions makes them acceptable and routine for the securely attached infant.

The anxiously attached infant, on the other hand, has often experienced its caregiver's rejection when it sought comfort for its distress. Such an infant learns that some emotions are not acceptable and may not even be safe. It develops a wariness and avoidance of its caregiver and begins to regulate its emotions by minimizing their expression when in the presence of the caregiver. Cassidy cites a couple of studies that indicated that insecurely attached infants interacted responsively with their mothers when not distressed or needing care. But when experiencing emotional distress, they ended up suppressing their negative emotional display so as *to maintain* caregiver involvement. In other words, the infant's emotional regulation strategy seems to be, "Mom will stay with me if I don't raise any fuss." The cost, however, to the infant is constant emotional vigilance and suppression of normal distress, which, if it becomes a chronic pattern, is often maladaptive in other close relationships. This takes us to the next issue, does the quality of attachment with one's primary caregivers *predictably* affect one's social and emotional functioning later in life? This question raises a number of theoretically controversial issues about continuity and change in human development, and longitudinal research has not been able to definitively answer this question. Many caveats remain.

Retrospective research with 18-year-olds does suggest a link between their emotional functioning and their attachment style.[32] When these young adults were interviewed about their family-of-origin relationships,[33] the securely attached individuals emerged as less hostile, less anxious, more ego-resilient, experienced less distress, and enjoyed more social support than the avoidant/attachment-dismissing group or the excessively preoccupied group. Thus, relative to emotion regulation and associated social efficacy, it would appear that within the family of origin warmth, responsiveness, and empathy with the child's emotional experience contribute to the development over time of competent self-regulation. These same experiences may prove to be centrally involved in the acquisition of emotional competence as well. I turn now to a brief presentation of the skills and capabilities involved in emotional competence.

SKILLS OF EMOTIONAL COMPETENCE

An important point to bear in mind as we review these emotional competencies is that they are intimately linked with cultural values. In many respects, these skills of emotional competence reflect Western societies' notions of "how emotion works." I refer to such beliefs as folk theories of emotion. For example, consider how many people in the United States believe in the "volcano theory" of emotion—namely, that unexpressed emotions will somehow build up inside an individual and "explode" if they are not otherwise "vented." Other non-Western cultures do not necessarily view unexpressed emotions as accumulative or as explosive. Variants on North American folk theories of emotion also include the "tidal wave theory" (emotions are overwhelming), the "out-of-sight-out-of-mind theory" (if emotions are not thought about, they will somehow evaporate), and the "Mr. Spock (*Star Trek*) theory" (emotions are irrelevant when compared to the importance of logical thinking). Perhaps the reader can think of additional metaphors for characterizing how emotion works in our society; I would be interested in hearing them.

It should be noted that many research investigations have been carried out in recent years that are relevant to the skills and capabilities of emotional competence listed in the following. For the sake of brevity, I will not review those studies here.[34]

1: *Awareness of one's emotional state, including the possibility that one is experiencing multiple emotions, and at even more mature levels, awareness that one might also not be consciously aware of one's feelings due to unconscious dynamics or selective inattention.*

A vignette illustrates this first skill of emotional competence in the life of a young adolescent:

> Fourteen-year-old Elijah lived with his Mom and younger brother; his dad lived across town and remained involved in both of his sons' lives. Recently Elijah announced to his Mom that he wanted to live with his dad, and although Dad was barely consulted, Elijah rather quickly showed up at his apartment with a suitcase and his computer, a gift from his maternal grandmother. Dad worked as a truck driver for a moving van company and frequently experienced layoffs; Mom worked as a dental hygienist. Mom worried about a clash in values, especially around educational achievement, but she let her son go. He would still attend the same diocesan high school, regardless of where he lived.
>
> Elijah set about fixing up his computer in a corner of the living room, which necessitated his cleaning up the place in order just to find a corner to use. He felt irritated with his dad, yet recognized that tidiness was not his dad's "thing." He briefly wondered if his dad would spill something on his keyboard or somehow mess up his computer. Dad came home, noticed the cleanup, and somewhat sheepishly thanked Elijah. He set about making supper and asked Elijah to show him "some stuff" on his computer. Elijah readily did so and enjoyed impressing his dad with both the games as well as the programs he used for school.

As days turned into weeks, Elijah felt that he increasingly missed the support that his Mom gave him in his schoolwork; he realized that his dad acted strained and uncomfortable if he asked him a question or for help. On the other hand, he felt his dad "lets me be me and Mom lets me be her." He considered spending the weekdays with Mom and the weekends with Dad and wondered how each would feel about that arrangement. He was aware of his need for each of them, but he also knew he felt both sad and irritated around his dad, and with his Mom he had felt stifled and overprotected. With Dad he felt more grown up, and with Mom he felt he shared more of himself. He also thought that his dad was not paying as much attention to his little brother now that he was living with him, and he was aware of feeling a curious mix of resentment and smugness.

Elijah went through numerous internal imaginary dialogues with himself and his parents. He worried about hurting his father's feelings if he moved back to Mom's and then realized that she might have felt hurt when he initially moved out. Maybe she wouldn't let him move back again! On his computer he made lists of pros and cons, and then he began to make lists of "feelings for" and "feelings against." He looked up the definition for *ambivalence* on the thesaurus option of his word-processing program and saw that it included as entries "vacillation" and "indecision." No wonder it was so hard to figure out what to do. He would really have to know his own mind if he was going to explain his choice to his parents.

Elijah called his Mom and suggested his plan: He and his brother would alternate living with each parent, and some weeks both brothers would be together with one or the other parent. He thought it would be fair to everyone, and he wanted to have time with both parents and even with his little brother. Little did he know that his arrangement was exactly what many custody mediators might have recommended for this family.

Elijah's awareness of his feelings facilitated his problem solving, a capability central to emotional competence. Knowing that one feels scared instead of sad yields different avenues for figuring out what to do; in the former circumstance it might be a good idea to run away, but if one is sad, seeking support might be the most adaptive action to take. Elijah was also able to appreciate his having multiple and even seemingly contradictory feelings about his parents. As a result, his interpersonal world was enriched and provided him with additional options for how to interact with his parents. He even had an inkling of being aware that he might be unaware of some feelings; namely, when he recognized that despite feeling resentful about his dad's lesser attention to his brother, he also enjoyed a certain degree of smug self-satisfaction with that arrangement.

In contrast to Elijah, individuals who are impoverished in their awareness of their emotions would have parallel deficits in knowing how to respond adaptively to their environment. Their reduced capacity for experiencing multiple emotions toward the same person or situation would restrict the complexity of their appraisals of their relationships. Concurrently, their self-efficacy in emotion-eliciting social transactions would be limited or even impaired.

2: *Ability to discern others' emotions, based on situational and expressive cues that have some degree of cultural consensus as to their emotional meaning.*

The ability to understand what others are feeling develops in conjunction with awareness of one's own feelings, with one's ability to empathize, and with the ability to conceptualize causes of emotions and their behavioral consequences. In addition, the more we learn about how and why people act as they do, the more we can *infer* what is going on for them emotionally, even if it is not especially obvious or may even be counterintuitive.

Infants learn to scan others' facial expressions (especially their caregivers') in order to figure out the emotional meaning of ambiguous situations. This has been called social referencing, and much research has been devoted to it.[35] However, let us move beyond social referencing to examine what children have to understand in order to generate *sophisticated* insight into another's emotional experience: (a) They need to be able to decode the usual meanings of emotional facial expressions; (b) they need to understand situations that commonly elicit emotions; (c) they need to realize that others have minds, intentions, beliefs, or what has otherwise been referred to as "inner states"; (d) they need to take into account unique information about the other that might qualify or make comprehensible a nonstereotypic emotional response or a response that differs from how oneself would feel in the same situation; and (e) they need to be able to apply emotion labels to emotional experience so that they can verbally communicate with others about their feelings. (This last item is part of the next emotional competence skill.)

By 7 to 8 years of age, many children are able to demonstrate these aspects of this emotional competency in social interactions that are familiar to them. Research suggests that children who are particularly skilled at "reading" others' emotions also are generally those who enjoy higher social status among their peers.[36] In contrast, children who grow up in chronically abusive homes may show deficits in understanding others' emotions and often demonstrate a combination of aggression and withdrawal in their peer interaction.[37]

3: *Ability to use the vocabulary of emotion and expression terms commonly available in one's (sub)culture and at more mature levels to acquire cultural scripts that link emotion with social roles.*

The ability to represent our emotional experience through words, imagery, and symbolism of varied sorts leads to two major accomplishments: The first is we can communicate our emotional experiences to others across time and space, whether this takes the form of talking on the telephone about how we felt about what happened yesterday or painting a picture of a maelstrom to represent our inner turmoil. The second accomplishment is conceptual. By having access to representations of our emotional experiences, we can further elaborate them, integrate them across contexts, and compare them with others' representations about emotional experiences. Some of the developments in awareness of our own multiple feelings or in understanding others' atypical emotions described earlier could not occur if we did not have access to a language or representational system for symbolically encoding and communicating our emotional experiences.

As school-age children mature, we can study how their scripts for particular emotions become integrated with other belief networks such as sex role. I will use Russell's definition of scripts here: It is "a knowledge structure for a type of event whereby the event is thought of as a sequence of subevents."[38] To illustrate, the script sequence for anger in North America might be as follows: (a) An offensive act was undertaken that was both intentional and harmful to an undeserving person; (b) the recipient of the offense expresses negative emotion at the offender; (c) the recipient experiences physical changes accompanying the negative emotion, for example, flushing, clenched jaws; (d) the recipient contemplates retribution; and (e) reciprocal harm is done to the offender. Of course emotion scripts surround both positive and negative emotional experiences, but given that negative emotions might be more differentiated in their conceptualization,[39] our scripts for negative emotions when viewed as interacting with other belief systems may provide us with the richest scenarios for emotional experiences embedded in interpersonal contexts. I offer the following two anger episodes to illustrate contextual, sex-role, and individual differences.

Enrique accidentally bumped his cafeteria tray into Charlie, a notorious bully at the Cesar Chavez Middle School, and his pudding dish fell off onto Charlie's high-top shoe, making quite a mess. Enrique crossed himself mentally and began to apologize to Charlie. Some other boys began to laugh at Charlie, taunting him about his soiled shoe. Charlie flushed and grimaced briefly. Despite Enrique's apology and its clearly being an accident, Charlie grabbed Enrique behind the neck and forced his face to his shoe and said crudely, "Clean it up, now." The cafeteria supervisor noticed the crowd gathering and rushed over. He separated the boys, but not before Charlie had mashed Enrique's face into the pudding on his shoe. Charlie ran off from the cafeteria supervisor laughing and shouting out to the shamed Enrique that he should wash his face more often.

Darlene was getting ready for picture day at her middle school. She fussed over her hair and tried to apply mascara gingerly to her eyelashes and a bit of eyeliner to the base of her eyelids. Kids were not supposed to wear any makeup, but she thought she could get away with just a little, and it was worth the risk, because it would make her eyes look prettier in the photograph. Some lipstick wouldn't hurt either.

Later that morning, the vice principal, Mr. Smith, did indeed catch Darlene, and in front of a number of kids told her in a rather insulting manner that she wouldn't be allowed to have her picture taken if she didn't remove her lipstick. Darlene smiled demurely at Mr. Smith and turned toward the girls' bathroom, tossing her long hair over her shoulder in an exaggeratedly dramatic fashion. But as she entered the bathroom, she could feel she was clenching her teeth. Later she bragged to the other girls about how she had at least gotten her photo taken with her eye makeup on, because Mr. Smith was too stupid to notice it, and eye makeup is what really counts in photos anyway.

Charlie's anger script does not need the feature of intentionality in the actions of the offender, and his retribution is in excess of the presumed offense. Darlene's anger script appears by comparison to be very mild. Her emphasis is on maintenance of her image with her peers (also a major factor in Charlie's anger script) rather than on retribution toward the offender, although she does disparage him when out of his hearing. Darlene's anger script may also overlap with her shame script, a connection that Michael Lewis has discussed in detail in relating shame to women's sex-role socialization.[40] Certainly Charlie's vengeance was directed at shaming the unfortunate Enrique, for he had felt shamed himself by the taunts of bystanders about the pudding on his shoe. Turning shame into rage may be part of men's sex-role socialization, according to Lewis. The insightful clinician Helen Block Lewis referred to the *"humiliated fury"* directed at the instigators and witnesses of one's shame,[41] and she reasoned that when shamed individuals direct their rage at others, they anticipate restoring their sense of powerfulness and control. I think what is important to consider here is that scripts for different emotions may merge (or one emotion may cycle into another) under certain circumstances, particularly if individuals appraise a situation as salient for certain beliefs they hold about themselves.

4: *Capacity for empathic and sympathetic involvement in others' emotional experiences.*

In terms of emotional competence, empathic responsiveness may be one of the most significant components for promoting social bonds among people and fostering prosocial behavior. Without empathy as a component of emotional competence, one could conceivably demonstrate all the other "skills" of emotional competence in a very Machiavellian or even sociopathic fashion. Empathy, *feeling with* others, and sympathy, *feeling for* others, are emotional responses that connect us with others. On a larger scale, even society recognizes the importance of empathy and sympathy, for without them, we would have no sense of mercy or clemency when dispensing justice. Empathic arousal and the somewhat cognitively more "detached" sympathetic response appear to be critical emotional antecedents of prosocial behavior, although they do not guarantee prosocial behavior. Research also suggests that there needs to be felt a sense of responsibility for helping or comforting a distressed person.[42] Possession of a moral sense or character as described at the beginning of this essay is especially relevant here. Developmental research suggests that young children who are more likely to help and share with others are able to reason about others' needs and are likely to have sympathetic parents as well.[43]

In offenders and victimizers we see the breakdown of emotional competence, and, indeed, when people victimize others, they typically do not feel empathy or sympathy toward them. Some of the characteristics of the "mind-set" held by victimizers include the following:[44]

First, they have an impaired or distorted perspective-taking capacity in that the intended victim is viewed as *worthless,* as dispensable, as subhuman, as inferior. Bandura states that the attribution, on some level, of the victim as insensate, as unfeeling, is critical for short-circuiting the otherwise emotion-arousing response that would normally be evoked upon witnessing another's distress. Second, the attribution of *blame* to victims for what happened to them deflects self-evaluation and permits exoneration of the perpetrators' behavior toward them. Gibbs quotes delinquents as saying that a store owner "deserved" to get robbed, since he had not secured the premises adequately. Third, as Bandura argues, if harmdoers can make a comparison with someone else's destructive behavior and *view their own as less harmful,* then they can counter self-doubts and replace them with self-approving sanctions for the destructive exploits.

Such a cognitive "switch" may be occurring with drive-by shootings: The other gang did something bad to one's group, territory, or contacts, so now one not only seeks revenge but also condones it as a worthy act, despite the possible injury of innocent bystanders.

Empathy, sympathy, and prosocial behavior are multidimensional, and it is not surprising that contextual factors, including one's scripts regarding sex role and one's self-concept, may influence how one experiences empathy and concern for others' well-being in a particular situation. As an example, helping strangers has been found to be more frequent among males, but women do more long-term nurturing and helping of others in close relationships.[45] Our capacity for responding vicariously to another's emotional plight humanizes us and may well bring out the best in us; with empathic responsiveness we can extend ourselves beyond our immediate space and time.

5: *Ability to realize that an inner emotional state need not correspond to outer expression, both in oneself and in others, and at more mature levels the ability to understand that one's emotional-expressive behavior may impact on another and to take this into account in one's self-presentation strategies.*

I will introduce this significant skill of emotional competence with a vignette:

> Laura, a 12-year-old, was the newly elected captain of her all-girl soccer team. They had a good record so far this year and were scheduled to play against a team in another town who had previously always beaten them. Laura wanted very much to prove herself a worthy team captain and help her team win this game, but she was apprehensive about several players' skills. During practice she encouraged and tried to give support to everyone, including the weak players. The day of the game arrived, and everyone nervously gathered at the playing field.
>
> The game did not go well for Laura's team. They played as well as they could but the other team essentially demolished them. As they dismally gathered together after the game was over, Laura felt like crying, and her eyes smarted as she sought to regain composure. After gathering herself together, she said loudly to her teammates, "Those guys don't realize that we *LET* them win; we were just showing how generous we can be," and she lifted up her head, stuck out her flat chest, and pretended to strut. Her teammates cheered and began to mimic her gestures.

Laura keenly felt disappointment over losing the game and distress over letting her teammates down. However, she sought to keep these feelings to herself and present herself differently to her teammates and any other onlookers by adopting a posture of mock bravado. Her attempt at parody worked to pull her team together and distract them, at least temporarily, from their defeat. It was also a strategy that restored her leadership, again at least for the moment. Her management of her initial negative feelings was skillful and effective relative to the social goals she had in mind, and, indeed, her *emotional dissemblance* functioned as an interpersonal coping strategy. Emotional dissemblance is a strategy aimed at maintenance (or restoration) of social-emotional equilibrium by an individual's altering her verbal and/or nonverbal communication of her emotional experience to others. "Others" can also be an imaginary or anticipated audience.

Emotional dissemblance is effective when it serves the long-term well-being of the individual and facilitates interpersonal negotiation during conflict. In such instances emotional dissemblance will be fluidly applied, and "mixed messages" are commonly observed. For example, some people might have observed Laura's initial distress, or had they looked more closely at her "performance," they might have noticed some tension in the exaggerated strutting or in the shrillness of her voice. Interestingly, many people overlook these mixed messages, either by accepting the expressive gestures as part of the expected social interaction or by politely ignoring our minor social gaffes.[46] When emotional dissemblance is carried to an extreme and is used rigidly and inflexibly, it is likely to become maladaptive as an interpersonal negotiation strategy and may contribute to impoverished close relationships.[47]

Preschoolers are able to behave in ways that indicate that they can separate their internal feelings from their emotional-expressive behavior, although they may not be able to articulate their doing this.[48] School-age children are generally quite aware of not revealing their feelings in certain circumstances in order to avoid negative social consequences like teasing, getting in trouble, or being criticized. They also know that not revealing some feelings helps to protect the feelings of others. Yet school-age children also recognize that it is appropriate to express feelings in certain kinds of relationships, for example, with close friends. I use the term *emotion management* to refer to knowing when to express one's feelings genuinely and when to modify or even suppress their expression, depending on the social circumstances and on how important it is to the self to control or express the feeling.[49] Emotional dissemblance becomes, then, one strategy of emotion management among many.

6: *Capacity for adaptive coping with aversive or distressing emotions by using self-regulatory strategies that ameliorate the intensity or temporal duration of such emotional states (e.g., "stress hardiness").*

Effective coping in Western cultures involves acknowledgment of one's feelings, awareness of one's self as having some degree of agency, and a functional appraisal of the problematic situation and one's role in it. Adaptive problem solving can then be initiated. By late childhood or early adolescence, Western children who have enjoyed secure attachment within their supportive families and escaped severe trauma should generally be capable of this sort of emotionally competent coping. However, it should be noted that these are two rather significant contingencies, secure attachment relations and relative absence of trauma, that may be relatively scarce when one considers the incidence of divorce, poverty, community violence, and abuse in American families.

Types of Coping Strategies

The sorts of coping strategies commonly available to children and youth can be prioritized according to the degree to which they are thought to be adaptive. I have here constructed two such prioritized lists. The first list addresses coping strategies that are often used in situations in which *one has control* over the circumstances. The second list addresses what have been called *emotion-focused* coping strategies, and these strategies are typically evoked when we have relatively *little control* over the circumstances (e.g., undergoing aversive medical procedures).

Moderate to High Control over Circumstances:

1. Problem-solving strategies.
2. Support seeking (includes seeking both help and comfort or solace).
3. Distancing strategies (wary detachment).
4. Internalizing strategies (self-blaming, anxious, worried behavior).
5. Externalizing strategies (blaming others, aggressive behavior).

Children readily nominate problem solving and support seeking as the best strategies for dealing with situations in which one has at least moderate control. They view aggressive and externalizing strategies as the worst approach.[50]

For situations in which children perceive that they do not have much control, the following first three emotion-focused strategies are more adaptive than the last three.

Little or No Control over Circumstances:

1. Substitution or distraction from context or feeling.
2. Reframing or redefining the negative context or negative feeling.
3. Cognitive "blunting" or information-seeking strategies.
4. Avoidance of negative context or of negative feeling.
5. Denial of negative context or feeling.
6. Dissociation of self from situation.[51]

Development of Coping Strategies

Due to methodological variation, sample age differences, and rather profound contextual differences, we do not have a systematic empirical literature that tells us what coping strategies tend to emerge at what age for mainstream North American children. However, two general patterns have emerged with regard to age: As children get older, they generate *more* coping alternatives to stressful situations and they become more able to make use of cognitively oriented coping strategies for situations in which they have no control.[52] Embedded in both of these age-related patterns is greater cognitive complexity that is associated with becoming older: (a) the ability to appraise *accurately* when a situation is simply not under one's control; (b) the ability to shift intentionally one's thoughts to something else less aversive; (c) the ability to use symbolic thought in ways that transform the meaningfulness of a stressful encounter or situation; and (d) very importantly, the ability to consider a stressful situation from a number of different angles and thus consider different problem solutions relative to these different perspectives. As to when these two general developmental patterns in coping are clearly in place, I would suggest that by age 10 most children will have a fairly well developed coping repertoire that includes the emotion-focused strategies of cognitive distraction and transformation. This assumes, of course, that these children have received adequate support and that traumas have not preoccupied their emotional resources.

In summary, as children mature, their growing cognitive sophistication, exposure to varied social models, and breadth of emotional-social experience contribute to their being able to generate more coping solutions to problematic situations. The older they are when faced with severe trauma, the more able they are to see the situation from various perspectives (including those held by other people who may be part of the problematic situation) and figure out a way to resolve it. With maturity, they become more accurate in their appraisals of how much control they really have over the situation and of what risks might accompany taking control of a very difficult situation (e.g., intervening in a fight).

7: *Awareness that the structure or nature of relationships is in part defined by the quality of emotional communication within the relationship.*

With awareness of emotional communication within relationships, the individual now recognizes and uses emotional expression and experience to differentiate his or her relations with others. For example, mature intimacy is in part defined by mutual or reciprocal sharing of genuine emotions, whereas a parent-child relationship may have asymmetric sharing of genuine emotions. This requires the individual to take into account the interpersonal consequences of his or her emotional communication within the relationship. From an emotional competence perspective, self-efficacy is served if one is aware of how she communicated her feelings with others and recognizes that she communicated differently depending on the nature of the relationship. With awareness, we are better able to gauge our goals vis-à-vis a particular person (or set of people) and to alter our emotional communication in order to fine-tune the quality of the relationship and its boundaries. An example will make this more clear:

> Fourteen-year-old Alicia went through a conflict resolution training program given by the school counselor and some other counselors from a local youth services agency. A short time later she found out she had been selected to be a peer counselor in the middle school. She felt quite honored. However, her positive feelings were shaken when the selection was announced the next day at a school-wide assembly, and she overheard a couple of kids sitting behind her whispering none too softly, "She is such a brown-nose." She wanted to turn around and retort with some choice words of her own, but she did not, for it was immediately clear to her that an angry reaction to a couple of dumb kids' trying to "bait" her would affect her credibility as a peer counselor. How could she help others to solve their fights if she could be easily rattled by insults? She pondered how she would help kids deal with insults or "dissing," and noticed that for herself what worked was to focus on her goals, like what she

had just done: She had wanted to be seen as a fair and strong peer counselor by other kids.

Alicia is obviously an insightful and self-reflective girl and is very much aware of how expression of feelings affects social interaction. Her desire to be perceived as a fair and strong peer counselor helps her to manage her emotional communication so as to promote that goal and to define the boundaries between appropriate behavior as a peer counselor and vengeful behavior that she might have otherwise impulsively undertaken upon hearing herself described as a "brown-nose." The school counselor obviously recognized Alicia's emotional competence and especially her sensitivity to how emotional communication is inextricably intertwined with the dynamics of relationships.

Consistent with the aforementioned focus on goals of a relationship, much of North American emotional communication is also concerned with issues of power or dominance and closeness of relationship.[53] Asymmetric relationships are those in which one person might dominate over the other, yet they might still have a close relationship. Such asymmetry characterizes a parent-child relationship, and the parent clearly has the major responsibility for fostering the well-being of the child. We can think of other asymmetric relationships, such as two people who differ in power but are mutually distant with one another (e.g., supervisor and employee relationship) or a dyad in which power is equal, but one member views himself as being closer to the other, despite the feeling not being reciprocated (e.g., one-sided "friendships"). On the other hand, a genuine friendship or close relationship between peers would more likely be symmetric: Power or dominance would be equally shared, and mutuality would be a defining characteristic of the emotional communication.

Selman and his colleague have developed a model of interpersonal negotiation that is related to emotional communication within relationships.[54] They based their model on how two people define a problem between them, ranging from elementary (the problem is defined in terms of the wants of the person viewed as having the most power) to complex and mature (the problem is defined as a shared or mutual concern, taking into account both persons' needs or wants). A problem implies a goal, whether it is to restore relationship equilibrium or to achieve some common instrumental or task outcome. Whether the problem is defined in either an elementary or a complex fashion, its definition influences the nature of the goal as well, and this in turn sets the stage for emotional communication within the dyadic relationship. Consider a marital conflict: If one spouse overtly or covertly sees the conflict as a challenge to her or his power in the relationship, then resolution of the conflict will be seen by that spouse as "winning" the fight and getting what she/he wants with little regard for the needs and desires of the other partner. Extreme examples of this pattern are found in cases of domestic violence.[55]

There have been relatively few studies which have examined children's emotional communication within different kinds of relationships. However, one study conducted in Germany is relevant to this emotional competency.[56] Von Salisch investigated differences in emotional communication between friendship pairs and acquaintance pairs. All the children were 11 or 12 years old. She had the pairs of children play a computer game that had been rigged so that it would appear as though one of them had caused the pair to lose the game. In contrast to playing the game with a casual acquaintance, with their close friends the children smiled very frequently at one another, even as they uttered verbal reproaches or expressed contempt for their friend's "failure" in the game. Their smiling was often reciprocated, and the dance of smiles seemed to function as a mutual reassurance that the relationship between the children was maintained and not threatened—despite the occasional reproaches and expressions of contempt. The children's smiling behavior not only expressed positive feelings, it also contained important social messages about relationship durability (or equilibrium) and about how the interactants defined their relationship by their style of emotional communication.

8: *Capacity for emotional self-efficacy: The individual views her or himself as feeling, overall, the way he or she wants to feel.*

Emotional self-efficacy means that one accepts one's emotional experience, whether unique and eccentric or culturally conventional, and this acceptance is in alignment with the individual's beliefs about what constitutes desirable emotional "balance." In essence, one is living in accord with one's *personal* folk theory of emotion when one demonstrates emotional self-efficacy, as well as in accord with one's moral sense.

With emotional self-efficacy one feels relatively in control of one's emotional experience from the standpoint of mastery and self-regard. One does not feel overwhelmed by the enormity, intensity, or complexity of emotional experience, nor does one react to one's feelings by inhibiting, distrusting, or "damping down and numbing them out." The capacity for emotional self-efficacy probably also entails some understanding of how one's personality interfaces with one's emotional experience. Insight into one's foibles, talents, vulnerabilities, and strengths can be melded with emotional self-efficacy to generate a sense of self-acceptance.

Constructs related to emotional self-efficacy include *subjective well-being* and *positive appraisal style.*[57] The former functions much like a mood state that helps as a buffer when we do have to endure especially taxing or adverse circumstances. The latter, positive appraisal style, is also trait-like in that it functions like a dispositional "filter" through which we attribute meaningfulness to events in our lives. In the comparison of people who see a glass as half full versus those who see it as half empty, the former have a positive appraisal style.

Harter's research on the role of self-worth in mediating emotion and motivation is also very relevant to emotional self-efficacy.[58] Using path analytic techniques with data from older children, she found that global self-worth strongly influenced affect (defined here as happy versus sad), and affect in turn influenced motivation (defined as energy and interest versus their absence). Her model suggests that the overall evaluation of the self is laden with feeling, and it is this feeling about who we are as a person that energizes us or renders us lethargic. It should also be noted that the determinants she used for global self-worth consisted of social support, positive regard from others, and competence in domains viewed as important to the self.

The notion of emotional self-efficacy maps onto Harter's model very well. If we experience ourselves as generally well regarded by others who are significant to us, and we believe we function competently in the activities important to us, then the feedback we get from our behavior and relationships reinforces our belief in our *self-efficacy*. Assuming that people want to be efficacious—that is, they generally desire to succeed in their endeavors and attain their goals—then upon goal achievement, they will likely feel happy (or contented, or relieved, or perhaps even elated and joyful). If a child grows up experiencing goal attainment and the accompanying positive feelings more often than not, she will be more likely to develop a positive appraisal style and concomitant sense of subjective well-being. Then, when faced with serious and challenging circumstances, she has the resilience to weather adversity as well as the capacity to appraise the situation for problem-solving opportunities.

CONCLUSION

The skills of emotional competence are dynamic, and they are also interdependent with one another. Thus, one could strengthen one skill—for example, one's emotional lexicon—and it will facilitate gains in the other skills as well. This interdependence occurs in ordinary emotional development, and it could conceivably be used to enhance the emotional functioning of children thought to be at risk for maladaptive outcomes. For example, children who have survived trauma may show deficits in their ability to represent their emotional experience (i.e., alexithymia),[59] and abused children may show deficits in their understanding of what others are feeling. Victimized and neglected children have experienced little sympathy for their feelings, and not surprisingly, they have difficulty empathizing with the distress of others. Experiencing chronic humiliation is, needless to say, a formidable barrier to ever developing emotional self-efficacy. Thus, as we consider how to promote the emotional competence of vulnerable children, we will probably be most efficient if we design programs that address multiple facets of emotional competence in order to take advantage of the interdependence of the skills described here. However, I seriously doubt that any "instructional program" in the skills of emotional competence will have an effect on children at risk if there is no concurrent pragmatic effort to ameliorate the desperate circumstances of their daily life.

With children judged to be especially socially competent and self-confident, we can see how they use the skills of emotional competence to regulate themselves. Returning to the definition of self-regulation offered near the beginning of this essay, such emotionally competent children manage their actions, thoughts, and feelings in adaptive and flexible ways across a variety of contexts. They demonstrate self-efficacy, confidence, and a sense of connectedness with others. In short, they respect their emotional experience, whether they are joyful, scared, or sad, allowing them to respect themselves. I am quite confident that little Samuel, who was introduced at the beginning of this essay and whose competence may have saved a life, will grow up assured of his self-worth and self-respect.

GLOSSARY

Attachment—A reciprocal and enduring relationship between a child and its primary caregivers; optimal attachments are secure in that the child's needs for affection, comfort, protection, and guidance in the ways of its culture are met.

Efficacy—The capacity and skills to attain one's goals.

Emotional Dissemblance—Strategies aimed at maintenance or restoration of one's emotional equilibrium and social relationships by masking one's verbal and/or nonverbal emotional-expressive behavior; for example, we might adopt a "poker face" as a way of presenting an image of stoicism to others, despite our feeling distressed.

Emotion Management—Knowledge of when to express one's feelings genuinely and when to modify or even suppress their expression, depending on the social circumstances and on how important it is to oneself to express the feeling.

Emotion Regulation—The recruitment of those processes within the self that facilitate a person's monitoring, evaluating, and changing her emotional reactions to maximize her efficacy.

Self-regulation—The ability to manage one's actions, thoughts, and feelings in flexible ways such that one's efficacy is enhanced.

Self-system—The view that the self consists of several parts related to and/or coordinated with one another but that can differ in how they function. For example, the self can deceive itself, or one aspect of the self; for example, Neisser's ecological self may not have awareness of itself.

NOTES

References

Aldwin, C. (1994). *Stress, coping, and development.* New York: Guilford.

Altshuler, J., & Ruble, D. (1989). Developmental changes in children's aware-ness of strategies for coping with uncontrollable stress. *Child Development, 60,* 1337–1349.

Aristotle. (trans. 1985). *Nichomachean Ethics* (Trans. T. Irwin). Indianapolis, IN: Hackett.

Band, E., & Weisz, J. (1988). How to feel better when it feels bad: Children's perspectives on coping with everyday stress. *Developmental Psychology, 24,* 247–253.

Bandura, A. (1977). Self-efficacy: Toward a unifying theory of behavior change. *Psychological Review, 84,* 191–215.

Bandura, A. (1991). Social cognitive theory of moral thought and action. In W. Kurtines & J. Gewirtz (Eds.), *Handbook of moral behavior and development* (Vol. I, pp. 45–103). Hillsdale, NJ: Erlbaum.

Baumeister, R. (1993a). *The puzzle of low self-regard.* New York: Plenum.

Baumeister, R. F. (1993b). Lying to yourself: The enigma of self-deception. In M. Lewis & C. Saarni (Eds.), *Lying and deception in everyday life* (pp. 166–183). New York: Guilford.

Block, J., & Block, J. (1980). The role of ego-control and ego-resiliency in the organization of behavior. In W. A. Collins (Ed.), *Development of cognition, affect, and social relations: The Minnesota symposia on child psychology* (Vol. 13, pp. 39–101). Hillsdale, NJ: Erlbaum.

Bowlby, J. (1979). *The making and breaking of affectional bonds.* London: Tavis-tock.

Cassidy, J. (1994). Emotion regulation: Influences of attachment relationships. In N. Fox (Ed.), *Emotion regulation: Behavioral and biological considerations* (pp. 228–249). *Society for Research in Child Development Monographs, 59* (Serial No. 240).

Chapman, M., Zahn-Waxler, C., Cooperman, G., & Iannotti, R. (1987). Empa-thy and responsibility in the motivation of children's helping. *Developmental Psychology, 23,* 140–145.

Cole, P. M., & Putnam, F. (1992). Effect of incest on self and social function-ing: A developmental psychopathology perspective. *Journal of Consulting and Clinical Psychology, 60,* 174–184.

Compas, B., Malcarne, V., & Fondacaro, K. (1988). Coping with stressful events in older children and young adolescents. *Journal of Consulting and Clinical Psychology, 56,* 405–411.

Compas, B., Phares, V., & Ledoux, N. (1989). Stress and coping preventive in-terventions for children and adolescents. In L. Bond & B. Compas (Eds.), *Primary prevention and promotion in the schools* (pp. 319–340). London: Sage.

Cooley, C. H. (1902). *Human nature and the social order*. New York: Scribner's.

Cramer, P. (1991). *The development of defense mechanisms*. New York: Springer-Verlag.

DePaulo, B., Epstein, J., Wyer, M. (1993). Sex differences in lying: How women and men deal with the dilemma of deceit. In M. Lewis & C. Saarni (Eds.), *Lying and deception in everyday life* (pp. 126–147). New York: Guilford.

Edinger, J., & Patterson, M. L. (1983). Nonverbal involvement and social control. *Psychological Bulletin, 93*, 30–56.

Eisenberg, N., Fabes, R., Carlo, G., & Karbon, M. (1992). Emotional responsivity to others: Behavioral correlates and socialization antecedents. In N. Eisenberg & R. A. Fabes (Eds.), *New Directions for Child Development, 55*, 57–73.

Erickson, M., Egeland, B., & Pianta, R. (1989). The effects of maltreatment on the development of young children. In D. Cicchetti & V. Carlson (Eds.), *Child maltreatment* (pp. 647–684). New York: Cambridge University Press.

George, C., Kaplan, N., & Main, M. (1985). *The attachment interview for adults*. Unpublished manuscript, University of California, Berkeley.

Gibbs, J. C. (1991). Sociomoral developmental delay and cognitive distortion: Implications for the treatment of antisocial youth. In W. Kurtines & J. Gewirtz (Eds.), *Handbook of moral behavior and development* (Vol. III, pp. 95–110). Hillsdale, NJ: Erlbaum.

Gibson, E. J. (1982). The concept of affordance in development: The renascence of functionalism. In W. A. Collins (Ed.), *The concept of development. Minnesota symposium on child psychology* (Vol. 15, pp. 55–81). Hillsdale, NJ: Erlbaum.

Goffman, E. (1967). *Interaction ritual*. Chicago: Aldine.

Harris, P., & Lipian, M. S. (1989). Understanding emotion and experiencing emotion. In C. Saarni & P. Harris (Eds.), *Children's understanding of emotion* (pp. 241–258). Cambridge: Cambridge University Press.

Harter, S. (1986). Processes underlying the construction, maintenance, and enhancement of the self-concept in children. In J. Suls & A. Greenwald (Eds.), *Psychological perspectives on the self* (Vol. 3, pp. 137–181). Hillsdale, NJ: Erlbaum.

Harter, S. (1987). The determinants and mediational role of global self-worth in children. In N. Eisenberg (Ed.), *Contemporary issues in developmental psychology* (pp. 219–242). New York: Wiley.

Harter, S. (1990). Developmental differences in the nature of self-representations: Implications for the understanding, assessment, and treatment of maladaptive behavior. *Cognitive Therapy and Research, 14*, 113–142.

Higgins, E. T., Loeb, I., & Moretti, M. (1995). Self-discrepancies and developmental shifts in vulnerability: Life transitions in the regulatory significance of others. In D. Cicchetti & S. Toth (Eds.), *Emotion, cognition, and representation* (pp. 191–230). Rochester Symposium on Developmental Psychopathology, Vol. 6. Rochester, NY: University of Rochester Press.

Hoffman, M. (1977). Empathy: Its development and prosocial implications. *Nebraska symposium on motivation*. Lincoln, NE: University of Nebraska Press.

Hubbard, J., & Coie, J. (1994). Emotional correlates of social competence in children's peer relationships. *Merrill-Palmer Quarterly, 40,* 1–20.

James, W. (1892). *Psychology: The briefer course.* New York: Holt, Rinehart & Winston.

Josephs, I. E. (1993, March). *The development of display rules: Do you understand what you already do?* Paper presented at the biennial meeting of the Society for Research in Child Development, New Orleans, LA.

Kobak, R., & Sceery, A. (1988). Attachment in late adolescence: Working models, affect regulation, and representations of self and others. *Child Development, 59,* 135–146.

Lazarus, R. S. (1991). *Emotion and adaptation.* New York: Oxford University Press.

Lennon, R., & Eisenberg, N. (1987). Gender and age differences in empathy and sympathy. In N. Eisenberg & J. Strayer (Eds.), *Empathy and its development* (pp. 195–217). New York: Cambridge University Press.

Lewis, H. B. (1971). *Shame and guilt in neurosis.* New York: International Universities Press.

Lewis, M. (1992a). *Shame: The exposed self.* New York: Free Press.

Lewis, M. (1992b). The role of the self in social behavior. In F. Kessel, P. M. Cole, & D. Johnson (Eds.), *Self and consciousness: Multiple perspectives* (pp. 19–44). Hillsdale, NJ: Erlbaum.

Maccoby, E. (1983). Social-emotional development and response to stressors. In N. Garmezy & M. Rutter (Eds.), *Stress, coping, and development in children* (pp. 217–234). New York: McGraw-Hill.

Main, M. (1990). Cross-cultural studies of attachment organization: Recent studies, changing methodologies, and the concept of conditional strategies. *Human Development, 33,* 48–61.

Main, M., Kaplan, N., & Cassidy, J. (1985). Security in infancy, childhood, and adulthood: A move to the level of representation. In I. Bretherton & E. Waters (Eds.), *Growing points of attachment theory and research* (pp. 66–104). *Monographs of the Society for Research in Child Development* (Vol. 50, Serial No. 209).

Masten, A., Best, K., & Garmezy, N. (1990). Resilience and development: Contributions from the study of children who overcome adversity. *Development and Psychopathology, 2,* 425–444.

Mead, G. H. (1934). *Mind, self, and society.* Chicago: University of Chicago Press.

Miller, S. M., & Green, M L. (1985). Coping with stress and frustration: Origins, nature, and development. In M. Lewis & C. Saarni (Eds.), *The socialization of emotions* (pp. 263–314). New York: Plenum Press.

Murphy, L., & Moriarty, A. (1976). *Vulnerability, coping, and growth.* New Haven, CT: Yale University Press.

Neisser, U. (1988). Five kinds of self-knowledge. *Philosophical Psychology, 1,* 35–59.

Neisser, U. (1992). The development of consciousness and the acquisition of skill. In F. Kessel, P. M. Cole, & D. Johnson (Eds.), *Self and consciousness: Multiple perspectives* (pp. 1–18). Hillsdale, NJ: Erlbaum.

Russell, J. A. (1989). Culture, scripts, and children's understanding of emotion. In C. Saarni & P. L. Harris (Eds.), *Children's understanding of emotion* (pp. 293–318). New York: Cambridge University Press.

Saarni, C. (1988). Children's understanding of the interpersonal consequences of dissemblance of nonverbal emotional-expressive behavior [Special issue: Deception]. *Journal of Nonverbal Behavior, 12*(4, pt. 2), 275–294.

Saarni, C. (1990). Emotional competence: How emotions and relationships become integrated. In R. A. Thompson (Ed.), *Socioemotional development. Nebraska symposium on motivation* (Vol. 36, pp. 115–182). Lincoln, NE: University of Nebraska Press.

Saarni, C. (1995). *Children's coping with aversive emotions.* Paper presented at the biennial meeting of the Society for Research in Child Development, Indianapolis, IN. (Available through ERIC, #PS 023 350.)

Saarni, C. (in press). *Developing emotional competence.* New York: Guilford.

Saarni, C., & von Salisch, M. (1993). Socialization of emotional dissemblance. In M. Lewis & C. Saarni (Eds.), *Lying and deception in everyday life* (pp. 106–125). New York: Guilford.

Selman, R., & Demorest, A. (1987). Putting thoughts and feelings into perspective: A developmental view on how children deal with interpersonal disequilibrium. In D. Bearison & H. Zimiles (Eds.), *Thought and emotion* (pp. 93–128). Hillsdale, NJ: Erlbaum.

Sonkin, D., Martin, D., & Walker, L. (1985). *The male batterer.* New York: Springer-Verlag.

Sorensen, E. S. (1993). *Children's stress and coping.* New York: Guilford.

Staub, E. (1991). Psychological and cultural origins of extreme destructiveness and extreme altruism. In W. Kurtines & J. Gewirtz (Eds.), *Handbook of moral behavior and development* (Vol. I, pp. 425–446). Hillsdale, NJ: Erlbaum.

Thompson, R. (1994). Emotion regulation: A theme in search of definition. In N. Fox (Ed.), *Emotion regulation: Behavioral and biological considerations* (pp. 25–52). *Society for Research in Child Development Monographs, 59* (Serial No. 240).

von Salisch, M. (1991). *Kinderfreundschaften.* Göttingen, Germany: Hogrefe.

Walden, T. (1991). Infant social referencing. In J. Garber & K. Dodge (Eds.), *The development of emotion regulation and dysregulation* (pp. 69–88). Cambridge, UK: Cambridge University Press.

White, G. M. (1994). Affecting culture: Emotion and morality in everyday life. In S. Kitayama & H. Markus (Eds.), *Emotion and culture* (pp. 219–239). Washington, D.C.: American Psychological Association.

White, R. W. (1959). Motivation reconsidered: The concept of competence. *Psychological Review, 66,* 297–333.

White, R. W. (1963). Ego and reality in psychoanalytic theory: A proposal regarding independent ego energies. *Psychological Issues Monograph* (No. 11). New York: International Universities Press.

Wilson, J. Q. (1993). *The moral sense.* New York: Free Press.

1. This vignette was adapted from a news story in the *San Francisco Chronicle.*

2. Murphy and Moriarty (1976).
3. Masten, Best, and Garmezy (1990).
4. Saarni (1990; in press).
5. Bandura (1977).
6. White (1959, 1963).
7. *Nichomachean Ethics,* trans. T. Irwin (1985).
8. Wilson (1993).
9. J. and J. Block (1980).
10. Maccoby (1983).
11. Harter (1990).
12. See also Lewis's *Shame: The exposed self* (1992a).
13. "Expression of emotion" is intended to include both speech and nonverbal behavior.
14. Saarni (1988).
15. Thompson (1994, pp. 27–28).
16. Cooley (1902).
17. James (1892).
18. Lewis (1992b).
19. See Baumeister (1993a) for papers addressing the "puzzle of low self-regard."
20. Mead (1934).
21. Higgins, Loeb, and Moretti (1995) have reviewed how children develop this increasing attentiveness to others' responses to themselves; they conclude that this attentiveness comes to have a regulating function on one's own behavior.
22. For relevant reviews, see Baumeister (1993a).
23. Neisser (1988, 1992).
24. Gibson (1982).
25. Neisser (1992, p. 10).
26. Lewis (1992b).
27. See also Baumeister (1993b).
28. For example, Kobak and Skeery (1988); Main, Kaplan, and Cassidy (1985).
29. Cassidy (1994).
30. Bowlby (1979).
31. Main (1990).
32. Kobak and Sceery (1988).
33. *The Attachment Interview for Adults,* George, Kaplan, and Main (1985).
34. The interested reader may consult Saarni's *Developing Emotional Competence* (in press) for an extended discussion of research related to each of these competencies as well as a discussion of the influence of individual differences and culture on each of them.
35. For a review, see Walden (1991).
36. Hubbard and Coie (1994).
37. For example, Cole and Putnam (1992); Erickson, Egeland, and Pianta (1989).
38. Russell (1989, p. 303).
39. White (1994).
40. Lewis (1992a).
41. Lewis (1971).

42. For example, Chapman, Zahn-Waxler, Cooperman, and Ianotti (1987); Hoffman (1977).
43. For example, Eisenberg, Fabes, Carlo, and Karbon (1992).
44. Bandura (1991); Gibbs (1991); Staub (1991).
45. Lennon and Eisenberg (1987).
46. For example, DePaulo, Epstein, and Wyer (1993); Goffman (1967).
47. Saarni and von Salisch (1993).
48. Josephs (1993).
49. Saarni (in press).
50. Saarni (1995).
51. A rather large literature has developed examining these different strategies, and for further elaboration, the reader is referred to Aldwin's (1994) volume on stress, coping, and development; Compas, Phares, and Ledoux's (1989) review of coping interventions for children and adolescents; Cramer's (1991) volume on defense processes; Miller and Green's (1985) chapter on coping with stress and frustration; and Sorensen's (1993) text on children's stress and coping using their diaries and artwork.
52. For example, Altshuler and Ruble (1989); Band and Weisz (1988); Compas, Malcarne, and Fondacaro (1988); Harris and Lipian (1989); Miller and Green (1985).
53. For example, Edinger and Patterson (1983).
54. Selman and Demorest (1987).
55. For example, Sonkin, Martin, and Walker (1985).
56. von Salisch (1991).
57. Lazarus's comprehensive volume, *Emotion and Adaptation* (1991), contains an extended discussion of these constructs.
58. Harter (1986, 1987).
59. *Alexithymia* refers to the inability to access emotion-descriptive language when trying to describe one's experience. It is associated with individuals who have endured severe trauma.

EDUCATOR'S COMMENTARY

MARIANNE NOVAK HOUSTON

ALTHOUGH THE LISTING of individual emotional competencies in Saarni's work may seem theoretical and complicated, a careful reading has demonstrated the usefulness of such knowledge for the classroom teacher. Translating these competencies to simpler terms, I find that they are very practical touchstones in working with early adolescents at the middle-school level, and especially helpful when communications have broken down due to social/emotional problems. In counseling individual students, too, it has helped to define difficulties in terms of one or more of these competencies.

In the front of my lesson-plan book, in fact, I have a collection of "Notes to Myself"—reminders I turn to again and again to keep my own focus. I have added Saarni's competencies, in these terms: "To be healthy and happy, we should: (1) be aware of our own sometimes complex emotional state; (2) be able to discern others' emotional states; (3) be able to state and communicate our emotions; (4) be able to feel with and for others; (5) understand that we, and others, don't always show emotions accurately; (6) be able to cope with different emotional situations without 'losing it'; (7) be aware of the importance of emotional communication when relating to others; (8) be aware that one is in charge of one's feelings, and may choose one's emotional response in a given situation."

These are discrete competencies, as outlined by Saarni, but they also develop interdependently, so that as we direct our work to a specific one or two, it helps greatly to be aware of the others. Early adolescents have found these "touchstones" (a version of which also appears on my bulletin board) understandable and helpful.

On another front, Saarni's work leaves me with a renewed sense of the importance of viewing my students as specific individuals: children from frequently very different familial, ethnic, and racial systems. Each comes with his/her own bag of worldviews, self-views, and coping mechanisms; his/her own developed notions of good and bad, acceptable and unacceptable emotions and behaviors. What are these for this specific individual child? Where do I learn about his/her world? Can we—this student and I and our classroom community—come to some common understanding of what constitutes emotionally competent behavior?

As the essay states, most of the research in this area has been done on "mainstream American children." Although it's not entirely clear what this means, I think we can assume that the subjects were white, middle-class children. (As an aside, I am moved to point out that I think any such phrase has the potential to lead us to think that "mainstream America" is a homogeneous group, whereas there is great diversity in any classroom!) Returning to the research, however: How valid are the findings for other children? Can we assume their validity for all our students? In fact, millions of children who are not "mainstream American children" are currently being taught by "mainstream American adults"! Misunderstandings or misreadings of some of their principles and behaviors, it seems to me, can lead to a shutdown of communication, and increased emotional acting out. Again: How can we come to understand "where our children are coming from"? And should we assume that it is always best for those with nonmainstream American values to defer to "ours"?

Teachers need in-depth training to understand not only the fine points of emotional development, including the individual competencies enumerated in Saarni's work, but also the sociology of our major cultural groups. And for starters in this latter category, we need to understand just how culture-bound each of us teachers is—in general, living on automatic pilot as we all do, I believe we have little notion of how our own emotional responses to students and situations come from deep, culturally founded biases. The teaching staff in many of our schools is rather homogeneous, too, so we don't have the benefit of dialogue with adults who have racial or cultural backgrounds like those of our students, and whom we might use as sources of wisdom in this regard. We must come to realize that when a student says, "You just don't understand," she may be absolutely correct, and that we may need major consciousness-raising to begin to understand. Maintaining an awareness of this reality—that is, "I may not understand all that's going on here"—is a critical insight that will be helpful.

A friend's experiment in her multicultural classroom speaks volumes, I think. She showed her students pictures of individuals in high states of emotion and asked each child to tell which emotion was being displayed. The variety of responses was amazing; different children identified the same picture as variously showing anger, fear, hatred, surprise, sadness, and even "acting." Such differences in reading facial expressions and other signals most likely occur among themselves, too, and could very probably lead to emotional and social difficulties among them. Addressing directly the second emotional competency listed in Saarni's essay might prove helpful in investigating confusions like these.

How do we best approach the task of teaching emotional competency in a multidimensional classroom? It seems to me that putting rules in place and then simply expecting children to live by them is not enough. Such a modus operandi does little to teach or develop emotional competence or self-efficacy. In my experience, it is more helpful to treat the subject as worthy of direct address, teaching children to name what they are feeling, to identify what others are feeling, and to respond to their own and others' emotional needs in a constructive way. I believe that it makes eminent good sense to deal with *major* emotional or social knots that may arise in classrooms at the time they surface. Stopping a math or reading class to deal with the outrage and unhappiness that erupts right then is a good use of classroom time, because helping children develop emotional intelligence should have very high priority, and it is important to strike while the issue is hot. Stopping class to explore feelings and behaviors sends an important message to our students, too: It is important for a happy and satisfying life to work with our emotions, and we can learn to do that! Obviously, every difficulty does not warrant a class stoppage, but those major ones that give promise of major gains should dictate a "time-out."

In addition, it seems to me that lessons that deal with emotional competence directly are also very necessary. The return to the "home room" concept in many of our middle, junior high, and high schools is promising; in Vicksburg Middle School in Vicksburg, Michigan, where I teach, emotional competence is taught in small home room communities. Various elements, including the Quest Program developed and funded by Lions International, are used. Quest contains a parental component, and reaching out to families is critical, as Saarni points out. It continues, however, to be one of the most difficult things to accomplish: The parents who respond to efforts are typically not the ones we most need to reach. Encouraging students to make their skills *habits,* using them at home and outside school, and then sharing family successes do seem to provide some practical outreach, but this remains a most demanding aspect of the program.

Our Health and Life Skills classes also sometimes serve as a site for such programs, all of which should be based on the mushrooming information on emotional intelligence, maturity development, and competence. The move toward teaching problem-solving strategies across the board in our own and many other schools across the country is encouraging and could have significant impact, since this capability, according to Saarni, is central to emotional competence.

Finally, speaking as a teacher with nearly 40 years of experience in first-grade through college-level classrooms, I think we cannot exaggerate the importance of addressing these issues in our schools. It is essential not only for each student and for us teachers—for one of the fallouts of this work with students will almost certainly be our own continued personal emotional growth—but also, and most importantly, for the creation of a more peaceful and empathetic society.

CHAPTER 3

Friends, Diplomats, and Leaders in Kindergarten: Interpersonal Intelligence in Play

THOMAS HATCH

Ned, Bobby, Kenny, Gerald, and Darin are sitting in the dramatic play area.

They have been here for about 20 minutes talking about a variety of subjects, including which girls are hard to catch on the playground and what to play at recess. Finally, Ned suggests they begin to play something. "Guys, I'm gonna start playing Mad Scientists things."

"Not now," Bobby urges. Gerald, Darin, and Kenny loudly protest as well.

"Wait a minute you guys!" Kenny finally yells several times. "Today, Ned gets to decide who the leader is." He turns toward Ned and points. "And you can't choose yourself."

Ned thinks for a few moments. All the others begin to call out "Me!" "Me!" "Pick me."

"Don't just pick Kenny 'cause he already got a turn," Gerald warns. "No! That was Ned the last time," argues Kenny.

"Yeah it was me," Ned agrees.

"I want Ned to choose me to be the leader," reasons Kenny. "So I can choose Ned to be the leader."

Ned finally decides. "I think I'll pick Bobby 'cause yesterday he didn't get a turn to get a plan, so that means he gets to be the leader today."

There is intelligence in play, but not the kind that can be measured in a conventional paper-and-pencil test. These children control their own desires and recognize and respond to the thoughts and feelings of others. They have a knowledge of the kinds of rules and strategies that can be used to resolve conflicts in this culture. They can organize themselves and make group decisions.

Most of us are not used to considering such abilities as a distinct social or emotional intelligence. Instead, we are accustomed to equating intelligence with the kinds of linguistic, logical, and mathematical abilities measured in conventional tests. Such conventional tests are based on a view that suggests that intelligence is a general capacity that is reflected in a person's ability to solve abstract problems in language and mathematics. A person who does well on such a test is presumed to do well on all manner of tasks. Further, such performances are presumed to reflect innate abilities that are relatively fixed for life.[1]

In contrast, Howard Gardner suggests that intelligence is the capacity to solve problems or fashion products that are valued in one or more cultures. Gardner argues that there are at least seven different kinds of intelligence, including linguistic, logical-mathematical, bodily-kinesthetic, musical, spatial, interpersonal, and intrapersonal.[2] Gardner bases this claim on a review of a wide range of data that show these capacities develop relatively independently from other abilities; they can be damaged selectively, and they have a distinct developmental trajectory that culminates in different and valued adult roles within different cultures.

This view differs from others in this volume in several important respects. First, rather than focusing on a single "emotional intelligence," Gardner suggests that the capacities to deal with one's own feelings and those of others form two related but distinct intelligences—inter- and intrapersonal intelligence. While Gardner discusses these two intelligences together, for the purposes of this chapter I will focus on interpersonal intelligence. Second, this view differs from others in this volume by suggesting that interpersonal intelligence includes, but is not limited to, abilities in dealing with emotions. Thus, the core components of interpersonal intelligence encompass the abilities to notice and make distinctions among the motivations, intentions, and thoughts of others as well as among their moods and temperaments. These abilities enable adults to interpret other people's feelings and actions and to act upon this knowledge to influence others.

MULTIPLE INTELLIGENCES

Although there have been a number of critiques of MI theory,[3] the basic arguments about the nature of interpersonal intelligence are supported by a variety of studies carried out by researchers who focus on social and emotional competence. Several studies indicate that how effectively people monitor and interpret the feelings and motivations of others and relate to others may be independent of performance on IQ and other conventional measures of cognitive and academic achievement. Other studies also have shown that there is little or no relation between tasks involving leading or managing others and performance on conventional measures of achievement.[4] Further, many studies converge to suggest that there are core capacities that lie at the heart of effective interpersonal behavior. These core capacities have been described in a number of ways, but often include a sensitivity to social and/or emotional cues, a knowledge of and ability to generate appropriate responses, and the ability to achieve a desired affect on others by responding effectively.[5]

Researchers from several different perspectives have also shown that the development of these mechanisms depends upon social, contextual, and cultural factors as well as biological ones. These researchers suggest that interpersonal intelligence is not a general capacity evident across all situations. For example, popularity has been used as one index of social competence, yet studies show that children identified by peer nominations as popular are not successful in all situations; even they are often rejected by their peers when they attempt to enter into play. Correspondingly, children who appear to be of low status on sociometric tests are not equally ineffective in all contexts. In fact, while significant differences are observed between popular and rejected children in competitive situations, those differences diminish in cooperative activities. Differences are also evident in performance on tests of social abilities in laboratory settings and observations in natural contexts; for example, some children who show an understanding of appropriate responses to social and emotional cues fail to make those responses in real situations. In terms of cultural factors, the development and demonstration of social competence also require an understanding of the cultural conventions regarding acceptable social behavior, the display of emotions, and the use of rules and routines.[6]

These findings indicate that measuring interpersonal intelligence with a single indicator—such as popularity or performance on a test of social or emotional knowledge—or in a single situation will be difficult, if not impossible. MI theory suggests that one way to deal with this dilemma is to consider how interpersonal intelligence develops and is displayed within the context of culturally valued activities and roles. From this perspective, people demonstrate their interpersonal intelligence as they carry out a variety of roles like those of salespeople, diplomats, therapists, and leaders. Despite common roots in the core operations, the people who fill these roles can demonstrate their interpersonal intelligence in remarkably different ways. Thus, leaders need to be able to motivate and organize large groups of people, but therapists often work one on one to diagnose and explain the social and emotional behavior of others. Although salespeople and diplomats both need negotiation skills, a successful salesperson may not be as effective when acting in the role of diplomat (or vice versa).

Even young children's interpersonal intelligence may be demonstrated in their capacity to carry out several different kinds of social roles. Roles that young children may take on in their interactions with others include those of friend, negotiator, and leader (see Table 3.1). Although a wide range of intelligences and knowledge are used in carrying out all of these roles, each role emphasizes some components of interpersonal intelligence more than others. In order to be good friends, young children need to be able to enter into and sustain relationships with others. They need to be able to make connections to others and to establish "common ground" with them. Friends also show more attention and sensitivity to others and a greater willingness to provide help and support than other children. Friends also may be able to develop a reciprocal relationship by successfully balancing their own interests with those of others.[7]

TABLE 3.1

Roles Involving a High Degree of Interpersonal Intelligence

Friends   Effective friends are able to enter into and sustain relationships by making connections to other individuals, establishing common ground, balancing their interests, and providing help and support in times of need.

Negotiators Successful negotiators are able to resolve conflicts by generating alternative solutions to a problem, monitoring others' responses, and adjusting their actions accordingly.

Leaders   Effective leaders are able to organize groups by initiating activities, inspiring and motivating others, and keeping groups focused and "on track."

Like good friends, effective negotiators need to be sensitive to what others are thinking and feeling and to take the perspective of their peers. But negotiators need to be able to use their understanding of others to persuade, convince, and satisfy their peers, not necessarily to maintain a relationship. In fact, highly skilled negotiators may be very effective at resolving disputes while still advancing their own ideas. In order to be effective, negotiators need to be persistent and flexible, generating a number of possible solutions to a problem or conflict, monitoring the effects of any strategies they pursue, and offering other alternatives if necessary. Although children across cultures show a basic understanding of rules and social and moral conventions, negotiators are also likely to benefit from a knowledge of the specific problem-solving routines and strategies that are acceptable and useful in a given context and culture.[8]

Leaders may benefit from the ability to resolve conflicts, but they also need to be able to inspire and motivate others, initiate activities, direct and manage groups, and coordinate play. Recognizing and responding to the interests and concerns of their peers may help them to be successful, but they may be especially adept at keeping groups focused and "on track" by advancing a personal or group agenda or "story" over the desires of particular members of the group.[9]

In this chapter, I explore the extent to which performance in these roles can be differentiated at a young age and the extent to which performance in particular roles is consistent across situations. I pursue these issues by describing how three kindergartners carry out these different roles in interactions with their peers. These observations were conducted in their classroom—in a public school in a low- to middle-income urban area—during free play for 2 hours a day, 4 days a week over a 6-month period. The observations were supplemented by interviews with the three children, their parents, and their teacher. The observations were part of a larger study that sought to identify activities (like painting, writing, interacting with others) in which the children showed particular skill or interest and to document how those skills and interests developed.[10]

These observations suggest that while one of the children effectively carries out all three roles, the other two children appear to be more effective in some roles rather than others. Further, the analysis of children's interactions in different situations suggests that the contexts in which they interact have a strong impact on their ability to carry out these roles and, thereby, on the extent of interpersonal intelligence they can demonstrate at a given time. While these observations provide a glimpse of interpersonal intelligence in action, still to be explored are the precise contributions of different factors—such as linguistic skill, interests, and personality variables—to successful performance in these different roles.

DEVELOPING RELATIONSHIPS WITH OTHERS

When Mark arrives, he always says "hello." He is usually one of the first children to get to school in the morning, and, after hanging up his coat, he waits by the door to greet his peers. Mark frequently plays with Ned, Bobby, and Kenny, but he is one of the few boys who plays willingly, and happily, with almost all members of the class—even girls.

From the first moment that Mark walks through the classroom door, he takes every opportunity to make connections to others.

When the teacher asks Mark if he would like to be on the waiting list to play math games on the computer, he eagerly agrees. Yet he spends the next 20 minutes trying to find someone else to be his partner when it is his turn. Once Katie agrees to join him, he periodically reminds her of their upcoming venture.

For many children, working at the computer is an individual activity, but for Mark it is just another chance to find a friend. Mark's social interests are also evident at home, where he spends much of the time playing with his younger brother and sister. As his father explains, "He likes to be around other people a lot."

Beyond being interested in other people, Mark's interpersonal intelligence is reflected in his ability to develop and sustain relationships with a number of his peers. He has a specific circle of friends including both boys and girls that he plays with both inside and outside of school on a regular basis. In addition to being one of the only boys who plays with girls, he is also one of the few children to strike up a friendship with Tony, one of the most aggressive boys in the class.

Mark's success in developing friendships with many in his class rests on his abilities to identify, remember, and respond to what others are thinking, feeling, and doing. Mark displays his sensitivity to others both in the concern he shows when other children are upset and in his regular, almost constant, attention to what other children are doing. At the art table, one of the areas of the classroom where his peers are most likely to engage in independent activities, Mark turns drawing into a social occasion. Over half of the drawings he completes during the observations are related to the works of the children around him. He painstakingly copies the work of the children seated next to him, asks for their advice, and often solicits their help and assistance. Under these conditions, his drawings demonstrate a degree of skill not apparent in work he carries out on his own. Compared to his peers, Mark also shows an unusually good memory of the social interactions that take place all around him. As a result, even though Mark has very little to say about his own activities and overall is relatively quiet, I rely on him for information about what happens on the playground or for corroboration of his peers' accounts of their interactions.

While he shows an unusual sensitivity to and interest in others, Mark never acts as a negotiator or leader. When playing in a group, Mark willingly offers ideas, but he seems more interested in playing with his friends than following his own designs. When I ask him which Ninja Turtle he likes to be, he answers "Leonardo." But when I ask what happens when someone else wants to be Leonardo too, he responds simply: "They get to be Leonardo, and I get to be someone else." Mark implies that he would rather let his friends have their way than argue about it. As he explains in our interview when I ask him about leaders:

TOM: What happens when you want to be the leader and somebody else wants to be the leader?

MARK: Oh, I just let them be the leader.

TOM: How come?

MARK: 'Cause if they want to I'll let them.

TOM: Yeah, but I thought you wanted to be the leader?

MARK: Well, not really if somebody else did.

While other children often try to claim the role of leader, Mark's willingness to give his peers what they want gets him something he values more than a position of power: the chance to play with others.

This tendency to agree and follow the wishes of his friends helps to make Mark an easy child with whom to play and work. But Mark may go overboard in his sensitivity and concern for others and may not be interested in advancing his own ideas. Rather than embarking on activities of his own design, Mark usually asks what his playmates want to do and then eagerly joins them. At the conclusion of many group meetings, the teacher asks each of the children, one by one, to select an activity; Mark almost always asks to skip his turn unless Ned or Kenny has already picked. Once they have made their selection, Mark invariably chooses the same activity as one of them. In addition to copying the drawings of his peers, Mark constructs replicas of his friends' constructions with blocks, Legos, and other materials.

As a result, Mark appears dependent upon, and sometimes a burden to, his peers. Even though he has formed strong friendships with individual children, in group situations he sometimes gets rejected by his peers and, in several cases, others appear to take advantage of him and leave him with the most undesirable roles or tasks. Thus, Mark can carry out the role of friend effectively, particularly in one-on-one and small-group situations, but he seems to be unwilling or unable to take a more directive role in interactions with his peers. Conceivably, Mark's sensitivity to others needs to be accompanied by a greater independence and the further development of an interest and competence in advancing his own agenda.

RESOLVING THE PROBLEMS OF PLAY

Kenny enters slowly and looks around. He is one of the smallest boys in class and does not move as rapidly or as roughly as the rest. He surveys the scene, looks to see who else has arrived, and takes a few moments to decide what to do. Often, he gathers with the other boys in the block area. Chances are that Tony, Darin, Gerald, or perhaps even Kenny himself will demonstrate the latest toy that he has acquired. On other occasions, Kenny may simply walk around with Mark and Bobby and talk about television shows and movies that they have viewed recently. If an activity Kenny would like to join is already under way, he approaches quietly and sits off to the side. Silent at the start, he may begin to ask a few questions or make a comment that will connect him to the play.

Kenny can make connections to his peers and is usually able to enter into play relatively successfully. But while he shares a group of friends with Mark, he appears to be more interested in advancing his own agenda than in attending to the interests and concerns of others. As a result, more often than not, he plays the role of a negotiator, occasionally creating conflicts as well as solving them.

> Kenny wonders who the leader will be today.
> "How 'bout Ned is the leader?" Mark suggests.
> Ned says he thinks Mark should be the leader.
> Kenny says Mark already had a turn and adds that it should be his turn because his last turn was before Mark's. But then Ned says that since he (Ned) was the leader the last time, he gets to pick the new leader. Now Kenny says "actually," the last time he (Kenny) was the leader so he gets to pick the new one. "And that is exactly . . ." He pauses for a long time. "No one in this area."

As in the example at the beginning of this chapter, when Kenny enters into play he often has his own interests in mind. Nonetheless, he is not unaware of the concerns and interests of his peers. He seems to know that they probably would not be happy if he declares himself the leader. Faced with the prospect of picking either Ned or Mark, Kenny does what he does best: He discovers another option. He declares that no one is the leader, and the issue is dropped. A few minutes later, after the arguments have been forgotten, Kenny declares himself the leader. Magnanimously, he decides that they can play all the games they want.

In many—though not all—of his interactions with his peers, Kenny is very vocal, stating his opinion and trying to get others to see things his way. Rather than simply stating a position and sticking to it, he gradually makes adjustments—until, as in the cases above, he finds a suitable alternative. Although these conflicts are not always resolved or resolved easily, Kenny seems to have at his disposal a knowledge of a wide range of strategies that can help resolve disputes, and he knows how to employ them to his advantage.

> Kenny, Gerald, Mark, and Bobby have just come into the dramatic play area.
> Kenny announces that he is Cool Dude,[11] but Gerald claims that role for himself.
> "I said it first," Kenny points out.
> "I never get to be Cool Dude," Gerald laments.

"I know," adds Kenny, "'cause I always say it first."

The boys go on to discuss whether or not they are playing Ninja-gaidens or Ninja Turtles. Gerald suggests they have a vote.

"But we'll need another person to break the tie," Kenny argues.

In addition to using strategies such as "saying it first," voting, and naming a leader, I also observe Kenny using some common means of compromise. On several occasions, he suggests allowing all the children to make their own choice by arguing: "Why can't we just play Ninja Turtles, Superfriends, Carebears, Mad Scientists, monsters, and superheroes?" or "We can be whoever we want from our favorite cartoon or movie."

Despite his ability to act as a negotiator, this ability is not evident in all situations; and even when he does try to mediate he does not always succeed in leading the group or maintaining play. Thus, while Kenny often tries to lead the group, if Ned is present, Ned usually takes the lead role.

Bobby is the leader and struggles to decide what to play. When Kenny urges Bobby to play "monsters," Ned shakes his head. "No, I'm not playing that," Ned declares. "Even though he's the leader I'm not playing that."

Ned is the most popular boy in class, and, if necessary, Ned has the power to override the decisions of others.

While Kenny often has to take a secondary role to Ned, he does not give up easily. In fact, "picking a leader" may be a strategy that Kenny has helped to develop and employ precisely to give him more of a leadership role in groups with Ned. Of the four times when children are observed discussing the selection of a leader in the dramatic play area, Ned is the only child besides Kenny who is always involved. Of the five times that I observe Kenny and Ned playing together in the dramatic play area, on only one occasion do they play together without discussing who the leader is. On seven other occasions during the year, Kenny is observed in the dramatic play area with children other than Ned. Although the children often argue about what to play, they never attempt to pick a leader.

In other situations, however, Kenny appears to be more successful. When Ned is absent, Kenny is often able to use his negotiating skills to convince other children to listen to his ideas. In fact, after the first two months of the observations, he plays less frequently with Ned and appears to have formed a new friendship with Darin. Kenny's mother confirms that during this period of time Kenny no longer talks about Ned as frequently as he did earlier in the year. Conceivably, Kenny has found an alternative way to get his ideas into play. Instead of battling with Ned over the leadership of the group, he turns instead to Darin, who often is willing to go along with his ideas. Under these circumstances—with a change in the peers with whom he frequently plays—Kenny can be a leader.

INSPIRING AND COORDINATING ACTIVITIES

In September, Maggie walks directly to the art table. She immediately begins drawing rainbows, a series of hearts, and little girls jumping rope. While her laughter is not yet audible, the propeller on top of her hat hints that Maggie will not always be so serious. When she wears her heart-shaped sunglasses, her ensemble is complete. Later in the year, Maggie no longer needs the security of the art table. She walks straight through the doorway, deposits her backpack in her cubby, and finds Rosa, Jeanie, Edith, and the other girls and gets to work coming up with ideas for play scripts, building projects, and "worlds" they can make in sand.

In contrast to Mark and Kenny, Maggie's interpersonal intelligence is evident in all manner of situations. She is a leader among the girls in the classroom. She helps to resolve disputes. She shows an unusual sensitivity to those around her and smoothly and easily enters into play. During our interview, her mother talks about Maggie's social inclinations:

> She's comfortable anywhere just about. She likes to observe first, but she's always been around people from [when she was] very little, so she's very used to people. She's reserved but not shy. And then once she gets to know somebody, that's it. Friends for life or whatever.

When I interview Maggie, she also describes how she makes connections to others first by watching them and then approaching them if they seem nice.

MAGGIE: I gotta find out, first I just watch them to see if they would be good if they were my friend. To see if they were getting along well with the other person if they were playing with someone else. Most of the time they are. Then if they are, then I go and ask them if they want to be my friend.

TOM: Uh-huh. Can you tell me about it? Do you remember a time when that happened when you saw somebody and you watched them for a while?

MAGGIE: (Pause) Yep.

TOM: What happened? What was she doing?

MAGGIE: She was coloring with another little girl on a boat, and she was having a good time, and she wasn't looking at me but I was looking at her. And then I went up and asked her if she wanted to be my friend, and she said yes. And I was having fun when I was coloring with them.

At another point in the interview, Maggie describes how she took the same approach to making friends in kindergarten. She reports that on the first day of school, she saw Rosa, Edith, and Jeanie at the art table, concluded that they looked nice because "they were smiling," and went over and joined them.

Maggie's interpersonal proclivities lead her to spend much of her time playing with a number of different children (although usually girls). As with Mark, her school activities frequently reflect the influences of her peers, and she often makes a connection to her friends by copying them. But Maggie is not dependent on others. She builds on their work and generates new and creative possibilities of her own. Like Mark, she bases her choice of activity on her peers' selections, but she offers them something as well.

> At the end of group meeting, Linda asks each child to pick an area in which to work. Maggie picks art. Rosa does too. As they proceed to their common destination, Maggie explains, "You told me you wanted to go to art area. That's why I picked it."
>
> Maggie gets a piece of paper. "Wanna make a crown?" she asks Rosa. "I do."
>
> "Yeah, I wanna make a beautiful crown," answers Rosa.

At the art table, Maggie pays attention to the work around her but gives it her own personal twist. In her interview, she explains how she draws on the works of others in order to create her own pictures:

MAGGIE: Sometimes I copy Rosa, and Edith and Jeanie. Sometimes I just use some of each of their ideas.

TOM: Like what?

MAGGIE: Sometimes I drew, like Rosa was drawing a rainbow, so I put half of a rainbow, and Jeanie was drawing a sky so I decided to connect the half of the rainbow to the cloud.

TOM: Oh really?

MAGGIE: Uh-huh. Clouds . . .

TOM: Was that the first time . . .

MAGGIE: And I put a bird in the cloud.

TOM: What made you think of the bird?

MAGGIE: Jeanie had a picture of a bird on the picture.

In addition to building on other children's drawings, I observed her picking up on the ideas of her peers when she makes costumes, constructs block buildings, and creates designs with tiles.

This attention to others combined with Maggie's creativity enables her to serve as an initiator and organizer of play among the girls. After Katie announces that she is going to put on a play, Maggie is immediately flooded with ideas. By the end of the day, she has gathered together a number of children, including Rosa, Jeanie, Katie, Edith, and Julia, to take on specific parts. For the next few weeks, Maggie and her friends put on a series of productions. Maggie's peers look to her for role assignments, advice on their costumes, and instructions on what to say. In one instance, Maggie stands at the side of the stage and speaks for Jeanie while Jeanie stands on stage and opens and closes her mouth, lip-synching her lines.

Rather than controlling or directing others, Maggie seems to lead by suggestion, offering ideas that get play started and keep it going. In the block area, Maggie comes up with the idea of building a circus and invites Rosa and Edith to join her and Jeanie. The girls eagerly agree, but after a few minutes Jeanie and Edith seem to lose interest.

> Maggie is piling up blocks in one corner of the pit. Jeanie appears to be making a bridge, but stops and starts to read a book; Edith joins Jeanie. Rosa is making a merry-go-round at the far end of the pit.
>
> Maggie examines her construction. "Okay so what we need is something to bang." She looks up when Ned comes in a little late. She and the other girls talk about boys for a moment.
>
> "Let's go on the merry-go-round," Maggie decides.
>
> "No, it's not ready yet," Rosa protests.
>
> "We need to build some horses," Maggie adds, "or something to sit down on."
>
> "I'm not building them yet," Rosa orders. Maggie moves back toward her structure and bangs it at the bottom, with another block. Suddenly she gasps and says that they can pretend that her structure is the carnival game where you hit the bottom with a hammer to try and ring the bell at the top. She bangs on it a number of times and laughs. Then Maggie says, "Roller coaster, we have to make a roller coaster."

Excitedly, Jeanie and Edith return to help. In this case, as in many others, Maggie's ideas lead their play in new directions.

Maggie's skills as a leader are supported by her ability to act as a negotiator. She is firm and effective when it comes to resolving disputes and weighing the interests of different parties.

> Maggie, Edith, and Rosa are in the dramatic play area. Edith suggests that they pretend they are going to a ball. Unfortunately for Rosa, there are only two fancy gowns for dressing up, and Edith and Maggie have them. Rosa complains that she will be ugly, but, in a burst of inspiration, declares that she can be Cinderella. Edith immediately claims that she is Cinderella. Then Maggie steps in.
>
> "Let's *not* play Cinderella," Maggie declares.
>
> "Let's play Snow White," offers Edith.
>
> "I'm Snow White," Rosa calls.
>
> "No," Maggie decides, "it's not gonna be fair, we're just gonna make pretend that there's a ball. That's all."
>
> "A ball?" Rosa asks.
>
> "Yeah, that's all," explains Maggie. "We're gonna play no games, 'cause it won't be fair 'cause everyone else is a girl. Everyone will want to be a pretty lady, and there's no boys to be the prince." Maggie

goes on to suggest that they just play house so that it will be fair for everyone.

Instead of advancing her own agenda and fighting for her right to a fancy dress, Maggie finds a compromise fair to all.

Like Kenny, Maggie also appears to have a good knowledge of the strategies that can be used to resolve disputes.

TOM: What happens if the five of you [Maggie and four other girls Maggie frequently plays with] all get there [to dramatic play] at the same time? How do you decide who gets to be in?

MAGGIE: We're gonna see who wants to be in. Like we ask. We raise our hand. Like people ask who wants people to be in red area [the dramatic play area], and if, and the person who has the least people or nobody has to get out. Unless everyone wants everyone to stay in, and then we gotta ask for an exception [of the teacher]. Unless they say "no," and then we gotta decide by doing "eenie meenie minie moe," and the person who gets out, goes "y o u" 'cause they say "out."

TOM: What happens if someone wants to play school and someone wants to play house? What happens then?

MAGGIE: We gotta do eenie meenie minie moe again.

The contrast with others suggests the depth of Maggie's knowledge. When I ask the same question of Rosa—a child who normally answers my questions with more detail than any of her peers—she simply points to herself and then to me and back again. Together, Maggie's sensitivity to others, her ability to inspire and organize a group, and her capacity to act as a negotiator in conflicts enable her to carry out a full social agenda. As her teacher explains, Maggie "comes to school every day to be with other kids."

IMPLICATIONS FOR INTELLIGENCE: FROM "HOW MUCH?" TO "IN WHAT WAYS?"

These observations illustrate how young children's interpersonal intelligence is displayed as they carry out the roles of friends, negotiators, and leaders. While one could argue that Maggie has "the most" interpersonal intelligence because she seems to be able to carry out all roles effectively, such a simple judgment obscures much of the information revealed in this analysis. What is at issue here is not how much interpersonal intelligence these children have, but how they express it.

Thus, instead of casting interpersonal intelligence as a continuum that runs from less to more socially competent, a "social roles" approach begins to highlight the rich variety of ways that children can demonstrate their abilities in the social domain. Instead of asking "How much?" intelligence young children have, it may be beneficial to look for and expect to find different signs or "symptoms" of interpersonal intelligence in different children. Mark may not show particular skills in mediating conflicts or in acting as a leader. At the same time, in one-on-one interactions with many different children, Mark's attention and sensitivity to others may enable him to carry out the role of friend more effectively than many of his peers. Correspondingly, as he grows older, Mark might not fare as well in roles that require him to direct other people or to work in large groups, but he may excel in roles in which the focus is on individual interaction, personal relationships, and caring for others. Kenny can serve as a negotiator, and, in a situation where he has recognized authority or particular expertise, Kenny may well be able to lead a group effectively. As he matures, Kenny may be particularly successful in contexts where negotiation skills are paramount. Nonetheless, he may not always show as much sensitivity to or concern for others as peers like Mark and Maggie.

While Maggie's success in carrying out all three roles may stand her in good stead in many situations, her capacities do not necessarily guarantee her popularity, happiness, or success. She may be able to help inspire or organize groups, but she could be overshadowed or overwhelmed by more popular or powerful peers. Her sensitivity to others could enable her to develop close friendships, but she, like Mark, may also be more affected by the actions of those around her. Without peers with whom she can make a connection or whom she can draw upon for ideas, she may not fare as well. In fact, two years after these observations were completed, her former teacher reported that Maggie was not doing well in second grade because many of the close friends she had developed in previous years had left the school.

POSSIBILITIES FOR FURTHER STUDY

Predicting individual behavior and making broad generalizations on the basis of limited observations is an extremely risky business. While these observations suggest that young children may demonstrate different levels of intelligence in carrying out different roles and in different situations, such speculations need to be investigated systematically with larger numbers of children and in experimental as well as naturalistic studies.

In particular, such studies might focus on determining the extent to which young children can be identified reliably as friends, negotiators, or leaders. Relatedly, investigations of children's performances in these different roles over time would illuminate the stability and predictive value of these constructs. The relationship between children's performances in the different kinds of activities and tasks that tap their abilities to carry out these roles also bears further examination. For example, a number of studies have shown that friends are often involved in conflicts and have cited the ability to resolve such conflicts as an important contributor to the maintenance of those friendships.[12] If children are equally successful at entering into and maintaining relationships with other individuals and at resolving conflicts in one-on-one and group situations, then there may be little value in distinguishing between these two roles.

EDUCATIONAL IMPLICATIONS

If such social roles accurately reflect the interpersonal intelligence of young children, identifying and supporting children's abilities to carry out these roles may help to meet the specific needs of different individuals. Thus, it may be useful to assess children's strengths and weaknesses in different roles and to design interventions or educational experiences on the basis of those results. For example, the observations of Mark's abilities to connect and respond to other individuals suggest that Mark may not gain that much from interventions that focus on helping him to identify or understand the feelings of others. On the other hand, the observations of his lack of interest in or inability to act as a negotiator or a leader indicate that he may benefit from efforts to help him learn to assert himself in certain situations and to resolve hypothetical and real conflicts. In contrast, the observations suggest that Kenny might benefit most from educational efforts that focus on helping him to identify, understand, and respond to the feelings and concerns of others. The point, however, is not to label each child in a class as a friend, negotiator, or leader, or to design an individual "social development" program for every child. It is to use an understanding of the range of children's interpersonal abilities to help them build on their strengths and to address particular personal or interpersonal problems they may be experiencing.

In either case, an MI approach to interpersonal intelligence suggests that interventions and assessments carried out in the course of normal interactions may be particularly productive in supporting children's interpersonal development. This view suggests that the most effective programs are likely to be those that combine efforts to teach the "basics" of emotional literacy with strategies to reflect on real conflicts, to provide coaching during group activities, and to model appropriate behavior.

Unfortunately, efforts to provide such extensive and explicit support for social development in school present another problem. A focus on social development in schools often adds another set of courses and curriculum requirements on top of an already overburdened educational system. In order to have the most benefit for students, schools, and society as a whole, developing new interventions and courses may be too much. Efforts need to concentrate on how to integrate support for the development of social and emotional competence into students' everyday school experiences.

Eliminating many curriculum requirements and focusing on key questions and issues that cut across disciplines is one avenue for such integration that is reflected in numerous current reform efforts. Theodore Sizer, chairman of the Coalition of Essential Schools, argues that "less is more";[13] that only by removing the bureaucratic constraints that require teachers to cover, superficially, a wide range of subjects and topics will students be able to come to deep understandings of important issues in our society. Such integrated investigations of key questions not only allow students to develop their skills in traditional subjects but also enable them to engage directly the problems and challenges of the social, emotional, and moral domains. Similarly, projects in which students strive to achieve meaningful goals like the construction of a community playground or an evaluation of the quality of the town water supply require students to work together, to organize themselves effectively, and to develop productive relationships. Thus, efforts to expand the scope of schooling and to provide support for social development need to be accompanied by corresponding efforts to rethink the character and depth of learning that can be accomplished in schools.

INTERPERSONAL INTELLIGENCE IN PERSPECTIVE

Focusing on social and emotional issues and skills in the course of meaningful investigations and projects is only one way to support the development of a wider range of skills in school without simply adding on more courses or requirements. But it also serves as a reminder that interpersonal intelligence cannot be developed or expressed in isolation. The kinds of interpersonal intelligence a person can demonstrate in a particular situation are linked to other intelligences and to a host of other variables. The observations of Maggie, Kenny, and Mark reveal that tied up in the expression of interpersonal intelligence are interests (whether in other people or one's self; or in fairness or control) and a willingness or inclination to act in certain ways. Thus, even if Mark does develop more skills as a negotiator or a leader, he may have little interest in using his skills in those ways. In addition, the children use other abilities to help them carry out these different roles. In particular, all of them demonstrate linguistic skills and communicate effectively with their peers, and Maggie's creativity seems to help her take a leadership role. Finally, all of them depend on a basic cultural knowledge of the characters and scripts—from Ninja Turtles to the Little Mermaid—and the routines that guide their play. Thus, the descriptions here give a glimpse of the social roles that young children can carry out in different situations. They serve as a first step toward teasing out the different factors that contribute to success in these roles and provide another opportunity to look for the intelligence in play.

NOTES

References

Berndt, T. (1983). Social cognition, social behavior, and children's friendships. In E. Higgins, D. Ruble, & W. Hartup (Eds.), *Social cognition and social development*. Cambridge: Cambridge University Press.

Coie, J., Dodge, K., & Kupersmidt, J. (1991). Peer group behavior and social status. In S. Asher & J. Coie (Eds.), *Peer rejection in childhood*. Cambridge: Cambridge University Press.

Corsaro, W. (1981). Friendship in the nursery school. In S. Asher and J. Gottman (Eds.), *The development of children's friendships*. Cambridge: Cambridge University Press.

Corsaro, W., & Rizzo, T. (1990). Disputes in the peer culture of American and Italian nursery school children. In A. Grimshaw (Ed.), *Conflict talk*. Cambridge: Cambridge University Press.

Dodge, K., Coie, J., & Brakke, N. (1982). Behavior patterns of socially rejected and neglected preadolescents. *Journal of Abnormal Child Psychology, 10*, 389–409.

Dodge, K., McClaskey, C., & Feldman, E. (1985). A situational approach to the assessment of skills in children. *Journal of Consulting and Clinical Psychology, 53*, 344–353.

Dodge, K., Pettit, G., McClaskey, C., & Brown, M. (1986). Social competence in children. *Monographs of the Society for Research in Child Development, 51* (2, Serial No. 213).

Dunn, J. (1993). *Young children's close relationships*. Newbury Park, CA: Sage.

Fiedler, F., & Link, T. (1994). Leader intelligence, interpersonal stress, and task performance. In R. Sternberg & R. Wagner (Eds.), *Mind in context*. Cambridge: Cambridge University Press.

Foot, H., Chapman, A., & Smith, J. (1980). Patterns of interaction in children's friendships. In H. Foot, A. Chapman, & J. Smith (Eds.), *Friendships and social relations in children*. New Brunswick, NJ: Transaction.

Gardner, H. (1983). *Frames of mind*. New York: Basic Books.

Gardner, H. (1995a). Reflections on multiple intelligences. *Phi Delta Kappan, 77* (3), 200–209.

Gardner, H. (1995b). *Leading minds*. New York: Basic Books.

Gelb, R., & Jacobson, J. (1985). Popular and rejected children's interactions during cooperative and competitive peer group activities. Paper presented at the annual meeting of the Society for Research in Child Development, Toronto.

Goleman, D. (1995). *Emotional intelligence*. New York: Bantam Books.

Gordon, S. (1989). The socialization of children's emotions. In C. Saarni & P. Harris (Eds.), *Children's understanding of emotions*. Cambridge: Cambridge University Press.

Gottman, J. (1983). How children become friends. *Monographs of the Society for Research in Child Development, 48* (3, Serial No. 201).

Hartup, W. (1992). Friendships and their developmental significance. In H. McGurk (Ed.), *Childhood social development*. Hillsdale, NJ: Erlbaum.

Hartup, W., Laursen, B., Stewart, M., & Eastenson, A. (1988). Conflict and the friendship relations of young children. *Child Development, 59,* 1590–1600.

Hatch, T. (1990). Looking at leadership in a four-year-old's world. *Young Children, 45,* 11–17.

Hatch, T., & Gardner, H. (1992). Finding cognition in the classroom. In G. Salomon (Ed.), *Distributed cognitions.* Cambridge: Cambridge University Press.

Hernstein, R., & Murray, C. (1994). *The bell curve.* New York: Free Press.

Ladd, G., & Mize, J. (1983). A cognitive-social learning model of social skills training. *Psychological Review, 90,* 127–157.

Mayer, J., & Salovey, P. (1993). The intelligence of emotional intelligence. *Intelligence, 17,* 433–442.

McFall, R. (1992). A review and reformulation of the concept of social skills. *Behavioral Assessment, 4,* 1–25.

Mize, J., & Ladd, G. (1991). Toward the development of successful social skills training for preschool children. In S. Asher and J. Coie (Eds.), *Peer rejection in childhood.* Cambridge: Cambridge University Press.

Much, N., & Shweder, R. (1978). Speaking of rules. In W. Damon (Ed.), *New directions for child development, Vol. 2.* San Francisco: Jossey-Bass.

Parker, J. (1986). Becoming friends. In J. Gottman and J. Parker (Eds.), *Conversations of friends.* Cambridge: Cambridge University Press.

Putallaz, M., & Wasserman, A. (1991). Children's entry behavior. In S. Asher and J. Coie (Eds.), *Peer rejection in childhood.* Cambridge: Cambridge University Press.

Rizzo, T. (1989). *Friendship development among children in school.* Norwood, NJ: Ablex.

Rosnow, R., Skleder, A., Jaeger, M., & Rind, B. (1994). Intelligence and the epistemics of interpersonal acumen. *Intelligence, 19,* 93–116.

Rubin, K., & Krasnor, L. (1986). Social cognitive and social behavioral perspectives on problem-solving. In M. Perlmutter (Ed.), *Minnesota symposia on child psychology* (Vol. 18). Hillsdale, NJ: Erlbaum.

Saarni, C. (1990). Emotional competence. In R. Thompson (Ed.), *Socioemotional development. Nebraska symposium on motivation* (Vol. 36). Lincoln: University of Nebraska Press.

Scarr, S. (1985). An author's frame of mind. *New Ideas in Psychology, 3,* 95–100.

Selman, R. (1980). *The growth of interpersonal understanding.* New York: Academic Press.

Shantz, C. (1982). Children's understanding of social rules and the social context. In F. Serafica (Ed.), *Social-cognitive development in context.* New York: Guilford.

Shure, M. (1982). Interpersonal problem solving. In F. Serafica (Ed.), *Social-cognitive development in context.* New York: Guilford.

Sizer, T. (1984). *Horace's compromise.* Boston: Houghton-Mifflin.

Sternberg, R. (1994). Commentary: Reforming school reform: Comments on "Multiple Intelligences: The theory in practice." *Teachers College Record, 95,* 561–569.

Wagner, R. (1994). Context counts. In R. Sternberg and R. Wagner (Eds.), *Mind in context*. Cambridge: Cambridge University Press.

AUTHOR'S NOTE

For their help and support, I would like to thank the families, teachers, and students from the classroom in which this study was carried out. For comments on an earlier draft of this article, I would also like to thank Howard Gardner, the editors, and the authors of the other chapters and commentaries contained in this book. The work reported here was supported by a dissertation fellowship from the Spencer Foundation. The conclusions are solely those of the author.

1. See Hernstein and Murray (1994) for one statement of such a position.
2. Gardner originally made these claims in *Frames of Mind* (1983). In a more recent article, Gardner (1995a) has argued that there is an eighth intelligence—naturalist intelligence. Naturalist intelligence involves the recognition and classification of the numerous species in an environment and is reflected in the accomplishments of individuals like Charles Darwin and John James Audubon.
3. For critiques of MI see, for example, Scarr (1985) and Sternberg (1994).
4. See, for example, Goleman (1995); Mayer and Salovey (1993); and Rosnow et al. (1994) for reviews of emotional intelligence, and see Fiedler and Link (1994) and Wagner (1994) for studies of the relationship between aspects of interpersonal intelligence and achievement.
5. For converging views of the core capacities, see Dodge, Pettit, McClaskey, and Brown (1986); Coie, Dodge, and Kupersmidt (1991); Ladd and Mize (1983); McFall (1992); and Rubin and Krasnor (1986).
6. For investigations of the performance of popular and rejected children in different contexts, see Corsaro (1981); Dodge, Coie, and Brakke (1982); Dodge, McClaskey, and Feldman (1985); Gelb and Jacobson (1985); Mize and Ladd (1991); Putallaz and Wasserman (1991); and Rubin and Krasnor (1986). For discussions of cultural factors and social competence, see, for example, Corsaro and Rizzo (1990); Gordon (1989); and Saarni (1990).
7. Children's friendships have been a subject of considerable interest to researchers. For studies relevant to the issues of this chapter, see, for example, Asher and Rose (this volume); Berndt (1983); Dunn (1993); Foot, Chapman, and Smith (1980); Gottman (1983); Hartup (1992); Parker (1986); and Rizzo (1989).
8. For investigations of issues related to children's abilities to resolve conflicts, see, for example, Much and Shweder (1978); Rubin and Krasnor (1986); Selman (1980); Shantz (1982); and Shure (1982).

9. For discussions of leadership, see Gardner (1995b) and Hatch (1990).
10. Further reporting of the study of the display and development of children's strengths and interests can be found in Hatch and Gardner (1992).
11. Cool Dude is a character from the Ninja Turtles. The boys often claim that Cool Dude is Leonardo's (the "lead" Turtle's) brother.
12. See for example, Hartup, Laursen, Stewart, and Eastenson (1988) and Hartup (1992).
13. Sizer first made these arguments in *Horace's Compromise* (1984).

EDUCATOR'S COMMENTARY

LINDA LANTIERI

THIS PHENOMENOLOGICAL STUDY by Thomas Hatch offers a unique lens through which to view emotional development at work—through the play of three kindergartners, Kenny, Mark, and Maggie. I learned that Tom Hatch spent 6 months in a classroom observing many different behaviors in the children he got to know. For the purpose of this study, he especially looked more closely at the varied ways young children seem to exhibit "interpersonal intelligence" as described by Howard Gardner's work in multiple intelligence. As Tom was introducing these ideas to the other authors and respondents to this book at the Fetzer Institute, he described his perspective as one that was neither exactly a researcher's nor an educator's. He referred to this precarious point of view as "being out on a limb with a bunch of tree surgeons around."

Nevertheless, from his refreshing frame of reference, the insights, conclusions, and perspectives Tom Hatch has to offer can clearly inform and help those of us promoting emotional literacy in classrooms across the country.

My own background is as an educator for close to three decades. I have worked as classroom teacher, assistant principal, and director of an alternative middle school in East Harlem, New York City. Today I serve as national director for the Resolving Conflict Creatively Program (RCCP), a school-based program that combines the teaching of social and emotional skills with conflict resolution and intergroup relations. We are one of the largest and longest running programs of its kind in the country.

In our work at RCCP, we believe our society needs a new way of thinking about what it means to be an educated person. We need a vision of education that recognizes the ability to manage emotions, resolve conflicts, and interrupt bias as fundamental skills that can and must be taught. In fact, we would argue that every child's education should include the development of social and emotional competence through the teaching of these life skills as part of the curriculum.

Gardner believes that the intelligences can be best developed and assessed in terms of "culturally meaningful activities and roles." Three aspects of interpersonal competence emerge in Tom's study—in the roles of friend, leader, and mediator—which clearly indicate that there are many different ways to express and demonstrate interpersonal intelligence. Yet some of the children show greater propensity to taking on one of these roles more than others—for example, being good at forging friendships but not necessarily good at negotiating one's way through a conflict. Others like Maggie seem to exhibit strength in all three roles.

Several questions arise as I look at the significance of approaching interpersonal intelligence in this way. First, I would ask: Are we actually observing in these three young children specific abilities that will stay stable over a period of time, or is their way of relating more a style of interaction based on a particular social, emotional, and cultural context? Secondly, is it actually useful to assess children's strengths and/or weaknesses in these different roles, or can identifying children in such specific ways be limiting in how we approach each child's uniqueness? Thirdly, are the differences observed really fixed assets or deficits, or would these capacities be likely to change in each youngster over a period of time based on developmental issues and a variety of other factors?

As a practitioner in the field, I would consider the following factors as I reflect on Tom's helpful descriptive data, which lays the foundation for further research.

Although we observe youngsters displaying these natural capacities with a variety of distinct strengths and weaknesses, schooling can intentionally shape the "lessons of the heart" and equip young people with a *wide variety* of competencies that fall under the heading of "interpersonal intelligence." I would argue that young people would benefit greatly from having *all* these abilities in their active repertoire—good leadership skills, negotiation skills—the kind of human skills good friendships are based on—as well as other competencies. Tom's point is not necessarily proving the existence of only these three but to show us that there are many aspects to interpersonal competence.

And schools can be the vehicle to enhance these skills. Mark is described as a good friend, but with the addition of conflict resolution skills he would be more likely to be a better friend to himself, allowing his own needs to also be met in any interaction. Kenny may have strong conflict resolution skills, but he would probably benefit from having some perspective-taking skills so that he learns to consider others' needs as well. In other words, we can offer young people concrete skills for managing emotions, resolving conflict, and participating as responsible citizens in a democratic process. And although some young people may choose to develop and work with one area of interpersonal intelligence more than another, I would sooner offer young people a wide range of people skills to have at their disposal.

For this to happen, the mission of our schools must be expanded to include these critical human skills as part of young people's regular education—not only when they arrive at the principal's office and are labeled "troubled." In our work in classrooms, we see the distinct roles of friend, mediator, and leader as very interrelated. When we teach skills in conflict resolution, we help young people identify and implement nonviolent solutions to conflict, ones that meet the needs of those involved and keep relationships intact as well. So we are also strengthening the qualities good friendships are based on. And although RCCP's curriculum is skill-based, the development and promotion of social responsibility and active leadership is an expected outcome as well. In our work, we create the kind of classrooms where young people can experience a sense of community, a community where cooperation, empathy, negotiation, and leadership are encouraged. As a result, young people can be more hopeful about what the larger world could be like and can be equipped with a wide repertoire of skills to bring to any given situation. Knowing how to be a friend, diplomat, and leader all in one can prove very useful. I'm reminded of an incident that illustrates the benefits of having developed various aspects of interpersonal competence.

One day, I received a phone call from a woman who had seen an amazing interaction at a local playground in New York City after school hours. A group of students, probably in about third or fourth grade, playing basketball, were being harassed by another group of slightly older kids who evidently wanted to play, too. The older kids were about to start a fight. The woman wanted to intervene but wasn't sure if or how she should. All of a sudden, another group of young people who had been standing nearby surrounded the arguing kids in a circle and started to sing a song, "Peacemakers talk about it, they don't fight about it, they want to make up and be friends." The kids who were starting the fight were so surprised by this behavior that they quickly dispersed, and the clash never took place. The woman, stunned and moved to tears by the actions of these young people, asked them who they were and where they were from. It turns out that they were RCCP mediators from the school nearby and had learned the song during mediation training.

These courageous young people displayed a great deal of interpersonal competence—from using mediation skills to de-escalate a conflict, to being a leader and taking a stand in a difficult situation, to befriending that young boy being bullied. In this small, caring act, they epitomized what interpersonal intelligence is all about.

CHAPTER 4

Brain Development and Emotional Development: The Role of Teaching in Organizing the Frontal Lobe

MARK T. GREENBERG AND
JENNIE L. SNELL

Sharmaine is described by her teachers as well liked, easy to get along with, and empathic with others. She can take a role of leadership, but is comfortable working with others no matter what her status in the group. When upset she is able to verbalize her feelings and use the support of adults and peers. When she does something that hurts others, she tries to repair it.

Nick is described by his teacher as disruptive, confrontational, and inattentive. He does poorly in school (at least more poorly than his teacher thinks he should). He is hotheaded, easily loses his temper, and behaves immaturely. He is both aggressive and disliked. He acts impulsively without accurately identifying what is happening or why. He is egocentric (self-focused), and while he often shows regret after he has calmed down, it appears that this regret is more for the consequences/negative reinforcement he received for his misbehavior than for the damage/pain he causes others. In this sense he is often seen as a bully, but feels as if he is a victim.

Jennifer is described by her teacher as unpredictable. She is quite intelligent, scores high on standard achievement tests, and is verbally facile. In general, she gets along pretty well with adults. However, especially in her peer relations she is bossy, controlling, and unable to follow the lead of others. She is easily hurt by the actions of others and responds by either verbal aggressiveness or sulking. She is quick to blame others and to hold a grudge, but is not able to effectively communicate when she is upset (disappointment explodes into anger and blaming).

Alonzo is a child who often is off-task and in "another world"; he meets the criteria for attentional "disorder" and is very distractible. He gets along OK with peers but is not very interactive or involved. He is a quiet child and often attempts to avoid confrontations of any kind. Thus, some children easily overpower him and he acts compulsively compliant; he both wants to be liked and to avoid confrontation. He often plays with younger children. He is highly anxious and often unable to identify how he feels. He has experienced a history of physical abuse and maltreatment. He has "good days" and "bad days."

INTRODUCTION

These emotional/behavioral profiles present a small part of the variability that is contained in almost any classroom of elementary-school-aged children. Children vary greatly in their developmental level and ability to understand, express, and regulate their emotional lives. Further, an important aspect of teaching effectiveness is creating a classroom atmosphere that encourages the development of emotional and social competence simultaneously and in an integrated fashion with academic and cognitive competence. An understanding of the basic developmental issues in brain organization regarding emotional competence should be an important linkage in developing better strategies for understanding and educating the "whole child."

Although developmental psychology has a relatively long history of investigating emotional development in children, only recently have researchers begun to consider the neurobiological underpinnings of emotion. Many of the chapters in this volume provide support for the importance of emotion in multiple aspects of development, including for the parent-child relationship (attachment) and for children's relationships with peers.[1] In addition, many childhood psychological disorders can be viewed in part as failures in emotion regulation processes.[2] Recent advances in procedures available to study the brain (e.g., neuroimaging techniques, EEG), along with a changing zeitgeist that accords emotion a more central role in behavior and development, have resulted in an increased interest in the neurobiology of emotion.[3]

The long-held notion of mind–body dualism espoused by Descartes contributed to the traditional separation of emotion from the brain. Under this theory, emotions were viewed as originating primarily in the body, with rational thought being the primary concern of the "mind." That is, we feel in our "gut and heart" and think in our brain. Gradually, this view has been changing, and the brain is now viewed as playing a critical role in emotion processing. In fact, some investigators have begun to emphasize the importance of emotion for what has traditionally been viewed as the domain of rational thought, for example, for effective decision making.[4] The integration of cognition and emotion has significant implications for education.

In humans, both socioemotional and brain development undergo a protracted course of development, with much room for external influence. Immense postnatal brain development occurs, with some areas of the brain (e.g., the frontal lobes) not fully maturing until adolescence. Current views of the neurobiology of emotional development emphasize the interplay and reciprocal influence that social development and brain development exert on one another. For instance, Panksepp provides examples of developmental milestones in emotion (e.g., social bonding, the development of sexuality during puberty) that may have a bidirectional tie to central nervous system development.[5] Fascinating new research is also beginning to uncover the ways in which early experience may impact brain development with possible long-term impact on emotional responding.[6]

This chapter will review current research on the neurobiology of emotion, including evolution of the brain and the brain systems believed to be involved in emotion. The practical implications of this knowledge for development and for early childhood intervention and education will also be addressed. Although there are numerous mutual paths of influence between the brain and various aspects of development (e.g., cognitive and language development), the primary focus of this analysis will be on the *neurobiology of emotion*. Readers interested in a more general review of brain systems and function are referred to a recent book written specifically for educators.[7]

At least two aspects of brain development might be considered relevant to social development and education. The first is the development of structures in the brain and their networks of association. The second is the neurochemical aspects of the moment-to-moment functioning of the brain. We primarily address the development of brain structure in this chapter. The study of neurochemical processes such as neurotransmitters (dopamine, norepinepherine, serotonin), amino acids (e.g., GABA), neuropeptides, and hormones and how they influence both development and function are beyond the scope of this chapter. However, these neurochemical processes are critical to understanding the excitation and inhibition of neural pathways. Further, some forms of "treatment" for such difficulties as ADD (attention deficit disorder), depression, anxiety, and panic in both children and adults are based on this neurochemical information.

We refer the reader to other sources for current reviews of these areas of brain development.[8]

DEFINING EMOTION

Definitions of *emotion* are numerous and often conflicting.[9] The controversy arises in part because there are numerous facets of emotion. Emotion includes at least the following four components: (1) an expressive or motor component, (2) an experiential component, (3) a regulatory component, and (4) a recognition or processing component. Further, each of these components is recognized as involving particular neural/brain processes.

The first component is the ability to express emotion through facial expression, body posture, and vocal tone and content. Infants come equipped with facial and body actions that we believe reflect their emotional experience. As with many aspects of development, these expressions become more differentiated and refined over time. For example, the early expression of distress is later differentiated into expressions of sadness and anger.

A second component is our conscious recognition of our emotions, or what we often call "feeling." Feeling states are the result of our awareness of cues that come from our central nervous system (e.g., heart rate, neurochemical changes in our bodies, and so forth), feedback from our facial expressions, and our interpretation of what is happening both internally and from environmental cues. These feeling states are normally expressed after language acquisition, by our verbal report of our experience. However, it should be recognized that for at least two reasons there is often a lack of concordance between what our body is experiencing and our ability to be aware of it. The first reason is that often the processing of emotional context occurs outside of our conscious awareness (unconscious processing). Secondly, feeling states are often complex, and we are frequently inaccurate at verbally reporting what we are consciously experiencing.

The third component of emotion is the regulation of emotion. There are certain action tendencies that are the direct result of experiencing emotions. For example, joy is translated into exuberant activity level; in contrast, sadness leads to a very low activity level. While anger is directly associated with the action tendency to hit or strike out at a target/person, fear leads to freezing and then withdrawal from the target/person. This is nowhere so obvious as in watching an infant, because infants directly express their emotional states. With increasing age and cognitive/neural maturity, children become better able to regulate their emotions and to control the natural action tendency associated with a particular emotion. Thus, when a 7-year-old is hit by another and feels quite angry, he or she can often control the desire to strike back and instead use a different strategy. However, there are wide individual differences, as reflected in our opening descriptions of Nick and Jennifer versus Sharmaine. Similarly, a 9-year-old who is being painfully teased by a peer may be able to hide that emotion and instead react with humor in order to stop or defuse the teasing. This chapter primarily concerns this component of emotion regulation because of its immediate concern for educators.

The final component of emotion is the ability to recognize emotions in others; that is, the ability to recognize what emotion another person is having by processing their facial expression, body posture (including head and eye movements), and vocal tone and speed. As discussed by Saarni (in chapter 2), this ability develops during infancy and early childhood.

EVOLUTION OF THE HUMAN BRAIN

In order to understand current work on the neurobiological underpinnings of emotion, it is useful to consider the evolution of the brain and of emotion, along with their interaction. The human brain has evolved over a period of millions of years through a process largely characterized by the growth and expansion of higher brain structures from lower parts. The lower parts consist of structures, primarily in the brain stem, that regulate basic survival functions (e.g., breathing, hunger). This is also the part of the brain that humans have in common with most other animals.[10]

Over the course of millions of years, emotional brain systems evolved from the brain stem, due partially to the increase in skills necessary for survival in more complex environments. Sylwester emphasizes the role of emotion in providing a quick assessment of danger and, overall, in assigning importance to and sorting the vast array of incoming sensory information from both the external environment and from internal bodily signals.[11] One of the earliest stages in the evolution of the emotional brain began with the evolution of the olfactory bulb for sensing smell, a critical ability for detecting danger as well as potential mates. For many species lower on the phylogenetic tree, this is still the primary brain structure involved in what could be considered emotional or drive-oriented behavior. However, as evolution progressed—mammalian evolution in particular—new levels of complexity were added to the emotional brain. At this stage, the "limbic system," a set of subcortical brain structures surrounding the brain stem, first appeared. The components of the limbic system and their connections with other brain areas are hypothesized to provide many of the neural underpinnings for emotion in humans.

Approximately 100 million years ago, a decisive development in the evolution of the mammalian brain occurred. At this time, multiple new layers were added to the cortex, the outermost layer of the brain. The human neocortex is much larger than that of any other species and is believed to be responsible for the development of the higher order mental functions that are viewed as uniquely human (e.g., rational thought, planning ability, inhibition of impulses). Although the neocortex has traditionally been associated with rationality and the intellect, recent work has also begun to focus more on the involvement of this area of the brain in emotions.[12] The cortex and, in particular, the frontal lobes of the brain undergo a protracted course of development in humans, continuing to develop through adolescence.

The triune brain model, which roughly corresponds to the evolutionary developments previously discussed, was proposed by Maclean as a conceptual model for describing the different brain systems (see Figure 4.1).[13] Maclean's model is hierarchical and divides the brain into three sections based on their functions: survival, emotional, and rational. Although this model is useful for delineating the global categories of brain function roughly by area, more recent models of neural organization are much more complex and focus to a greater extent on the role of interconnections *between* different neural systems in determining behavior. We now know that survival and emotional activities occur at all levels of the brain and that the dualism between emotion and rational cognition is misleading.

The following sections will review what is known about the parts of the brain involved in emotion. Although certain areas of the brain may be involved in emotional experience to a greater degree than others, it is important to remember that the brain functions as a highly complex, interrelated system, with multiple connections between different regions. There are also different levels of analysis for studying emotional processes in the brain, ranging from the cellular to gross anatomical level. In addition, multiple technologies are available for studying the brain, including neuroimaging (e.g., PET scan and functional MRI) and electroencephalogram (EEG). Research on the brain's involvement in emotion is occurring at each of these levels, but a review of each is beyond the scope of the chapter. The primary focus here will be on what research on larger brain systems tells us about the neurobiology of emotion regulation and its implications for education.

REGIONS OF THE BRAIN CENTRAL TO EMOTIONAL DEVELOPMENT

The Limbic System

Although much earlier research on the neurobiology of emotion exists, Maclean expanded upon earlier work by identifying the limbic system as the central site for emotion in the brain.[14] Currently, controversy exists regarding the usefulness of this global term and whether the component parts of the limbic system indeed function as a system.[15] For example, while the amygdala is centrally involved, other "limbic" structures such as the hippocampus are only peripherally involved. In addition, impor-

FIGURE 4.1

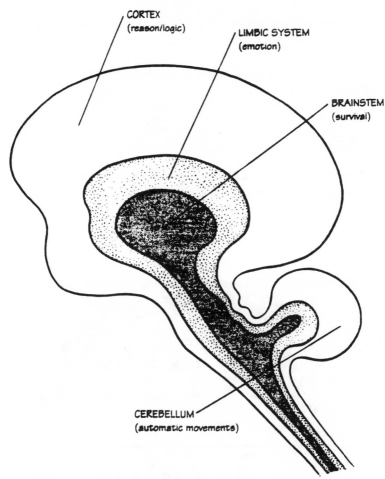

tant aspects of emotion processing utilize other parts of the brain, outside the limbic system. Nevertheless, it is apparent that many of the structures comprising the limbic system play an important role in regulating feelings. Limbic system structures are involved in multiple aspects of emotion, including the recognition of emotional expressions on the face, action tendencies, and the storage of emotional memories. The limbic system also is very rich in peptide receptors that are involved in drive-related behaviors such as eating and sexual behavior, another fact that makes it especially well suited to its involvement in emotions.[16] Limbic structures are also poised to receive signals from the body regarding what the person is experiencing internally, in addition to incoming sensory information from the environment. Through its initial appraisal of the emotional meaning of this information, along with its extensive connections with other brain systems, the limbic system sets into motion responses to this incoming information.

Most definitions of the limbic system include the following set of subcortical structures surrounding the brain stem: the amygdala, hippocampus, thalamus, and hypothalamus (see Figure 4.2). The thalamus and hypothalamus can be considered akin to relay stations for incoming information. The thalamus receives incoming sensory information from the external environment, whereas the hypothalamus receives signals from the body and is involved in the regulation of sexuality and appetite. Both of these structures relay information to the amygdala, the brain structure that has been referred to as the primary limbic structure involved in the neurobiology of emotion.[17]

The amygdala is a relatively small, almond-shaped structure with mul-

FIGURE 4.2

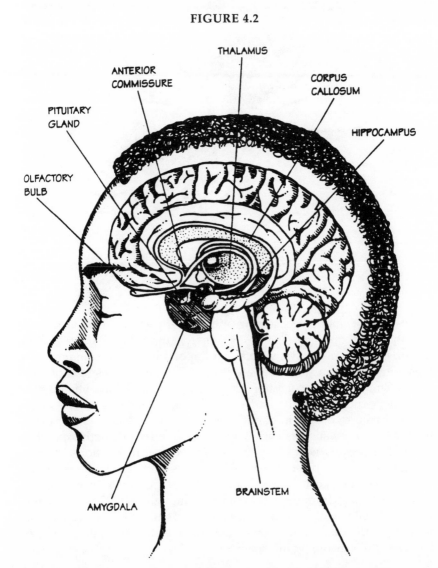

tiple connections to other brain regions. The primary function of the amygdala appears to be the interpretation of incoming sensory information within the context of the individual's survival needs and emotions. Through its connections with other brain areas, the amygdala influences a person's response to this incoming information on multiple levels. Operationally, the amygdala can be likened to the body's "alarm system."[18] That is, using incoming sensory information, the amygdala scans experience, examining even minute changes in context. It is asking the question, is there something important here? Something to fear? Something attractive?

Another crucial function of the amygdala is the assigning of emotional meaning to memories. When a powerful emotion is experienced, especially under conditions of emotional stress, it appears that the amygdala imprints this memory with an added degree of strength. This may account for the fact that people tend to have strong memories for emotionally charged, personal experiences.[19] Some have speculated that the amygdala has the ability to store emotional memories outside of consciousness that can still exert an impact on behavior without ever entering conscious awareness.[20] Thus, it is believed that many early childhood experiences, particularly emotionally charged ones, such as in the infant-caregiver relationship, may exert a long-term impact on behavior through this mechanism. That is, emotional reactions to these early childhood events are stored in the amygdala and because they were stored before language and other representational skills were developed, they are not easily accessible to our conscious minds. Nevertheless, these emotional memories affect our current functioning. This phenomenon is termed "infantile amnesia" because of the inability to regain these memories in our conscious mind.[21] The implications of this knowledge for children who have experienced extreme emotional deprivation or abuse will be discussed later.

The hippocampus is another limbic system structure involved in memory. The hippocampus and amygdala appear to act as a team in the process of memory storage, with the hippocampus providing the memory for context or nonemotional details and the amygdala adding the emotional imprint to the memory. Sylwester refers to the hippocampus as the "card catalog for our library of memories" due to its role in assigning memories to memory networks in different brain areas.[22] As the hippocampus is believed to mature later in development (postbirth), this may be part of the reason that early memories are not available to us; that is, they have been stored in the amygdala rather than in the hippocampus.[23]

The Frontal Lobes

The frontal lobes are another brain area critically involved in emotion regulation. The frontal lobes are one of the brain regions comprising the neocortex, or outermost and evolutionarily most recent, layer of the brain (see Figure 4.3). This area also receives the largest projection of sensory information from the thalamus and, hence, is the primary site for the analysis of incoming sensory information.[24] In examining the role played by the frontal lobe in emotion, it is important to consider the complex interwoven connections of this region with the limbic system. The frontal cortex (sometimes termed the "prefrontal" cortex) has a unique connection with the limbic system in that it is the only neocortical site in which information processed in this system is represented.[25]

FIGURE 4.3

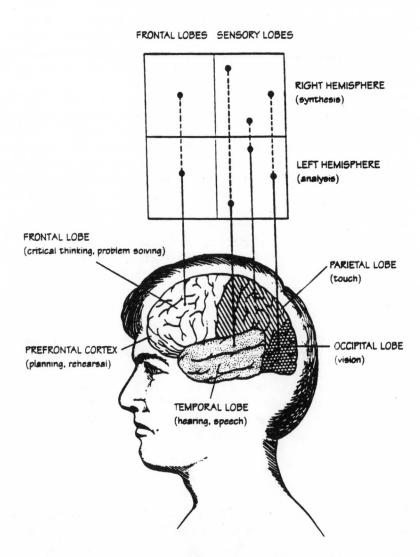

These connections between the frontal lobe and limbic system have led some to conclude that the frontal cortex provides the arena for the interplay between cognition and emotion.[26] For instance, Dawson and colleagues hypothesized that the frontal lobe plays a regulatory role in emotional processes, in particular guiding coping and the control of emotional expression.[27] Goleman refers to the frontal lobe as the "emotional manager" due to its apparent role in controlling emotion and overriding emotional impulses.[28] He states,

> In the neocortex a cascading series of circuits registers and analyzes that information, comprehends it, and through the prefrontal lobes, orchestrates a reaction. If in the process an emotional response is called for, the prefrontal lobes dictate it, working hand-in-hand with the amygdala and other circuits in the emotional brain. (p. 25)

Numerous case studies show that injuries and lesions specific to the frontal lobe are associated with dramatic changes in emotion regulation and social competence in adulthood.[29] However, some of the most dramatic evidence demonstrating the importance of the frontal lobe for many aspects of normal socioemotional development is taken from case reports of brain-injured children with documented frontal damage.[30] Across studies, some of the most pervasive signs of injury involve deficits in self-regulatory behavior and in social awareness, which persisted for years postinjury. Although the children in these case reports often performed in the normal range on tests of cognitive functioning (intelligence testing, reading, mathematics), marked deficits in social functioning were observed from childhood throughout the lifespan, primarily in the domains of emotion regulation, adapting to novel situations, and general social behavior. In the area of emotion regulation, limited frustration tolerance, increased impulsivity, emotional lability, and frequent mood swings are frequently described.[31] In the social domain, virtually all of these patients exhibited a failure to sustain meaningful relationships, extending across developmental levels. Grattan and Esslinger contend that frontal injury in childhood can preclude the development of social and emotional maturity through influencing empathic understanding, identity formation, and moral development.

THE DEVELOPMENT OF EMOTION REGULATION

> We know that emotion is very important to the educative process because it drives attention, which drives learning and memory. We've never really understood emotion, however, and so don't know how to regulate it in school—beyond defining too much or too little of it as misbehavior and relegating most of it to the arts, PE, recess, and the extracurricular program. Thus, we've never incorporated emotion comfortably into the curriculum and classroom.[32]

There is little doubt that the manner in which behavior, emotions, and cognitions become integrated in the first decade of development has important implications for psychological and emotional functioning throughout the lifespan.[33] Implicit in our developmental model is the idea that during the maturation process, some components of emotional development precede later forms of cognition. As a result, in early development, affect is an important precursor of other modes of thinking, and subsequently must be integrated with other developmental functions for optimal maturation. This appears to be supported by neurobiological study indicating that the emotional/limbic system is operative prior to networks in the brain primary for cognition (e.g., the neocortex).

Infancy and Toddlerhood

During infancy, emotions provide infants and toddlers with a mode for communicating with others as well as within themselves.[34] Although communication through affective expression remains available to an individual throughout his or her lifetime, it is *the* major mode of communication available during infancy. We hypothesize that infants can also monitor their own affective states (albeit at a nonconscious level), which provides them with signals for behavioral responding.

Through the caregiver's reactions to the infant's emotional displays, the infant slowly builds expectancies regarding the nature of social interaction. Thus, the manner in which such emotions are socialized in early development is believed to have a major impact on the child's later ability to monitor and share emotions.[35] Daniel Stern eloquently details how the caregiver's selective responsiveness to the infant's emotional displays informs the infant which emotions are permissible and thus socializes the infant's subsequent affective displays.[36]

During the first three years of life, the entire repertoire of affective signals develops, and these signals/displays are subsequently available for use throughout the rest of an individual's lifetime.[37] Thus, by the time children are beginning to use language to express internal states of being, most of their habitual affective responses have already been established. By the end of toddlerhood, most children have become skilled in both showing and interpreting emotional displays, although there are considerable individual differences in children's emotional profiles.

Although emotional development proceeds rapidly during infancy and toddlerhood, cognitive and linguistic processes are less developed. As a result, when the infant experiences emotional stress (anxiety, fear, excitement, boredom, sadness, etc.), only sensorimotor processes are available for emotion regulation (e.g., gaze aversion, self-stimulation). In most cases the infant must rely on the parent to help modulate emotions during times of either high or insufficient levels of arousal. Sroufe emphasizes the importance of the child's early attachment relationships and the impact that such relationships have on both the organization of the child's affect and his or her coping strategies.[38]

The Preschool Years

One of the crucial developmental tasks during the preschool and early elementary–school-age years is to learn to integrate previously developed modes of thinking and feeling with the newly acquired ability to use language-based codes. This achievement has been noted by various developmental theorists and plays a critical role in diverse theories of development.[39] As the child acquires language, he or she can begin to express in a more coherent and organized fashion what before could be expressed only in action, image, or affectivity.[40] Through the verbal labeling of emotional states, the child develops a new and powerful form of self-control and self-expression. In fact, the use of language to express emotions may facilitate control over nonverbal emotional expressions and thus enhance regulation of emotions themselves.[41]

Language serves the child's behavior and emotional control in at least three ways. First, it serves the internal executive function of mediating between intention or desire and behavioral action. Deficiencies in this "second signal system," often termed verbal self-control,[42] have been clearly related to impulsivity and behavior problems.[43] The second function of language is to communicate one's internal state to others. Greenspan and Greenspan have described the toddler's progression from "being their affect" to representing their affective states symbolically; in this manner, they become able to work through affective conflict with the use of fantasy and pretend play, as well as through conversation.[44] Finally, language (and possibly other forms of symbolic representation) allows the child to become consciously aware of how he or she is feeling. Thus, speech *begins* as a way of indicating to others, but later provides a self-guidance function; speech ceases to merely accompany action and begins to help organize behavioral processes. Thus, we believe that the role of language during early childhood is of particular importance in understanding the development of emotional and social competence during the preschool years. Language and communication serve many important functions that are new to this phase: They provide a means to (1) symbolize one's attitudes toward others, (2) debate and act on problems both intrapsychically and interpersonally, (3) increase self-control, and (4) enhance self-awareness.

With the advent of the child's ability to use self-talk, the control of behavior first comes under conscious cognitive control. The use of internal self-talk presumes that the child has some recognition of a problem situation. During the preschool years, the child also begins to differentiate the emotions, needs, and desires of different people in a particular context. Adults play a critical role in helping children to make effective plans during peer interactions that can facilitate frustration tolerance.

The Elementary–School-Age Years

Between the ages of 5 and 7 (sometimes referred to as the "5–to–7 shift,"[45] children undergo a major developmental transformation that generally includes increases in cognitive processing skills, a growth spurt, and changes in brain size and function.[46] This transition and the accompanying changes allow children to undertake major changes in responsibilities, independence, and social roles.

One hallmark of the 5–to–7 shift involves the young elementary–school-age child having internalized or "automatized" much of what could previously be accomplished only with conscious effort. The use of inner speech, which we have previously discussed, is one example of this process. The ability to think through problem situations and to anticipate their occurrence is critical for socially competent behavior at this age.[47] However, it is important to recognize that these "cold" cognitive processes are likely to be effective only if the child has accurately processed the emotional context of a particular situation. For example, if children misidentify their own feelings or those of others, they are likely to generate maladaptive solutions to the problem, regardless of their intellectual capacities. Thus, the relationships between affective understanding, cognition, and behavior are of crucial importance in problem solving.

A second critical issue in the use of problem-solving skills involves the child's ability to calm down when highly aroused in order to engage in problem solving; this is a concern in our portrayals of both Nick and Jennifer. An inability to calm down in emotionally charged situations often results in poor problem solving and maladaptive behavior. Language plays a key role in this area. Although the preschooler begins to use language to facilitate self-control and begins to engage in cognitive planning in the service of frustration tolerance, the ability to effectively and automatically use these processes transpires primarily during the elementary school years.

LINKAGES BETWEEN THE PSYCHOLOGICAL MODEL AND NEURAL MODELS

How compatible is this psychological model of development with neurobiology? Although the direct links at the neuronal level are still barely explored, recent advances in developmental neuropsychology provide striking physiological parallels to our psychological observations of emotional development and its linkages to language and cognitive function.

Returning to the model of the "triune brain," by birth the brain stem is well developed and the baby is more or less able to sustain its own vital life functions.[48] The limbic system appears to develop less quickly than the brain stem, but matures faster than the neocortex. At birth, the cerebral cortex is quite immature,[49] and the behavior of the neonate is primarily directed by the brain stem and midbrain.[50] During the first few years of life, the neocortex develops rapidly, and this development continues throughout childhood and adolescence.[51]

The brain develops by overproducing synapses during the prenatal and early infancy period. The synapses are pruned away or strengthened as a result of early experience as well as maturational processes. Thus, the brain in part develops by loss of connections that are not used. The adage is "Neurons that fire together wire together!" For example, in the monkey (macaque) brain, over 2 trillion synapses are lost by the fifth year of life. This process is often called "ontogenetic sculpting," or synaptic death. Thus, Dawson and her colleagues suggest that "the nature of early parent-child interactions are likely to influence patterns of neuronal connectivity that mediate social behavior. We know that infancy is an important period for establishing such neuronal networks."[52]

The frontal lobes undergo an extremely protracted course of development throughout childhood, a fact that mistakenly has led some to conclude that they are essentially nonfunctional until adolescence.[53] Although they are not fully developed until adolescence, research has shown the crucial role the frontal lobes play in regulating behavior and emotions at each stage of development. Research indicates that beginning before the end of the first year of life, the frontal lobe begins to play an increasing role in emotional development. A number of researchers have recently produced exciting findings that show evidence for the specialized role of the frontal lobe in mediating emotional behavior in infancy (e.g., EEG results showed that increases in frontal activity were associated with increases in different types of emotional arousal).[54] Thus, even in the early years, it is believed that the frontal lobes are where information is integrated between subcortical structures such as the hippocampus and amygdala, as well as from other neocortical structures such as the parietal and temporal lobes—it is the "command center" of projections from diverse brain areas.

Over the course of childhood, interconnections between the limbic system and neocortex increase and differentiate, which allows for the processing of emotional experience to become linked with other areas of the brain and also allows for qualitative changes in emotional development. More specifically, neuronal connections and pathways to and from the limbic system develop. The specific organization of brain organization between the limbic system and both cortical areas and the lower brain stem is unique and will depend on both social experience and genetic factors.

In summary, it is clear that the frontal lobes play an essential role in regulating emotional behavior from infancy on, particularly in the areas of self-control or the overriding of emotional impulses. Research has been complicated by the fact that the frontal lobes continue developing throughout adolescence. However, the fact that they undergo such a protracted course of development, much of which is characterized by the formation of connections with other brain regions, has critical implications for the potential effects of environmental influences on the development of these connections. It is likely that neural templates are being laid down for the management of emotion through connections formed as a result of critical learning experiences during childhood. It is also likely that these patterns become much more difficult to alter once development is complete. The implications of this knowledge for intervention and prevention programs will be addressed in a later section.

THE ROLE OF ATTENTION

Because of the role of attention in the educational process and children's classroom behavior (see our opening description of Alonzo), neural processes underlying attention will be briefly discussed. Although attention is not considered an emotion, attentional processes and emotion are mutually influential. Attention is both influenced by a child's current emotional state and is important in achieving control over that emotional state.

According to Sylwester, a well-functioning attentional system must fulfill several tasks, including identification of important elements in the environment, the ability to ignore irrelevant stimuli while sustaining attention to the primary focus, the ability to access inactive memories, and the capacity to shift attention rapidly as a result of new information.[55] Different brain regions are involved in these varied tasks. It is likely that the pathway from the thalamus to the amygdala, discussed previously, is involved in focusing attention on emotionally loaded stimuli in the environment, where a rapid response may be required. The frontal lobes, on the other hand, play an important role in processing more complex information, sustaining attention to relevant versus irrelevant stimuli, and integrating incoming information with prior knowledge.

The important point for the purposes of this chapter is the fact that the development of the attentional system is complex and involves several brain areas. Also important is the interaction of attentional processes with emotions, with each influencing the other. Emotions often drive attention, as people attend to information that they find positively reinforcing or, conversely, threatening. They can, however, also interfere with attentional focusing, as is seen in the case of post-traumatic stress disorder (see next section). Children's attentional difficulties in the classroom, in particular ADHD, have been the focus of much research. Given the complexity of the brain systems involved in attention, along with their interaction with emotion, it is important to keep in mind that the reason for a given child's attentional difficulties is likely multifaceted and requires thorough evaluation prior to intervention.

NEURAL MECHANISMS UNDERLYING SPECIFIC EMOTIONS

Although there is much work to be done in this area, research suggests that different brain regions may contribute in varying degrees to the *experience* of different emotions. Much work in this area has focused on the emotions of fear and sadness. Most research on the neural underpinnings of emotion has focused on primary emotions, with much less known about the neural involvement in more complex human emotions, such as shame and pride.

Many researchers working in this area, instead of focusing on the neural substrate for specific emotions, have divided emotions into two distinct systems: the approach and withdrawal systems.[56] The approach system is hypothesized to control approach-related positive affect, such as interest and goal-directedness, while the withdrawal system is proposed to govern withdrawal-related negative emotions, such as fear and disgust. Differences in these systems have been shown to have implications for childhood temperament.[57]

Sadness

Most of the research done on possible brain mechanisms underlying sadness has focused on hemispheric differences in brain activity in the left and right frontal lobes of adults.[58] Early studies of adult patients with cortical lesions indicated striking differences in the emotional behavior of those who experienced injury in the left versus right hemisphere. Patients with damage to the right hemisphere typically displayed more negative affect symptoms, characterized as "catastrophic depression"; whereas symptoms such as indifference to the injury, euphoria, and mania were more commonly manifested in patients with damage to the left hemisphere.[59] More recent research on hemispheric differences in EEG activation in adults has demonstrated patterns of frontal asymmetry, with depressed adults showing less left-frontal activation than nondepressed adults.[60] These same researchers also were able to show that baseline differences in activation in the left- and right-frontal hemispheres of adults could predict proneness to depression, with less left-frontal activation increasing the likelihood of depression. Davidson and colleagues have introduced the notion of "affective style" to explain individual differences in the thresholds at which people experience different emotions and the implications that these differences might have for personality and the development of psychological disorder.[61]

Davidson and colleagues have also studied patterns of frontal activation in infants and children, partly with the goal of revealing patterns that may increase a child's risk for emotional difficulties later in life. This work is closely related to work on infant temperament, which can be defined as "characteristic individual differences in the way basic emotions are experienced and expressed."[62] Much research on temperament has focused on "behaviorally inhibited" children, a group described by Kagan, Reznick, and Snidman as timid in social situations, and particularly anxious in unfamiliar situations of all types.[63] Fox reviews research demonstrating that children who exhibit inhibited behavior in a preschool setting were more likely to show right-frontal EEG asymmetry that was a result of lower left-frontal activation, whereas highly sociable children showed left-frontal asymmetry due to increased left-frontal activation.[64] Early patterns of frontal asymmetry in infancy have been shown to predict behavioral inhibition in the preschool years, and frontal asymmetry patterns have also been shown to relate to infants' responses to separation from their mothers.[65] In summary, the research on frontal asymmetry patterns suggests that there are important individual differences in the patterns of activation of different cortical areas that relate to emotional reactivity, including proneness to depression in adults and behavioral inhibition in children. Crucial questions that remain partially unanswered concern the degree to which these patterns are malleable over time and the extent to which they are influenced by experience throughout childhood.

Fear

There is a large body of research on the neurobiology of fear. There are well-established experimental procedures for studying fear conditioning, the process through which a nonthreatening stimulus becomes threatening over time through pairing with the threatening stimulus, that are applicable to both animals and humans. Joseph LeDoux and his colleagues have conducted extensive research on the neural pathways through which fear conditioning occurs.[66] The amygdala plays a crucial role in the emotion of fear and appears to function as an "alarm system," appraising and reacting instantaneously to perceived threat by sending messages to multiple parts of the brain.[67] These signals then trigger the activation of bodily responses, such as the fight-or-flight response.

During this research LeDoux has made two revolutionary discoveries, with far-reaching implications for human behavior. The first discovery is that LeDoux demonstrated the existence in rats of a pathway directly from the thalamus (the area of the brain that receives incoming sensory information) to the amygdala separate from the pathway that is routed from the thalamus through the neocortex. This subcortical route provides a basic emotion structure with rapid/crude information processing as a basis for action. This subcortical system may contain innate neuromotor programs for a small number of basic emotions, including fear. Rapid response to fear has obvious survival value and suggests the reason for a "quick and dirty" subcortical pathway. Goleman states, "This circuit does much to explain the power of emotion to overwhelm rationality."[68]

This contrasts with the cortical route in which emotion is further processed and evaluated for its meaning and reaction. In this system, emotional information becomes integrated into complex intentional plans for social interaction involving the frontal lobe. LeDoux has hypothesized that, if for genetic or experiential reasons, the lower order pathways are more efficiently triggered by the amygdala than are the higher order pathways, then we might expect the person to have little insight into their emotional reactions and also less emotional control.[69]

A second discovery by LeDoux regards emotional memory. LeDoux conditioned a rat to fear a certain stimulus and then tried to extinguish that fear; fear conditioning is important because it is probably a component in many anxiety, panic, and post-traumatic stress disorders. He found that damage to the frontal lobe made extinction very difficult. Thus, overcoming early conditioning is not the result of passive forgetting but instead of new learning. These early emotional memories are indelible and cannot be erased. As a result, new learning probably includes frontal lobe control or inhibition of the actions fired by these memories. Educational or therapeutic experiences may allow the cortex to establish more effective and efficient synaptic links with the amygdala that lead to better emotional control.

Post-traumatic stress disorder, a particularly extreme case of fear conditioning, typically occurs following extreme, uncontrollable trauma and is characterized by hypervigilance, emotional numbing, and intrusive reexperiencing of the trauma (e.g., nightmares and flashbacks). A wide range of traumatic experiences can result in PTSD (e.g., combat, car accidents, natural disasters, and childhood abuse). Research has begun to identify the neural mechanisms underlying this disorder, with far-reaching implications for the emotional development of children who have experienced trauma.

It appears that PTSD occurs as a result of an extreme case of the fear conditioning discussed in the previous section. Goleman describes the neural underpinnings of this disorder as follows:

> These vivid, terrifying moments, neuroscientists now say, become memories emblazoned in the emotional circuitry. The symptoms are, in effect, signs of an overaroused amygdala impelling the vivid memories of a traumatic moment to continue to intrude on awareness.[70]

One of the effects of this neural imprinting of the trauma is to lower the brain's setpoint for responding to potentially retraumatizing experiences, resulting in a state of hyperarousal, in which the individual responds to ordinary life events as though he/she was reexperiencing the original trauma.

Critically important from the standpoint of development is the fact that clinical studies of traumatic stress in humans have revealed that a single highly stressful episode, such as severe beating by a parent, or observing the murder of a loved one, has the potential to alter arousal responses and emotional stability for many years.[71] This conditioning of a child's relatively young neural network may produce rippling effects throughout the developing nervous system, constraining the child's flexibility to adapt to challenging new situations with new strategies instead of old habits.

Positive Emotion

Very little work has been done on the brain structures underlying positive emotion. Davidson provides preliminary evidence for involvement of the dorsolateral frontal cortex in the implementation of approach-related positive affect and, in the case of the left prefrontal cortex, the inhibition of negative affect generated in the right hemisphere.[72] Other researchers have also emphasized the importance of the inhibition of negative emotion for positive emotional experience and have suggested that there may be important individual differences in people's capacity to "turn off" negative emotions once they are aroused.[73] This preliminary research indicates that individual differences in the ability to bounce back from negative emotions may directly influence the experience of positive emotions. Goleman posits a role for the frontal lobes, in particular, in the experience of more complex positive emotions such as love.[74] For instance, although structures in the limbic system set into motion feelings of sexual arousal and pleasure, the frontal lobe may be responsible for the linking of these more primitive feelings with the capacity for longer term love and connection with others, or the development of empathy.

IMPLICATIONS OF THE NEUROBIOLOGY OF EMOTION FOR EDUCATION

We conclude this overview of brain development and structure by drawing five implications of our current knowledge on brain processes and growth underlying emotional development for educational practice.

1: *The nature and quality of teacher-child and peer-peer social and academic interactions impacts brain development, attention, and learning.* During development the nature of social and educational interactions plays an active role in shaping brain growth. It is clear that brain development is highly malleable and strongly impacted by experience. Experience throughout childhood leads to the strengthening and integration or the fragmentation of neural networks. Of special importance is how education and social experience create healthy neural networks between the frontal lobes and subcortical emotion centers (primarily the amygdala). However, it should be noted that there has been no experimental data with humans illustrating how educational experience alters brain structure.

2: *Education can be considered to be a critical influence on strengthening neocortical control and self-awareness.* Teaching should be conceived of as facilitating the process of neural integration; that is, teachers have the potential to play an important role in strengthening pathways that lead to the integration of affect, language, and cognition. Although teaching content or subject matter is important, the manner in which it is taught requires further attention. Of particular importance is the manner in which teachers promote cognitive and interpersonal decision making and problem solving in the classroom.

3: *The strengthening of frontal lobe capacities (maintenance of attention, social problem-solving skills, frustration tolerance, and the management of negative and positive affect) is critical to academic, social, and personal outcomes.*

4: *Helping children develop awareness of emotional processes (both in themselves and in others), applying verbal labels to emotions, and encouraging perspective taking and empathic identification with others are the first steps in developing these frontal lobe functions of interpersonal awareness and self-control.* In our own work we have shown that children who show the most impulsive and aggressive behavior have the least access to verbalizing and discussing their emotions.[75] Further, our work over the past 15 years on the PATHS Curriculum with normal, special-needs, and deaf children (a school-based curriculum focused on emotional development and social problem solving) has demonstrated that curricula focused in this domain can lead to significant changes in both level of emotional awareness and behavior.[76] We refer the reader to *Emotional Intelligence* for further discussion of school-based curricula and approaches that seek to "educate the emotions."[77]

5: *Attending patiently to children's emotions and their effects as a central part of classroom processes will lead to improved personal and academic outcomes.* Teaching healthy strategies for coping with, communicating about, and managing emotions assists children in maintaining attention and focus during academic and interpersonal learning contexts.

NOTES

References

Aggleton, J. P. (1992). *The amygdala: Neurobiological aspects of emotion, memory, and mental dysfunction.* New York: Wiley-Liss.

Benton, A. (1991). Prefrontal injury and behavior in children. *Developmental Neuropsychology, 7,* 275–281.

Bruner, J. (1979). *On knowing.* Cambridge, MA: Harvard University Press.

Ciaranello, R., Aimi, J., Dean, R. R., Morilak, D. A., Porteus, M. H., & Cicchetti, D. (1995). Fundamentals of molecular neurobiology. In D. Cicchetti & D. Cohen (Eds.), *Developmental psychopathology: Vol. 1. Theory and methods* (pp. 109–160). New York: Wiley Interscience.

Cicchetti, D. (1994). Development and self-regulatory structures of the mind. *Development and Psychopathology, 6,* 533–549.

Cicchetti, D., & Tucker, D. (1994). Development and self-regulatory structures of the mind. *Development and Psychopathology, 6,* 543–549.

Cook, E. T., Greenberg, M. T., and Kusche, C. A. (1994). The relations between emotional understanding, intellectual functioning, and disruptive behavior problems in elementary school-aged children. *Journal of Abnormal Child Psychology, 22,* 205–219.

Damasio, A. R. (1994). *Descartes' error: Emotion, reason, and the human brain.* New York: Grosset/Putnam.

Davidson, R. J. (1994). Asymmetric brain function, affective style, and psychopathology: The role of early experiences and plasticity. *Development and Psychopathology, 6,* 741–758.

Dawson, G. (1994). Frontal electroencephalographic correlates of individual differences in emotion expression in infants: A brain systems perspective on emotion. In N. Fox (Ed.), *Monographs of the Society for Research in Child Development: Vol. 59. The development of emotion regulation: Biological and behavioral considerations* (pp. 135–151).

Dawson, G., Hessl, D., & Frey, K. (1994). Social influences on early developing biological and behavioral systems related to risk for affective disorder. *Development and Psychopathology, 6,* 759–779.

Dawson, G., Panagiotides, H., Klinger, L. G., & Hill, D. (1992). The role of frontal lobe functioning in the development of infant self-regulatory behavior. *Brain and Cognition, 20,* 152–175.

Dodge, K. A. (1986). A social-information processing model of social competence in children. In M. Perlmutter (Ed.), *Cognitive perspectives on children's social behavior and behavioral development. The Minnesota symposium on child psychology* (Vol. 18). Hillsdale, NJ: Erlbaum.

Eisenberg, N., & Fabes, R. (1992). Emotional responsivity to others: Behavioral correlates and socialization antecedents. In N. W. Damon (Series Ed.), and N. Eisenberg & R. Fabes (Vol. Eds.), *New Directions for Child*

Development: Vol. 55. Emotion and its regulation in early development (pp. 57–73). San Francisco: Jossey-Bass.

Falkner, F., & Tanner, J. M. (1978). *Human growth*. New York: Plenum.

Fox, N. A. (1994). Dynamic cerebral processes underlying emotion regulation. In N. Fox (Ed.), *Monographs of the Society for Research in Child Development: Vol. 59. The development of emotion regulation: Biological and behavioral considerations* (pp. 152–166).

Freud, S. (1957). The unconscious. In J. Strachey, (Ed. and Trans.), *The standard edition of the complete psychological works of Sigmund Freud* (Vol. 14, pp. 159–215). London: Hogarth Press. (Original work published 1915)

Gainotti, G. (1972). Emotional behavior and hemispheric side of lesion. *Cortex, 8*, 41–55.

Golden, C. J. (1981). The Luria-Nebraska Children's Battery: Theory and formulation. In G. W. Hynd & J. E. Obrzut (Eds.), *Neuropsychological assessment and the school-aged child* (pp. 277–302). New York: Grune and Stratton.

Goldsmith, H. H. (1994). Parsing the emotional domain from a developmental perspective. In P. Ekman & R. J. Davidson (Eds.), *The nature of emotion: Fundamental questions* (pp. 68–73). New York: Oxford University Press.

Goldsmith, H. H., & Campos, J. J. (1982). Toward a theory of infant temperament. In R. N. Emde & R. J. Harmon (Eds.), *The development of attachment and affiliative systems*. New York: Plenum.

Goleman, D. (1995). *Emotional intelligence*. New York: Bantam Books.

Grattan, L. M., & Esslinger, P. J. (1991). Frontal lobe damage in children and adults: A comparative review. *Developmental Neuropsychology, 7*, 283–326.

Greenberg, M. T., & Kusche, C. A. (1993). *Promoting social and emotional development in deaf children: The PATHS project*. Seattle, WA: University of Washington Press.

Greenberg, M. T., Kusche, C. A., Cook, E. T., and Quamma, J. P. (1995). Promoting emotional competence in school-aged deaf children: The effects of the PATHS Curriculum. *Development and Psychopathology, 7*, 117–136.

Greenberg, M. T., Kusche, C. A., & Speltz, M. (1991). Emotional regulation, self-control and psychopathology: The role of relationships in early childhood. In D. Cicchetti & S. Toth (Eds.), *Rochester symposium on developmental psychopathology* (Vol. 2). New York: Cambridge University Press.

Greenspan, S. I., & Greenspan, N. T. (1985). *First feelings*. New York: Viking.

Henriques, J. B., & Davidson, R. J. (1991). Left frontal hypoactivation in depression. *Journal of Abnormal Psychology, 100*, 535–545.

Hesse, P., & Cicchetti, D. (1982). Perspectives on an integrated theory of emotional development. In D. Cicchetti & P. Hesse (Eds.), *New Directions for Child Development: Vol. 16. Emotional development* (pp. 3–48). San Francisco: Jossey-Bass.

Huttenlocher, P. R. (1979). Synaptic density in human frontal cortex-developmental changes and effects of aging. *Brain Research, 63*, 195–205.

Izard, C. E. (1991). *The psychology of emotions*. New York: Plenum.

Izard, C. E. (1993). Four systems for emotion activation: Cognitive and noncognitive processes. *Psychological Review, 100,* 68–90.

Jacobs, W. J., & Nadel, L. (1985). Stress-induced recovery of fears and phobias. *Psychological Review, 92,* 512–531.

James, W. (1884). What is emotion? *Mind, 9,* 188–205.

Kagan, J. (1994). *Galen's prophecy.* New York: Basic Books.

Kagan, J., Reznick, J. S., & Snidman, N. (1987). The physiology and psychology of behavioral inhibition in children. *Child Development, 58,* 1459–1473.

Kendall, P. C., & Braswell, L. (1985). *Cognitive-behavioral therapy for impulsive children.* New York: Guilford.

Kendler, T. S. (1963). Development of mediating responses in children. In J. C. Wright & J. Kagan (Eds.), *Monographs of the Society for Research in Child Development: Vol. 28. Basic cognitive processes in children* (pp. 33–51).

LeDoux, J. E. (1991). Emotion and the limbic system concept. *Concepts in Neuroscience, 2,* 169–199.

LeDoux, J. E. (1993). Emotional memory systems in the brain. *Behavioural Brain Research, 58,* 69–79.

LeDoux, J. E. (1995). Emotion: Clues from the brain. *Annual Review of Psychology, 46,* 209–235.

LeDoux, J. E., Iwata, J., Cicchetti, P., & Reis, D. J. (1988). Different projections of the central amygdaloid nucleus mediate autonomic and behavioral correlates of conditioned fear. *Journal of Neuroscience, 8,* 2517–2529.

Lewis, M., & Michalson, L. (1982). The socialization of emotions. In T. Field & A. Fogel (Eds.), *Emotion and early interaction* (pp. 189–212). Hillsdale, NJ: Erlbaum.

Lewis, M., & Michalson, L. (1983). *Children's emotions and moods: Developmental theory and measurement.* New York: Plenum.

Luria, A. R. (1976). *Cognitive development: Its cultural and social foundations.* Cambridge, MA: Harvard University Press.

Maclean, P. D. (1952). Some psychiatric implications of physiological studies on frontotemporal portion of limbic system (visceral brain). *Electroencephalography and Clinical Neurophysiology, 4,* 407–418.

Maclean, P. D. (1978). A mind of three minds: Educating the triune brain. In J. Chall & A. Mirsky (Eds.), *Education and the brain, 77th national society for the study of education yearbook.* Chicago: University of Chicago Press.

Maclean, P. D. (1990). *The triune brain in evolution: Role in paleocerebral functions.* New York: Plenum.

Malatesta, C. Z., & Izard, C. E. (1984a). The facial expression of emotion: Young, middle-aged, and older adult expressions. In C. Z. Malatesta & C. E. Izard (Eds.), *Emotion in adult development* (pp. 253–273). Beverly Hills: Sage Publications.

Malatesta, C. Z., & Izard, C. E. (1984b). The ontogenesis of human social signals: From biological imperative to symbol utilization. In N. A. Fox & R. J. Davidson (Eds.), *The psychobiology of affective development* (pp. 161–206). Hillsdale, NJ: Erlbaum.

Marlowe, W. B. (1992). The impact of a right prefrontal lesion on the developing brain. *Brain and Cognition, 20,* 205–213.

Mateer, C. A., & Williams, D. (1991). Effects of frontal lobe injury in childhood. *Developmental Neuropsychology, 7,* 359–376.

Panksepp, J. (1994). Emotional development yields lots of "stuff" . . . especially mind "stuff" that emerges from brain "stuff." In P. Ekman & R. J. Davidson (Eds.), *The nature of emotion: Fundamental questions* (pp. 367–368). New York: Oxford University Press.

Pine, F. (1985). *Developmental theory and clinical process.* New Haven: Yale University Press.

Post, R. M., Weiss, S. B., & Leverich, G. S. (1994). Recurrent affective disorder: Roots in developmental neurobiology and illness progression based on changes in gene expression. *Development and Psychopathology, 6,* 781–813.

Schore, A. (1994). *Affect regulation and the origins of the self: Neurobiology of emotional development.* Hillsdale, NJ: Erlbaum.

Sroufe, L. A. (1979). Socioemotional development. In J. D. Osofsky (Ed.), *Handbook of infant development.* New York: Wiley.

Stern, D. (1985). *The interpersonal world of the infant.* New York: Basic Books.

Sylwester, R. (1995). *A celebration of neurons: An educator's guide to the human brain.* Alexandria, VA: Association for Supervison and Curriculum Development.

Teicher, M., Glod, C., Surrey, S., & Swett, C. (1993). Early childhood abuse and limbic system ratings in adult psychiatric outpatients. *Journal of Neuropsychiatry, 5,* 301–306.

Thatcher, R. W. (1994). Psychopathology of early frontal lobe damage: Dependence on cycles of development. *Development and Psychopathology, 6,* 565–596.

Todd, R. D., Swarzenski, B., Rossi, P. G., & Visconti, P. (1995). Structural and functional development of the human brain. In D. Cicchetti & D. Cohen (Eds.), *Developmental Psychopathology: Vol. 1. Theory and methods* (pp. 161–194). New York: Wiley Interscience.

Tronick, E. Z. (1989). Emotions and emotional communication in infants. *American Psychologist, 44,* 112–119.

Trotter, R. J. (1983). Baby face. *Psychology Today, 7,* 4–20.

van der Kolk, B., & Greenberg, M. (1987). The psychobiology of the trauma response: Hyperarousal, constriction, and addiction to traumatic reexposure. In B. van der Kolk (Ed.), *Psychological trauma* (pp. 63–87). Washington, DC: American Psychiatric Press.

Vygotsky, L. S. (1972). *Thought and language.* Cambridge, MA: MIT Press.

Vygotsky, L. S. (1978). *Mind in society.* Cambridge, MA: Harvard University Press.

Weinberger, D. R. (1993). A connectionist approach to the prefrontal cortex. *Journal of Neuropsychiatry and Clinical Neurosciences, 5,* 241–253.

White, S. H. (1965). Evidence for a hierarchical arrangement of learning processes. In L. P. Lipsett & C. C. Spiker (Eds.), *Advances in child development and behavior* (Vol. 2). New York: Academic Press.

1. Eisenberg and Fabes (1992).
2. Greenberg, Kusche, and Speltz (1991).
3. Damasio (1994); Goleman (1995).

4. Damasio (1994); LeDoux (1995).
5. Panksepp (1994).
6. Cicchetti and Tucker (1994); Dawson, Hessl, and Frey (1994); Post, Weiss, and Leverich (1994); Teicher, Glod, Surrey, and Swett (1993).
7. Sylwester (1995).
8. Ciaranello et al. (1995); Todd, Swarzenski, Rossi, and Visconti (1995).
9. Kagan (1994); James (1884); Izard (1993); Lewis and Michalson (1982).
10. Maclean (1978).
11. Sylwester (1995).
12. Damasio (1994); Goleman (1995); LeDoux (1995).
13. Maclean (1978).
14. Maclean (1952).
15. LeDoux (1991).
16. Aggleton (1992).
17. Aggleton (1992); Sylwester (1995).
18. Goleman (1995); LeDoux et al. (1988); LeDoux (1995).
19. Goleman (1995).
20. LeDoux (1995).
21. Jacobs and Nadel (1985).
22. Sylwester (1995, p. 45).
23. Izard (1993).
24. Goleman (1995).
25. Weinberger (1993).
26. Maclean (1990).
27. Dawson, Panagiotides, Klinger, and Hill (1992).
28. Goleman (1995).
29. Damasio (1994).
30. Benton (1991); Grattan and Esslinger (1991); Marlowe (1992); Mateer and Williams (1991).
31. Grattan and Esslinger (1991).
32. Sylwester (1995, p. 72).
33. Greenberg, Kusche, and Speltz (1991); Luria (1976).
34. Lewis and Michalson (1982, 1983); Malatesta and Izard (1984b).
35. Tronick (1989).
36. Stern (1985).
37. Trotter (1983); Malatesta and Izard (1984a)
38. Sroufe (1979).
39. Bruner (1979); Freud (1957); Vygotsky (1972).
40. Pine (1985).
41. Hesse and Cicchetti (1982).
42. Vygotsky (1978).
43. Kendall and Braswell (1985).
44. Greenspan and Greenspan (1985).
45. Kendler (1963); White (1965).
46. Thatcher (1994).
47. Dodge (1986).
48. Schore (1994).
49. Falkner and Tanner (1978).
50. Schore (1994).
51. Huttenlocher (1979).

52. Dawson (1994, p. 764).

53. Golden (1981).

54. Dawson (1994); Fox (1994).

55. Sylwester (1995).

56. Davidson (1994).

57. Fox (1994).

58. Davidson (1994).

59. Gainotti (1972).

60. Henriques and Davidson (1991).

61. Davidson (1994).

62. Goldsmith (1994); Goldsmith and Campos (1982).

63. Kagan, Reznick, and Snidman (1987).

64. Fox (1994).

65. Dawson, Hessl, and Frey (1994).

66. LeDoux, Iwata, Cicchetti, and Reis (1988); LeDoux (1995).

67. Goleman (1995).

68. Goleman (1995, p. 17).

69. LeDoux (1995).

70. Goleman (1995, p. 201).

71. van der Kolk and Greenberg (1987).

72. Davidson (1994).

73. Goleman (1995); Davidson (1994).

74. Goleman (1995).

75. Cook, Greenberg, and Kusche (1994).

76. Greenberg and Kusche (1993); Greenberg, Kusche, Cook, and Quamma (1995).

77. Goleman (1995).

EDUCATOR'S COMMENTARY

JO-AN VARGO

TEACHING WEAVES THE BRAIN'S NEURON CONNECTIONS

The implication of current research into the brain's processes is of crucial importance to education today. Students can be taught and do learn to make positive choices for themselves and support others by using process tools such as reflective listening, responsible decision making, empathy, compassion, and conflict resolution techniques. This wisdom supports the creation of a neurological environment for academic and cognitive learning.

The Nueva School incorporates a life skills class called Self-Science® into its curriculum's scope and sequence. Its focus is to recognize as well as address the emotional and social aspects of the student—the person who has to do the processing before learning can take place. Our experiences during 28 years of teaching Self-Science clearly demonstrate the efficacy of a curriculum that strives to enhance self-awareness, social interaction, and problem-solving skills. Its content and teaching methodology are one model for implementing a curriculum that supports the current findings.

The act of teaching can be described as an art form. Since I am a weaver, I consider teaching to be like creating a basket or other sculptural form. When I teach I use the "fibers" of the brain's neural system and my understanding of neural processes. This results in new neuron connections leading to knowledge in my students.

The warp of any weaving is the vertical foundation upon which the complete structure is built. The general warp of my teaching has a foundation of themes: specific skills that prepare for lifelong learning, an awareness of the persistence of themes (within life, nature, disciplines), an ability to see and value diverse viewpoints, an appreciation of one's own and others' learning styles, some avenue of creative expression, and the development of intrinsic motivation.

The warp of the Self-Science curriculum has a foundation of underlying principles. They are:

- Children have valuable insights and information to share.
- Children need an opportunity to express themselves.
- Children readily generate alternatives.
- The evolutionary process of group development enhances children's relationships with themselves and others.

These principles are translated into general goals: Children will be able to:

- Use appropriate communication skills.
- Master conflict resolution techniques.
- Recognize patterns in their own and others' behavior.
- Recognize that an individual can choose to change patterns of behavior.
- Examine specific overarching issues, such as peer pressure, stress management, making choices, fears, self-confidence, risk taking, sibling rivalry, and friendship building.

The weft of a weaving is the horizontally woven material that gives form, texture, color, and interest to the piece. The weft of my teaching contains many different types of material based on the course content, but it always contains metaphor. Why? Because language is most effective through metaphor's creation of a visual understanding that is more complex than literal description. Metaphor uses the visual, linguistic, and emotional pathways of the brain's nervous system.

The weft of the Self-Science curriculum is the set of process skills that develop into a cognitive library for the individual: reflective listening, acknowledging and appreciating others, acting assertively, making responsible decisions and choices. A successful Self-Scientist has acquired and uses this cognitive library. The weft of the Self-Science curriculum also includes a cognitive understanding of the brain's biology and functioning as well as practice in applying it in real, personally valuable, and meaningful ways.

This practice has developed a set of significant abilities—the brain's own synaptic work of art—to focus attention and energy and to resist distractions, to be a sensitive observer and become aware of one's needs and those of others, to learn to understand and select meaningful communication styles and techniques, and to consider a range of possible responses to conflict.

It is the student who is his/her own teacher and I am the facilitator or guide in this process. My job is to help students come to their own wisdom, not just disseminate information. Ronald Edmunds expresses it another way: "Children know how to learn in more ways than we know how to teach them."[1] A successful Self-Scientist is one who leaves Nueva making a conscious choice to live the fundamentals of emotional intelligence.[2]

THE BRAIN'S FUNCTIONING WITHIN THE CONTEXT OF SOCIAL AND EMOTIONAL LEARNING

Learning uses the brain's three major layers—the reptilian system, the limbic system, and the neocortex. The neocortex comprises two hemispheres, left and right, with separate specialized functions. "The left hemisphere analyzes over time, whereas the right hemisphere synthesizes over space."[3] They communicate and work together.

Learning always involves both conscious and unconscious processes. Nueva's students begin to learn about the brain's biology and functioning beginning in the third and fourth grades. We explore our left and right hemispheres' strengths by drawing Mind-Maps (both literally and figuratively). I teach them Tony Buzan's mind-mapping technique, and each student begins to learn that the brain is always searching for meaning by looking for patterns, patterns that become the brain's own spatial map for understanding and memory.[4] This idea becomes personally meaningful when we each make Mind-Maps of our minds that show our individual strengths located in their respective places in the triune brain.

This experience is one of many opportunities for students to develop the first aspect of Goleman's definition of emotional intelligence, self-awareness, which involves the language areas of the neocortex.[5] Our Self-Science curriculum also develops self-awareness, which we define as observing yourself and recognizing your feelings, building a vocabulary for those feelings, and knowing the relationship between thoughts, feelings, and actions. First- and second-graders begin developing these skills by identifying their feelings on our Rating Scale. A personal mental thesaurus of emotional adjectives such as excited, sad, wonderful, worried, happy, and frustrated begins to develop. It grows as the Rating Scale activity (for a "check-in," as the kids call it) repeats throughout the grades.

Students in the fifth grade were recently involved in a discussion of the following questions. A sampling of their responses is included.

Question: "What questions would you like to ask about your brain, emotional intelligence, or Self-Science skills?"
"Why do some people think kids can't realize their feelings or that they are changing from one feeling to another. I know they can."
Christen, grade 5

"Can anyone think of a situation that occurred today when your feelings changed and you were very conscious of it at that moment in time?"
"I don't want to mention names so I'll just say that I was feeling fine and then someone did something and I felt mad; I didn't like it."
Zack, grade 5

"I wasn't very interested and bored in a class early today and then someone said something and I became very interested and had a great idea.

I was surprised at how quickly it changed from boring to interesting and exciting."

Sophie, grade 5

"Today, at lunch recess, we were having a game called 'knock-out.' It's a kind of basketball game and I was excited that I had won two games. All of a sudden somebody who was in third grade got me out. Since I'm in fifth grade and in those last two games I had gotten them out, I was mad that they'd beaten me and felt that I should have beaten them. I knew right away that I was mad at myself."

Ryan, grade 5

Recognizing one's emotions is a first step in the development of Self-Science skills. Managing both positive and negative feelings involves conscious self-control. The challenge here is to learn how to use our "thinking brain" and avoid what Goleman terms an "emotional hijacking" by our limbic system. He explains how our limbic system is always in a state of "action-readiness" in order to step into action when needed. The amygdala releases a surge of chemicals called catacholamines when necessary. These chemicals then flow in waves throughout the adrenal branch of our nervous system.[6]

Lara, a sixth-grade student, recently stated that "It's important to remember to use your thinking brain when you are angry. All the adrenaline and other chemicals are pumping through your brain and the rest of your body. Your thinking brain has to learn how to control your temper." And in another discussion, fifth-grader Devin gave the following example in sports. "Indoor soccer can be really rough. It's easier to get slammed up against the walls. You want to go up and punch the person when that happens, but you have to think, 'That person was trying to get the ball and not hurt me so it was an accident. It's like a mental wake-up call.'"

The concept of regulating emotions was integrated with a history unit of study about civil rights. As part of a culminating assessment, students read a magazine article about the 1991 Crown Heights, N.Y., riots in the African American and Hasidic Jewish communities.[7] They also viewed the PBS broadcast of Anna Devere Smith's "Fires in the Mirror," her dramatic treatment of the incident and its implications on the issues of race in our country.[8] This thought-provoking lesson contained the following assignment: to write a response to this incident as a letter to the editor or a newspaper editorial incorporating the knowledge gained in the study of civil rights as well as in Self-Science. Assignments like this allow the learner to actively process multiple overlapping experiences, in what Caine and Caine describe as an immersion curriculum.[9] It uses functions in both hemispheres of the brain by allowing the learner to reorganize information for personalized meaning, creatively elaborate concepts/ideas/facts, and, it is hoped, evolve into new viewpoints, insights, and understandings.

Motivation is the key to developing a mind-set that allows the individual to remain optimistic in discouraging or adverse conditions instead of giving up and experiencing distress. That optimism can further motivate a person to persevere and perhaps change the course of events or at least feel positive about the attempt. Devin related an additional incident involving her soccer team. "When I'm playing indoor soccer and I know my team is going to lose, I've noticed that I start thinking really negatively about it. Then I catch myself doing this and think, 'I don't need to think this way. We tried as hard as we could.'"

We recognize that not all stress is harmful. In the right doses it can even be a motivator to achieve, and that life without stress is not an option in our modern world. Jacobs and Nadel found that under high levels of negative stress, the indexing capabilities of the brain are limited and short-term memory and the ability to form permanent new memories are suppressed.[10] Nine-year-old Nick recently wrote in his journal, "I convinced myself that I wouldn't know the answers on the math contest and I didn't during the test. But I could easily figure them out a little later. I need to give myself a break!" Eleven-year-old Zoe gave these examples: "There are times when your amygdala *really* takes over; then you can't hear words even though you know the person is talking to you and sometimes it's even hard to breathe. Times like when a pet dies or you're told that something bad like a divorce or separation is happening. You want to . . . run away and say, 'I didn't hear that.'" Our students enter their classroom with a mental backpack filled with emotions lingering from recent experiences. Those emotions can seriously limit their attentiveness and performance in class.

Contrast this level of functioning to that which occurs during an optimum performance. For example, Janice comes to school worried because her grandfather is seriously ill. Nevertheless, she is confident that she is well prepared for debating the following issue in her literature class: The world government is justified in breeding military geniuses to insure that Earth will not be destroyed by aliens (*Ender's Game* by Orson Scott Card).[11] She mentally reassures herself that she will go to the hospital right after school and reminds herself that her grandfather will be proud if she does her best. Her ability to concentrate is increased as is the accessibility of higher order thinking skills. She expresses her thoughts eloquently and wins the debate. Later Janice remarks in a puzzled tone that the experience felt easy, almost effortless. Actually, her brain *really wasn't* working as hard. The brain's cortex *was* less activated than it would have been if she'd continued worrying and tried to concentrate on the debate at the same time. By taking the time to practice motivating and encouraging themselves, students are more likely to avoid the harmful effects of distress.

Academic learning is therefore enhanced when supported by these emotional skills. Empathy also plays a major role. Research now shows us that three areas of the brain—the visual cortex, the amygdala, and the right prefrontal lobe of the neocortex—are involved when we exhibit empathy for another. We pick up nonverbal communication unconsciously and respond to it. How many times do we as educators expect our students to identify and empathize with how harsh or adverse conditions might have affected the people during a particular historical event? Or how certain events might affect a book's characters and therefore their motivations and actions? Some students simply haven't had enough practice empathizing with others in their own lives to be able to transfer this skill to an educational setting.

The richest environment in which to begin to learn this skill is our classrooms, school buses, and sports fields. The opportunities to explore empathy and the other inter- and intrapersonal skills are endless. A student recently tried to empathize or at least understand a historic figure in World War II and became stuck. He raised his hand and asked, "Are there people who have a damaged or less developed part of their emotional brain? I'm thinking of Hitler, who did terrible things in his life and didn't seem to realize it." It is in circumstances such as this that those "Aha!" moments in learning exist. Real learning of lessons never to be forgotten occur.

Learning is a lifelong process, and the application of its lessons will affect all areas of a person's life. I was reminded of this while sitting at the computer composing a draft of this section. A parent asked if she could interrupt me for a moment. I almost said no, but something in her facial expression stopped me. Taking the time to listen allowed her to give me a gift.

She wanted to express her appreciation for the lessons her 11-year-old is learning in Self-Science and tell me about an incident that had occurred the night before. A heated discussion had taken place and the voice levels were rising quickly. In the middle of a particularly upsetting comment, her son stopped, turned to his father, and said, "Dad, you don't practice what we've been taught in Self-Science!" His irritated father asked gruffly, "And what is that!?" Their son's reply was, "We're told that when we notice a change of feeling coming on, it's important to stop and think about what that change means instead of just acting it out." That comment broke the tension enough to allow father and son to take a different approach to solving their conflict. Andi's comment was, "The good news is Zack's increasing mastery of social and problem-solving skills." We chuckled over her husband's response when they discussed the incident, "The 'bad' news is that Zack was completely right!"[12]

NOTES

References

Bock, M., Shanitz, B., & Mabry, M. (1991, September 9). Bonfire in Crown Heights. *Newsweek*, p. 48.

Buzan, T. (1977). *Speed memory* (Rev. ed.). North Pomfret, VT: Newton Abbot.

Caine, R., & Caine, G. (1994). *Making connections: Teaching and the human brain.* Menlo Park, CA: Addison-Wesley.

Card, O. S. (1985). *Ender's game.* New York: Tom Doherty Associates.

Edmunds, R. (Program Consultant). (1991). *Effective schools for children at risk* [videotape]. Alexandria, VA: ASCD.

Goleman, D. (1995). *Emotional intelligence.* New York: Bantam Books.

Jacobs, W. J., & Nadel, L. (1985). Stress-induced recovery of fear and phobias. *Psychological Review, 92,* 512–531.

Levy, J. (1974). Psychobiological implications of bilateral asymmetry. In S. J. Dimond & J. G. Beaumont (Eds.), *Hemisphere function in the human brain.* New York: John Wiley and Sons.

Smith, A. D. (1993). *Fires in the mirror* [videotape]. New York: Public Television Playhouse, Inc.

1. Edmunds (1991).
2. Goleman (1995).
3. Levy (1974).
4. Buzan (1977).
5. Goleman (1995).
6. Goleman (1995).
7. Bock, Shanitz, and Mabry (1991).
8. Smith (1993).
9. Caine and Caine (1994).
10. Jacobs and Nadel (1985).
11. Card (1985).
12. In recognition of the Self-Science® students and staff at the Nueva School®, 6565 Skyline Boulevard, Hillsborough, CA, 94010, and especially its executive director, Anabel Jensen, Ph.D., for giving me the opportunity to explore and help develop a curriculum that has truly changed my life.

PART II

Social and Emotional Competencies

CHAPTER 5

Emotional Responding: Regulation, Social Correlates, and Socialization

NANCY EISENBERG, RICHARD A. FABES, AND SANDRA LOSOYA

JENNY, AN 8-YEAR-OLD, is disruptive in class, aggressive on the playground, and often seems unable to control her anger and frustration. In addition, she tends to breaks rules of conduct.

John, also aged 8, is prone to anxiety and has numerous fears. He is shy, frightened of novel objects and new situations, frequently withdraws from social interactions, and sometimes appears depressed.

These two children exhibit patterns of behavior and emotional expression that frequently are labeled as externalizing (Jenny) and internalizing (John) problems. Although their behaviors are quite different, both seem to have difficulties with negative emotion and with regulating their behavior in optimal ways. In our recent research, we have been concerned with how

This research was supported by a grant from the National Science Foundation (DBS–9208375) to both authors and Research Scientist Development and Research Scientist Awards from the National Institute of Mental Health (K02 MH00903 and K05 M801321) to Nancy Eisenberg. Address correspondence to Nancy Eisenberg, Psychology, Arizona State University, Box 871104, Tempe, AZ 85287–1104.

individual differences in children's typical emotion and their ability to regulate their emotion and behavior predict the quality of children's social
functioning at school and home. The purpose of this chapter is to review
some of the research findings related to this topic. Specifically, our goals
are (a) to differentiate among various ways of conceptualizing emotionality and regulation in children, (b) to discuss differences among children
in emotionality and regulation and their role in both problem behavior
and variations in social functioning among normal children, (c) to consider the relevance of differences among children in their emotionality
and regulation for children's empathy-related responding, and (d) to
summarize some of the research findings on the socialization of optimal
emotional responding and regulation among children.

In recent years, there has been an increasing appreciation of the inter-
relatedness of emotion, motivation, and behavior, and of the role of emotion in normal development and social functioning. In the past emotions
generally were seen as playing little causal role in normal social behavior.
Emotions are now viewed as both a product of and a process in social
interaction.[1]

Despite the growing importance of the topic of emotion in developmental and personality psychology, research and theory pertaining to the
role of emotion and its regulation in normal social functioning are limited. For example, Hubbard and Coie noted the dearth of research on the
relation of the ability to regulate emotions effectively to social competence with peers.[2] Much of the literature pertaining to emotion during
childhood concerns children's understanding of others' emotions and
when emotions are masked rather than the experience, expression, and
regulation of emotion.[3] Of the limited work on the latter topics, most pertains to early socioemotional functioning (e.g., temperament and emotion in early relationships).[4]

Recently, Eisenberg and Fabes[5] argued that individual differences in
emotional intensity and in regulatory capabilities play a pivotal role in a
variety of aspects of social functioning. In potentially emotional situations, individual differences in emotional reactivity (often considered a
temperamental or personality trait) undoubtedly influence degree of
emotional responding.[6] Moreover, the ways individuals experience, express, and cope with feelings would be expected to influence the quality
of associated behavior, as well as long-term outcomes such as quality of
social relationships and feelings of competence.[7] In addition, the way
people react to and cope with emotions is likely influenced by how others in one's social world handle and respond to emotion. Conversely, it is
probable that how individuals experience, express, and regulate their
emotions influence the socialization process.

We have begun to explore, theoretically and empirically, the roles of individual differences in emotionality and regulation in individuals' social
functioning, including their social competence, peer acceptance, anger-
related behavior, and vicarious emotional responding to others (empathy-

related responses such as sympathy). Further, we are studying associations between children's social functioning and the ways in which adults react to, talk about, and model emotion and emotion regulation. In this chapter, we summarize some of the findings (ours and others') on these issues, with an emphasis on findings of practical interest.

CONCEPTIONS OF EMOTIONALITY AND REGULATION: A FRAMEWORK

Based on work concerning infants' and children's emotional reactivity and inhibition of emotionally driven behavior,[8] it seems reasonable to assume that people who easily become emotionally overaroused are relatively unlikely to behave in socially competent ways in situations involving social conflict or others' negative emotions. Eisenberg and Fabes[9] proposed that whether people become overaroused in social contexts likely varies as a function of at least two variables: (1) their dispositional level of reactivity, particularly intensity of emotional responding (an aspect of temperament), and (2) their abilities to regulate their emotional reactions and emotionally driven behavior and to cope with an evocative situation.

Currently there is limited evidence that differences among people in dispositional emotional intensity are associated with reactions in specific distressing or stressful situations. For example, Derryberry and Rothbart[10] found positive relations between measures of dispositional arousability and adults' sadness. Further, initial evidence suggests that adults high in emotional intensity tend to react vicariously to others in distress and exhibit skin conductance reactions (i.e., they sweat) to empathy-inducing stimuli.[11]

At least three types of regulation processes are relevant to the quality of social functioning: regulation of emotion, regulation of the context itself, and regulation of emotionally driven behavior. Further, aspects of regulation pertinent to socioemotional functioning have been discussed in the literature from a variety of perspectives. For example, regulation is viewed by some temperament theorists as involving several mechanisms for the regulation or modulation of stimuli impinging from outside the individual and an individual's internal states. These mechanisms include shifting attention away from an arousing or unpleasant stimulus (attentional shifting), sustaining attention (attentional focusing), voluntarily initiating or continuing action (activation control), and inhibiting action (inhibition control). People who can regulate their emotional reactivity in social or nonsocial contexts through allocating attention would be expected to react relatively positively to stressful events. Shifting attention from a distressing stimulus can decrease arousal; focusing attention on positive aspects of the situation or means by which to cope also can decrease negative emotion. In fact, the ability to shift and refocus attention has been associated with lower levels of distress, frustration, and other negative emotions, although until recently most of the relevant work had been conducted with infants and adults.[12] Further, relatively extreme problems with sustaining attention (as evidenced in attention-deficit hyperactivity disorder) have been associated with social deficits.[13]

Coping also can be viewed as a type of regulation—specifically, effortful regulation in stressful contexts. Coping is defined as changing cognitive and behavioral efforts to manage specific external or internal demands that are appraised as taxing or exceeding the resources of the individual. Coping theorists focus primarily on the regulation of emotional distress (i.e., emotion-focused coping) and efforts to regulate the source of the problem (i.e., the problem context; problem-focused coping). Both types of strategies frequently may be useful in dealing with negative emotional arousal in social contexts; Lazarus and Folkman[14] argued that in most situations people first need to regulate emotional distress in order to facilitate problem-solving coping. In social circumstances in which people have some control, some strategies (e.g., positive reappraisal, planful problem solving) tend to be more adaptive than others (e.g., denial, confrontative strategies). However, different strategies (e.g., emotion-focused strategies, cognitive distraction) may be more adaptive in uncontrollable contexts.[15] For example, cognitive strategies such as thinking about something else may be most appropriate and adaptive for a child who is fearful while waiting to get a shot at the doctor's office, whereas active problem solving may be more appropriate for dealing with anxiety about a test that is scheduled.

Research on regulation of emotionally driven behavior has been discussed under the rubric of ego or impulse control,[16] disinhibition in the adult personality literature,[17] and temperamental inhibition control and impulsivity.[18] Degree of regulation of emotionally driven behavior occasionally has been linked to both acting-out types of behavior and highly inhibited behavior, particularly the former.[19]

Arousability and regulation—although separate constructs—are interrelated. The individual's temperament, including arousal components, may influence the style that characterizes the child's coping/regulation and vice versa. However, these two constructs also are distinctive and may be associated in a variety of ways. For example, some people who are easily overaroused may exhibit behavioral inhibition in response to a stressful stimulus, whereas others seem to become undercontrolled in their behavior. Further, the emotions associated with under- and overcontrol may differ; for example, hostility appears to be associated with underregulation, whereas overcontrolled, shy people often are anxious.[20] Thus, it is useful to study both individual differences in emotionality and in regulation.

EMOTIONALITY, REGULATION, AND CHILDHOOD PROBLEM BEHAVIOR

Although there is considerable research on the relations of emotional re-activity and negative emotionality to social and problem behaviors, much of this research has been conducted with clinical samples rather than normal children. We briefly summarize this clinically oriented work before turning to our own research with samples of normal children.

In research on psychopathology in childhood, two categories of disorders frequently are distinguished: internalizing and externalizing disorders. Internalizing disorders include behaviors that are inner-directed such as anxiety, tendencies to behave in a withdrawn fashion, depressed behaviors, and somatic complaints. Externalizing problems, on the other hand, include outwardly expressed behaviors such as hyperactivity, aggression, antisocial behaviors, and conduct problems.[21] Links between internalizing/externalizing disorders and emotionality and regulation have been articulated and studied primarily by researchers interested in early childhood temperament and its role in the development of psychopathology.[22]

The defining characteristics of these problems suggest aspects of emotionality and regulation that are likely to be related to the development and maintenance of specific disorders. For instance, externalizing disorders, which often involve aggression and hostile behavior, suggest under-regulation of the experience and expression of anger, a diminished ability to inhibit socially prohibited behavior, and perhaps a lack of fear, which would also serve to inhibit behavior in some situations.[23] In contrast, internalizing disorders would appear to involve negative emotionality (e.g., anxiety and despair), lack of adaptive modes of regulation such as attentional control, and perhaps extreme levels of behavioral inhibition. However, it is important to keep in mind that internalizing and externalizing symptoms tend to co-occur and usually are substantially correlated; for example, there is a group of children characterized by depression, aggression, and social withdrawal.[24]

Internalizing Disorders

Research on the roles of dispositional emotionality and regulation in internalizing behavior is somewhat limited. However, there is some evidence that elementary school children with internalizing disorders are (and have been when younger) intense, prone to negative moods including anxiety, and distractible (unable to focus attention).[25] In a sample of 10- to 17-year-old boys and girls, depressed youth reported more negative emotions (e.g., sadness, anger, shame, shyness, guilt, and self-directed hostility) and less joy than did youth who were diagnosed with other nondepressive, nonpsychotic conditions.[26] Similar findings in regard to anger, sadness, and happiness were obtained by Garber.[27] Further, some evidence suggests that behavioral overcontrol in infancy and childhood may be associated with internalizing problems.[28] For example, Block and colleagues[29] found that depressed mood in girls (but not boys) tended to be related to overcontrolled behavior, including anxiety and a somewhat rigid self-focus. In contrast, undercontrolled, aggressive tendencies have been related to depression for boys.[30] Depression also has been linked to low attentional control (distractibility) among young adults.[31]

Extreme shyness and inhibition in new situations may be an expression of some kind of internalizing disorder. Researchers have found that behavioral inhibition, which is an aspect of temperament characterized by extreme shyness/cautiousness and behavioral inhibition of responses, is indeed a risk factor for the onset of anxiety disorders in childhood. Rosenbaum and his colleagues[32] compared children of parents with agoraphobia and/or panic disorder with children whose parents had other disorders and found that rates of behavioral inhibition were significantly higher in the children of phobic parents. Moreover, rates of childhood-onset anxiety disorders were significantly higher in children with behavioral inhibition than those without, regardless of experimental group membership. The findings were similar at a 3-year follow-up, indicating the stability of behavioral inhibition over time and providing support for the link between overcontrolled, emotion-related regulatory processes and the development of later anxiety disorders.

Similar results also emerged in a longitudinal study of the temperamental origins of childhood behavior disorders.[33] In this study, behaviorally based observations were used to derive measures of temperament for over 800 children. For girls but not boys, higher rates of *sluggishness,* a factor of characteristics related to behavioral inhibition, were found to be linked to the development of anxiety over the course of 12 years (from ages 3 to 15). Girls with higher rates of sluggishness also were more likely to experience attentional problems in adolescence. For boys, internalizing problems were weakly predicted by lower ratings on approach (i.e., adaptability to new situations, self-confidence, self-reliance, and friendliness) and higher ratings on lack of control (e.g., emotional lability, negativity, restlessness, impulsivity).

In summary, it appears that internalizing disorders in children are associated with anxiety, low emotion regulation, and highly inhibited behavior, suggesting rigid overcontrol of behavior for girls.

Externalizing Disorders

In studies of general behavioral problems (e.g., aggression, noncompliance), negative behaviors have been linked to characteristics such as high intensity or reactivity, negative emotionality, and low adaptability.[34] In many of these studies, different types of behavioral problems that might be differentially related to emotionality and regulation were not examined separately. Further, the severity and status of the problems (e.g., if they were diagnosed with a problem) varied across studies.

As noted previously, emotional reactivity and regulation frequently have been linked to externalizing disorders. For instance, Losoya[35] found that boys with attention deficit hyperactivity disorder (ADHD) were rated by their mothers as higher on negative emotionality and lower on characteristics related to self-regulation (e.g., attention control, motor arousal, and activity level) than were age-matched boys without ADHD. Aspects of emotion regulation also were related to maternal ratings of social competence and peer relations. Mothers who rated their sons as low on attentional capabilities and activity level and high on negative emotionality (i.e., irritability, sadness, and shyness) also rated their sons as having relatively poor social skills and few friends.

In a longitudinal study, Sanson, Smart, Prior, and Oberklaid[36] obtained parent, nurse, and then teacher ratings of the temperament and behavior of children who were followed from infancy to 8 years of age. Three groups of children were targeted for study: hyperactive but not aggressive (H); aggressive but not hyperactive (A); hyperactive and aggressive (H+A); matched control children also were studied. Compared to the normal control group, all three diagnosed groups evidenced poor emotion regulation, even from infancy. Descriptions of the children included references to emotionality (i.e., negative mood and high emotional intensity or overreactivity), as well as self-regulation (i.e., lack of persistence, suggesting poorly developed attentional processes, nonadaptability, and inflexibility). Those infants who developed one or more problems with aggression (particularly the H+A groups) were rated as particularly unregulated and temperamentally difficult in childhood. However, the hyperactive and aggressive group also was characterized by lower socioeconomic status, larger families, more negative life events, and poorer self-perceived coping with these events. Thus, in addition to being poorly self-regulated, children in the hyperactive plus aggression group apparently were placed at greater risk by being members of families characterized, to some degree, by instability and dysregulation. These findings suggest an interaction between emotional reactivity and regulation with family variables as one developmental pathway to more serious kinds of externalizing disorders.

In another series of studies, Caspi and colleagues have demonstrated the predictive power of behaviorally based, observationally derived measures of early childhood temperament to externalizing disorders.[37] Early temperament and behavior problems for a sample of over 800 children from New Zealand were assessed longitudinally across 12 years. Measures of individual differences in temperamental behavioral styles of approach and response to novelty were derived from examiners' ratings of behavior of children at ages 3, 5, 7, and 9. Caspi et al. found that a factor labeled *lack of control*, defined as emotional lability, restlessness, distractibility, and negativity, predicted parents' and teachers' reports of inattention, hyperactivity, and antisocial behavior at ages 9, 11, and 13. Moreover, this factor was negatively related to parental reports of their children's competencies (e.g., self-confidence and determination for both sexes; popularity for girls) at ages 13 and 15. Parental reports of undercontrolled behavior at age 5 also predicted antisocial outcomes in later childhood and adolescence.[38] At age 18, individuals' reports of low regulation and the tendency to experience negative emotions (e.g., fear, anxiety, and anger, as well as breaking down under stress) were related to delinquency, as assessed with variables such as self- and informant-reported delinquency and court convictions.[39] Similarly, in another study, behavioral impulsivity at age 10 was linked to delinquency at ages 10 and 12 to 13.[40] In addition, observations or teachers' reports of preschoolers' impulsivity and hostility, but not anxiety, have been related to parent-referred problems (aggression-noncompliant and hyperactive-distractible behavior).[41]

In a follow-up study of the males in the previously discussed New Zealand sample, Henry, Caspi, Moffitt, and Silva[42] found that family characteristics and early childhood temperament were differentially related to convictions for violent and nonviolent offenses. Three groups of males were identified on the basis of their conviction status at age 18: those who had never been convicted, those who were convicted for nonviolent offenses, and those who had been convicted for violent offenses. Men convicted of violent or nonviolent crimes tended to come from unstable families (characterized by changes in residence and parents). However, membership in the violent conviction category was specifically associated with temperamental lack of control. Moreover, only this aspect of temperament discriminated between nonviolent and violent group membership, with men who committed violent offenses scoring lower in control. Consistent with these findings, there is mounting evidence that adult psychopaths may have inhibitory control failures in some situations and have difficulty switching attention to new information that is relatively low in salience but important to guiding ongoing action.[43]

Finally, it appears that the appropriateness of children's emotional reactions in social situations, even positive contexts, is associated with psychological status. Casey and Schlosser[44] examined 7- to 14-year-olds' facial and cognitive reactions to positive peer praise. Children with and without externalizing disorders were complimented by same-sex, same-age confederates in another room (observed through a monitor). Casey and Schlosser found that although the children in the disordered group reported positive reactions to the compliments of the confederate, they displayed more facial expressions of hostility and surprise, suggesting an inability to regulate facial emotional expressions. The groups did not differ on their appraisals of emotions; however, the externalizing children demonstrated less sophistication in their understanding of their own emotions.

Thus far in our review, we have focused on emotion- and regulation-related characteristics of children with psychological disorders. However, it is important to note that researchers frequently have found that the child's social context (e.g., quality of interactions with parents, socioeconomic status, hassles) is related, and may interact with, dispositional characteristics when predicting psychopathology.[45] For example, the relation of stress to symptoms of psychological disorders may be less for children who are temperamentally prone to approach new situations and strangers with positive affect rather than withdraw from the situation.[46] We return to the issue of family influence on emotionality shortly.

RELATIONS OF EMOTIONALITY AND REGULATION TO CHILDREN'S SOCIAL FUNCTIONING

As is evident from the previous review, the literature on the links between psychopathology and both emotionality and regulation is growing. However, research on the relation of emotionality and regulation to social functioning in normal samples, particularly in regard to positive aspects of behavior rather than problem behavior, is relatively scant. Indeed, as noted previously, little is known about the relation of emotionality to peer relationships and interactions,[47] although there is some evidence that intense, moody, or emotionally negative children are less popular with peers than are other children.[48] Moreover, our knowledge of the role of emotionality and regulation in children's social functioning is limited because most investigators have studied frequency of children's experiencing negative affect or the broader construct of reactivity (which can involve behavioral as well as emotional reactivity) rather than intensity of emotion. In addition, in many studies on temperament and social functioning, both temperament and behavior/adjustment were assessed by means of reports from a single adult (e.g., a parent). Thus, it is difficult to know whether associations are due to using the same reporter and/or methods when collecting data on emotionality/regulation and social functioning.

Socially Appropriate Behavior, Peer Acceptance, and Anger-Related Reactions

In an ongoing longitudinal study, we have started to explore linkages between normal children's emotionality or regulation and their social functioning.

Findings for 4- to 6-Year-Olds

When children in the study were aged 4 to 6 and in preschool or kindergarten, their social behaviors with peers and their anger reactions were observed over an extended period of time. In addition, mothers and teachers reported their perceptions of the children's intensity of negative emotional responding, the frequency of children's negative emotions, children's abilities to regulate their attention, and coping styles.[49] Peers also rated how much they liked to play with each child in the study, and the children themselves acted out with puppets what they would do in peer conflict situations (such as when another child knocked over a block tower that the child was building, teased the child, or would not play with him or her).[50]

We expected children high in intensity and frequency of negative emotions, particularly if they were low in attentional control and constructive modes of coping, to be low in positive social functioning. Specifically, such children were expected to be viewed by school personnel as low in socially appropriate behavior, to be relatively unpopular with peers, and to exhibit inappropriate reactions in real-life anger situations and when enacting the puppet vignettes. Constructive coping was assessed with a composite measure of teachers' and teacher aides' reports of children's instrumental problem solving (i.e., the tendency to take constructive action to try to improve a problem situation) and seeking social support when dealing with problems. Similarly, nonconstructive coping styles were assessed with school personnel's reports of children's tendencies to aggress and vent emotion (e.g., cry, yell) rather than avoid the situation, distract themselves, or look at the positive side of the situation (i.e., positive cognitive restructuring). Mothers' reports of these same coping strategies were obtained but were not combined into constructive/nonconstructive categories for statistical reasons.

In general, we found support for our predictions. For example, boys who were viewed by their teachers as low in frequency of negative emotion and high in constructive coping and attentional control (the ability to shift and focus attention) were rated as socially appropriate by adults who observed the children at school. These same boys were liked by their peers. For both boys and girls, low levels of intense negative emotion and nonconstructive coping were associated with observers' reports of socially appropriate behavior; for boys, these aspects of functioning also were related to peer acceptance. For boys and girls combined, those high in negative emotional intensity and low in constructive coping and attentional regulation were low in both peer acceptance and social skills (as rated by teachers). In combination, school personnel reports of negative emotionality and regulation were fairly good predictors of children's, especially boys', social functioning.

Mothers' reports of children's emotionality and regulation were less frequently related to children's behavior as observed at school and peer acceptance. However, for boys, negative emotional intensity was negatively related to social skills and peer acceptance at school. For the combined group of boys and girls, children high in emotional intensity and low in constructive coping were likely to be relatively low in peer acceptance; such boys also were rated as low in socially appropriate behavior.

Children's observed, real-life anger reactions also were related to individual differences in emotionality and regulation. For example, children who reacted with nonabusive verbalizations (labeled verbal objections, e.g., "Stop that," "I want to play," "Go away") when angered were low in teacher-reported nonconstructive coping and emotional intensity. Boys high in the use of verbal objections also were high in teachers' reports of attentional control and constructive coping, whereas girls who used verbal objections tended to be low in observed intensity of anger when angered. Venting of emotion (i.e., crying or yelling) when angered was related to observed anger intensity, and girls' nonconstructive coping and emotional intensity. Aggressive reactions when angered were associated with teachers' reports of nonconstructive coping and high emotional intensity. The tendency simply to escape (leave) the anger situation was associated with low constructive or nonconstructive coping, as well as low emotional intensity and real-life anger intensity for girls. Thus, children who escaped when angered typically exhibited few coping reactions of any type at school, and girls were low in expressions of intense negative emotion.

Mothers' reports of children's emotionality and regulation also were related to children's tendencies to react in various ways to anger. For example, children who used verbal objections when angered were reported by their mothers to be relatively likely to seek support or engage in instrumental coping when stressed, and relatively unlikely to aggress when stressed. Further, such children were viewed by their mothers as low in negative emotional intensity. Children who were likely to try to escape in anger conflicts were viewed by their mothers as relatively aggressive and high in the tendency to experience negative emotions (such as sadness and fear). Further, children who were likely to try to defend themselves or objects when angered were viewed by mothers as low in attentional control, whereas those who used physical retaliation (e.g., aggression) were reported to be low in the tendency to cope by seeking social support.

Finally, relations between children's enacted responses in the puppet vignettes to teachers' and parents' reports of children's negative emotionality and regulation were examined. Children's verbal descriptions of what they would do in the conflict situations, as well as their enactments with the puppets, were scored for friendliness versus hostility; further, aggressive actions were noted for boys (girls engaged in few). Children rated high in negative emotionality by teachers and mothers were low in enacted friendliness and enacted more aggression with the puppets. These findings were especially true when one considered intensity of children's negative emotions rather than mere frequency of negative emotions.[51] Further, mothers who reported that their sons were high in attentional control had boys who were relatively unlikely to exhibit aggressive responses in the puppet enactments.[52]

In summary, when the children were aged 4 to 6, those who were relatively high in negative emotionality (especially intensity of negative emotion) and low in regulation were doing more poorly in regard to a variety of measures of social functioning. The tendencies to regulate one's own attention and to engage in constructive modes of coping were predictive primarily for boys, whereas negative emotionality and nonconstructive coping were predictive of social outcomes for both sexes.

Findings in Early Elementary School

In a 2-year follow-up, in addition to the measures of negative emotionality and regulation previously discussed, we assessed more types of regulation (e.g., inhibition control, or the ability to inhibit action), as well as positive emotionality. Further, teachers rated children's socially skilled behavior, social insecurity, peer acceptance, and disruptive or aggressive behaviors, and mothers and fathers provided information about children's problem behaviors at home.

Our findings suggest that individual differences in emotionality and regulation predict social functioning among 6- to 8-year-olds, as well as at a younger age. In this study, a composite score of children's regulation (comprised of a number of scales reflecting attentional, behavioral, and inhibition control) was computed. Children viewed as well regulated by teachers or parents (most parents were mothers) were likely (according to teacher reports) to behave in socially appropriate, nonaggressive ways at school and were likely to be relatively popular, prosocial, and socially secure.[53] In addition, they were viewed as doing well academically.[54] Further, children viewed by teachers as high in negative emotionality and nonconstructive coping were relatively low in quality of social functioning at school. Parents' reports of general emotional intensity (i.e., the tendency to react with strong emotions once emotionally aroused, regardless of the valence of the emotion) also were associated with low social functioning at school. In addition, children viewed by teachers as high in expression of positive emotion (excited, inspired, enthusiastic) were reported to be accepted by their peers and low in social insecurity.

Teachers' reports of children's emotionality and regulation 2 years earlier also predicted their functioning at school (as reported by elementary school teachers). Children viewed by school personnel 2 years earlier as being emotionally intense, nonconstructive rather than constructive copers, and low in attentional control were rated by their elementary school teachers as relatively low in social functioning. There were few relations between mothers' reports of children's emotionality/regulation at age 4 to 6 and children's social functioning at school 2 years later, although boys viewed by mothers as aggressive in their coping at the earlier age were reported by teachers to be relatively low in socially appropriate behavior 2 years later.[55]

Parents' reports of problem behaviors (primarily acting-out types of behaviors) at age 6 to 8 also were associated with children's concurrent emotionality and regulation. Findings were primarily for parents' (rather than teachers') reports of children's emotionality and regulation, although children viewed by their elementary school teachers as unregulated tended to be those with problem behaviors at home (as reported by mothers). Children viewed by their mothers as unregulated, nonconstructive copers or high in negative emotionality (including intensity and frequency of negative emotions) were rated by both mothers and fathers as having a relatively high number of problem behaviors. These findings generally were somewhat stronger for boys than girls, and links between emotionality/regulation and fathers' reports of problem behaviors were significant only for boys. Further, mothers' reports of boys' use of seeking support as a means of coping were associated with mothers' reports of fewer problem behaviors. Adults' reports of children's positive emotionality were not related to problem behaviors. Thus, regulation and negative emotionality were linked to children's problem behaviors as reported by both parents, but particularly for boys.

Mothers' reports of children's emotionality and regulation at age 4 to 6 also were related to parents' reports of problem behavior at age 6 to 8 years. Boys high in negative emotional intensity at the younger age tended to have problems, as reported by both parents, during elementary school. Further, children who reportedly used constructive (seeking support, cognitive restructuring) rather than aggressive coping at age 4 to 6 generally were viewed as having fewer problem behaviors at age 6 to 8 by parents (i.e., by both parents for cognitive restructuring and aggressive coping, and by mothers for seeking social support).[56]

Summary

In summary, the results of this study provide support for the assumption that children's expression of emotion and regulatory capabilities are related to their social functioning at home and at school. Relations between social functioning and emotionality/regulation generally were stronger if assessed in the same context (e.g., if both were assessed at school or both at home). However, relations were obtained not only across reporters and measures but sometimes across settings.

Interestingly, although we have found moderate agreement between parents' and teachers' reports of children's coping behaviors, there is little agreement about children's emotionality across settings. It is likely that children's expression of emotion does differ across settings; further, teachers and parents likely focus on different negative emotions. For example, teachers seem to be more likely than mothers to take into account children's displays of anger and frustration when rating negative emotional intensity.[57] This is probably because anger reactions both are more noticeable than other more subtle negative emotions (and teachers are watching many children) and are particularly salient in the school environment. In any case, there appears to be a need to study the relations of emotionality and regulation to social functioning in both the home and school setting, as well as in a variety of age groups.

RELATIONS OF EMOTIONALITY AND REGULATION TO EMPATHY-RELATED RESPONDING

For years, we have been studying empathy-related responding, including its links to prosocial behaviors (e.g., helping, caring, and sharing) and its socialization correlates. More recently, however, we have begun to examine the roles of emotionality and regulation in empathy and related emotional reactions. In fact, our findings in regard to empathy first stimulated the previously discussed work concerning the roles of emotionality and regulation in socially competent responding; we view sympathetic rather than distressed responding to another's distress as one of many indices of socially competent socioemotional functioning.

In work on empathy, it is essential to differentiate among various emotional reactions that have been labeled "empathy." *Sympathy* often is defined as feelings of sorrow for another or concern for another based on the perception of another's emotional state or condition. In contrast, *personal distress* is an aversive emotional reaction such as discomfort or anxiety resulting from exposure to another's emotional state or condition.[58] Both of these emotional responses are viewed as often stemming from *empathy* (an emotional response resulting from the recognition of another's emotional state or condition, which is very similar or identical to what the other individual is perceived to experience). Sympathy is defined as involving other-oriented, altruistic motivation, whereas personal distress is viewed as reflecting the self-focused, egoistic motivation of alleviating one's own distress.[59]

Psychologists frequently have hypothesized that sympathy is positively related to other-oriented behavior, including altruism, whereas personal distress is negatively related. In general, results of empirical studies are consistent with this hypothesis.[60] Thus, sympathy and personal distress appear to play an important role in children's and adults' positive social behavior.

Eisenberg and her colleagues[61] suggested that individual differences in the tendency to experience sympathy rather than personal distress are due in part to stable differences among people in their typical level of vicarious emotional responding. In our view, some people are susceptible to emotional overarousal, and those people are likely to experience high levels of vicariously induced negative emotion. Empathic overarousal, when empathizing with another's negative emotion or situation, is likely to be experienced as aversive and, consequently, would be expected to result in concern about oneself (i.e., personal distress).[62] For example, a child who views another child crying and bleeding after falling down may feel very anxious and distressed, with the consequence that he or she simply goes elsewhere to avoid looking rather than trying to help the injured child. Consistent with this view, general negative emotional arousal has been found to result in a self-focus.[63]

In contrast, Eisenberg and her colleagues[64] suggested that people who can maintain their emotional reactions within a moderate, tolerable range are more likely to experience sympathy when confronted with empathy-inducing situations. Such individuals are likely to experience how needy or distressed others feel, but are relatively unlikely to become overwhelmed by their negative emotion and self-focus. As an example, a child who views an injured peer may be able to avoid focusing on the blood and, consequently, can avoid high levels of distress or anxiety that are likely to undermine concern for the peer.

Based on this line of reasoning, Eisenberg and Fabes[65] proposed that individual differences in the tendency to experience sympathy versus personal distress vary as a function of dispositional differences in both typical level of emotional intensity (EI) and people's ability to regulate their emotional reactions. Individuals high in constructive modes of regulation such as attentional control (e.g., attention focusing and shifting) and the ability to inhibit behavior were hypothesized to be relatively high in sympathy regardless of emotional intensity. People at least moderately high in emotional intensity were expected to be particularly sympathetic if they also were well regulated. This is because well-regulated people should be able to modulate their negative vicarious emotion and maintain an optimal level of emotional arousal—one that has emotional force but is not so aversive that it engenders a self-focus. In contrast, people low in the ability to regulate their emotion, especially if they are emotionally intense, would be expected to be prone to personal distress rather than sympathy.

There is some empirical support for this line of reasoning, but most of the relevant research has been conducted with adults. Measures of emotional intensity, emotionality, and arousability have been associated with adults' reports of vicarious emotional responding in empathy-inducing contexts,[66] reported stable individual differences in the tendency to experience empathy, sympathy, and personal distress,[67] and skin conductance (sweating, which is a physiological marker of arousal) while viewing a sympathy-inducing film.[68] Carlo and colleagues[69] found that personal distress, but not dispositional sympathy, grouped in statistical analyses with emotional intensity. In addition, children and adults exhibit higher skin conductance in response to distressing than to sympathy-inducing stimuli[70]—a finding that supports the idea that personal distress involves higher emotional arousal than does sympathy.

In support of the importance of regulation in empathy-related reactions, Rothbart, Ahadi, and Hershey[71] found that mothers' reports of their children's effortful control were positively correlated with mothers' reports of their 7-year-olds' empathy. In this study, effortful control was operationalized as temperamental inhibitory control, attentional focusing, low intensity pleasure (pleasure in situations involving lower stimulus intensity, rate, complexity, novelty, and incongruity), and perceptual intensity (detection of low-intensity stimuli from the external environment). Further, high regulation has been linked to low levels of infants' vicariously induced distress.[72]

In recent work in which both emotional intensity and regulation were assessed in the same study, both younger[73] and older[74] adults' self-reported personal distress was associated with low levels of regulatory skills and high emotional intensity (in regard to negative emotions). Findings for sympathy were mixed. Among older adults, self-reported dispositional sympathy was associated with high levels of both emotionality and regulation; among younger adults, sympathy was correlated with relatively high emotional intensity, but evidence of a positive relation to regulation was very weak. In another study of preschoolers' responses to an empathy-inducing film, children high in concerned facial reactions to a tape of distressed others were rated by their teachers as high in attentional regulation and low in nonconstructive coping (viewed as evidence of regulation). High negative emotional intensity (as rated by teachers) and aggressive coping (as rated by mothers) were related to low levels of young children's facial concern.[75] The negative relation between children's concerned reactions and negative emotional intensity likely was due to teachers' weighing disruptive negative emotions highly when rating emotional intensity.[76]

In a recent study, we examined the relations of children's stable tendencies to be sympathetic (as rated by teachers and the children themselves) and teachers' and parents' reports of emotionality and regulation.[77] Contemporaneously and 2 years earlier, parents and teachers reported on children's dispositional positive and negative emotionality, regulation, and social functioning (this is the same longitudinal sample discussed previously). In addition, social functioning was assessed with sociometric evaluations and children's enacted puppet behavior in hypothetical conflict situations; negative emotionality was assessed with physiological responses to a distress stimulus. In general, sympathy was associated with high levels of regulation, high levels of teacher-reported positive emotionality and general emotional intensity, and, particularly for boys, low levels of negative emotionality (including physiological reactivity to the distress stimulus). Also of interest, higher levels of sympathy tended to be associated with higher level social functioning, with the pattern being somewhat more consistent for boys than girls.

In this same study, we examined the associations between vagal tone and sympathy. Vagal tone is a heart-rate variability measure believed to reflect temperamental physiological regulation (by assessing aspects of the functioning of the nervous system).[78] It was positively related to boys' self-reported sympathy, whereas the pattern was reversed for girls. This pattern of findings was consistent with the other data in the same study suggesting that vagal tone was associated with socially competent functioning for boys but not girls. One explanation for this pattern of findings is that uninhibited, assertive girls and boys are viewed differently, and come to view themselves differently. High vagal tone and heart rate variability have been linked to uninhibited rather than shy behavior;[79] in addition, we found that preschoolers with high vagal tone were more assertive in defending their possessions and territory.[80] Perhaps due to gender stereotypes and resulting differential expectations for boys and girls, boys' uninhibited, assertive behavior is viewed more positively than is that of girls. Consistent with this view, inhibited, shy behavior has been associated with positive social interactions and outcomes for girls but not boys.[81]

In summary, initial data generally are consistent with the view that sympathetic individuals are well regulated, although they may be high in emotional intensity. In contrast, people prone to personal distress tend to be emotional but not well regulated. Because sympathy appears to motivate positive behaviors such as helping and sharing, these findings have considerable relevance for understanding and predicting the quality of children's social functioning.

SOCIALIZATION OF EMOTIONAL EXPRESSION AND REGULATION

Up to this point, we have focused our discussion on individual characteristics of children that may influence their social-emotional competencies. However, it is clear from the existing research that social agents' (particularly parents') practices and behaviors are linked to children's socioemotional responding.[82] Although the family is considered to be the primary agent for socializing children's social-emotional competence, until recently few researchers have examined the socialization of emotion and its regulation. Because family situations often involve the need for family members to communicate their emotional needs and desires, the family likely is the primary context in which children's emotional competencies develop.

Parents may influence how children respond to, or cope with, emotionally evocative situations in a number of ways. Parke and his colleagues[83] noted that parental influence generally can be divided into direct and indirect influences. These two types of socializing influences are distinguished by the parents' intent or objective in socializing the child. Direct socialization influences are intentional attempts by parents to influence or facilitate children's emotional behavior; parents usually do this by taking an instructive or organizing role. An example of direct influence is directing or coaching children about appropriate emotional expressions, for example, telling children that it will hurt a girl's feelings if they laugh at her because she fell down. In this situation, rules about the appropriate display of felt emotions are conveyed directly by the parent to the child with the intent to help the child develop socially appropriate emotional competencies.

With indirect socializing influences, parents are not explicitly or intentionally trying to modify their children's emotional behavior. Children's observing the emotional expressions of parents is thought to reflect an indirect influence because parents usually are not trying to influence children's emotional development when they express emotions. Of course, parental influences on children's emotional competence consist of both direct and indirect types.

Two parental behaviors that have received attention in recent work on the socialization of emotion are parental expression of emotion and parental reactions to children in emotional situations (and when their children express emotion). These two behaviors have been examined in relation to two child variables: (a) children's overt expression of emotion, and (b) children's social and emotional competence.

Parents' expression of emotion likely influences children's social and emotional competence by means of multiple mechanisms. It influences children's social competence indirectly through its effects on children's own emotional expressivity. The degree to which children express positive and negative emotions has been found to affect how children are perceived and whether peers like them.[84] Parental expressiveness also may influence children's abilities to interpret and understand others' emotional reactions (for better or worse). In turn, accuracy of interpreting others' emotions is thought to be related to how well children interact with others.[85] Further, parental expression of emotion (e.g., hostility toward the child, anger) may influence children's socioemotional competence relatively directly through mechanisms such as shaping children's feelings about themselves and others.

Similarly, parental emotion-related practices would be expected to affect both the degree to which children express their emotions and their ability to regulate their emotion and emotionally driven behavior in appropriate ways. Parents may teach their children how and when to express emotion, how to interpret others' emotional displays and behaviors, and ways to manage their emotion so that they are able to behave in an appropriate manner. Of course, the direction of causation is likely bidirectional. Children's dispositional emotionality may influence parents' emotional displays and the types of emotion-relevant practices used by socializers.[86]

The limited empirical research has provided some support for the role of parents in children's expression of emotion. Parents' emotional displays appear to have at least some relation to children's expression and reports of their own emotions. Some researchers[87] found that college students who rated their families as relatively more expressive tended to be more expressive themselves than did those students who rated their families as less expressive. Similarly, Denham[88] found that mothers who displayed positive emotions had toddlers who tended to display positive rather than negative emotion. In addition, mothers who displayed more anger had toddlers who tended to display negative emotional expressions and relatively low levels of positive emotion. In a study involving many of the same children, preschoolers whose mothers reported intense emotions displayed more emotions at preschool.[89] In regard to vicariously induced emotions, Fabes, Eisenberg, and Miller[90] found that mothers' tendencies to feel and express sympathy were associated with daughters' (but not sons') sympathetic expressions and inversely related to inappropriate positive emotional expressions during a sympathy-inducing film.[91]

The mechanisms that account for similarities in parents' and children's expressiveness are not clear. Modeling of parents' expressive style is one possible explanation; genetic factors also may account for the parent-child similarities. In addition, maternal reactions in particular situations likely influence the valence and intensity of children's emotional reactions, as well as their interpretations of potentially evocative situations.[92]

Family emotional expressiveness also has been linked to children's socioemotional competencies. Children's social competence (assessed by teachers) has been associated with mothers' reports of intense happiness and relatively infrequent tension.[93] Frequent but low-level anger and anger caused by factors other than disobedience were related to social competence, whereas frequency of anger was negatively related to children's prosocial responses.[94] The expression of nonhostile negative emotions in the home also has been associated with daughters' vicarious emotional responding to others in distress (e.g., sympathy)[95] and with the ability to display (but not decode or decipher) emotion clearly.[96] Further, parental expressiveness has been related to children's social status and, to some degree, with socially appropriate behavior (for boys) and low levels of psychological problems among older children.[97]

Expression of negative emotion in the family may be positively related to social competence and prosocial behavior primarily when the expression of negative affect leads to discourse about feelings and explanations by parents for the negative affect.[98] Indeed, high overall levels of strong negative emotions such as anger by family members seem to be linked with low social competence in children, as indexed by low levels of prosocial behavior and sympathy,[99] less negotiation in conflict,[100] and poor performance on emotion-understanding tasks.[101] Findings regarding the relation of the expression of softer negative emotions in the family (e.g., loss, sadness) to empathy and prosocial behavior are contradictory.[102]

The view that children's emotionality and emotion regulation are associated with the quality of the parent-child relationship (as expressed through emotion in the home) is reflected in recent conceptualizations of the parent-child attachment. Specifically, attachment styles and relationships have been viewed as reflecting strategies for regulating emotion in interpersonal relationships.[103] For example, the securely attached infant whose parent is consistently and appropriately responsive to the infant's distress signals is viewed as learning that it is acceptable to exhibit distress and to actively seek out the assistance of others for comfort when stressed. In contrast, the avoidant infant, due in part to the parent's non-responsiveness to his or her distress signals, appears to learn to inhibit emotional expressiveness as well as other-directed self-regulatory strategies (e.g., contact-seeking and -maintaining behaviors).[104] Thus, attachment relationships are viewed as influencing children's socioemotional competence.

There is empirical support for this perspective. The ability of the mother to be appropriately responsive to the child's interactive behaviors is associated with infants' increasing positive emotionality[105] and maternal support has been linked with the variety of coping strategies used by children to deal with stress, as well as the use of relatively appropriate strategies (e.g., avoidant strategies in uncontrollable situations).[106] Furthermore, Kestenbaum, Farber, and Sroufe[107] found that preschool children with secure attachments at 12 and 18 months of age were more empathic and more prosocial toward others. In contrast, antiempathy responses (delight in others' discomfort, attempts to aggravate victims' condition, etc.) were observed to occur more often in children with anxious-avoidant attachment histories. Similarly, college students who were classified as secure in their attachment style were perceived as low in anxiety and ego-resilient and reported little distress and high levels of social support. Students classified as avoidant or dismissive (i.e., insecure) in their attachment style were rated by their peers as higher in hostility than were students who were identified as secure.[108] This hostility toward peers may be the result of displaced hostility that resulted from the parent-child relationship or may be the result of the increased dysregulation experienced by children whose parents are generally punishing or non-responsive to their children's negative emotional states and conditions.[109]

Specific emotion-related parental practices also appear to be associated with children's expression of appropriate emotion, as well as their social and emotional competence. Buck[110] hypothesized that children who are punished for the expression of negative emotion gradually learn to hide or inhibit these emotions. However, such individuals are likely, as they age, to become more physiologically aroused than other people in situations likely to involve negative emotions because of the association between negative sanctions and situations involving negative emotions.

Consistent with Buck's theorizing, how parents respond to children's displays of negative emotions has been linked to children's displays and reports of vicariously induced emotion (i.e., sympathy and personal distress). For example, parental encouragement to control one's emotions has been correlated with children's self-monitoring behavior and boys' reports of low levels of dispositional sympathy. Similarly, boys whose mothers reported restrictive reactions to their sons' displays of negative emotion tended to become physiologically distressed (overaroused) by exposure to others' negative emotions but denied feeling distressed.[111] The fact that the findings in regard to control were primarily for boys is likely due to the cultural norms regarding emotion[112] and suggest that males may be more likely than females to express their emotions internally.

Maternal discouragement of children's expression of emotion may curtail opportunities to learn about others' emotions. For example, parents who discouraged children's expression of emotion were relatively unlikely to recognize angry situations.[113] Deficits in the understanding of others' emotions likely are linked to lower levels of social competence and peer acceptance.[114]

The effects of discouraging the expression of emotion vary with the specific emotion. Although restrictiveness of children's expression of their own negative emotion has been associated with negative outcomes, Eisenberg and others found that parents who were relatively restrictive of inappropriate and potentially hurtful emotional displays had same-sex children who reported high levels of sympathy[115] (although such restrictiveness may induce distress in young girls).[116] Presumably parents teach children when it is not appropriate to display emotions that are hurtful, although the restrictiveness involved in such teachings may cause anxiety in younger children. Additionally mothers' reinforcement of children's focusing on others' distress (in contrast to mothers' focusing on their own children's distress) has been associated with girls' (but not boys') displays of sympathy.[117] Mothers who verbally highlighted the similarity between their children's own experiences and those of another person in distress had children who were relatively likely to exhibit sympathy, sadness, or distress when viewing the distressed individual. Thus, reinforcing or inducing children to think about the emotions they experience or the similarity of their problems to those of others in distress may foster the development of children's tendencies to feel sympathy or empathic sadness (as well as empathic distress in some cases) when exposed to others in distress.

Parental responses to children's negative emotions are linked to aspects of children's social functioning beyond their vicarious emotional responding. Denham[118] found that 2-year-olds whose mothers reacted with optimal responsiveness when confronted with children's anger were less likely to become angry and were more capable of responding positively to other people when mother was absent. Mothers who were relatively responsive to children's anger had children who expressed more happiness and interest in their environment. In addition, children whose mothers responded optimally to fear were less fearful in other situations. In studies of preschoolers, parental encouragement of children's emotional expressiveness when they were distressed was related to popularity and low use of socially inappropriate methods of coping with anger provocations, whereas maternal comforting was associated with appropriate and less intense anger reactions. In contrast, parental efforts to minimize children's emotional responses (e.g., to tell them not to make such a big deal out of things that bother them) were inversely related to teachers' reports of children's social competence.[119]

There may be an optimal level of parental encouragement of the expression of emotion. Roberts and Strayer[120] found that a moderate level of parental expression of negative affect was linked to preschoolers' social competence. However, the decline in children's social competence at high levels of parental encouragement was small.

Nonetheless, Denham[121] found that maternal tenderness to 2-year-old children's sadness was related to low levels of children's positive affiliation. Perhaps calming a sad child is effective in reducing the child's distress, but does not capitalize on opportunities for the child to learn to cope effectively. Alternatively, mothers may be particularly likely to calm children who tend to be sad, anxious, or shy and withdrawn, and such children would be expected to have deficits in their social skills.[122]

Some parental reactions in evocative situations are problem-focused rather than designed to deal directly with children's emotion. Roberts and Strayer[123] found that parental instrumental problem-solving responses when their children were upset (e.g., putting a bandage on the child when he/she was hurt) were related to children's social competence. Furthermore, parental emphasis on children's instrumental problem solving has been associated with sons' sympathy[124] and children's popularity.[125] Thus, parental modeling and encouragement of problem-focused coping may foster children's emotional and social competence.

Parental discussion of children's emotion also has been linked to children's understanding of emotion and their social competence. For example, Dunn and her colleagues reported that mother–child discussions about feelings and their causes and their consequences were associated with later success on affective perspective-taking tasks.[126] They also found that by 2 years of age most children were talking with their mothers about feelings and that mothers appeared to be using these conversations to guide the child's behavior or explain another's emotions, rather than merely taking note of someone's feelings. Results of a follow-up study conducted when these children were 6 years of age showed that early family emotion-related talk predicted later understanding of emotions, even after controlling for children's verbal abilities and frequency of family conversations.[127] Consistent with Dunn and her colleagues' findings, other researchers have found that mothers' discussions of emotions with their 4-year-olds and kindergartners predicted children's peer acceptance.[128] Similarly, Putallaz[129] reported that mothers of high-status children focused more on feelings in their interactions with their children than did mothers of low-status children.

As noted previously, it is likely that parents' emotion-related socialization practices are in part a reaction to their children's emotion-related tendencies. At this time, there is relatively little research on this topic.

However, initial data from our studies support this conclusion. Eisenberg and Fabes[130] found that mothers tended to be relatively punitive and avoidant in response to children's negative emotions if they viewed their children as high in negative affectivity and low in their abilities to regulate their attention. In contrast, mothers tended to report more supportive and constructive socialization practices if they viewed their children as able to regulate their attention.

In another study, mothers were asked to tell emotionally evocative stories to their children. Mothers' behaviors in these story contexts varied according to their perceptions of their children's emotional reactivity. Moreover, these perceptions were influenced by the age of their children. Specifically, kindergartners were viewed by their mothers as more emotionally reactive to others' distress than were second-graders. In addition, mothers tended to use more positive facial expressions when telling the emotionally evocative stories to their kindergarten-aged children than they did when telling the stories to the older children. It appears that mothers of the younger children in our study attempted to minimize children's negative responses to the stories by trying to induce a positive mood in their children (or avoid inducing a negative one). This tendency was especially true for those younger children whose mothers believed were prone to become emotionally aroused when exposed to the emotions of others. Thus, mothers' actions appeared to be influenced by their perceptions of their children's vulnerability to become dysregulated as a consequence of exposure to others' negative emotions.[131]

In contrast, mothers' beliefs about the emotional reactivity of older children were inversely related to their responsiveness while telling the stories. Mothers who viewed their older children (i.e., second-graders) as emotionally reactive tended to be less involved and warm in the storytelling context than were mothers who believed their children were emotionally controlled. Thus, it seems that mothers who perceived their older children to be emotionally reactive may have "backed off" from socialization efforts that actively involved their children in a particular distressing experience.

Importantly, the ways that stories were told by mothers also were related to children's vicarious emotional responses and to their prosocial behavior. For younger children, mothers' relative use of positive facial expressions was positively related with children's helpfulness. In contrast, second-graders' emotional and prosocial responses were predicted by maternal responsiveness rather than maternal expressiveness. Maternal responsiveness was related to lower levels of distress-related responses and to increased sympathetic and prosocial responding. These results suggest that mothers employ different strategies when addressing emotionally evocative contexts for younger and older children, and that these tendencies predict how their children respond in contexts involving sympathetic and prosocial responses when the mother is not present.

SUMMARY

The findings reviewed in this study are consistent with the conclusion that individual differences in emotionality and regulatory capabilities are associated with social functioning in childhood, including socially appropriate behavior, anger reactions, peer acceptance, and externalizing and internalizing behaviors and disorders. In general, negative emotionality, intense emotional responding, and lack of regulation are associated with negative outcomes; overcontrol also has been linked to internalizing disorders, particularly for girls. Much more information is needed to clarify the role of different kinds of emotional responses such as anger, anxiety, sadness, and fear in social functioning, as well as the varied ways in which regulatory processes influence children's social and emotional functioning. Further consideration of the role of the social environment in children's emotional development and behavior is needed to complement the work on individual differences in emotionality and regulation.

What do these findings mean for educators? It is important to know that individual differences in children's emotionality and regulation are associated with the quality of children's social functioning. Children prone to intense negative emotion and who are unregulated likely elicit negative responses from both peers and teachers, which may diminish other people's regard for the child and decrease opportunities for learning positive social skills. However, it also is useful to note that socializers such as parents and teachers probably play a role in teaching children how to manage their emotions and behavior based on intense emotion. Children who feel that it is okay to feel negative emotions but have learned constructive ways to deal with these emotions are likely to feel sympathy for others, to engage in socially appropriate, positive behavior, and, consequently, to be liked by both teachers and peers. Learning to manage one's emotions is, no doubt, particularly important for those children who are temperamentally prone to anxiety, fear, anger, frustration, and other negative emotions that are likely to overwhelm the child. If emotional children do not learn to manage the experience and expression of emotion, they are at risk for a variety of social and emotional (as well as academic) problems.

GLOSSARY

Coping—Regulation in stressful contexts; changing cognitive and behavioral efforts to manage specific external or internal demands that are appraised as taxing or exceeding the resources of the individual.

Empathy—An emotional response resulting from the recognition of another's emotional state or condition, which is very similar or identical to what the other individual is perceived to experience.

Personal Distress—An aversive emotional reaction such as discomfort or anxiety resulting from exposure to another's emotional state or condition.

Regulation—The process of initiating, maintaining, or modulating the occurrence, intensity, or duration of internal feeling states and emotion-related physiological processes, behavior driven by emotion, as well as attempts to change the external situation that elicits an emotional response.

Sympathy—Feelings of sorrow for another or concern for another based on the perception of another's emotional state or condition.

NOTES

References

Achenbach, T.M., & Edelbrock, C. (1983). *Manual for the Child Behavior Checklist and the Revised Child Behavior Profile.* Burlington, VT: Queen City Printers.

Altshuler, J. L., & Ruble, D. N. (1989). Developmental changes in children's awareness of strategies for coping with uncontrollable stress. *Child Development, 60,* 1337–1349.

Balswick, J., & Avertt, C. (1977). Differences in expressiveness: Gender, interpersonal orientation, and perceived parental expressiveness as contributing factors. *Journal of Marriage and the Family, 39,* 121–127.

Bates, J. E., Bayles, K., Bennett, D. S., Ridge, B., & Brown, M. M. (1991). Origins of externalizing behavior problems at eight years of age. In D. J. Pepler & K. H. Rubin (Eds.), *The development and treatment of childhood aggression* (pp. 93–120). Hillsdale, NJ: Erlbaum.

Batson, C. D. (1991). *The altruism question: Toward a social-psychological answer.* Hillsdale, NJ: Erlbaum.

Block, J. H., & Block, J. (1980). The role of ego-control and ego-resiliency in the organization of behavior. In W. A. Collins (Ed.), *Development of cognition, affect, and social relations. The Minnesota symposia on child psychology* (Vol. 13, pp. 39–101). Hillsdale, NJ: Erlbaum.

Block, J. H., & Gjerde, P. F. (1986). Distinguishing between antisocial behavior and undercontrol. In D. Olweus, J. Block, & M. Radke-Yarrow (Eds.), *Development of antisocial and prosocial behavior: Research, theories, and issues* (pp. 177–206). Orlando: Academic Press.

Block, J. & Gjerde, P. F. (1990). Depressive symptoms in late adolescence: A longitudinal perspective on personality antecedents. In J. Rolf, A. S. Masten, D. Cicchetti, K. H. Nuechterlein, & S. Weintraub (Eds.),

Antecedents of adolescent depression (pp. 334–360). New York: Cambridge University Press.

Block, J., Gjerde, P. F., & Block, J. H. (1991). Personality antecedents of depressive tendencies in 18-year-olds: A prospective study. *Journal of Personality and Social Psychology, 60,* 726–738.

Braungart, J. M., & Stifter, C. A. (1991). Regulation of negative reactivity during the strange situation: Temperament and attachment in 12-month-old infants. *Infant Behavior and Development, 14,* 349–364.

Bridges, L. J., & Grolnick, W. S. (1995). The development of emotional self-regulation in infancy and early childhood. In N. Eisenberg (Ed.), *Review of Personality and Psychology* (pp. 185–211). Newbury Park, CA: Sage.

Brody, L. R. (1985). Gender differences in emotional development: A review of theories and research. *Journal of Personality, 53,* 102–149.

Bronstein, P., Fitzgerald, M., Briones, M., Pieniadz, J., & D'Ari, A. (1993). Family emotional expressiveness as a predictor of early adolescent social and psychological adjustment. *Journal of Early Adolescence, 13,* 448–471.

Buck, R. (1984). *The communication of emotion.* New York: Guilford.

Campbell, S. B. (1991). Longitudinal studies of active and aggressive preschoolers: Individual differences in early behavior and in outcome. In D. Cicchetti & S. L. Toth (Eds.), *Internalizing and externalizing expressions of dysfunction: Rochester symposium on developmental psychopathology* (Vol. 2). Hillsdale, NJ: Erlbaum.

Campos, J. J., Campos, R. G., & Barrett, K. C. (1989). Emergent themes in the study of emotional development and emotion regulation. *Developmental Psychology, 25,* 394–402.

Carey, T. C., Finch, A. J., & Carey, M. P. (1991). Relation between differential emotions and depression in emotionally disturbed children and adolescents. *Journal of Consulting and Clinical Psychology, 59,* 594–597.

Carlo, G., Eisenberg, N., Troyer, D., Switzer, G., & Speer, A. L. (1991). The altruistic personality: In what contexts is it apparent? *Journal of Personality and Social Psychology, 61,* 450–458.

Casey, R. J., & Schlosser, S. (1994). Emotional responses to peer praise in children with and without a diagnosed externalizing disorder. *Merrill-Palmer Quarterly, 40,* 60–81.

Caspi, A., Bem, D., & Elder, G. H., Jr. (1989). Continuities and consequences of interactional styles across the life course. *Journal of Personality, 57,* 375–406.

Caspi, A., Henry, B., McGee, R. O., Moffitt, T. E., & Silva, P. A. (1995). Temperamental origins of child and adolescent behavior problems: From age three to age fifteen. *Child Development, 66,* 55–68.

Caspi, A., Moffitt, T. E., Silva, P. A., Stouthamer-Loeber, M., Krueger, R. F., & Schmutte, P. S. (1994). Are some people crime-prone? Replications of the personality-crime relationship across countries, genders, races, and methods. *Criminology, 32,* 163–195.

Cassidy, J., Parke, R. D., Butkovsky, L., & Braungart, J. M. (1992). Family-peer connections: The roles of emotional expressiveness within the family and children's understanding of emotion. *Child Development, 63,* 603–618.

Compas, B. E. (1987). Coping with stress during childhood and adolescence. *Psychological Bulletin, 101,* 393–403.

Compas, B. E., Banez, G. A., Malcarne, V., & Worsham, N. (1991). Perceived control and coping with stress: A developmental perspective. *Journal of Social Issues, 47,* 23–34.

Davis, M. H. (1994). *Empathy: A social psychological approach.* Madison, WI: Brown & Benchmark.

Denham, S. A. (1989). Maternal affect and toddlers' social-emotional competence. *American Journal of Orthopsychiatry, 59,* 368–376.

Denham, S.A. (1993). Maternal emotional responsiveness and toddlers' social-emotional competence. *Journal of Child Psychology and Psychiatry, 34,* 715–728.

Denham, S. A., & Grout, L. (1992). Mothers' emotional expressiveness and coping: Relations with preschoolers' social-emotional competence. *Genetic, Social, and General Psychology Monographs, 118,* 73–101.

Denham, S. A., & Grout, L. (1993). Socialization of emotion: Pathway to preschoolers' emotional and social competence. *Journal of Nonverbal Behavior, 17,* 205–227.

Derryberry, D., & Rothbart, M. K. (1988). Arousal, affect, and attention as components of temperament. *Journal of Personality and Social Psychology, 55,* 958–966.

Dodge, K. A. (1985). A social information processing model of social competence in children. In M. Perlmutter (Ed.), *Cognitive perspectives on children's social and behavioral development: Minnesota symposium on child psychology* (Vol. 18, pp. 77–125). Hillsdale, NJ: Erlbaum.

Dunn, J., & Brown, J. (1994). Affect expression in the family, children's understanding of emotions, and their interactions with others. *Merrill-Palmer Quarterly, 40,* 120–137.

Dunn, J., Bretherton, I., & Munn, P. (1987). Conversations about feeling states between mothers and their young children. *Developmental Psychology, 23,* 132–139.

Dunn, J., Brown, J., & Beardsall, L. (1991). Family talk about feeling states and children's later understanding of others' emotions. *Developmental Psychology, 27,* 448–455.

Dunn, J., Brown, J., Slomkowski, C., Telsa, C., & Youngblade, L. (1991). Young children's understanding of other people's feelings and beliefs: Individual differences and their antecedents. *Child Development, 62,* 1352–1366.

Eisenberg, N., & Fabes, R. A. (1990). Empathy: Conceptualization, assessment, and relation to prosocial behavior. *Motivation and Emotion, 14,* 131–149.

Eisenberg, N., & Fabes, R. A. (1992). Emotion, regulation, and the development of social competence. In M. S. Clark (Ed.), *Review of personality and social psychology: Emotion and social behavior* (Vol. 14, pp. 119–150). Newbury Park, CA: Sage.

Eisenberg, N., & Fabes, R. A. (1994). Mothers' reactions to children's negative emotions: Relations to children's temperament and anger behavior. *Merrill-Palmer Quarterly, 40,* 138–156.

Eisenberg, N., & Fabes, R. A. (1995). The relation of young children's vicarious emotional responding to social competence, regulation, and emotionality. *Cognition and Emotion, 9,* 203–229.

Eisenberg, N., & Miller, P. (1987). The relation of empathy to prosocial and related behaviors. *Psychological Bulletin, 101,* 91–119.

Eisenberg, N., & Okun, M. A. (1996). The relations of dispositional regulation and emotionality to elders' empathy-related responding and affect while volunteering. *Journal of Personality, 64,* 157–183.

Eisenberg, N., Fabes, R. A., Bernzweig, J., Karbon, M., Poulin, R., & Hanish, L. (1993). The relations of emotionality and regulation to preschoolers' social skills and sociometric status. *Child Development, 64,* 1418–1438.

Eisenberg, N., Fabes, R. A., Carlo, G., & Karbon, M. (1992). Emotional responsivity to others: Behavioral correlates and socialization antecedents. In N. Eisenberg & R. A. Fabes (Eds.), *New Directions in Child Development, 55,* 57–73.

Eisenberg, N., Fabes, R. A., Carlo, G., Troyer, D., Speer, A. L., Karbon, M., & Switzer, G. (1992). The relations of maternal practices and characteristics to children's vicarious emotional responsiveness. *Child Development, 63,* 583–602.

Eisenberg, N., Fabes, R. A., Miller, P. A., Shell, C., Shea, R., May-Plumee, T. (1990). Preschoolers' vicarious emotional responding and their situational and dispositional prosocial behavior. *Merrill-Palmer Quarterly, 36,* 507–529.

Eisenberg, N., Fabes, R. A., Minore, D., Mathy, R., Hanish, L., & Brown, T. (1994). Children's enacted interpersonal strategies: Their relations to social behavior and negative emotionality. *Merrill-Palmer Quarterly, 40,* 212–232.

Eisenberg, N., Fabes, R. A., Murphy, B., Karbon, M., Maszk, P., Smith, M., O'Boyle, C., & Suh, K. (1994). The relations of emotionality and regulation to dispositional and situational empathy-related responding. *Journal of Personality and Social Psychology, 66,* 776–797.

Eisenberg, N., Fabes, R. A., Murphy, B., Karbon, M., Smith, M., & Maszk, P. (1996). The relations of children's dispositional empathy-related responding to their emotionality, regulation, and social functioning. *Developmental Psychology, 32,* 195–209.

Eisenberg, N., Fabes, R. A., Murphy, B., Maszk, P., Smith, M., & Karbon, M. (1995). The role of emotionality and regulation in children's social functioning: A longitudinal study. *Child Development, 66,* 1360–1384.

Eisenberg, N., Fabes, R. A., Nyman, M., Bernzweig, J., & Pinuelas, A. (1994). The relations of emotionality and regulation to children's anger-related reactions. *Child Development, 65,* 109–128.

Eisenberg, N., Fabes, R. A., Schaller, M., Carlo, G., & Miller, P. A. (1991). The relations of parental characteristics and practices to children's vicarious emotional responding. *Child Development, 62,* 1393–1408.

Eisenberg, N., Fabes, R. A., Schaller, M., Miller, P. A., Carlo, G., Poulin, R., Shea, C., & Shell, R. (1991). Personality and socialization correlates of vicarious emotional responding. *Journal of Personality and Social Psychology, 61,* 459–471.

Fabes, R. A., Eisenberg, N., Karbon, M., Bernzweig, J., Speer, A. L., & Carlo, G. (1994). Socialization of children's vicarious emotional responding and prosocial behavior: Relations with mothers' perceptions of children's emotional reactivity. *Developmental Psychology, 30,* 44–55.

Fabes, R. A., Eisenberg, N., & Miller, P. (1990). Maternal correlates of children's vicarious emotional responsiveness. *Developmental Psychology, 26,* 639–648.

Fox, N. A. (1989). Psychophysiological correlates of emotional reactivity during the first year of life. *Developmental Psychology, 25,* 364–372.

Frick, P. J., & Lahey, B. B. (1991). The nature and characteristics of attention-deficit hyperactivity disorder. *School Psychology Review, 20,* 163–173.

Garber, J., Quiggle, N. L., Panak, W., & Dodge, K. A. (1991). Aggression and depression in children: Comorbidity, specificity, and social cognitive processing. In D. Cicchetti & S. L. Toth (Eds.), *Internalizing and externalizing expressions of dysfunction: Rochester symposium on developmental psychopathology* (Vol. 2). Hillsdale, NJ: Erlbaum.

Garner, P. W., Jones, D. C., & Miner, J. L. (1994). Social competence among low-income preschoolers: Emotion socialization practices and social cognitive correlates. *Child Development, 65,* 622–637.

Gianino, A., & Tronick, E. Z. (1988). The mutual regulation model: The infant's self and interactive regulation, coping, and defense. In T. Field, P. McCabe, & N. Schneiderman (Eds.), *Stress and coping* (pp. 47–68). Hillsdale, NJ: Erlbaum.

Goldsmith, H. H., & Rothbart, M. K. (1991). Contemporary instruments for assessing early temperament by questionnaire and in the laboratory. In A. Angleitner & J. Strelau (Eds.), *Explorations in temperament* (pp. 249–272). New York: Plenum.

Halberstadt, A. G. (1984). Family expression of emotion. In C. Z. Malatesta & C. E. Izard (Eds.), *Emotion and adult development* (pp. 235–252). Beverly Hills, CA: Sage.

Halberstadt, A. G. (1986). Family socialization of emotional expression and nonverbal communication styles and skills. *Journal of Personality and Social Psychology, 51,* 827–836.

Halberstadt, A. G., Fox, N. A., & Jones, N. A. (1993). Do expressive mothers have expressive children? The role of socialization in children's affect expression. *Social Development, 2,* 48–65.

Hardy, D. F., Power, T. G., & Jaedicke, S. (1993). Examining the relation of parenting to children's coping with everyday stress. *Child Development, 64,* 1829–1841.

Henry, B., Caspi, A., Moffitt, T. E., & Silva, P. A. (1994). Temperamental and familial predictors of violent and non-violent criminal convictions: From age 3 to age 18. Manuscript submitted for editorial review.

Hoffman, M. L. (1982). Development of prosocial motivation: Empathy and guilt. In N. Eisenberg (Ed.), *The development of prosocial behavior* (pp. 281–313). NY: Academic Press.

Hubbard, J., & Coie, J. D. (1994). Emotional determinants of social competence in children's peer relationships. *Merrill-Palmer Quarterly, 40,* 1–20.

Kagan, J. (1989). The concept of behavioral inhibition to the unfamiliar. In J.

S. Reznick (Ed.), *Perspectives on behavioral inhibition* (pp. 1–23). Chicago: University of Chicago Press.

Kestenbaum, R., Farber, E. A., & Sroufe, L. A. (1989). Individual differences in empathy among preschoolers: Relation to attachment history. In N. Eisenberg (Ed.), *New directions for child development: Empathy and related emotional responses* (Vol. 44, pp. 51–64). San Francisco: Jossey-Bass.

Kobak, R. R., & Sceery, A. (1988). Attachment in late adolescence: Working models, affect regulation, and perception of self and others. *Child Development, 59,* 135–146.

Krueger, R. F., Schmutte, P. S., Caspi, A., Moffitt, T. E., Campbell, K., & Silva, P. A. (1994). Personality traits are linked to crime among men and women: Evidence from a birth cohort. *Journal of Abnormal Psychology, 103,* 328–338.

Kyrios, M., & Prior, M. (1990). Temperament, stress and family factors in behavioural adjustment of 3–5-year-old children. *International Journal of Behavioral Development, 13,* 67–93.

Laird, R. D., Pettit, G. S., Mize, J., Brown, E. G., & Lindsey, E. (1994). Mother–child conversations about peers: Contributions to competence. *Family Relations, 43,* 425–432.

Landau, S., & Moore, L. A. (1991). Social skill deficits in children with attention-deficit hyperactivity disorder. *School Psychology Review, 20,* 235–251.

Larsen, R. J., Diener, E., & Cropanzano, R. A. (1987). Cognitive operations associated with individual differences in affect intensity. *Journal of Personality and Social Psychology, 53,* 767–774.

Laursen, B., & Hartup, W. W. (1989). The dynamics of preschool children's conflicts. *Merrill-Palmer Quarterly, 35,* 281–297.

Lazarus, R. S., & Folkman, S. (1984). *Stress, appraisal, and coping.* New York: Springer.

Losoya, S. H. (1994). The patterns of vicarious emotional responding in boys with and without Attention Deficit Hyperactivity Disorder. Unpublished doctoral dissertation data. University of Oregon.

Masters, J. C. (1991). Strategies and mechanisms for the personal and social control of emotion. In J. Garber & K. A. Dodge (Eds.), *The development of emotion regulation and dysregulation* (pp. 182–207). Cambridge, England: Cambridge University Press.

Maziade, M., Cote, R., Bernier, H., Boutin, P., & Thivierge, J. (1989). Significance of extreme temperament in infancy for clinical status in pre-school years I: Value of extreme temperament at 4–8 months for predicting diagnosis at 4.7 years. *British Journal of Psychiatry, 154,* 535–543.

Mehrabian, A. (1977). Individual differences in stimulus screening and arousability. *Journal of Personality, 45,* 237–250.

Parke, R. D. (1994). Progress, paradigms, and unresolved problems: Recent advances in our understanding of children's emotions. *Merrill-Palmer Quarterly, 40,* 157–169.

Parke, R. D., MacDonald, K. B., Burks, V. M., Carson, J., Bhavnagri, N., Barth, J. M., & Beitel, A. (1989). Family and peer systems: In search of linkages. In K. Kreppner & R. M. Lerner (Eds.), *Family systems and life span development* (pp. 65–91). Hillsdale, NJ: Erlbaum.

Patterson, C. M., & Newman, J. P. (1993). Reflectivity and learning from aversive events: Toward a psychological mechanism for the syndromes of disinhibition. *Psychological Review, 100,* 716–736.

Patterson, G. R., & Capaldi, D. M. (1990). A mediational model for boys' depressed mood. In J. Rolf, A. S. Master, D. Cicchetti, K. H. Neuchterlin, & S. Weintraub (Eds.), *Risk and protective factors in the development of psychopathology* (pp. 141–163). New York: Cambridge University Press.

Porges, S. W. (1991). Vagal one: An autonomic mediator of affect. In J. Garber & K. A. Dodge (Eds.), *The development of emotion regulation and dysregulation* (pp. 111–128). Cambridge, England: University of Cambridge Press.

Pulkkinen, L. (1982). Self-control and continuity from childhood to late adolescence. In P. B. Baltes & O. G. Brim, Jr. (Eds.), *Life-span development and behavior* (Vol. 4). New York: Academic Press.

Putallaz, M. (1987). Maternal behavior and children's sociometric status. *Child Development, 58,* 324–340.

Quay, H. C. (1986). Classification. In H. C. Quay & J. S. Werry (Eds.), *Psychopathological disorders of childhood* (3rd ed.). New York: Wiley.

Reznick, J. S. (1989). *Perspectives on behavioral inhibition.* Chicago: University of Chicago Press.

Roberts, W., & Strayer, J. (1987). Parents' responses to the emotional distress of their children: Relations with children's competence. *Developmental Psychology, 23,* 415–432.

Rosenbaum, J. F., Biederman, J., Bolduc-Murphy, E. A., Faraone, S. V., Chaloff, J., Hirshfeld, D. R., & Kagan, J. (1993). Converging evidence for behavioral inhibition as a risk factor for childhood-onset anxiety disorders: The MGH-Harvard collaborative project. *Harvard Review of Psychiatry, 1,* 2–16.

Rothbart, M. K., & Ahadi, S. A. (1994). Temperament and the development of personality. *Journal of Abnormal Psychology, 103,* 55–66.

Rothbart, M. K., & Derryberry, D. (1981). Development of individual differences in temperament. In M. E. Lamb & A. L. Brown (Eds.), *Advances in developmental psychology* (Vol. 1, pp. 37–86). Hillsdale, NJ: Erlbaum.

Rothbart, M. K., Ahadi, S. A., & Hershey, K. L. (1994). Temperament and social behavior in childhood. *Merrill-Palmer Quarterly, 40,* 21–39.

Rothbart, M. K., Posner, M. I., & Hershey, K. L. (1995). Temperament, attention and developmental psychopathology. In D. Cicchetti & D. Cohen (Eds.), *Manual of developmental psychopathology* (pp. 315–340). New York: Wiley.

Rothbart, M. K., Ziaie, H., & O'Boyle, C. G. (1992). Self-regulation and emotion in infancy. *New Directions in Child Development, 55,* 7–23.

Rubin, K. H., Chen, X., & Hymel, S. (1993). Socioemotional characteristics of withdrawn and aggressive children. *Merrill-Palmer Quarterly, 39,* 518–534.

Saarni, C. (1990). Emotional competence: How emotions and relationships become integrated. In R. A. Thompson (Ed.), *Socioemotional development* (pp. 115–182). Lincoln: University of Nebraska Press.

Sanson, A., Smart, D., Prior, M., & Oberklaid, F. (1993). Precursors of hyperactivity and aggression. *Journal of American Academy of Child and Adolescent Psychiatry, 32,* 1207–1216.

Shields, A. M., Cicchetti, D., & Ryan, R. M. (1994). The development of emotional and behavioral self-regulation and social competence among maltreated school-age children. *Development and Psychopathology, 6*, 57–75.

Skinner, E. A., & Wellborn, J. G. (1994). Coping during childhood and adolescence: A motivational perspective. In R. Lerner, D. Featherman, & M. Perlmutter (Eds.), *Life-span development and behavior* (Vol. 12, pp. 91–123). Hillsdale, NJ: Erlbaum.

Sroufe, L. A., Schork, E., Motti, F., Lawroski, N., & LaFreniere, P. (1984). The role of affect in social competence. In C. E. Izard, J. Kagan, & R. B. Zajonc (Eds.), *Emotion, cognition, and behavior* (pp. 289–319). Cambridge, England: Cambridge University Press.

Stevenson-Hinde, J. (1989). Behavioral inhibition: Issues of context. In J. S. Reznick (Ed.), *Perspectives on behavioral inhibition* (pp. 125–138). Chicago: University of Chicago Press.

Stocker, C., & Dunn, J. (1990). Sibling relationships in childhood: Links with friendships and peer relationships. *British Journal of Developmental Psychology, 8*, 227–244.

Strauss, C. C. (1988). Social deficits of children with internalizing disorders. In B. B. Lahey & A. E. Kazdin (Eds.), *Advances in clinical child psychology* (Vol. 11, pp. 159–191). New York: Plenum.

Thompson, R. A. (1994). Emotional regulation: A theme in search of definition. *Monographs of the Society for Research in Child Development, 59* (Serial No. 240), 25–52.

Ungerer, J. A., Dolby, R., Waters, B., Barnett, B., Kelk, N., & Lewin, V. (1990). The early development of empathy: Self-regulation and individual differences in the first year. *Motivation and Emotion, 14*, 93–106.

Watson, D., & Clark, L. A. (1993). Behavioral disinhibition versus constraint: A dispositional perspective. In D. M. Wegner & J. W. Pennebacker (Eds.), *Handbook of mental control* (pp. 506–527). Englewood Cliffs, NJ: Prentice-Hall.

Wertlieb, D., Weigel, C., Springer, T., & Feldstein, M. (1987). Temperament as a moderator of children's stressful experiences. *American Journal of Orthopsychiatry, 57*, 234–245.

White, J. L., Moffitt, T. E., Caspi, A., Bartusch, D. J., Needles, D. J., & Stouthamer-Loeber, M. (1994). Measuring impulsivity and examining its relationship to delinquency. *Journal of Abnormal Psychology, 103*, 192–205.

White, J. L., Moffitt, T. E., Earls, F., Robins, L., & Silva, P. (1990). How early can we tell? Predictors of childhood conduct disorder and adolescent delinquency. *Criminology, 28*, 507–533.

Windle, M., Hooker, K., Lenerz, K., East, P. L., Lerner, J. V., & Lerner, R. M. (1986). Temperament, perceived competence, and depression in early and late adolescents. *Developmental Psychology, 22*, 384–392.

Wood, J. V., Saltzberg, J. A., & Goldsamt, L. A. (1990). Does affect induce self-focused attention? *Journal of Personality and Social Psychology, 58*, 899–908.

1. Parke (1994).
2. Hubbard and Coie (1994).

3. Saarni (1990).

4. Bridges and Grolnick (1995); Thompson (1994).

5. Eisenberg and Fabes (1992).

6. Larsen, Diener, and Cropanzano (1987).

7. Masters (1991); Bridges and Grolnick (1995); Skinner and Wellborn (1994).

8. See Kagan (1989); Laursen and Hartup (1989); Pulkkinen (1982).

9. Eisenberg and Fabes (1992).

10. Derryberry and Rothbart (1988).

11. Eisenberg, Fabes, Murphy, Karbon, Maszk et al. (1994); Eisenberg, Fabes, Schaller, Miller et al. (1991); Larsen, Diener, and Cropanzano (1987).

12. Bridges and Grolnick (1995); Derryberry and Rothbart (1988); Rothbart, Ziaie, and O'Boyle (1992).

13. Frick and Lahey (1991); Landau and Moore (1991).

14. Lazarus and Folkman (1984).

15. Altshuler and Ruble (1989); See Compas, Banez, Malcarne, and Worsham (1991).

16. Block and Block (1980).

17. Watson and Clark (1993).

18. Caspi, Henry, McGee, Moffitt, and Silva (1995); Goldsmith and Rothbart (1991).

19. Block and Block (1980); Caspi et al. (1995); Pulkkinen (1982); Watson and Clark (1993).

20. Bates, Bayles, Bennett, Ridge, and Brown (1991); Rubin, Chen, and Hymel (1993).

21. Achenbach and Edelbrock (1983); Quay (1986).

22. Bates et al. (1991); Rothbart and Ahadi (1994).

23. See Rothbart, Posner, and Hershey (1995).

24. Garber, Quiggle, Panak, and Dodge (1991).

25. Bates et al. (1991); Wertlieb et al. (1987).

26. Carey, Finch, and Carey (1991).

27. Garber et al. (1991).

28. Maziade, Cote, Bernier, Boutin, and Thivierge (1989).

29. Block and Gjerde (1990); Block, Gjerde, and Block (1991).

30. Block et al. (1991); Patterson and Capaldi (1990).

31. Windle et al. (1986).

32. Rosenbaum et al. (1993).

33. Caspi et al. (1995).

34. Caspi et al. (1994); Kyrios and Prior (1990); Shields, Cicchetti, and Ryan (1994).

35. Losoya (1994).

36. Sanson, Smart, Prior, and Oberklaid (1993).

37. Caspi et al. (1995); White, Moffitt, Earls, Robins, and Silva (1990).

38. White et al. (1990).

39. Krueger, Schmutte, Caspi, Moffitt, Campbell, and Silva (1994).

40. White et al. (1994).

41. Campbell (1991).

42. Henry, Caspi, Moffitt, and Silva (1994).

43. Patterson and Newman (1993).

44. Casey and Schlosser (1994).

45. See Bates et al. (1991); Sanson et al. (1993); Wertlieb et al. (1987).
46. Wertlieb et al. (1987).
47. Hubbard and Coie (1994).
48. Stocker and Dunn (1990).
49. Eisenberg, Fabes, Bernzweig et al. (1993); Eisenberg, Fabes, Nyman et al. (1994).
50. Eisenberg, Fabes, Minore et al. (1994).
51. Eisenberg, Fabes, Minore et al. (1994).
52. Unpublished data from Eisenberg, Fabes, Minore et al. (1994).
53. Eisenberg et al. (1995).
54. Unpublished data from Eisenberg et al. (1995).
55. Eisenberg et al. (1995).
56. See Eisenberg et al. (1995).
57. Eisenberg, Fabes, Bernzweig et al. (1993).
58. See Batson (1991); Davis (1994); Eisenberg and Fabes (1990).
59. Batson (1991); Eisenberg and Fabes (1990).
60. Batson (1991); Davis (1994); Eisenberg and Fabes (1990); Eisenberg and Miller (1987).
61. Eisenberg, Fabes, Murphy, Karbon et al. (1994).
62. Also see Hoffman (1982).
63. Wood, Saltzberg, and Goldsamt (1990).
64. Eisenberg, Fabes, Murphy, Karbon et al. (1994).
65. Eisenberg and Fabes (1992).
66. Eisenberg, Fabes, Schaller, Miller et al. (1991); Larsen, Diener, and Cropanzano (1987).
67. Davis (1994); Mehrabian (1977).
68. Eisenberg, Fabes, Schaller, Miller et al. (1991).
69. Carlo et al. (1991).
70. Eisenberg, Fabes, Schaller, Carlo, and Miller (1991); Eisenberg, Fabes, Schaller, Miller et al. (1991).
71. Rothbart, Ahadi, and Hershey (1994).
72. Ungerer et al. (1990).
73. Eisenberg, Fabes, Murphy, Karbon et al. (1994).
74. Eisenberg and Okun (1996).
75. Eisenberg and Fabes (1995).
76. See Eisenberg, Fabes, Nyman et al. (1994).
77. Eisenberg, Fabes, Murphy et al. (1996).
78. Porges (1991).
79. Reznick (1989).
80. Unpublished data from Eisenberg et al. (1990).
81. Caspi, Bem, and Elder (1989); Stevenson-Hinde (1989).
82. Dunn and Brown (1994); Eisenberg and Fabes (1994).
83. Parke et al. (1989).
84. Sroufe, Schork, Motti, Lawroski, and LaFreniere (1984).
85. Dodge (1985).
86. See Eisenberg and Fabes (1994); Eisenberg, Fabes, Carlo, and Karbon (1992).
87. Balswick and Avertt (1977); Halberstadt (1986).
88. Denham (1989).
89. Denham and Grout (1993).

90. Fabes, Eisenberg, and Miller (1990).
91. Also see Eisenberg, Fabes, Schaller, Carlo, and Miller (1991); Eisenberg, Fabes, Carlo, Troyer et al. (1992).
92. See Campos, Campos, and Barrett (1989); Eisenberg, Fabes, Carlo, Troyer et al. (1992).
93. Denham and Grout (1992).
94. Also see Denham (1989); Denham and Grout (1993).
95. Eisenberg, Fabes, Carlo, Troyer et al. (1992); Eisenberg, Fabes, Schaller, Carlo, and Miller (1991).
96. Halberstadt (1986).
97. Bronstein et al. (1993).
98. Denham and Grout (1993); Dunn and Brown (1994).
99. Denham and Grout (1992); Eisenberg, Fabes, Carlo, Troyer et al. (1992).
100. Dunn and Brown (1994).
101. Dunn and Brown (1994).
102. Eisenberg, Fabes, Carlo, Troyer et al. (1992); Garner et al. (1994).
103. Bridges and Grolnick (1995); Sroufe et al. (1984).
104. Bridges and Grolnick (1995); Braungart and Stifter (1991).
105. Gianino and Tronick (1988).
106. Hardy, Power, and Jaedicke (1993).
107. Kestenbaum, Farber, and Sroufe (1989).
108. Kobak and Sceery (1988).
109. Bridges and Grolnick (1995).
110. Buck (1984).
111. Eisenberg, Fabes, Schaller, Carlo, and Miller (1991).
112. Brody (1985).
113. Garner et al. (1994).
114. Cassidy et al. (1992); also see Saarni, this volume.
115. Eisenberg, Fabes, Schaller, Carlo, and Miller (1991).
116. Eisenberg, Fabes, Carlo, Troyer et al. (1992).
117. Eisenberg, Fabes, Carlo, Karbon et al. (1992).
118. Denham (1993).
119. Eisenberg and Fabes (1994); also see Eisenberg, Fabes, Carlo, and Karbon (1992).
120. Roberts and Strayer (1987).
121. Denham (1993).
122. Strauss (1988).
123. Roberts and Strayer (1987).
124. Eisenberg, Fabes, Schaller, Carlo, and Miller (1991).
125. Eisenberg, Fabes, Carlo, and Karbon (1992).
126. Dunn, Brown, Slomkowski, Telsa, and Youngblade (1991); Dunn, Bretherton, and Munn (1987).
127. Dunn, Brown, and Beardsall (1991).
128. Laird, Pettit, Mize, Brown, and Lindsey (1994).
129. Putallaz (1987).
130. Eisenberg and Fabes (1994).
131. Fabes et al. (1994).

EDUCATOR'S COMMENTARY

REBECCA NELLUM-WILLIAMS

I SHARED NANCY EISENBERG and her coauthors' chapter with several of my colleagues. We gained many insights from their research. Perhaps the most important point we came away with was that an individual's emotions, the intensity of those emotions, and the individual's ability to control those emotions make up the formula that reveals that person's level of social functioning. Further, a well-regulated child is more likely to engage in nonaggressive behavior, be popular among his or her peers, be prosocial, feel secure, and do well academically. We believe this body of research supports the idea that as teachers, we need to be versed in emotional development and be aware of the relationship between emotionality, intensity, and regulation. Armed with this expertise, we must impart the essentials to our students via direct teaching, modeling, and on-the-spot crisis intervention. In addition, this body of research as well as our own experiences suggest that it is necessary to share this knowledge, its implications, and related suggestions with parents.

I must admit that my colleagues' immediate reaction to this research and to the topic of emotion-related curriculum mirrored my own: OVERLOAD! So you're telling us that we need to add yet another subject to a plate that is without exaggeration piled high. So in addition to teaching upwards of 10 subjects, grading papers, meeting with parents, attending in-services, attending faculty and team meetings, writing lesson plans, reviewing textbooks, participating in two pilot programs, reading current research, decorating bulletin boards (on top of getting to know 25 to 30 students who come from every walk of life with varying abilities, personalities, abnormalities, and home lives, whom we must engage, assess, remediate, challenge, reassess, evaluate, celebrate, love, and nurture), you want us to train children to identify, read, and regulate their emotions. We should be experts on this as well as ADD, multiple intelligences, inclusion, reading recovery, developmental spelling, teaching the gifted, alternative assessment, new math, telecommunicating, and whole-language versus basal-driven instruction. Sure, no problem.

However, not seconds later, we all concluded that we cannot afford *not* to add this to our plate. And that we were already modeling and teaching about emotions and emotional regulation every single day. We agreed that it would be helpful and extremely worthwhile if a formal curriculum were adopted by our school districts, combined with essential teacher training and support. We recognized three facts that led us to the conclusion that we must teach emotion management. First, we care very deeply about children; that is why most of us became teachers. We care about the education and well-being of every child. We know that we must educate the whole child. We also recognize that we are lifelong learners ourselves. So we stand ready to continue to do what we are doing, as well as read, understand, and apply any new information about this or any other education-related topic.

Second, we are keenly aware that a child is not able to participate in the learning process until certain basic needs are met. Included in these "needs," it seems reasonable to conclude, are the child's emotional needs. Just yesterday as I was about to begin my math lesson on division rules, Jessi, a student in my third-grade class, began wailing hysterically. Besides the fact that I was genuinely concerned about Jessi, it was obvious that I was going to get nowhere with $x \div 1 = x$ until I helped Jessi understand and control her emotions. I further understood that as far as Jessi was concerned, nothing was more important than getting to the root of her frustration and hopefully learning to regulate the situation.

Third, and sadly, we as a society are failing to regulate our emotions. The evening news teems with examples of citizens who have "lost control." Unregulated anger and frustration often turn violent, if not deadly. My colleagues and I recounted the report of two drivers on a local highway who were angry with one another for improper lane changes. They let the situation escalate into a race/argument that resulted in an accident that killed one of them and three other drivers. We could not help but see a connection between this incident and the student who becomes so angry because another student "butted in line" that he stomps on that student's foot or punches that student in the face.

What can we as teachers do? We can do a number of things. First, we can continue to do what we are already doing. In my case, this includes teaching the portion of our health curriculum that deals with emotions, as well as teaching students to send "I Messages" and supporting our school counselor's instruction on Kelso's Choices. I have had great success using "I Messages" or "I Care Language." It involves beginning with "I," stating how you feel, what incident made you feel that way, why you feel that way, and what you would like the other person to do. For example, Michael said to Jason last week, "I feel *angry* when you *jump on my back and pat me on the head* because *it hurts and I always end up in trouble for making noise in the hall*, so would you *please not stand next to me in line?*" In the beginning of the year, I teach my students how to use "I Care Language" and then we practice together. Our school counselor does a series of lessons on using Kelso's Choices to solve small problems. Kelso's Choices include: (1) Wait and cool off, (2) Go to another activity, (3) Share and take turns, (4) Talk it out, (5) Walk away, (6) Ignore it, (7) Tell them to stop, (8) Apologize, (9) Make a deal. Kelso recommends that students try two of these choices. For larger problems Kelso recommends talking to an adult you trust.

Second, we can employ certain strategies referred to in Eisenberg and her colleagues' chapter. Some points were derived from research on parents as socializers; however, these points are definitely applicable in the classroom. For example, we can encourage students to express emotion, positive or negative, rather than punish. We can help students explore the causes and consequences of various emotions. We can also teach them the three levels of regulation: (1) regulation of your emotions, (2) regulation of how you express that emotion, and (3) regulation of the situation. When Jessi becomes unraveled by Ryan's constant teasing, she might choose "Wait and cool off" and "Talk it out" from Kelso's Choices. After she cools off, I would encourage her to use "I Care Language" with Ryan. I would also help Jessi examine what control she has over the situation; what she can do to change what is going on. She did in fact decide to make every effort to avoid Ryan and to do her best not to buy into his teasing. As the teacher, I can make decisions regarding this conflict. For example, I might avoid seating them next to each other or placing them in a cooperative group together. I would also attempt to help Ryan examine his emotions and reasons for picking on Jessi.

Another way we as teachers can promote emotional competence among our students, perhaps the most important way, is through modeling. It is the old adage "Actions speak louder than words." I frequently use "I Care Language" with my students to express my negative emotions. It has proved very effective in many instances. I can also make an effort to express my positive emotions. I can model discussing emotions by discussing my own emotions, their causes, and their consequences.

Although my colleagues and I were able to identify ways we as teachers can promote the positive socioemotional development of our students, we are cognizant of several obstacles that make it difficult for us to have as much of an impact as we would like. These obstacles include parental practices, lack of curriculum and training, and the general public's apathy. Eisenberg states, "social agents' (particularly parents') practices and behaviors are linked to children's socioemotional responding" (p. 145). She continues, "the family . . . is the primary context in which children's emotional competencies develop." Thus, our impact as educators is limited. I can't help but think of Brandon, a former student of mine. The counselor and I worked hard to promote constructive expression of his anger and also to help him regulate the situation. However, violence and profanity were accepted expressions of anger at home. Perhaps schools and other institutions should play a greater role in educating parents with regard to socializing their children emotionally. Seminars and information sessions could be offered to share research and strategies with parents such as "I Statements" and the importance of expressing and discussing emotions.

The second obstacle that we noted is the lack of curriculum and training. Unfortunately, the school systems in our area do not have a specific emotion curriculum. What we use in our classrooms comes from the school counselor, fellow teachers, or our own socialization. We agreed that our school systems should adopt such a curriculum. However, we feel very strongly that any such program must go hand in hand with adequate and ongoing teacher training and support. We are tired of programs being piloted with little or no training. We realize that professional development is expensive, but it is central to the success of any program.

We fear that the greatest obstacle is the current attitude of the general public and those clutching the educational pursestrings. The current attitude, evident from local political battles and editorials, seems to be that we spend entirely too much on education already. Many think we need to cut the education budget, not increase it. Such individuals think that we can easily trim education spending by eliminating "social programs" and "extra fluff." They include school counselors in "social programs"! We should stick to the basics, they say. We should not be teaching about things like feelings or recycling. The reality is that growing evidence points to the need to teach emotional responding at all levels, now.

As a result of reading Eisenberg and her colleagues' chapter on emotional responding and other articles published on this subject, my colleagues and I will pay particular attention to the emotional development of our students. We look forward to the adoption of comprehensive programs that promote this end. If we can overcome the obstacles previously mentioned, we as a society can look forward to children who are socially and emotionally competent as well as well educated. In the meantime, we will do our best to educate "the whole child."

CHAPTER 6

Emotion Regulation During Childhood: Developmental, Interpersonal, and Individual Considerations

ELIOT M. BRENNER AND
PETER SALOVEY

Rachel is a 5-year-old girl who often cries when she attempts to complete difficult tasks in her kindergarten classroom. When Rachel's teacher offers support and comfort and redirects her to a different activity, such as a game or coloring task, Rachel engages readily with the new task and her sadness dissipates.

Michael is a 10-year-old boy who sometimes becomes sad and irritable when he fails to understand arithmetic or science problems. At these times, he is prone to make angry remarks at peers whom he perceives as making noise and interfering with his concentration. Michael has told his teacher that when he thinks about something else for a while, his mood and concentration improve. The teacher notices that Michael's mood also improves when he exercises during lunch or physical education class.

Jennifer is a 13-year-old adolescent who for the past 4 months has avoided socializing and interacting with her classmates, and looks sad for much of the day. Although Jennifer used to talk with friends to comfort herself when she was sad or angry about being teased by boys, lately she threatens them or withdraws and isolates herself.

Jennifer's teacher has encouraged her to socialize more and not to take seriously the boys' insensitive remarks, but Jennifer is not comforted by this support, and she continues to isolate herself from her classmates. When the teacher met Jennifer's mother at a school conference, she also seemed quite sad. At that time, the teacher learned that Jennifer's parents were divorced and that Jennifer had been physically abused by her father as a young child.

These three examples illustrate the important role that emotion regulation plays in children's everyday functioning. In recent years, considerable empirical research has been published on children's regulation of emotion, although much of this research has not been accessible to educators, child psychologists, and other people working with children and adolescents.[1] In this chapter, we attempt to summarize this research in a manner that is accessible to these professionals. Where appropriate, we employ the case examples of Rachel, Michael, and Jennifer to illustrate important empirical findings.

In the first section of this chapter, we define emotion and emotion regulation. In the second section, we discuss age-related, developmental changes in how children and early adolescents regulate emotion.[2] We show how research can help us understand how children of different ages—like 5-year-old Rachel, 10-year-old Michael, and 13-year-old Jennifer—regulate emotion. We illustrate how, as children mature, they become better able to regulate emotion internally and without the help of others, and how their ability to select situationally appropriate regulatory strategies improves. Differences in the strategies that boys (like Michael) and girls (like Jennifer) use to manage emotions are discussed in the second section, as is the important role that children's knowledge about emotion plays in their regulatory ability. In the third section of this chapter, we focus on interpersonal influences on emotion regulation, paying particular attention to how parents and other adults socialize children's emotion regulation. In the fourth section, we discuss how individual differences can influence children's regulation, paying particular attention to children who are depressed, have conduct problems, or have been maltreated. Finally, we discuss some of the implications for educators and child psychologists of the findings reviewed in this chapter. The focus of this chapter is on how the individual child regulates emotion and on the influence of important adults in the child's environment. We recognize that social systems (e.g., schools, churches, communities) also affect the child's emotion regulation, although we do not discuss these influences here.

DEFINING EMOTION REGULATION

In our society, emotions are often viewed as disorganizing forces that disrupt one's ability to reason.[3] In chapter 2 of this volume, for example,

Carolyn Saarni discusses the "volcano" theory, a typical lay theory of emotion that holds that unless feelings are vented or discharged from within the individual, they may accumulate and burst forth, impairing the individual's ability to reason and function adaptively. In contrast to most lay theories of emotion, much of the research that we discuss in this chapter derives from functionalist views of emotion.[4] Functionalist perspectives conceptualize emotions as *responses that guide the individual's behavior and serve as information that helps the individual achieve goals.*[5] Emotions can be thought to have three components: cognitive-experiential, behavioral-expressive, and physiological-biochemical.[6] The cognitive-experiential component comprises one's thoughts and awareness of emotional states (i.e., what most people refer to as "feelings"). The behavioral-expressive component comprises such domains as speech, body movement, facial expression, posture, and gesture (i.e., the visible signs of emotion). The physiological-biochemcal component comprises physical states and is reflected in such measures as brain activity, heart rate, skin response, and hormone levels. (Like the cognitive-experiential component, this dimension of emotion is generally not visible to others.)

Some functionalist theorists include regulation as a fourth component of emotion, although we prefer to view regulation as distinct from emotion.[7] We define emotion regulation as *the process of managing responses that originate within cognitive-experiential, behavioral-expressive, and physiological-biochemical components.*[8] In this chapter, we emphasize the development of regulation within cognitive-experiential and behavioral-expressive components because emotional literacy frameworks emphasize these components[9] and because educators and clinicians are most likely to target interventions that use them. The development of physiological-biochemical regulation is discussed by Greenberg and Snell in chapter 4 of this book.

THE DEVELOPMENT OF EMOTION REGULATION STRATEGIES

Understanding developmental changes in children's capacity to regulate emotion can help educators and practitioners assist children when they become emotionally distressed. Much of our knowledge of the development of children's emotion regulation derives from research in which children are asked to report the things they do to cope with stressful experiences. Most of this research views coping as a *process* comprising two principle *components:* stressor and strategy.[10] Any event that evokes distress in the child is considered a *stressor*. Any effort to manage distress is considered a *strategy*. We believe that coping is synonymous with emotion regulation; both are processes in which the child uses available strategies to manage stressful encounters. Successful coping or emotion regulation is determined by the range of strategies available, the ability to select strategies that meet the demands of particular stressors, and the ability to implement these strategies.

Although researchers have described coping strategies in a number of different ways, we describe strategies along two dimensions: external-internal and social-solitary. First, strategies can exist at any point along an external-internal continuum: At the external end are strategies that involve altering the individual's behavior or the environment (e.g., using physical exercise to reduce anxiety or tension), while at the internal end are strategies that involve altering the individual's internal experience (e.g., substituting positive thoughts for negative ones to reduce sadness). Strategies that exist in the middle of the continuum involve altering both behavior and internal experience, for example, writing about one's reasons for feeling sad (an external strategy), then substituting positive thoughts to minimize the sad feelings (an internal strategy). The external end of this continuum resembles what Nancy Eisenberg and colleagues (chapter 5 of this volume) refer to as "regulating externally driven behavior"; the internal end of this continuum resembles what they refer to as "regulating emotion." Second, coping strategies also exist at any point along the social-solitary continuum: At one end are strategies that involve other people (e.g., going to a party with friends), while at the other end are strategies that involve the individual (e.g., watching television alone).

Different dimensions have also been used to describe the types of *stressors* that children face.[11] One important dimension of the stressor is its degree of controllability: At one end of the continuum are stressors that are largely within the child's control (e.g., an upcoming arithmetic test), while at the other end are those that are largely outside of the child's control (e.g., airplane turbulence).[12]

Understanding the strategies that children use to regulate emotion and the types of stressors that they face serves two purposes. First, it provides us with a practical way of communicating with children about the things they can do to manage particular kinds of stressful or unpleasant experiences. Second, it allows us to delineate developmental changes in the types of strategies that children use and in their ability to implement these strategies to manage stressful encounters. Our review suggests three age-related, developmental trends: (a) Children's use of internal strategies increases throughout development, (b) their use of solitary strategies increases throughout development, and (c) their ability to distinguish between controllable and uncontrollable stressors, and to effectively match strategy to stressor, improves with development. We now discuss the research supporting these trends.

Use of Internal Strategies Increases with Development

Describing coping strategies as primarily internal or external is one way to summarize the many ways researchers have conceptualized or categorized different strategies. For example, researchers have distinguished between cognitive and behavioral strategies, which can be thought of as internal and external strategies, respectively. Research suggests that there is an age-related increase in children's use of cognitive strategies, while children's use of behavioral strategies remains relatively constant throughout development.[13] The reader will recall the case examples presented at the beginning of this chapter: five-year-old Rachel's sad feelings dissipated when she engaged in *behavioral* tasks (i.e., games or coloring), while 10-year-old Michael's angry and sad feelings dissipated when he engaged in *cognitive* distraction (i.e., thinking about something else). These case examples are consistent with most empirical research. For example, Altshuler and Ruble asked 5-, 8-, and 11-year-old children to read stories and identify strategies that the characters in these stories could use to cope with negative emotions resulting from an uncontrollable stressor. Older children were more likely than younger children to report that story characters could employ cognitive distraction strategies (e.g., "think about something else"), while there were no age differences in the frequency with which children reported behavioral strategies (e.g., "do something else"). In a similar study, 7- and 10-year-old children reported strategies that they used to manage self-reported stressful situations.[14] Older children reported using significantly more cognitive strategies (e.g., "I am not inadequate") than younger children. In yet another study, 10-year-old children reported greater use of cognitive problem-solving strategies (e.g., "I thought about what I could do to make the problem better") to cope with stressful experiences than did 7-year-old children.[15] Thus, studies asking children to report strategies they use to cope with distress suggest that children's use of internal, cognitive strategies increases with age, while their use of external, behavioral strategies remains relatively constant throughout development.

Researchers have distinguished between *emotion-focused* and *problem-focused* coping strategies, which can also be viewed as internal and external regulatory strategies, respectively.[16] Emotion-focused coping involves managing directly the negative emotions that result from a problem; problem-focused coping involves the individual's attempts to manage or change a problem that is generating negative emotions. To take an example, when Compas, Malcarne, and Fondacaro asked 10- to 14-year-olds to identify the strategies they used to cope with interpersonal or academic stressors, they found that the use of emotion-focused strategies (e.g., "tried to calm down") increased with age, whereas use of problem-focused strategies (e.g., "did more homework") did not. Thus, research using this conceptual approach also suggests that as children develop, they begin to rely more upon internal, emotion-focused strategies, while their use of external, problem-focused approaches is relatively constant throughout childhood.

Researchers have distinguished between *secondary control* and *primary control* strategies, which can also be viewed as internal and external coping strategies, respectively.[17] Secondary control involves coping to adjust oneself to events or conditions as they are; primary control involves coping to alter conditions or events. In research using this conceptual perspective, for example, Band and Weisz asked 6-, 9-, and 12-year-old children to describe the strategies they used to cope with everyday stressors such as a time when their mothers were mad at them. These researchers found that the number of primary coping strategies children reported (e.g., "yelling back, with the goal of convincing their mothers not to be so mean to them") decreased with age, while the number of secondary coping responses reported (e.g., "showing compassion for the fact that their mothers had a bad day") increased with age.

Additional evidence for developmental increases in children's use of internal strategies comes from a study of the effects of emotion on problem solving. Terwogt showed that 10-year-old children, but not 5-year-old children, were able to self-implement cognitive strategies to mitigate the effects of emotional arousal on problem solving.[18] Immediately prior to inducing in children sad moods and asking them to complete a problem-solving task, Terwogt activated cognitive regulation strategies in one-half of the children by asking them whether they thought that their moods might affect their schoolwork. The results indicated that 5-year-olds who were not cued to regulate their moods prior to the mood induction performed worse on a problem-solving task than 5-year-olds who were cued to regulate their moods, presumably because the cued children used internal regulatory strategies such as cognitive distraction to attenuate the adverse effects of emotional arousal on problem solving. In contrast, the problem-solving performances of 10-year-olds who were and were not cued did not differ significantly. This experiment implies that young children possess internal strategies, although they may not be able to access and implement these strategies readily. Toward the end of middle childhood, however, children may learn to employ internal strategies without cuing, thus enhancing their repertoire of regulatory strategies. These findings of age-related developmental increases in use of internal regulatory strategies are consistent with research distinguishing between cognitive/behavioral, emotion-focused/problem-focused, and secondary control/primary control regulatory strategies, and suggest that while children use external strategies throughout childhood, their use of internal strategies increases throughout childhood and appears to be in place by approximately age 10.

Use of Solitary Strategies Increases with Development

Children's ability to regulate emotions without the assistance of others, particularly parents, improves with age. We recall that 5-year-old Rachel needed help from her teacher to manage sad feelings, whereas 10-year-old Michael was able to regulate his sad and angry feelings without assistance. These case examples are consistent with most research.

For instance, Kliewer found that 7-year-old children relied more upon support from others (e.g., "I talked to my Mom about how I was feeling"; "I asked my friends to help me hunt for my lost dog") than did 10-year-old children to cope with stressful experiences.[19] A similar study found that kindergarten through sixth-grade children were more likely to seek the support of others after losing at a game than were seventh- and eighth-graders.[20] Finally, in a study that asked children to report the things they do when they "feel bad, nervous, or worried," 8-year-olds reported more social support strategies (e.g., "talk to my Mom") than did 12-year-olds.[21] Taken together, these studies suggest that, as children develop, their ability to regulate emotion without the assistance of others improves.

Ability to Match Strategy to Stressor Improves with Development

As children develop, their ability to use both internal and external regulatory strategies allows them to manage stressful situations with increased flexibility. Children also become better at distinguishing between controllable and uncontrollable stressors, and at choosing the most effective strategies for these stressors. Miller tested this idea directly by distinguishing between *monitoring* and *blunting* coping strategies, and controllable and uncontrollable stressors.[22] Monitoring involves attending to the aversive aspects of experiences (e.g., thinking about airplane turbulence); blunting entails using distraction, reappraisal, or avoidance to minimize the aversive aspects of experiences (e.g., playing cards to distract oneself from airplane turbulence).[23] Research with adults suggests that monitoring, which is largely an external regulatory strategy, is more effective for managing controllable stressors, whereas blunting, which is largely an internal strategy, is more effective for managing uncontrollable stressors.[24] Recall that 10-year-old Michael usually recognizes that his noisy classroom is beyond his control (i.e., it is an uncontrollable stressor), and that an internal, blunting regulatory strategy (i.e., thinking about something else) is most effective for managing this situation.

Michael's responses are typical of those gathered in research with other children his age. For instance, Hoffner asked 6- to 12-year-old children to report strategies they would use to cope with uncontrollable stressors described in several stories.[25] She found that 10- to 12-year-old children reported more blunting coping strategies than 6- to 9-year-old children, whereas there was no difference between the two age groups in the number of monitoring strategies reported. Similarly, 7- to 12-year-old children suffering from cancer reported using fewer emotion management strategies to cope with uncontrollable medical tests than did 13- to 17-year-old adolescents, although the use of problem-focused strategies did not differ significantly between age groups.[26] Taken together, these studies suggest that the abilities to evaluate the controllability of different stressors and to select situationally appropriate regulatory strategies improves with development, and that these abilities are often used during middle childhood and early adolescence.

Sex Differences in Strategy Use

The case examples at the beginning of this chapter suggest that the use of emotion regulation strategies differs not only as a function of age but also as a function of sex. Recall that Rachel felt better after she received comfort and emotional support from her teacher, while Michael felt better when he exercised. Research is consistent with these case examples and indicates that there are at least three salient differences in girls' and boys' use of regulatory strategies. First, studies suggest that girls are more likely than boys to rely upon social support to cope with distress.[27] For instance, when Wierzbicki asked 8- to 12-year-old children to "write down things to do that help a person who is feeling sad or depressed to feel better" (p. 1253), he found that girls were more likely to report help-seeking strategies (e.g., "talk about it"; "call someone") than boys.[28] Similarly, in a study of 11- to 14-year-olds, girls endorsed more "stress-recognition" coping strategies (e.g., "talk to my brother or sister"; "talk to my friend") than boys.[29] Finally, another study found that junior and senior high school girls were more likely than their male classmates to endorse using social support strategies (e.g., "talk to a friend about how you feel") to cope with stressful experiences.[30] Taken together, these studies suggest that during middle childhood through adolescence, girls are more likely than boys to rely upon social support strategies to regulate emotion.

Second, girls are more likely than boys to use emotion-focused regulation that involves attending to the cognitive-experiential component of emotion.[31] This has been found in 7- to 17-year-old children with active cancer or cancer in remission,[32] and with healthy junior high school[33] and senior high school students.[34] For example, one study reported that when faced with personal and cancer-related stressors, 7- to 17-year-old girls were more likely than boys of the same age to use emotion management strategies such as actively trying to forget about painful emotion.[35] It appears that throughout middle childhood and adolescence, girls are more likely than boys to cope with stressful experiences by attending to the internal, cognitive-experiential component of emotion.

Finally, research with 8- to 14-year-olds suggests that boys are more likely than girls to use physical exercise to manage distress.[36] For instance, Ryan found that boys were three times more likely than girls to report using physical exercise to manage events that made them feel "bad, nervous, or worried" (p. 113). A similar study found that the third most frequently endorsed coping strategy reported by young adolescent males was to "do a strenuous physical activity," whereas adolescent females were not likely to endorse this strategy.[37]

To summarize, there are at least three salient differences in girls' and boys' use of strategies to regulate negative emotion: (a) Girls are more likely than boys to seek support and guidance from others, (b) girls are more likely than boys to use emotion-focused coping, and (c) boys are more likely than girls to use physical exercise.

Emotional Knowledge and Expressive Regulation

The increase during development in children's use of internal regulatory strategies reflects their cognitive development more generally.[38] As children develop cognitively, their fund of general knowledge, which includes their knowledge about emotional experiences, grows. We define emotional knowledge as *a child's fund of information about emotion and emotional experience in the self and others that is used to understand and interpret events in the environment.* Research has documented age-related increases in children's knowledge of the duration of emotion,[39] the ability to discriminate and verbalize different basic emotions (e.g., fear, sadness, anger),[40] the capacity to determine others' emotional states,[41] the ability to describe the simultaneous experience of different emotions,[42] and knowledge of cultural rules about emotional expressiveness (i.e., display rules; see definition in next paragraph).[43]

Research suggests that children may use emotional knowledge to help themselves regulate their emotions.[44] This is important to teachers and practitioners because they may need to help children understand and interpret emotional cues in the environment before they can suggest a particular regulatory strategy. For example, if Michael's teacher were to suggest a regulatory strategy, she may initially need to help him understand that his noisy classmates are just having fun and aren't *intending* to impair his concentration. Consistent with this case example, Altshuler et al. found that 5- to 10-year-old children's knowledge of adaptive emotion coping strategies predicted their ability to use these strategies when hospitalized for elective surgery.[45] In a related area of research, positive associations have been observed between young children's ability to label emotions in themselves and others and their tendency to help, cooperate with, and share with other children, suggesting that children may use their emotional knowledge to guide social interactions.[46] Given the findings of Altshuler et al., one would expect that emotional knowledge might precede developmentally or emerge concurrently with strategies for regulating emotion.[47] For example, research on *display rules,* or the learned cultural norms that dictate appropriate emotional expressiveness, suggests that *knowledge* of display rules probably emerges concurrently with the *use* of display rules.[48] To illustrate, numerous studies suggest that 6-year-old children *know* about display rules and that this knowledge develops throughout middle childhood and early adolescence.[49] At the same time, when Saarni presented 6-, 8-, and 10-year-olds with an undesirable prize, she found that the youngest children *used* display rules by masking disappointment with positive facial expressions, and that the ability to mask disappointment improved with age. Given that children may use emotional knowledge to guide their regulation of expressive behavior, it is important for teachers and practitioners to be aware of children's funds of knowledge before they attempt to assist children in regulating their experiences.

INTERPERSONAL INFLUENCES ON EMOTION REGULATION

In this chapter, we distinguish between *interpersonal* and *individual* influences on emotion regulation because most previous research has done so. However, we believe that the two influences are inextricably interrelated and that emotions arise when the individual, who is pursuing goals, interacts with the environment and others. Positive emotions usually arise when the individual progresses toward a goal; negative emotions usually arise when the individual has difficulty accomplishing a goal. In this section, we discuss some of the ways parents can shape children's ability to regulate emotion. We hope to show how being aware of how parents shape emotion regulation can help teachers and practitioners create environments that are pleasant and conducive to learning and growth.

Parke has proposed three ways in which parents socialize emotion in their children: (a) by indirect exposure to parental and familial interactions, (b) by teaching and coaching, and (c) by regulating opportunities in the environment.[50] Before we review research in these domains, we note that teachers socialize emotion in the same ways by indirectly exposing children to their interactions with other students and teachers, by directly teaching and coaching children (e.g., the teacher who encouraged Jennifer not to ruminate over boys' insults), and by regulating opportunities in the environment (e.g., the teacher who allowed Michael to attend physical education class).

Indirect Influences

Research on two types of home environments illustrates how children can learn indirectly about emotion by observing family interactions. First, Cummings and colleagues have found that children are adversely affected when their parents have frequent, angry conflicts.[51] For example, these investigators found that 6- to 7-year-old children who had been repeatedly exposed to angry parental conflicts tended to cope with these conflicts by using maladaptive strategies (e.g., physical aggression).[52] Along the same line, children of mothers with high scores on an anger measure were more likely to verbalize anger when provoked than children of mothers who scored low on the anger measure.[53] Finally, when preschool children whose parents were high in marital conflict viewed an interaction between two angry adults, these children displayed more overt behavioral distress and different patterns of heart rate reactivity than did children whose parents were low in marital conflict.[54] Taken together, these studies suggest that the ways parents manage anger and conflict may influence the development of their children's strategies for regulating emotions through the process of indirect observation.

Second, research suggests that depressed parents possess a number of deficits in parenting that may indirectly influence the development of their children's regulatory abilities.[55] Compared with nondepressed mothers, depressed mothers tend to be more critical, hostile, and negative and less emotionally expressive and cooperative when they negotiate with their children and with adults. Given that depressed mothers' interactions model for their children how to regulate their own emotions, it is not surprising that parents' and children's strategies for managing depression are positively associated.[56] For example, it is quite possible that Jennifer, who withdraws from her peers to manage distress, may have learned this strategy from her depressed mother. The correspondence between mothers' and children's regulatory styles was borne out in a study by Garber and colleagues that found that depressed mothers and their 8- to 13-year-old children reported fewer strategies to regulate sad moods, and that judges rated these strategies as less effective than strategies endorsed by nondepressed mothers and their children.[57] To summarize, children may learn maladaptive strategies for regulating emotion by observing parents who are depressed, angry, or experience marital conflict. Although research has focused on the acquisition of maladaptive strategies, children also learn adaptive ways of regulating emotion by observing parents, teachers, and other adults interacting with one another in positive and productive ways.

Direct Influences

Children can also learn how to regulate emotion by having their parents teach or coach them. For example, Nolen-Hoeksema and colleagues found that when mothers encouraged their 5- to 7-year-old children to complete a difficult puzzle task, children were more enthusiastic and persistent and less frustrated than children whose mothers did not encourage them.[58] In contrast, the more critical and hostile mothers were, the less enthusiastic and persistent and the more frustrated their children were while completing the task. In a longitudinal study of children's strategies for coping with divorce, mothers' encouragement at the beginning of the study of coping strategies like distraction, avoidance, support seeking, and cognitive reframing was related positively to their children's use of these strategies 5 months later.[59] Further, mothers' reports of their own use of active, avoidance, and support-seeking strategies were related positively to their suggestions of these strategies to their children, suggesting that parents are likely to teach their children the strategies they use.

Along the same line, a number of studies have found that parents who encourage their children to express emotion in socially appropriate ways are likely to have empathic, emotionally expressive children.[60] For example, Eisenberg and colleagues found that parents' acknowledgment of their children's appropriate expressive behavior was related positively to their 8- and 11-year-old children's scores on a measure of empathy.[61] Similarly, Eisenberg observed that parents' permissiveness of their children's expressive behavior was related positively to same-sex children's sympathy.[62] Taken together, these studies suggest that one way children learn to regulate emotion is through direct teaching or coaching by their parents.

Environmental Opportunities

The opportunities that parents afford their children, which include the types of games that children play, the television programs they watch, and the friends with whom they play, may influence the development of children's emotion regulation.[63] The development of children's emotion regulation may also be influenced by the degree to which parents are absent from the home. When parents work long hours or their jobs require considerable travel, they may not be able to control the situations to which their children are exposed, and children may develop maladaptive or ineffectual strategies for regulating emotion in these situations. For example, it is possible that young, latchkey children who are exposed to violent programs on cable television or sexually explicit pictures on the Internet may develop maladaptive regulatory strategies because they are not able to understand or manage these experiences without assistance from adults.

INDIVIDUAL INFLUENCES ON EMOTION REGULATION

Children's capacity to manage emotion is associated with a number of dispositional differences. In this section, we discuss three of these dispositional differences: (a) depression, (b) conduct problems, and (c) maltreatment. Educators and practitioners who are aware of these differences may be able to assist children in compensating for the deficits in emotion regulation that often accompany these differences.

Depression

A number of studies suggest that clinically depressed and dysphoric (i.e., mildly depressed) children regulate emotions differently than nondepressed children.[64] We recall that Jennifer, who appears depressed, often avoids or withdraws from her peers when she is distressed. Her reaction is typical of depressed and dysphoric children, who tend to use more avoidant strategies for coping with distress and negative emotion than do nondepressed children.[65] For example, when Quiggle et al. asked 9- to 12-year-old schoolchildren to identify strategies they would use to cope with stressful situations, these investigators found that dysphoric children were more likely than nondysphoric children to report withdrawal strategies and to find assertive strategies ineffective. In a similar study of 8- to 17-year-olds, those who were clinically depressed were less likely to endorse active, problem-focused, or cognitive distraction strategies than children who were not depressed.[66]

Jennifer's difficulty in cognitively distracting herself from peers' teasing and insensitive remarks is typical of depressed children and adolescents, who are less likely than their nondepressed peers to use cognitive strategies (e.g., positive self-statements) to cope with negative moods.[67] For example, we found that 9- and 10-year-old dysphoric children reported less frequent use of cognitive distraction (e.g., "thinking about something else") to ameliorate sad moods in their everyday lives than nondysphoric children.[68] In addition, after watching mood-inducing videotapes in their school classrooms, dysphoric children were not as proficient as nondysphoric children in using distraction to ameliorate sad moods or in using distraction to maintain happy moods.[69] Similarly, a longitudinal study by Sandler and colleagues of the effects of divorce on 10-year-old children found that children who relied less upon active, cognitive coping strategies at the beginning of the study were more likely to report depressive symptoms 4 months later.[70] Finally, research suggests that depressed children are more likely than nondepressed children to use negative behavior (e.g., yelling at someone) to cope with sad moods.[71] Taken together, it appears that clinically depressed and dysphoric children do not manage distress, ameliorate negative moods, or maintain positive moods as well as nondepressed children. The direction of causality between deficits in emotion regulation and depression is not clear at this time, although the study by Sandler and colleagues suggests that regulatory deficits may predispose children to later depression.

Conduct Problems

Research has found a positive relationship between maladaptive styles of emotion regulation and conduct problems (e.g., fighting, lying, and defiance).[72] For example, when 4- to 5-year-old children described how they would cope with stressful situations, those with conduct problems reported greater use of angry and aggressive strategies than did children without these problems.[73] A similar study found that when preschool children were exposed to situations involving adults in distress, children with conduct problems tended to exhibit angry facial expressions toward the adults.[74] Finally, in a study of 7- to 14-year-old children's responses to positive feedback from a peer, children with conduct problems showed more hostile facial expressions to the feedback than children without these problems.[75] Following the feedback, children with conduct problems were also less accurate than other children in identifying the facial expressions they exhibited, suggesting that children with conduct problems may have less insight into their emotional experiences than children without these problems. Taken together, these studies suggest that children with conduct problems tend to regulate emotion with aggressive strategies in which they vent their anger. These children may rely upon these strategies to a greater degree than other children because children with conduct problems have less insight into their own and others' emotional experiences.

Maltreatment

Jennifer, who was physically abused as a young child, was inclined to threaten peers when they teased her. Her response is consistent with empirical research that has found that children who have been physically abused or neglected often exhibit aggressive emotion regulation strategies that are similar to those of children with conduct problems. For example, when 8- to 12-year-old children were observed during free play sessions at a summer day camp, those who had been physically abused were found to use more physically and verbally aggressive strategies to regulate emotion than those who had not been abused.[76] Likewise, after 5-year-old boys viewed a staged angry conflict between their mothers and an adult, children who had been physically abused showed more physical and verbal aggression than nonabused children.[77] Recent studies have also found that the severity, frequency, and chronicity of maltreatment are associated with the severity and frequency of conduct problems in 5- to 11-year-old children.[78] Studies by Dodge and colleagues[79] have found that the tendency for physically abused children to display aggressive regulatory strategies and conduct problems may be partially mediated by their unique ways of processing social and emotional cues in which they (a) are especially aware of hostile cues in the environment, (b) perceive peers' neutral actions as hostile, (c) access aggressive responses from memory, and (d) believe that aggressive strategies lead to positive outcomes.

Maltreated children have also been found to cope with distress by withdrawing from and avoiding peers during free play sessions.[80] Given maltreated children's frequent use of avoidant and aggressive regulatory strategies, it is not surprising that they tend to experience depression and anxiety[81] and to be less popular and socially competent than their nonmaltreated peers.[82] To summarize, maltreated children have been found to exhibit maladaptive regulatory strategies in which they verbally or physically vent their anger, in much the same ways as children with conduct problems. Unlike children with conduct problems, however, maltreated children also tend to rely upon avoidance and withdrawal strategies to cope with distress.

EDUCATIONAL AND PRACTICAL IMPLICATIONS

The development of flexible, adaptive ways of regulating emotion is essential to the emergence of children's emotional literacy and to their everyday adaptive functioning. Our review outlined three age-related trends in the development of children's regulation of emotion, each of which has practical implications for teachers, child psychologists, and other people working with children. As children develop, they rely more upon internal strategies that regulate the cognitive-experiential component of emotion. Children's ability to regulate emotion without the assistance of others and to implement situationally appropriate regulatory strategies also improves with age. This suggests that young children (i.e., 5 or 6 years old) who are having difficulty managing negative emotion may require considerable individualized attention and that they will respond most readily to behavioral tasks, such as games or other engaging activities. Older children (i.e., 9 or 10 years old), on the other hand, are capable of coping with distress by thinking about other things and are often able to assess the needs of situations and apply appropriate regulatory strategies without requiring adult intervention.

There are times when being aware of sex differences in children's strategy use could help educators and practitioners direct children to use appropriate strategies. For example, the research we reviewed suggests that girls are more likely than boys to attempt to regulate emotion by thinking about their feelings and seeking out the support of others, while boys are more likely to use physical exercise. Children's ability to regulate emotion is probably influenced to some degree by their fund of emotional knowledge, which implies that teaching children about how to recognize and label emotions in others could help them regulate adaptively.

The three age-related, developmental trends that we outlined are moderated by a number of interpersonal and individual factors. Research suggests that children's ability to regulate emotion is affected by their parents, who influence them indirectly by observational learning, directly by teaching and coaching, and by controlling children's exposure to different situations. Teachers and other practitioners influence children in the same three ways. For instance, teachers, through their interactions with students, teachers, and administrators, model for children how to regulate emotion appropriately in the classroom. Teachers and practitioners also instruct children directly about how to manage distress, as Jennifer's teacher did when she encouraged her not to take to heart the boys' insensitive remarks. In the process of designing and creating a comfortable learning environment, teachers also dictate the opportunities that children are afforded to learn about emotion regulation. The use of media (e.g., computers, television, books) affords children a range of opportunities for learning how to manage emotion.

Children who are depressed, have conduct problems, or have been maltreated are likely to have more difficulty regulating emotion adaptively than other children. Teachers and practitioners who are aware of these problems may be able to assist children in compensating for the deficits in emotion regulation that often accompany these problems.

GLOSSARY

Emotion—Responses that guide the individual's behavior and serve as information that helps the individual achieve goals. Emotions are thought to have three components. The cognitive-experiential component comprises thoughts and awareness of emotional states (i.e., one's feelings). The behavioral-expressive component comprises such domains as speech, body movement, facial expression, posture, and gesture (i.e., the visible signs of emotion). The physiological-biochemical component comprises physical states, and is reflected in such measures as brain activity, heart rate, skin response, and hormone levels. (Like the cognitive-experiential component, this dimension is generally not visible to others.)

Emotional Knowledge—A child's fund of information about emotion and emotional experience in the self and others that is used to understand and interpret events in the environment.

Emotion Regulation—The process of initiating, altering, or maintaining responses within or between cognitive-experiential, behavioral-expressive, and physiological-biochemical components of emotion.

External Regulatory Strategy—A way of managing emotion that involves the individual altering his or her behavior or the environment.

Internal Regulatory Strategy—A way of managing emotion that involves the individual altering his or her inner experience (i.e., thoughts and subjective feelings).

NOTES

References

Altshuler, J. L., & Ruble, D. N. (1989). Developmental changes in children's awareness of strategies for coping with uncontrollable stress. *Child Development, 60,* 1337–1349.

Altshuler, J. L., Genevro, J. L., Ruble, D. N., & Bornstein, M. H. (1995). Children's knowledge and use of coping strategies during hospitalization for elective surgery. *Journal of Applied Developmental Psychology, 16,* 53–76.

Asarnow, J. R., Carlson, G. A., & Guthrie, D. (1987). Coping strategies, self-perceptions, hopelessness, and perceived family environments in depressed and suicidal children. *Journal of Consulting and Clinical Psychology, 55,* 361–366.

Ballard, M. E., Cummings, E. M., & Larkin, K. (1993). Emotional and cardiovascular responses to adult's angry behavior and to challenging tasks in children of hypertensive and normotensive parents. *Child Development, 64,* 500–515.

Band, E. B., & Weisz, J. R. (1988). How to feel better when it feels bad: Children's perspectives on coping with everyday stress. *Developmental Psychology, 24,* 247–253.

Brenner, E. M., & Salovey, P. (1997). The influence of distraction, negative affectivity, and self-reported coping on children's regulation of happy and sad moods. Manuscript in preparation.

Bretherton, I., Fritz, J., Zahn-Waxler, C., & Ridgeway, D. (1986). Learning to talk about emotions: A functionalist perspective. *Child Development, 57,* 529–548.

Brown, K., Covell, K., & Abramovitch, R. (1991). Time course and control of emotion: Age differences in understanding and recognition. *Merrill-Palmer Quarterly, 37,* 273–287.

Buck, R. (1985). Prime theory: An integrated view of motivation and emotion. *Psychological Review, 92,* 389–413.

Bull, B. A., & Drotar, D. (1991). Coping with cancer in remission: Stressors and strategies reported by children and adolescents. *Journal of Pediatric Psychology, 16,* 767–782.

Bullock, M., & Russell, J. A. (1986). Concepts of emotion in developmental psychology. In C. E. Izard & P. B. Reed (Eds.), *Measuring emotions in infants and children.* New York: Cambridge University Press.

Campos, J. J., Campos, R. G., & Barrett, K. C. (1989). Emergent themes in the study of emotional development and emotion regulation. *Developmental Psychology, 25,* 394–402.

Campos, J. J., Mumme, D. L., Kermoian, R., & Campos, R. G. (1994). A functionalist perspective on the nature of emotion. In N. Fox (Ed.), *The development of emotion regulation. Monographs of the Society for Research in Child Development* (Vol. 59, pp. 284–303).

Carlo, G., Knight, G. P., Eisenberg, N., & Rotenberg, K. J. (1991). Cognitive processes and prosocial behaviors among children: The role of affective attributions and reconciliations. *Developmental Psychology, 27,* 456–461.

Casey, R. J., & Schlosser, S. (1994). Emotional responses to peer praise in children with and without a diagnosed externalizing disorder. *Merrill-Palmer Quarterly, 40,* 60–81.

Cole, P. M. (1985). Display rules and the socialization of affective displays. In G. Zivin (Ed.), *The development of expressive behavior* (pp. 269–290). New York: Academic Press.

Cole, P. M. (1986). Children's spontaneous control of facial expression. *Child Development, 57,* 1309–1321.

Cole, P. M., Jenkins, P. A., & Shott, C. T. (1989). Spontaneous expressive control in blind and sighted children. *Child Development, 60,* 683–688.

Compas, B. E., Malcarne, V. L., & Fondacaro, K. M. (1988). Coping with stressful events in older children and young adolescents. *Journal of Consulting and Clinical Psychology, 56,* 405–411.

Crittenden, P. M., Claussen, A. H., & Sugarman, D. B. (1994). Physical and psychological maltreatment in middle childhood and adolescence. *Development and Psychopathology, 6,* 145–164.

Cummings, E. M., Hennessy, K. D., Rabideau, G. J., & Cicchetti, D. (1994). Responses of physically abused boys to interadult anger involving their mothers. *Development and Psychopathology, 6,* 31–41.

Cummings, E. M., Simpson, K. S., & Wilson, A. (1993). Children's responses to interadult anger as a function of information about resolution. *Developmental Psychology, 29,* 978–985.

Cummings, E. M., Zahn-Waxler, C., & Radke-Yarrow, M. (1984). Developmental changes in children's reactions to anger in the home. *Journal of Child Psychology and Psychiatry, 25,* 63–74.

Denham, S. A. (1986). Social cognition, prosocial behavior, and emotion in preschoolers: Contextual validation. *Child Development, 57,* 194–201.

Denham, S. A., Renwick-DeBardi, S., & Hewes, S. (1994). Emotional communication between mothers and preschoolers: Relations with emotional competence. *Merrill-Palmer Quarterly, 40,* 488–508.

Dise-Lewis, J. E. (1988). The Life Events and Coping Inventory: An assessment of stress in children. *Psychosomatic Medicine, 50,* 484–499.

Dix, T. (1991). The affective organization of parenting: Adaptive and maladaptive processes. *Psychological Bulletin, 110,* 3–25.

Dodge, K. A. (1989). Coordinating responses to aversive stimuli: Introduction to a special section on the development of emotion regulation. *Developmental Psychology, 25,* 339–342.

Dodge, K. A., Pettit, G. S., Bates, J. E., & Valente, E. (1995). Social information-processing patterns partially mediate the effects of early physical abuse on later conduct problems. *Journal of Abnormal Psychology, 104,* 632–643.

Downey, G., & Coyne, J. C. (1990). Children of depressed parents: An integrative review. *Psychological Bulletin, 108,* 50–76.

Ebata, A. T., & Moos, R. H. (1991). Coping and adjustment in distressed and healthy adolescents. *Journal of Applied Psychology, 12,* 33–54.

Eisenberg, N., Fabes, R. A., Carlo, G., & Karbon, M. (1992). Emotional responsivity to others: Behavioral correlates and socialization antecedents. In N. Eisenberg & R. A. Fabes (Eds.), *New Directions for Child Development, 55,* 57–73.

Eisenberg, N., Fabes, R. A., Nyman, M., Bernzweig, J., & Pinuelas, A. (1994). The relations of emotionality and regulation to children's anger-related reactions. *Child Development, 65,* 109–128.

Eisenberg, N., Fabes, R. A., Schaller, M., Carlo, G., & Miller, P.A. (1991). The relations of parental characteristics and practices to children's vicarious emotional responding. *Child Development, 62,* 1393–1408.

Eisenberg, N., Fabes, R. A., Murphy, B., Maszk, P., Smith, M., & Karbon, M.

(1995). The role of emotionality and regulation in children's social functioning: A longitudinal study. *Child Development, 66*, 1360–1384.

Eisenberg, N., Schaller, M., Fabes, R. A., Bustamante, D., Mathy, R. M., Shell, R., & Rhodes, K. (1988). Differentiation of personal distress and sympathy in children and adults. *Developmental Psychology, 24*, 766–775.

El-Sheikh, M. (1994). Children's emotional and physiological responses to interadult angry behavior: The role of history of interparental hostility. *Journal of Abnormal Child Psychology, 22*, 661–678.

Fabes, R. A., Eisenberg, N., & Eisenbud, L. (1993). Behavioral and physiological correlates of children's reactions to others in distress. *Developmental Psychology, 4*, 655–663.

Fischer, K. W., Shaver, P. R., & Carnochan, P. (1990). How emotions develop and how they organize development. *Cognition and Emotion, 4*, 81–127.

Franko, D. L., Powers, T. A., Zuroff, D. C., & Moskowitz, D. S. (1985). Children and affect: Strategies for self-regulation and sex differences in sadness. *American Journal of Orthopsychiatry, 55*, 210–219.

Frijda, N. H. (1988). The laws of emotion. *American Psychologist, 43*, 349–358.

Fuchs, D., & Thelen, M. H. (1988). Children's expected interpersonal consequences of communicating their affective state and reported likelihood of expression. *Child Development, 59*, 1314–1322.

Garber, J., Braafladt, N., & Weiss, B. (1995). Affect regulation in depressed and nondepressed children and young adolescents. *Development and Psychopathology, 7*, 93–115.

Garber, J., Braafladt, N., & Zeman, J. (1991). The regulation of sad affect: An information-processing perspective. In J. Garber and K. Dodge (Eds.), *The development of emotion regulation and dysregulation* (pp. 208–240). New York: Cambridge University Press.

Gnepp, J. (1989). Children's use of personal information to understand other people's feelings. In C. Saarni & P. L. Harris (Eds.), *Children's understanding of emotion* (pp. 151–177). New York: Cambridge University Press.

Greenberg, M., & Snell, J. L. (1997). Brain development and emotional development: The role of teaching in organizing the frontal lobe. In P. Salovey & D. Sluyter (Eds.), *Emotional development and emotional intelligence: Educational implications*. New York: Basic Books.

Harris, P. L. (1985). What children know about the situations that provoke emotion. In M. Lewis & C. Saarni (Eds.), *The socialization of emotion* (pp. 161–185). New York: Plenum.

Harris, P. L. (1989). *Children and emotion: The development of psychological understanding*. New York: Basil Blackwell.

Hoffner, C. (1993). Children's strategies for coping with stress: Blunting and monitoring. *Motivation and Emotion, 17*, 91–106.

Ianotti, R. J. (1985). Naturalistic and structured assessments of prosocial behavior in preschool children: The influence of empathy and perspective taking. *Developmental Psychology, 21*, 46–55.

Izard, C. E. (1993). Four systems for emotion activation: Cognitive and noncognitive processes. *Psychological Review, 100*, 68–90.

Izard, C. E., & Kobak, R. R. (1991). Emotions system functioning and emotion regulation. In J. Garber & K. A. Dodge (Eds.), *The development of emotion regulation and dysregulation* (pp. 303–321). New York: Cambridge University Press.

Kaslow, N. J., Deering, C. G., and Racusin, G. R. (1994). Depressed children and their families. *Clinical Psychology Review, 14*, 39–59.

Kaufman, J., & Cicchetti, D. (1989). Effects of maltreatment on school-age children's socioemotional development: Assessments in a day-camp setting. *Developmental Psychology, 25*, 516–524.

Kliewer, W. (1991). Coping in middle childhood: Relations to competence, type A behavior, monitoring, blunting, and locus of control. *Developmental Psychology, 27*, 689–697.

Kopp, C. B. (1989). Regulation of distress and negative emotions: A developmental view. *Developmental Psychology, 25*, 343–354.

Kurdek, L. A. (1987). Gender differences in the psychological symptomatology and coping strategies of young adolescents. *Journal of Early Adolescence, 7*, 395–410.

Lazarus, R. S., & Folkman, S. (1984). *Stress, appraisal, and coping.* New York: Springer.

Manly, J. T., Cicchetti, D., & Barnett, D. (1994). The impact of subtype, frequency, chronicity, and severity of child maltreatment on social competence and behavior problems. *Development and Psychopathology, 6*, 121–143.

McCoy, C. L., & Masters, J. C. (1990). Children's strategies for the control of emotion in themselves and others. In B. S. Moore & A. M. Isen (Eds.), *Affect and social behavior* (pp. 231–268). New York: Cambridge University Press.

Miller, P. A., Kliewer, W., Hepworth, J. T., & Sandler, I. N. (1994). Maternal socialization of children's postdivorce coping: Development of a measurement model. *Journal of Applied Developmental Psychology, 15*, 457–487.

Miller, S. M. (1979). Controllability and human stress: Method, evidence, and theory. *Behavior Research and Therapy, 17*, 287–304.

Miller, S. M. (1990). To see or not to see: Cognitive informational styles in the coping process. In M. Rosenbaum (Ed.), *Learned resourcefulness: On coping skills, self-control and adaptive behavior* (pp. 95–126). New York: Springer.

Miller, S. M., & Green, M. L. (1985). Coping with stress and frustration. In M. Lewis & C. Saarni (Eds.), *The socialization of emotions* (pp. 263–314). New York: Plenum.

Nolen-Hoeksema, S., Wolfson, A., Mumme, D., & Guskin, K. (1995). Helplessness in children of depressed and nondepressed mothers. *Developmental Psychology, 31*, 377–387.

Parke, R. D. (1994). Progress, paradigms, and unresolved problems: A commentary on recent advances in our understanding of children's emotions. *Merrill-Palmer Quarterly, 40*, 157–169.

Patterson, J. M., & McCubbin, H. I. (1987). A-COPE: Adolescent Coping Orientation for Problem Experiences. In H. I. McCubbin & A. I. Thompson (Eds.), *Family assessment inventories for research and practice* (pp. 225–243). Madison: University of Wisconsin Press.

Quiggle, N. L., Garber, J., Panak, W. F., & Dodge, K. A. (1992). Social information processing in aggressive and depressed children. *Child Development, 63*, 1305–1320.

Roberts, W., & Strayer, J. (1987). Parents' responses to the emotional distress of their children: Relations with children's competence. *Developmental Psychology, 23*, 415–422.

Rothbaum, F., Weisz, J. R., & Snyder, S. S. (1982). Changing the world and changing the self: A two-process model of perceived control. *Journal of Personality and Social Psychology, 42*, 5–37.

Rudolph, K. D., Dennig, M. D., & Weisz, J. R. (1995). Determinants and consequences of children's coping in the medical setting: Conceptualization, review, and critique. *Psychological Bulletin, 118*, 328–357.

Ryan, N. M. (1989). Stress-coping strategies identified from school age children's perspective. *Research in Nursing and Health, 20*, 111–122.

Saarni, C. (1984). An observational study of children's attempts to monitor their expressive behavior. *Child Development, 55*, 1504–1513.

Saarni, C. (1988). Emotional Competence: How emotions and relationships become integrated. In R. A. Thompson (Ed.), *Socioemotional development: Nebraska symposium on motivation* (Vol. 36, pp. 115–182). Lincoln: University of Nebraska Press.

Saarni, C. (1989). Children's understanding of the strategic control of emotional expression in social transactions. In C. Saarni & P. L. Harris (Eds.), *Children's understanding of emotion* (pp. 181–208). New York: Cambridge University Press.

Salovey, P., & Mayer, J. D. (1990). Emotional intelligence. *Imagination, Cognition, & Personality, 9*, 185–211.

Sandler, I. N., Tein, J. Y., & West, S. G. (1994). Coping, stress, and the psychological symptoms of children of divorce: A cross-sectional and longitudinal study. *Child Development, 65*, 1744–1763.

Scherer, K. R. (1984). On the nature and function of emotion: A component process approach. In K. R. Scherer & P. Ekman (Eds.), *Approaches to emotion* (pp. 293–317). Hillsdale, NJ: Erlbaum.

Shields, A. M., Cicchetti, D., & Ryan, R. M. (1994). The development of emotional and behavioral self-regulation and social competence among maltreated school-age children. *Development and Psychopathology, 6*, 57–75.

Spirito, A., Stark, L. J., & Williams, C. (1988). Development of a brief coping checklist for use with pediatric populations. *Journal of Pediatric Psychology, 13*, 555–574.

Strassberg, Z., Dodge, K. A., Pettit, G. S., & Bates, J. E. (1994). Spanking in the home and children's subsequent aggression toward kindergarten peers. *Development and Psychopathology, 6*, 445–461.

Taylor, D. A., & Harris, P. L. (1984). Knowledge of strategies for the expression of emotion among normal and maladjusted boys: A research note. *Journal of Child Psychology and Psychiatry, 24*, 141–145.

Terwogt, M. (1986). Affective states and task performance in naive and prompted children. *European Journal of Psychology of Education, 1*, 31–40.

Terwogt, M., & Olthof, T. (1989). Awareness and self-regulation of emotion in young children. In C. Saarni & P. L. Harris (Eds.), *Children's understanding of emotion* (pp. 209–237). New York: Cambridge University Press.

Terwogt, M., Koops, W., Oosterhoff, T., & Olthof, T. (1986). Development of processing of multiple emotional situations. *Journal of General Psychology, 113,* 109–119.

Thompson, R. A. (1988). Emotion and self-regulation. In R. A. Thompson (Ed.), *Socioemotional development: Nebraska symposium on motivation* (Vol. 36, pp. 367–467). Lincoln: University of Nebraska Press.

Thompson, R. A. (1993). Socioemotional development: Enduring issues and new challenges. *Developmental Review, 13,* 372–402.

Underwood, M. K., Coie, J. D., & Herbsman, C. R. (1992). Display rules for anger and aggression in school-age children. *Child Development, 63,* 366–380.

Weiss, B., Dodge, K. A., Bates, J. E., & Pettit, G. S. (1992). Some consequences of early harsh discipline: Child aggression and a maladaptive social information processing style. *Child Development, 63,* 1321–1335.

Wertlieb, D., Weigel, C., & Feldstein, M. (1987). Measuring children's coping. *American Journal of Orthopsychiatry, 57,* 548–560.

Wierzbicki, M. (1989). Children's perceptions of counter-depressive activities. *Psychological Reports, 65,* 1251–1258.

Wierzbicki, M., & Carver, D. (1989). Children's engagement in antidepressant activities. *Journal of Genetic Psychology, 150,* 163–174.

Wintre, M. G., & Vallance, D. D. (1994). A developmental sequence in the comprehension of emotions: Intensity, multiple emotions, and valence. *Developmental Psychology, 30,* 509–514.

Zahn-Waxler, C., Cole, P. M., Richardson, D. T., Friedman, R. J., Michel, M. K., & Belouad, F. (1994). Social problem-solving in disruptive preschool children: Reactions to hypothetical situations of conflict and distress. *Merrill-Palmer Quarterly, 40,* 98–119.

Zahn-Waxler, C., Cole, P. M., Welsh, J. D., & Fox, N. A. (1995). Psychophysiological correlates of empathy and prosocial behaviors in preschool children with behavior problems. *Development and Psychopathology, 7,* 27–48.

1. For recent empirical research, see special issues of *Developmental Psychology, 1989; Development and Psychopathology, 1995; Journal of Research on Adolescence, 1994; Monographs of the Society for Research on Child Development, 1994.* For reviews of this literature, see McCoy and Masters (1990) or Thompson (1988).

2. For reviews of emotion regulation during infancy and early childhood, see Kopp (1989) or Thompson (1988).

3. See Salovey and Mayer (1990) for a brief historical account of this view of emotions.

4. See Bretherton, Fritz, Zahn-Waxler, and Ridgeway (1986), Campos, Campos, and Barrett (1989), or Campos, Mumme, Kermoian, and Campos (1994), for recent functionalist accounts of emotion.

5. We have adapted our definition from Bretherton et al. (1986), Buck (1985), and Campos et al. (1989).

6. Dodge (1989).
7. Campos et al. (1989); Frijda (1988); Izard and Koback (1991); Scherer (1984).
8. Our definition of emotion regulation is adapted from Dodge (1989) and Thompson (1993).
9. Fischer, Shaver, and Carnochan (1990); Saarni, this volume; Salovey and Mayer, this volume.
10. Lazarus and Folkman (1984); Miller and Green (1985).
11. See Rudolph, Dennig, and Weisz (1995) for a recent review of conceptual perspectives on coping and different types of stressors.
12. Miller (1985).
13. Altshuler, Genevro, Ruble, and Bornstein (1995); Altshuler and Ruble (1989); Brown, Covell, and Abramovitch (1991); Franko, Powers, Zuroff, and Moskowitz (1985); Harris (1985, 1989); Kliewer (1991); Ryan (1989); Wertlieb, Weigel, and Feldstein (1987).
14. Wertlieb et al. (1987).
15. Kliewer (1991).
16. This distinction was originally proposed by Lazarus and Folkman (1984); Compas, Malcarne, and Fondacaro (1988).
17. This distinction was initially proposed by Rothbaum, Weisz, and Snyder (1982); Band and Weisz (1988).
18. Terwogt (1986).
19. Kliewer (1991).
20. Garber, Braafladt, and Weiss (1995).
21. Ryan (1989).
22. Miller (1979).
23. See Miller and Green (1985) for a review of this conceptual distinction.
24. Miller (1990).
25. Hoffner (1993).
26. Bull and Drotar (1991).
27. Dise-Lewis (1988); Kurdek (1987); Patterson and McCubbin (1987); Ryan (1989).
28. Wierzbicki (1989).
29. Dise-Lewis (1988).
30. Patterson and McCubbin (1987).
31. Bull and Drotar (1991); Spirito, Stark, and Williams (1988); Wertieb et al. (1987); Wierzbicki (1989).
32. Bull and Drotar (1991).
33. Wierzbicki (1989).
34. Spirito, Stark, and Williams (1988).
35. Bull and Drotar (1991).
36. Kurdek (1987); Ryan (1989).
37. Kurdek (1987).
38. Altshuler et al. (1995).
39. See Harris (1985) for a review of this literature.
40. See Bullock and Russell (1986) for a review of this literature.
41. See Gnepp (1989) for a review of this literature.
42. Wintre and Vallance (1994).
43. See Cole (1986) for a review of this literature.
44. Children can sometimes regulate emotion without demonstrating

knowledge of this regulation. For example, Terwogt, Koops, Oosterhoff, and Olthof (1986) found that 6-year-old children were able to inhibit sad feelings while listening to a story, but were unable to verbalize their strategies for doing so. We would argue that in studies relying on verbal self report, the emotional knowledge that children demonstrate is often constrained by their verbal abilities (Kopp, 1989; Thompson, 1988). This is why some investigators gather data from children by using a "funneling" process of inquiry in which children are asked open-ended questions and then focused probes (Saarni, 1989).

45. Altshuler et al. (1995).
46. Carlo, Knight, Eisenberg, and Rotenberg (1991); Denham (1986); Denham, Renwick-DeBardi, and Hewes (1994); Ianotti (1985).
47. Altshuler et al. (1995).
48. See Cole (1985) for a review of this literature.
49. Cole (1986); Cole, Jenkins, and Shott (1989); Fuchs and Thelen (1988); Taylor and Harris (1984); Underwood, Coie, and Herbsman (1992); Saarni (1984); Parke (1994).
50. Parke (1994).
51. Ballard, Cummings, and Larkin (1993); Cummings, Simpson, and Wilson (1993); Cummings, Zahn-Waxler, and Radke-Yarrow (1984); see also Eisenberg, Fabes, Nyman, Bernzweig, and Pinuelas (1994).
52. Cummings et al. (1984).
53. Ballard et al. (1993).
54. El-Sheikh (1994).
55. See Dix (1991); Downey and Coyne (1990); and Kaslow, Deering, and Racusin (1994) for reviews of this literature. See *Developmental Psychology, 1995* for a special issue of empirical research on this topic.
56. Garber, Braafladt, and Zeman (1991); Wierzbicki and Carver (1989).
57. Garber et al. (1991).
58. Nolen-Hoeksema, Wolfson, Mumme, and Guskin (1995).
59. Miller, Kliewer, Hepworth, and Sandler (1994).
60. Eisenberg, Fabes, Carlo, and Karbon (1992); Eisenberg, Fabes, Schaller, Carlo, and Miller (1991); Eisenberg, Schaller, Fabes, Bustamante, Mathy, Shell, and Rhodes (1988); Fabes, Eisenberg, and Eisenbud (1993); Roberts and Strayer (1987).
61. Eisenberg et al. (1988).
62. Eisenberg et al. (1991).
63. Parke (1994).
64. Asarnow, Carlson, and Guthrie (1987); Brenner and Salovey (1997); Ebata and Moos (1991); Eisenberg, Fabes, Murphy, Maszk, Smith, and Karbon (1995); Garber, Braafladt, and Weiss (1995); Garber, Braafladt, and Zeman (1991); Quiggle, Garber, Panak, and Dodge (1992).
65. Ebata and Moos (1991); Garber, Braafladt, and Zeman (1991); Quiggle et al. (1992).
66. Garber et al. (1991).
67. Asarnow et al. (1987); Garber et al. (1995); Sandler, Tein, and West (1994).
68. Brenner and Salovey (1997).
69. Ibid.
70. Sandler et al. (1994).
71. Garber et al. (1991); Quiggle et al. (1992).

72. Casey and Schlosser (1994); Dodge, Pettit, Bates, and Valente (1995); Eisenberg et al. (1995); Zahn-Waxler, Cole, Richardson, Friedman, Michel, and Belouad (1994); Zahn-Waxler, Cole, Welsh, and Fox (1995).
73. Zahn-Waxler et al. (1994).
74. Zahn-Waxler et al. (1995).
75. Casey and Schlosser (1994).
76. Shields, Cicchetti, and Ryan (1994).
77. Cummings, Hennessy, Rabideau, and Cicchetti (1994).
78. Manly, Cicchetti, and Barnett (1994); Strassberg, Dodge, Pettit, and Bates (1994).
79. Dodge, Pettit, Bates, and Valente (1995); Weiss, Dodge, Bates, and Pettit (1992).
80. Kaufman and Cicchetti (1989); Shields, Cicchetti, and Ryan (1994).
81. Crittenden, Claussen, and Sugarman (1994).
82. Shields et al. (1994).

EDUCATOR'S COMMENTARY

PATRICIA MOORE HARBOUR AND JILL STEWART

IT IS GRATIFYING TO HAVE Eliot Brenner and Peter Salovey provide a firm foundation for understanding what teachers experience daily in the classroom concerning students' emotion regulation. It is disturbing, however, that the development of emotion regulation does not currently have a definable place in the curriculum. It is most often incidental or sporadic, receiving sustained attention only during crisis situations.

The stressors in children's lives have increased dramatically in the past few years. Children are involved in serious situations with drugs, divorce, death, and physical and sexual abuse. They live with the stress of contemplating the likelihood of their own death. Juvenile suicide, gang behavior, and violent behavior have become commonplace. They signal the need for a comprehensive and holistic teaching approach that encompasses the development and management of emotions. Strategies for developing new, appropriate responses to emotion regulation must be addressed *now,* and at *all* levels of a child's development.

Current approaches to handling problem situations include dismissal from school, referral to counseling or therapy, medication, and/or parent-teacher conferences. Such external management strategies rarely do more than provide temporary solutions, since the source of the disturbance remains untapped. These measures can become more effective, however, if they are used in conjunction with teaching children to identify stressors, develop effective coping skills, and choose appropriate management strategies.

Research tells us that stressors are defined as controllable and uncontrollable and this delineation can provide a framework for effective strategies. We know with age, children's uses of internal and solitary strategies become more fine-tuned. In the classroom, we can turn this fine-tuning to advantage as a natural, integral part of the subject matter. For instance, in reading *Charlotte's Web,* a discussion of Wilbur's controllable and uncontrollable stressors would be effective in developing the students' emotion regulation.

We also know that as children get older they use more emotion-focused, internal strategies to deal with emotion regulation. Teachers can fine-tune these self/solitary-centered approaches or develop other methods. Just as research shows that girls rely on social support while boys use more physical activity to handle stressors, girls could be encouraged to use physical activity and boys use group support to regulate emotion. Or, a teacher could manipulate these groups so that problem solving is done with physical activity available to everyone for emotion regulation.

In teaching academic courses, we know how to evaluate a student's prior knowledge of a subject. But how do we evaluate a student's prior knowledge of emotion regulation? One way is through emotional cues—from past records, interaction with parents and siblings, and observing the child in interpersonal relationships with peers. Aside from using emotional cues as assessment tools, they need to be taught. Often children identify then internalize the wrong reason why something happens to them. An objective look at interpreting emotional cues can help them understand their feelings and reactions and aid in reducing personal pressure.

To counteract negative influences on emotional regulation, many school systems are investing in support services such as school social workers who go into the homes to work with parents. But parents are not the only influence in the home. Television, the Internet, videos, and music also impact emotion regulation. These influences are most often at their peak during "latchkey" times. In response, many schools have developed this block of time with productive programming for organized physical and tutorial activities. Schools are also beginning to employ conflict resolution specialists who work with students in developing non-physical alternatives to conflict.

The school's role in assessing and developing emotional regulation is critical. It, therefore, cannot be an add-on to the existing curriculum, for example, a time set aside once a week to discuss emotion regulation. Instead, teachers must incorporate opportunities for developing emotion regulation into the curriculum at every level and in every subject. Character development as seen in high school Shakespeare or elementary reading texts provides a context through which emotion regulation can be developed. Frustration over an algebraic equation can be acknowledged and discussed as part of emotion regulation.

Since the classroom teacher has the child for the largest part of the day, his/her impact on the child is significant. Coaching and modeling are imperative. Teachers who are uncomfortable with "touch-feely" issues must be educated to realize that emotions are just as important as intelligence if one is to educate the whole child. The research stated in this chapter provides valuable data that emotion regulation in children can be supported and enriched through positive teaching experiences, coping skills, and management strategies.

Aside from developing strategies based on research, this brief commentary raises several questions: What are the implications for a clearly articulated scope and sequence curriculum, kindergarten through twelfth grade, dealing with emotion regulation? What effective techniques can teachers apply to diagnose the level of emotion maturity and prescribe developmental strategies? In what ways can teachers incorporate and integrate the development of emotion regulation in an integrated curriculum? And what are the implications for school districts to provide training opportunities for teachers in understanding and teaching emotion regulation?

Brenner and Salovey's work is exciting news for teachers, for ultimately it is they who must convey the message of the importance of a holistic education. A curriculum that employs instructional strategies encompassing the needs of the whole child—intellectual development *and* emotion regulation—is the only one that will meet twenty-first-century educational needs.

CHAPTER 7

Promoting Children's Social-Emotional Adjustment with Peers

STEVEN R. ASHER AND
AMANDA J. ROSE

One day a fourth-grade teacher intercepted a note that was being passed up and down the rows in class. The note read, "If you hate Graham, sign here." The note was about to reach Graham's desk, and all the children had signed![1]

Approximately 10% to 15% of children, like Graham, have serious peer relationship problems at school. Over the past two decades, a substantial research literature has developed that focuses on these children. Several considerations motivate this work. First, the study of peer rejection in childhood provides opportunities to learn about the functions served by peer relationships and the kinds of adverse consequences that result from serious peer relationship problems. Second, research in this area is designed to help us better understand the types of skills children need to function effectively with peers and the types of skill deficits that account for children's difficulties. Third, researchers in this area share a strong interest in helping children whose social relationship difficulties place them at risk for other problems. Many of the regular contributors to the literature on children's peer relations have conducted intervention research aimed at helping children cope more effectively with the challenges of social relationships.

This chapter focuses on the social and emotional significance of peer relations in children's lives. Our goals are to characterize what it means to make a successful peer adjustment in childhood, to describe the consequences of peer relationship problems, and to highlight the progress that has been made in teaching social relationship skills to children who are poorly accepted by peers and lack friends. We begin the chapter by describing three different indicators of children's peer adjustment. One is the extent to which children are accepted by peers, the second is whether children have a best friend, and the third is the extent to which children's best friendships are characterized by positive or supportive qualities. Following this discussion, we examine the benefits that children derive from their peer relationships and the emotional consequences and school adjustment outcomes that can result from children having good versus poor relations with peers. In the final major section, we focus on social skills training interventions to improve children's peer acceptance and friendship. Here we describe interventions that have been successful in helping children gain peer acceptance, and we propose that the games context is a useful one for teaching social relationship skills.

INDEXES OF PEER ADJUSTMENT

Peer Acceptance

Much of the research on peer relations has focused on children's acceptance versus rejection by the peer group.[2] This important dimension of peer adjustment refers to the extent to which a child is liked by peers and accepted or included into activities. Children who are rejected by peers lose out on several important relationship provisions or benefits, especially companionship and having someone to provide help or to share resources and information. This dimension of peer adjustment is also fairly stable over time. About 30% to 50% of children who are rejected by peers during the middle childhood years turn out to be rejected when assessments are made 5 years later.[3] Even this percentage range may somewhat underestimate stability. For example, a child could be rejected in the first year of a 5-year longitudinal study and not in the fifth, but still be rejected in the second, third, or fourth years. The rejection of such children appears to be unstable when only the first and last years of the study are considered, but is actually rather stable when viewed from the perspective of the entire 5-year period. Certainly, few children in school would like to be rejected by peers in 2 to 4 years out of 5!

One plausible explanation for the stability of rejection is that children acquire reputations that operate as biases against them as they move from one grade level to the next in school. We know that how children view the behavior of peers is strongly affected by the reputation of the child being viewed.[4] However, even when children are placed into entirely new groups of previously unfamiliar peers, the degree to which children are accepted versus rejected is quite stable. Consider, for example, a remarkable study by Coie and Kupersmidt.[5] In this investigation, children were brought into a new play group where they played for an hour with three other children they had not previously known. At the end of each session, children were privately interviewed about their liking for each member of the play group. Results indicated that within three one-hour sessions children's acceptance in these new peer groups correlated highly with their peer standing in their everyday classrooms. By the end of six sessions the correlation was even higher. This important finding indicates that even when reputational biases are not a factor (i.e., the children did not previously know anyone in the new groups), rejection is a fairly stable phenomenon.

How can educators or researchers identify children who are highly rejected by their peers? Although it is tempting to rely on teacher judgments, these prove to be only moderately related to peers' actual sentiments. For this reason, practitioners as well as researchers have long used sociometric measures in which children directly report their feelings toward other members of the group. One widely used sociometric method is to ask children to nominate three classmates they like most and three classmates they like least.[6] Older children can be asked to do this by circling the names of classmates, whereas young children who do not yet read can be individually interviewed and asked to point to photographs of classmates. With this method, children who receive large numbers of "like most" nominations and few "like least" nominations are considered to be popular or well accepted. Children who receive few "like most" nominations and many "like least" nominations are considered to be rejected or poorly accepted.

Rating-scale sociometric measures also have been regularly used to assess how well children are accepted versus rejected by other children.[7] Here children are given a roster of their class and are asked to rate how much they like to play with each child in their class. Typically a 1–5 rating scale is used for students in mid-elementary through secondary school, with a "1" indicating that a child is not at all liked and a "5" indicating that a child is liked a lot. A simpler 1–3 scale is used for young children. A child's acceptance score is the average rating received from classmates. Again, use of photographs of classmates is recommended for young children.

Using nominations and rating-scale sociometric measures reveals large differences between children in how accepted they are by their peers. In most classrooms, one can find children who are extremely disliked by their peers. Consider a third-grader named Biff, for example. No one names Biff as their most liked classmate, and a total of 16 children out of

25 classmates view him as their least liked classmate. On the rating-scale sociometric measure, he receives an average rating of 1.56. How different Biff's life must be from that of Gary, who receives 4 "liked most" nominations, no "liked least" nominations, and an average rating-scale score of 3.86.

Much of the research on acceptance versus rejection in the peer group has focused on the behavioral characteristics of children that are associated with being liked versus disliked by peers.[8] In general, well-accepted children are far more likely to display prosocial characteristics such as friendliness, cooperativeness, helpfulness, and kindness. Poorly accepted children are less likely to display these prosocial characteristics and are more likely to exhibit aggressive, disruptive, or extremely withdrawn behavior. Low-accepted children and better accepted children differ on other characteristics as well; for example, higher acceptance by peers is associated with having a good sense of humor and being competent at schoolwork and sports.[9]

One noteworthy feature of the research on the behavioral correlates of peer acceptance has been attention to how children function in specific social situations. Research on the social task of "entry" exemplifies this sort of work. Investigators have examined in detail how children go about the process of entering into an ongoing interaction.[10] Likewise, other studies have been conducted into how children respond to conflicts over limited resources[11] or to situations where someone causes the child harm but the intent is ambiguous.[12] These studies are extremely helpful in guiding the design of intervention efforts because they provide a detailed portrait of how socially successful versus unsuccessful children respond to the challenges of particular social situations.

Situation-specific studies of social competence also help qualify overly simple generalizations about the behavioral style of well-accepted children. Consider, for example, the generalization about well-liked children being more prosocial than less well accepted children. Although this generalization has some validity, it does not mean that highly accepted children are necessarily more prosocial in every situation they encounter. Clearly some situations call for other sorts of responses, and the hallmark of social competence would seem to involve the ability to respond in ways that are appropriate to the social task at hand. A situation studied recently by Hopmeyer and Asher helps to illustrate this point.[13] These authors described for children a situation in which they have possession of an object and another child comes along and tries to take it away. This type of rights infraction does not warrant a prosocial response such as sharing or taking turns. Indeed, Hopmeyer and Asher found that well-accepted children are not more prosocial than poorly accepted children in this situation. Instead, what they do is engage in verbally assertive strategies that are designed to keep possession of their property while not escalating the situation or doing damage to the possibility of a future relationship with the peer.

Friendship Participation

A second dimension of peer adjustment is children's participation in friendship.[14] Whereas acceptance refers to a child's inclusion in the group as a whole, friendship refers to the establishment of a particular dyadic relationship between two children, a relationship characterized by strong mutual liking, a mutually expressed preference for one another, and a sense of a shared history. Friendship in school can be assessed by asking children to indicate the names of their best friends. Older children can do this by circling names on a class roster, and younger children can do this in individual interviews by pointing to photographs. Children are identified as friends if they reciprocally nominate one another. Although children's acceptance by peers and their participation in best friendship might be thought to be so highly overlapping as to make them virtually redundant criteria, research suggests that the two dimensions are sufficiently independent to make them of separate interest. There are children who are well accepted yet lack best friends in school, and conversely there are some poorly accepted children who do have close friends. Figure 7.1a shows the relation between acceptance and friendship for a sample of 881 children in third through fifth grades.[15] Figure 7.1b shows this same relation for a sample of 710 fourth- and fifth-grade students.[16] Both studies make clear the partial independence of the two dimensions.

Friendship is a particularly rewarding context for children in terms of the kinds of benefits they derive from their peer relationships. Some of the benefits parallel the benefits of group acceptance or inclusion but are experienced in more intense form. Other benefits are probably more specific to friendship. Researchers can learn about the provisions of friendship by directly observing children's behavior with friends.[17] There is also value in interviewing children, since children can be quite insightful about the expectations of a friend and about the benefits that are derived from friendship.[18]

The various relationship provisions or benefits derived from friendship have been regularly described over the past two decades.[19] Those who study personal relationships agree that the most basic friendship benefit or provision is companionship. In fact, it is hard to even conceptualize a friendship in which two children do not seek each other out and enjoy one another's company, whether at school or at home. Indeed, companionship is one of the earliest provisions to develop. Young children have been found to spontaneously mention playing together more often than they mention other aspects of their relationship.

Another important relationship provision is the formation of a reliable alliance. One way a reliable alliance between two children could be expressed is by their being predictable companions for each other. Children with friends have someone they can count on to sit with on the bus or at lunch and to play with at recess. Having a reliable alliance also involves

FIGURE 7.1

Percentages of High-, Average-, and Low-Accepted Children Who Have a Best Friend

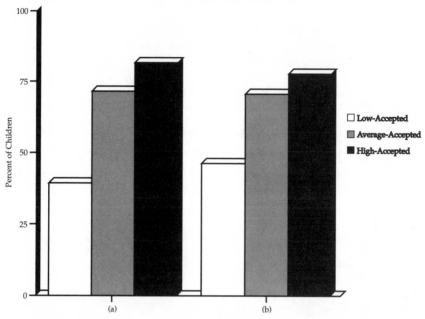

Note: (a) from Parker and Asher (1993b); (b) from a secondary analysis of Rose (1995).

being loyal. Friends stand up for each other and are trustworthy confidants for sharing problems or secrets.

Receiving help and guidance is also an important provision of peer relationships. Children need help and assistance with everyday tasks such as completing their homework and coping with personal problems. Children with close peer relationships can usually count on receiving help when it is needed, whereas children without social support may be left to carry their burdens alone.

All children at times experience insecurities about some aspects of themselves. Friends help children cope with insecurities and develop an image of themselves as competent and worthy. This process of validation and support can involve directly complimenting a friend or directly reassuring a friend about a problem or concern. A more indirect way that children can be validating is to provide a basis for social comparison. Friends are often similar to each other; by comparing values, beliefs, and abilities against one another, friends can gain confidence that their qualities as individuals are not aberrant. In addition, because friends generally admire and respect one another, finding similarities through social comparisons is even more validating than if the comparisons were made to another child who was not as respected.

Another provision, which can be seen as related to both helping and validation, is intimate exchange. Children with friends have someone with whom to talk over their worries and concerns. They have a sounding board, and they receive help in generating solutions to problems. Engaging in intimate self-disclosure may also be validating to a friend because it demonstrates trust in the friend and a respect for the friend's opinions and advice.

The argument has often been made that intimacy and emotional support and validation are provisions of friendship that do not develop until late childhood or even adolescence. Note, however, this conversation, which took place between Naomi (4 years, 6 months) and her best friend, Eric (3 years, 6 months). Young children will often express concerns or fears in the context of pretend play. In this pretend-play conversation, Naomi provides reassurance to Eric that he is liked and is not a "dumb-dumb."

NAOMI: No, it's time for our birthday. We better clean up quickly.
ERIC: Well, I'd rather play with my skeleton. Hold on there everyone. Snappers. I am the skeleton.
ERIC: I'm the skeleton. Ooh, hee . . . Hugh, ha, ha. You're hiding.
NAOMI: Hey, in the top drawer, there's the . . .
ERIC: I am the skeleton, whoa.
NAOMI: There's the feet [clattering].
ERIC: [Screams] A skeleton, everyone, a skeleton.
NAOMI: I'm your friend the dinosaur.
ERIC: Oh, hi dinosaur. You know, no one likes me.
NAOMI: But I like you. I'm your friend.
ERIC: But none of my other friends like me. They don't like my new suit. They don't like my skeleton suit. It's really just me. They think I'm a dumb-dumb.
NAOMI: I know what. He's a good skeleton.
ERIC: I am not a dumb-dumb, and that's so.
NAOMI: I'm not calling you a dumb-dumb. I'm calling you a friendly skeleton.[20]

Conversations such as this illustrate that even very young children rely on their friends for support and validation.

Friendship Quality

Psychologists have begun to focus on a third aspect of friendship adjustment, namely, the specific features or qualities of children's friendships. Friendships vary considerably with regard to how much they provide companionship and recreation, help and guidance, emotional support, and shared intimacy. They also vary in terms of how much conflict exists in the friendship and how easily conflict gets resolved. So it's possible to think of children's peer adjustment not only with regard to their level of peer acceptance and whether they have friends but also with regard to the nature of the friendships they develop.

Children can be quite articulate about the salient dimensions of their best friendships. By way of illustration, consider these quotes from a sample of third- through fifth-grade children. The children had participated in a large-scale study of children's friendships[21] and were asked to write down anything else they would like to about their best friend. The quotes are from a chapter by Parker and Asher.[22]

"He is my very best friend because he tells me things and I tell him things. He shows me a basketball move and I show him, too, and he never makes me sad."

"Me and Diana can count on trusting one another. Yesterday me and Diana talked about how our parents got a divorce and how the world is going to end."

"My friend is really nice. Once my nose was bleeding about a gallon every thirty minutes and he helped me."

"Jessica has problems at home and with her religion and when something happens she always comes to me and talks about it. We've been through a lot together."

"We love to be weird. We're never weird when the other's not there."

"Me and Tiff share our deepest darkest secrets and we talk about boys, when we grow up, and shopping."

"Someone bullied me and Carl stuck up for me and the kid hardly does it anymore."

"Me and Lamar makes each other laugh and we play kick soccer."

"Me and Kelly really don't talk about personal things. We mostly just play with each other."

"Me and Alexis act like we're cousins. We play a lot together. She comes over to my house a lot. Alexis comes and talks with me when I'm sad. She says we are best friends. I help her with homework. She helps me with my homework. And we play a lot together."

"I fight with Michelle too much and I really feel bad about it, but I can't stop. I'm afraid she wouldn't like me anymore."

"Angie is very special to me. If we get in a fight we always say we are sorry. And if she says she would play with me, she plays with me."

"She has another friend in our class named Charlene. Charlene always plays with Cindy. Me and Charlene don't always get along so I don't get to do too much with Cindy because Charlene won't let me."

"Tammy is really forgiving. She understands when I pick partners other than her."

"Becky always talks behind my back. It hurts my feelings. I will tell Becky something and she tells her other friends. And she always calls me and pranks me. And sometimes she can't keep a secret. And lies to me. Sometimes she isn't a great friend. But sometimes she's a fine friend!"

"Paul is not a critic."

These quotes suggest the richness, complexity, and challenges that friendship provides. It makes sense that children would differ not only in their degree of participation in best friendship but in the qualities or features of their friendships as well. Parker and Asher[23] recently created a measure of friendship quality (the Friendship Quality Questionnaire), which was adapted from a measure developed by Bukowski, Hoza, and Newcomb[24] and also built on the work of other investigators interested in qualitative features of children's friendships.[25] Third- through fifth-grade children were asked on a 40-item questionnaire to describe the nature of their best friendship. Each child's questionnaire was individually customized by inserting the name of the child's best friend into the questionnaire. Children were asked about six different friendship features: (a) *Companionship and Recreation* (e.g., "Jamie and I always play together at recess"); (b) *Help and Guidance* (e.g., "Jamie and I help each other with school work a lot"); (c) *Validation and Caring* (e.g., "Jamie cares about my feelings"); (d) *Intimate Exchange* (e.g., "Jamie and I talk about the things that make us sad"); (e) *Conflict and Betrayal* (e.g., "Jamie and I get mad at each other a lot"); and (f) *Conflict Resolution* (e.g., "Jamie and I always make up easily when we have a fight"). Each of these dimensions of best friendship was reliably measured. Furthermore, as will be discussed in the next section, each of these qualities predicted children's feelings of well-being at school. So it appears that there is validity to the idea of including friendship quality as one of the indicators of a child's adaptation to the world of peers.

One of the important questions that needs attention is whether the behavioral correlates of children's participation in friendship (and of children's participation in friendships of higher quality) are at all distinct from the characteristics associated with being accepted versus rejected by peers. In other words, does it take any special skills to make and keep (high-quality) friends, skills that go beyond the skills required to be accepted by others? Asher, Parker, and Walker[26] recently proposed that special skills are involved because there are certain social tasks that are unique to making and keeping friends. The social tasks of friendship described by Asher, Parker, and Walker are listed in Figure 7.2.

FIGURE 7.2

The Social Tasks of Friendship

1. Children must recognize and respect the "spirit of equality" that is the heart of friendship.
2. Children must be able to help when their friends are in need.
3. Children must be reliable partners.
4. Children must be able to manage disagreements and to resolve (and to the extent possible, prevent) more serious conflicts.
5. Children must recognize that friendships are embedded within the broader social network of the peer group and classroom, and children must be prepared to address issues within and outside the relationship that result from this fact.
6. Children must conceive of friendships as relationships that transcend a specific context, and children must possess social skills for initiating contact outside of the settings where they first met or typically interact.
7. Children must possess the skills and dispositions necessary to be perceived as fun, resourceful, and enjoyable companions.
8. Children must possess skills for self-disclosure.
9. Children must be able to express caring, concern, admiration, and affection in appropriate ways.
10. Children must be able to forgive.

Note: This figure is based on Asher, Parker, and Walker (1996).

Rose and Asher recently studied how children differ in their ways of responding to certain friendship tasks.[27] We wanted to learn whether responding competently to certain friendship tasks helps children make friends and achieve friendships of higher quality. We focused on the first five tasks listed in Figure 7.2 because these share the similar property of requiring children to manage the tension or conflict between their own individual self-interests and the interests of the friend or the relationship.

The first task was maintaining the "spirit of equality" of friendship. In friendships, children must participate as equals and be able to maintain reciprocity and balance in the relationship. This can be as simple as taking turns or sharing. A conflict of interests might arise in this task if it's the friend's turn to pick a movie they are going to see, but the child wants to pick the movie that he is excited about seeing. The second task was helping a friend when the friend is in need. In this task, a conflict of interests could arise if the friend wants help with homework or wants to talk over a problem, but the child has an alternative activity that she believes would be more enjoyable. The third task involved being a reliable partner to a friend. Children need to be available for their friends consistently rather than sporadically. In this task, a conflict of interests might occur if the friend wanted to sit together on the bus, but the child wanted to sit with a different classmate. The fourth task involved managing disagreements. A conflict of interests could arise if there were a dispute over a valued object, with the friend wanting it, but the child also wanting the object for herself. Lastly, the fifth task involved managing a friendship in the larger social context of the classroom and peer group. This means being able to coordinate multiple friendships and dealing with issues such as exclusivity and jealousy. A conflict of interests could arise in this task if a child wanted to play only with his friend, but his friend wanted to include other children. The child would have to either spend time with his friend under his friend's conditions or try to get what he wanted—time alone with his friend.

The Rose and Asher study, building on earlier investigations of children's goals and strategies in social situations,[28] was designed to test whether children's goals and strategies in response to these friendship tasks predicted children's friendship adjustment even after statistically controlling for how well children were accepted by peers. Fourth- and fifth-grade children were presented with 30 different hypothetical situations, with 6 situations representing each of the five social tasks of friendship.

For each situation, children were presented with six goals and asked to indicate on a 1 to 5 scale how much they agreed that each goal would be their goal. Because the five tasks each had the common characteristic of balancing one's own needs and the relationship's needs, the same six goals could be used in response to all 30 hypothetical situations. Some of the goals were rather prosocial, including a relationship goal ("I would be trying to stay friends") and a moral goal ("I would be trying to make sure things are done fairly"). Other goals were not prosocial. These included a retaliation goal ("I would be trying to get back at my friend") and a control goal ("I would be trying not to let my friend push me around"). Also assessed were a tension reduction goal ("I would be trying to keep myself from getting upset") and an instrumental goal that was worded differently for each vignette, but always involved trying to obtain something of personal value such as trying to see the particular movie the child wanted to see.

In a separate testing session, children were given the same 30 hypothetical situations, but in this case they were presented with six strategies after each vignette. They rated on a 1 to 5 scale how likely they would be to enact the strategies listed. Certain strategies were quite prosocial.

There was an accommodating strategy (e.g., "I would tell my friend that he could pick the movie") and a compromising strategy (e.g., "I would say that I would go to his movie this time if I could pick the movie next time"). Other strategies were not prosocial, including a verbally aggressive strategy (e.g., "I would tell him to shut up because I want to pick"), a friendship termination strategy (e.g., "I would tell my friend I won't be friends with him unless we go to the movie that I want to see"), and a leaving strategy (e.g., "I would just go away"). The final strategy was a self-interest pursuit strategy (e.g., "I would tell my friend that we should go to the movie I want to see").

Children's goals and strategies were found to predict both the number of best friends children had and also their friendship quality. Children with retaliation goals had fewer best friendships. In terms of strategies, children who proposed compromising strategies had a larger number of best friendships, whereas children with verbally aggressive strategies, leaving strategies, and friendship termination strategies had fewer best friendships.

Children's goals and strategies were also related to what the quality of their best friendship was like, as indexed by Parker and Asher's Friendship Quality Questionnaire. Specifically, children with relationship goals had less conflict in their best friendships. By contrast, children with retaliation goals, instrumental goals, and control goals had more conflict in their best friendships. Children's strategies were also related to how conflictual their best friendships were. Children who proposed compromising strategies had less conflict in their friendships. By contrast, verbal aggression, self-interest pursuit, leaving, and friendship termination were associated with more conflictual friendships. Of all goals and strategies, the retaliation goal was the strongest predictor of conflict within children's best friendships.

In sum, it appears that children's strategies and goals in friendship situations uniquely contribute to a child's friendship adjustment. Furthermore, it appears that children who have difficulty in their friendships engage in certain maladaptive patterns with regard to the sorts of benign conflicts that can arise in a friendship. It does not bode well for a child's friendships that the child wants to retaliate when the child and a friend disagree over which movie to see!

THE CONSEQUENCES OF PEER ADJUSTMENT

What consequences result from difficulties in peer relationships in school? The research we will discuss in this section focuses on children's emotional lives in school and on their academic adjustment as they proceed through school. Although more research is needed on these important topics, the evidence to date clearly indicates that adverse consequences are associated with peer relationship problems.

Emotional Consequences

It seems plausible that children who are poorly accepted by peers and lack friends would experience negative emotional consequences. Low acceptance and lack of friends mean that children will miss out on positive opportunities for inclusion, companionship and recreation, emotional support, and help and guidance. It is also known that children who are low in acceptance are more likely to receive negative responses from peers to their overtures.[29] Peer rejection is also associated with being victimized by peers.[30]

Many of the rejection experiences children have take place in school contexts that are relatively hidden from the eyes of teachers or other adults. Asher and Gabriel recently observed children all day at a school for a year to learn about the day-to-day lives of children with peer relationship problems.[31] Their sample of 35 children took turns wearing a wireless microphone and lightweight transmitter that transmitted to an observer who was standing up to 300 feet away. The observer wore audio-receiving equipment and held a camcorder. Observations of children on the playground, in the lunchroom, physical education, and the classroom indicated that children experience a wide variety of rejection experiences often outside of adult surveillance. Our preliminary attempts to code the kinds of rejection children encounter have resulted in a coding system with 5 broad types of rejection and 33 different subtypes![32] The following conversation took place in the lunchroom and illustrates the kind of overt rejection children experience in school. Maria, Ruth, Jeff, Jim, Mark, and Glen are negotiating their places in the lunch line:

RUTH TO GLEN: Get in front of him. Go on down. [Ruth is trying to get Glen to move away from her.]

GLEN TO RUTH: Where, here?

RUTH TO GLEN: Yeah. [Glen is still close enough he can hear the other children].

RUTH TO MARIA: He's sick [referring to Glen].

MARIA TO RUTH: He's a [unintelligible].

RUTH TO MARIA: I don't want to sit by him.

RUTH TO JIM: Will you stand right here? [Ruth asks Jim to stand next to Glen, which he does reluctantly].

RUTH TO JIM: I really don't want to stand by him. [Jim tries to get Mark and Jeff to take his place standing next to Glen. They refuse.]

Given this sort of rejection experience, it is not surprising that children who are rejected by peers suffer various sorts of emotional consequences. Indeed, children who are poorly accepted by their peers experience lower self-esteem[33] and more social anxiety[34] and depression.[35]

The largest body of research on the emotional consequences of peer relationship problems comes from studies of children's loneliness at school. Although much remains to be learned about loneliness in childhood, some important discoveries have been made. First it is clear that children have a basic understanding of the meaning of loneliness,[36] even as early as 5 and 6 years of age.[37] Furthermore, self-reports of loneliness can be reliably measured throughout childhood and adolescence.[38] Indicators of internal consistency of children's reports of loneliness are very high from age 8 and beyond, and are satisfactory with 5- and 6-year-olds. The level of loneliness that children report is also rather stable, even across a one-year period.[39]

As for connections between peer adjustment and loneliness, children with peer relationship difficulties have been found to report more loneliness than other children. This holds true at various age levels. Rejected children report more loneliness than other children in early adolescence,[40] middle childhood,[41] and in kindergarten and first grade.[42] Furthermore, none of the major school contexts where children spend time appears to provide a safe haven for poorly accepted children. In one recent study, children's feelings of loneliness were assessed in four school contexts: the classroom, the lunchroom, the playground, and physical education. In each of these contexts, low-accepted children were significantly more lonely than other children.[43]

Children's participation in friendship also is related to loneliness. Two recent studies found that participation in friendship and acceptance by peers made independent and additive contributions to children's well-being at school.[44] In other words, highly liked children reported more loneliness if they did not have a friend than if they did. Likewise, poorly accepted children reported less loneliness if they had a friend than if they did not.

Not only is having a friend an important buffer against feelings of loneliness, but the quality of that friendship is important as well. Parker and Asher[45] examined how features of friendship (companionship and recreation, help and guidance, validation and caring, intimate exchange, conflict and betrayal, and conflict resolution) related to children's feelings of loneliness at school. Each friendship quality predicted loneliness above and beyond the effects of acceptance. How friends function together, then, is an important determinant of loneliness. In sum, it appears that acceptance, friendship, and friendship quality make unique contributions to a child's emotional well-being.

School Adjustment

Children spend over 30 hours a week in school and are required to do so for at least 10 years of their lives. For most children, this is not a problem, since most children enjoy the social side of school regardless of whether they enjoy the academic side. As we know from research on loneliness, however, school can be very unpleasant for children who lack friends and are not accepted by their classmates. Consistent with this picture is growing evidence that children's peer relationships play an important role in children making a favorable school adjustment.

Two main lines of research demonstrate that the nature of a child's peer relationships is associated with good school adjustment. One area of research is concerned with the effects of peer relationships on children's transition to kindergarten. Studies here suggest that having positive peer relationships fosters positive school adjustment in children. In fact, children who become rejected by their peers during their first year of kindergarten are found to be less well adjusted to school than other children.[46] They report less positive attitudes, exhibit more school avoidance (as assessed by school absence and visits to the school nurse), and display lower school achievement.

As in research on loneliness, both participation in friendship and acceptance by peers are related to making a good school adjustment. In an initial study, Ladd and Price found that children who had familiar peers in their kindergarten class reported more positive attitudes about school and exhibited less school avoidance than did children without familiar peers in their class.[47] In a follow-up study, Ladd found that having friends (as opposed to just familiar acquaintances) in the kindergarten class was associated with having more positive school attitudes. Maintaining these friendships over time was also predictive of positive school adjustment.[48] These findings fit with earlier research from laboratory-based assessments suggesting that children are more comfortable exploring a novel context when they are with a friend.[49] Having a friend in the classroom should make school a more comfortable, less threatening environment.

Ladd's research also suggests that children who make new friends in kindergarten are more likely to achieve academically.[50] As Ladd notes, kindergarten children are encouraged to work in dyads or small groups for many of their activities, and those children who have been making new friends in the classroom may have the best opportunities for collaboration.

Recent research by Ladd and colleagues also suggests that not all friendships are equally helpful in encouraging school adjustment.[51] They examined the relationship between friendship quality and school adjustment in kindergarten. Positive features of friendship generally promoted positive school adjustment; kindergarteners who perceived their friends as validating and providing aid (both instrumental and emotional) were more likely to perceive their classmates as increasingly supportive throughout the school year. Furthermore, for boys, the more problematic aspects of friendship were related to making a poorer school adjustment. Specifically, boys who perceived their friendships as conflictual were more likely to show decreases in their school adjustment during the school year. They became more lonely at school, avoided school more, liked school less, and were less engaged in school as the year progressed.

The second area of research pointing to the link between peer relationships and school adjustment examines school dropouts. Two extensive literature reviews have been published on the topic of early peer relations and later life outcomes.[52] Each of these reviews gives major attention to school retention versus withdrawal. For example, Parker and Asher[53] reviewed 11 studies on this topic. Although the exact proportion of accepted and rejected children who dropped out of school varied from study to study, the finding was consistent across the 11 studies that children who were disliked were more likely than other children to drop out of school before graduation. In fact, averaging across studies, approximately 25% of rejected children dropped out of school compared to only 8% of other children.[54] In one study that examined both the effects of peer rejection and academic difficulties on dropping out, peer rejection was found to predict school dropout above and beyond the effects of academic difficulties.[55] Younger children, of course, do not have the legal option of dropping out of school. However, a longitudinal study of second- through seventh-grade children showed that rejected children were absent more often than other children.[56]

From these studies, we know that rejected children are more likely to be absent from school or drop out of school than other children. Many factors may account for the linkage between peer relationship problems and school adjustment. One can imagine that rejected students who avoid or leave school are attempting to avoid encountering aversive everyday life circumstances. It is also possible that rejected children get less help from their peers with schoolwork. Consider all of the ways friends call upon one another to succeed in school. These include getting missed notes, studying for a test together, and occasionally relying on one another for peer tutoring. Finally, it should be emphasized that many rejected children do not have good relationships with teachers.[57] As a result, adult as well as peer support is often lacking for these students.

SOCIAL RELATIONSHIP SKILLS INTERVENTIONS

The research discussed thus far provides strong justification for efforts to intervene with children who are rejected by their peers or lack friends. Children who are poorly accepted by their peers and who lack friends miss out on relationship benefits, experience negative emotional consequences, and make a less favorable school adjustment.

We also know that many low-accepted children would like help with peer relationship problems. In several recent studies, we asked children if they would like help with peer relationship problems.[58] In some studies, children were asked if they want to talk to the school social worker. In other studies, they were asked if they would like to get help from a "friendship expert" (rather than a specific school professional) if such a person worked at their school. Regardless of which way the question was asked, a substantial proportion of children expressed interest in getting help. For example, in one sample, about 47% of low-accepted children said "yes," 38% said "maybe," and only 15% said "no."

A striking pattern emerges when samples of low-accepted children are subclassified according to whether they are aggressive versus withdrawn in their behavioral style. The more withdrawn subgroup expresses a much greater interest in getting help.[59] This finding is interesting given that it is aggressive children rather than withdrawn children who are typically referred for services in schools.[60] Apparently, for low-accepted children overall, and for withdrawn children in particular, there is a special window of opportunity for providing help. These data on children's desire for help provide further rationale for intervening with children having peer relationship problems.

Two decades ago, a line of research began that is focused on improving children's peer acceptance in school by directly instructing children in social relationship skills.[61] The instructional procedures in these studies are cognitively based in that children are taught core concepts or principles of social interaction and are asked to reflect on their experience in light of the concepts. This approach to intervention is grounded in social learning theory, cognitive-behavioral modification, and experiential learning.

The children in these studies are selected using sociometric measures of peer acceptance. All of the studies provide either one-to-one or small-group instruction in which children are taught specific relationship concepts or principles. The particular relationship skills they are taught have been found to be correlated with peer acceptance in previous research. This approach to designing intervention content has been termed a "competence-correlates approach."[62] The effects of social skills intervention in these studies are typically assessed in terms of changes in behavioral style and changes in peer acceptance. With respect to research design, all of the studies compare intervention to no treatment (control) groups, with low-accepted children being randomly assigned to intervention or control conditions.

Although these intervention studies have the common goal of teaching children social skills in order to improve their relationships with peers, there are also significant differences among these studies. They differ in the age of the children selected, the specific sociometric measures and criteria used to select children, the types of social skills taught, the number of instructional sessions employed, the context in which instruction was offered, the types of outcomes assessed, and the degree of intervention success achieved.

In 10 out of 14 intervention studies reviewed most recently,[63] social skills intervention led to increased peer acceptance. This is a very encouraging pattern indicating that adults can make a substantial difference in the social lives of children. To illustrate the types of interventions that have been conducted, three studies will be described. These studies are a subset of those finding evidence of sociometric change.

Oden and Asher's study used a game context to teach social relationship concepts to third- and fourth-grade children.[64] Students were identified as low-accepted based on rating-scale sociometric measures. These children were then randomly assigned to one of three conditions. In the coaching condition, children were individually instructed for about 10 minutes in four broad social interaction concepts (participation, cooperation, communication, and validation-support). Children then had a chance to "try out the ideas" while playing a game for about 15 minutes with a same-sex, average-accepted classmate. Following the play session, children met individually once again for about five minutes with the adult, who asked them to reflect on each concept in light of their play experiences. Children participated in six of these sessions, each time with a different classmate and each time with a different game. During each session, the coach asked the children to describe instances when they used or did not use each of the ideas being coached. They were also asked whether each of the ideas helped "make the game fun to play." This may have had the effect of promoting attention to a particular game-playing goal, namely, having a good time with another child. In the second (peer-pairing) condition, children were paired with the same children who served as partners for the coached children. These children played the same games as the coached children for the same number of sessions, but they received no social skills instruction. The children in the third (control) condition also received no social skills instruction, nor did they get to play games with other children. Rather, they played games by themselves for the same number of sessions as in the coaching condition and in the peer-pairing condition. Results from this study indicated that coached children made significant gains in how well accepted they were by peers. A follow-up assessment made one year after the intervention indicated that these gains were maintained. Children in the two other conditions did not show comparable gains.

In Ladd's study, third-grade children were selected to participate based on low sociometric ratings and based on behavioral observations indicating that children were low on the skills to be taught.[65] The children were then randomly assigned to one of three groups. In the social skills training condition, children were paired with a same-sex child who also participated in the intervention. These dyads participated in a total of eight sessions. For the first six sessions, children were coached on and participated in guided rehearsal for three social skills: asking questions, leading (offering useful suggestions and directions), and offering support. During guided rehearsal, children practiced using the skills while playing games, and they were given feedback on their performance. In the seventh and eighth training sessions, the children first were asked to review from memory the concepts that had been taught. Then two other children, not otherwise participating in the intervention, were brought in to play the game with the focal children. After the game, the children discussed with the experimenter their perceptions of their performance and the other children's reactions. In the second condition, the attention-control condition, children received experience with peers and with the experimenter, but no social skills training. Children were paired in same-sex dyads for the same number of sessions as in the coaching condition. For the first six sessions, they received instructions from the experimenter on how to play the games, and they practiced playing the games. In the last two sessions, the children were asked to recall their activities from the previous sessions. Then two other classmates were brought in to play games with the dyad, and after the games the experimenter discussed with each child of the dyad what they learned by playing the games. In the third (nontreatment control) condition, children did not receive any training and were not brought out of the classroom. Results from this study indicated that children in the social skills training condition improved on two of the three skills (they did not improve on offering support), and they improved in their level of peer acceptance directly after the study and at the 4-week follow-up assessment.

An intervention study by Lochman, Coie, Underwood, and Terry addressed the importance of recognizing differences between subtypes of rejected children.[66] They examined the effects their intervention program had on aggressive-rejected and nonaggressive-rejected third-graders. Rejected children were identified using "like most" and "like least" nominations, and then were subclassified into aggressive-rejected and nonaggressive-rejected subsamples based on peer assessments of children's behavior. The intervention program consisted of 26 individual sessions and 8 small-group sessions. The aggressive-rejected children and the nonaggressive-rejected children were assigned either to the social skills training condition or the control condition. There were four components to the social skills training. First, children were taught social problem-solving skills (recognizing problem situations, not acting impulsively, examining alternative solutions). Second, children were taught skills such as negotiation and cooperation to enhance playing with other children and maintaining positive relationships. Third, children were taught how to enter a group of children more effectively. Fourth, the children were coached on how to cope with anger. This four-component intervention procedure involved direct instruction in concepts, role-playing, and practicing the concepts in small groups. The control condition received no social skills training or any other type of attention from the experimenters.

Results indicated that, following intervention, the coached aggressive-rejected children were seen as less aggressive by their teachers. They were also less rejected according to sociometric nominations and to teacher reports. Interestingly, at this same posttest the nonaggressive-rejected children did not evidence change as a result of the intervention. At a one-year follow-up test, teachers reported aggressive-rejected children who were coached to be less aggressive and more prosocial than children who were not coached. Also, at the one-year follow-up, rejected children (both aggressive and nonaggressive) who were coached were found to be more accepted by their peers and were perceived as less aggressive by their peers than rejected children (both aggressive and nonaggressive) who were not coached.

Studies such as these provide cause for optimism. Teaching children social relationship skills appears to be effective with many children who have peer relationship problems. Still, there is much to learn about the particular skills that should be taught, the particular training methods to be used, and the kinds of teaching contexts that are maximally effective.

We would like to conclude this chapter by suggesting that the game context may be a particularly useful setting in which to teach relationship skills. Two of the three studies just discussed used games as a context for intervention, and several of the other studies from the larger set of prior intervention studies also used games. The game context is very rich in terms of the wide variety of important social tasks that children are likely to face. These include initiating interaction, managing disagreement, coping with teasing, asking for help, cooperating, dealing with failure, and dealing with success. There is also a wide variety of goals children might pursue (see Figure 7.3).[67] As a result, the game context is one that provides an opportunity to help children with much of the complex goal coordination of everyday social life.[68]

FIGURE 7.3

Children's Goals in the Game-Playing Context

Goal Type	Description
Task Mastery	To master and develop game-playing skills; to enjoy involvement in task for its own sake
Performance	
Approach	To attain positive performance outcomes and positive peer judgments of game-playing competence
Avoidant	To avoid negative performance outcomes and negative peer judgments of game-playing competence
Rule-oriented/Fairness	To make sure the game is played by the rules
Relationship	
Approach	To initiate and maintain positive or neutral interactions and relationships with peers
Avoidant	To avoid negative interactions and relationships with peers
Self-protection	To protect oneself or retaliate against peer hostility and aggression
Dominance	To control or dominate others

Note: This figure is from Taylor and Asher (1984).

Using games as a context for social skills training has other advantages as well. First, children enjoy their participation so there is no problem motivating children to participate. Second, a positive mood has beneficial effects on learning so it is more likely that children will learn the concepts being taught. Third, just as low-accepted children tend to be less competent at schoolwork and sports, we suspect that they also tend to be less competent at games. One by-product of game-based interventions is that children have the opportunity to acquire new competencies at games. A personal experience brought this point home in a dramatic fashion. Several years ago, one of us (S.A.) and Angela Taylor were asked by a parent to coach their youngster, a 10-year-old with learning disabilities. We coached the child following Oden and Asher's procedure but were a bit discouraged that the child wasn't learning the ideas as quickly as we hoped. We did not look forward to our follow-up meeting with the parents and were therefore surprised to learn that they were thrilled with how their child was doing. When we asked why, they reported that their son was now inviting children over to play at home because he now knew lots of games!

Finally, we believe that games will provide a context for addressing some of the emotional challenges posed by peer relationships. Much of what makes social relationships difficult for children involves the kinds of emotions they have to deal with. Several of the game-playing tasks discussed above are likely to illicit strong emotions such as anger, anxiety, embarrassment, humiliation, relief, pleasure, pride, and joy. To date, school-based social skills interventions have given relatively little attention to children's emotional reactions to peer situations. There are many reasons for this, including the desire to maintain a boundary between education and therapy. Game situations may provide a productive and safe context for helping children with the emotional side of their lives with peers.

NOTES

References

Asher, S. R. (1978). Children's peer relations. In M. E. Lamb (Ed.), *Social and personality development* (pp. 91–113). New York: Holt, Rinehart, & Winston.

Asher, S. R. (1985). An evolving paradigm in social skill training research with children. In B. H. Schneider, K. H. Rubin, & J. E. Ledingham (Eds.), *Children's peer relations: Issues in assessment and intervention* (pp. 157–171). New York: Springer-Verlag.

Asher, S. R. (1993, March). Inviting children to self-refer. In C. Fisher (Chair), *Ethical issues in the reporting and referring of research participants.* Symposium conducted at the meeting of the Society for Research in Child Development, New Orleans.

Asher, S. R., & Coie, J. D. (1990). *Peer rejection in childhood.* New York: Cambridge University Press.

Asher, S. R., & Gabriel, S. W. (1993). Using a wireless transmission system to observe conversation and social interaction on the playground. In C. H. Hart (Ed.), *Children on playgrounds: Research perspectives and applications* (pp. 184–209). Albany, NY: State University of New York Press.

Asher, S. R., & Gottman, J. M. (1981). *The development of children's friendships.* New York: Cambridge University Press.

Asher, S. R., & Hymel, S. (1986). Coaching in social skills for children who lack friends in school. *Social Work in Education, 8,* 205–218.

Asher, S. R., & Parker, J. G. (1989). The significance of peer relationship problems in childhood. In B. H. Schneider, G. Attili, J. Nadel, & R. P. Weissberg (Eds.), *Social competence in developmental perspective* (pp. 5–23). Amsterdam: Kluwer Academic Publishing.

Asher, S. R., & Wheeler, V. A. (1985). Children's loneliness: A comparison of rejected and neglected peer status. *Journal of Consulting and Clinical Psychology, 53,* 500–505.

Asher, S. R., Gabriel, S. W., & Hopmeyer, A. (1993, March). *Children's loneliness in different school contexts.* Paper presented at the biennial meeting of the Society for Research in Child Development, New Orleans.

Asher, S. R., Hymel, S., & Renshaw, P. D. (1984). Loneliness in children. *Child Development, 55,* 1456–1464.

Asher, S. R., Parker, J. G., & Walker, D. L., (1996). Distinguishing friendship from acceptance: Implications for intervention and assessment. In W. M. Bukowski, A. F. Newcomb, & W. W. Hartup (Eds.), *The company they keep: Friendship during childhood and adolescence* (pp. 366–405). New York: Cambridge University Press.

Asher, S. R., Singleton, L. C., Tinsley, B. R., & Hymel, S. (1979). A reliable sociometric measure for preschool children. *Developmental Psychology, 15,* 443–444.

Asher, S. R., Zelis, K. M., Parker, J. G., & Bruene, C. M. (1991, April). Self-referral for peer relationship problems among aggressive and withdrawn low-accepted children. In J. T. Parkhurst and D. L. Rabiner (Chairs), *The behavioral characteristics and the subjective experiences of aggressive and withdrawn/submissive rejected children.* Symposium conducted at the meeting of the Society for Research in Child Development, Seattle.

Berndt, T. J. (1984). Sociometric, social-cognitive, and behavioral measures for the study of friendship and popularity. In T. Field, J. L. Roopnarine, & M. Segal (Eds.), *Friendships in normal and handicapped children* (pp. 31–52). Norwood, NJ: Ablex.

Berndt, T. J., & Ladd, G. W. (1989). *Peer relationships in child development.* New York: Wiley.

Berndt, T. J., & Perry, T. B. (1986). Children's perceptions of friendships as supportive relationships. *Developmental Psychology, 22,* 640–648.

Bigelow, B. J., & La Gaipa, J. J. (1975). Children's written descriptions of friendship: A multidimensional analysis. *Developmental Psychology, 11,* 857–858.

Boivin, M., Poulin, F., & Vitaro, F. (1994). Depressed mood and peer rejection in childhood. *Development and Psychopathology, 6,* 483–498.

Bukowski, W. M., Hoza, B., & Newcomb, A. F. (1987). *Friendship, popularity, and the "self" during adolescence.* Unpublished manuscript. University of Maine, Department of Psychology.

Bukowski, W. M., Newcomb, A. F., & Hartup, W. W. (Eds.). (1996). *The company they keep: Friendship during childhood and adolescence.* New York: Cambridge University Press.

Cassidy, J., & Asher, S. R. (1992). Loneliness and peer relations in young children. *Child Development, 63,* 350–365.

Chung, T., & Asher, S. R. (1996). Children's goals and strategies in peer conflict situations. *Merrill-Palmer Quarterly, 42,* 125–147.

Coie, J. D., & Dodge, K. A. (1983). Continuities and changes in children's social status: A five-year longitudinal study. *Merrill-Palmer Quarterly, 29,* 261–282.

Coie, J. D., & Koeppl, G. K. (1990). Adapting intervention to the problems of aggressive and disruptive rejected children. In S. R. Asher & J. D. Coie (Eds.), *Peer rejection in childhood* (pp. 309–337). New York: Cambridge University Press.

Coie, J. D., & Kupersmidt, J. B. (1983). A behavioral analysis of emerging social status in boys' groups. *Child Development, 54,* 1400–1416.

Coie, J. D., Dodge, K. A., & Coppotelli, H. (1982). Dimensions and types of status: A cross-age perspective. *Developmental Psychology, 18,* 557–570.

Coie, J. D., Dodge, K. A., & Kupersmidt, J. (1990). Peer group behavior and social status. In S. R. Asher & J. D. Coie (Eds.), *Peer rejection in childhood* (pp. 17–59). New York: Cambridge University Press.

Cole, D. A., & Carpentieri, S. (1990). Social status and the comorbidity of child depression and conduct disorder. *Journal of Consulting and Clinical Psychology, 58,* 748–757.

Crick, N. R., & Ladd, G. W. (1993). Children's perceptions of their peer experiences: Attributions, social anxiety, and social avoidance. *Developmental Psychology, 29,* 244–254.

DeRosier, M. E., Kupersmidt, J. B., & Patterson, C. J. (1994). Children's academic and behavioral adjustment as a function of the chronicity and proximity of peer rejection. *Child Development, 65,* 1799–1813.

Dodge, K. A. (1980). Social cognition and children's aggressive behavior. *Child Development, 51,* 162–170.

Dodge, K. A., Asher, S. R., & Parkhurst, J. T. (1989). Social life as a goal coordination task. In C. Ames & R. Ames (Eds.), *Research on motivation in education* (Vol. 3, pp. 107–135). Orlando: Academic Press.

Dodge, K. A., & Frame, C. L. (1982). Social cognitive biases and deficits in aggressive boys. *Child Development, 53,* 620–635.

Dodge, K. A., Schlundt, D. G., Schocken, I., & Delugach, J. D. (1983). Social competence and children's sociometric status: The role of peer group entry strategies. *Merrill-Palmer Quarterly, 29,* 309–336.

Duck, S. (1983). *Friends for life: The psychology of close relationships.* New York: St. Martin's Press.

Erdley, C. A., & Asher, S. R. (1996). Children's social goals and self-efficacy perceptions as influences on their responses to ambiguous provocation. *Child Development, 67,* 1329–1344.

Faust, J., Baum, C. G., & Forehand, R. (1985). An examination of the association between social relationships and depression in early adolescence. *Journal of Applied Developmental Psychology, 6,* 291–297.

Fine, G. A. (1981). Friends, impression management, and preadolescent behavior. In S. R. Asher & J. M. Gottman (Eds.), *The development of children's friendships* (pp. 29–52). New York: Cambridge University Press.

Franke, S., & Hymel, S. (1984, May). *Social anxiety in children: The development of self-report measures.* Paper presented at the third biennial meeting of the University of Waterloo Conference on Child Development. Waterloo, Ontario, Canada.

Furman, W., & Bierman, K. L. (1984). Children's conceptions of friendship: A multimethod study of developmental changes. *Developmental Psychology, 20,* 925–931.

Furman, W., & Robbins, P. (1985). What's the point? Issues in the selection of treatment objectives. In B. H. Schneider, K. H. Rubin, & J. E. Ledingham (Eds.), *Children's peer relations: Issues in assessment and intervention* (pp. 41–54). New York: Springer-Verlag.

Gottman, J. M., & Parker, J. G. (1986). *Conversations of friends: Speculations on affective development.* New York: Cambridge University Press.

Gottman, J. M., & Parkhurst, J. (1980). A developmental theory of friendship and acquaintanceship processes. In W. A. Collins (Ed.), *Minnesota symposia on child psychology* (Vol. 13, pp. 197–253). Hillsdale, NJ: Erlbaum.

Hartup, W. W., & Sancilio, M. F. (1986). Children's friendships. In E. Schopler & G. B. Mesibov (Eds.), *Social behavior in autism* (pp. 61–80). New York: Plenum.

Hayden, L., Tarulli, D., & Hymel, S. (1988, May). *Children talk about loneliness.* Paper presented at the biennial meeting of the University of Waterloo Conference on Child Development, Waterloo, Ontario, Canada.

Heinlein, L., & Spinner, B. (1985, April). *Measuring emotional loneliness in children.* Paper presented at the biennial meeting of the Society for Research in Child Development, Toronto, Ontario, Canada.

Hopmeyer, A., & Asher, S. R. (in press). Children's response to conflicts involving a rights infraction. *Merrill-Palmer Quarterly.*

Hymel, S. (1986). Interpretations of peer behavior: Affective bias in childhood and adolescence. *Child Development, 57,* 431–445.

Hymel, S., Freigang, R., Franke, S., Both, L., Bream, L., & Borys, S. (1983, June). *Children's attributions for social situations: Variations as a function of social status and self-perception variables.* Paper presented at the annual meeting of the Canadian Psychological Association, Winnipeg, Manitoba, Canada.

Ispa, J. (1981). Peer support among Soviet day care toddlers. *International Journal of Behavioral Development, 4,* 255–269.

Kupersmidt, J. B. (1983, April). Predicting delinquency and academic problems from childhood peer status. In J. D. Coie (Chair), *Strategies for identifying children at social risk: Longitudinal correlates and consequences.* Symposium conducted at the biennial meeting of the Society for Research in Child Development, Detroit.

Kupersmidt, J. B., & Patterson, C. (1991). Childhood peer rejection, aggression, withdrawal, and perceived competence as predictors of self-reported behavior problems in preadolescence. *Journal of Abnormal Child Psychology, 19,* 427–449.

Kupersmidt, J. B., Coie, J. D., & Dodge, K. A. (1990). The role of poor peer relationships in the development of disorder. In S. R. Asher & J. D. Coie (Eds.), *Peer rejection in childhood* (pp. 274–305). New York: Cambridge University Press.

Kurdek, L. A., & Krile, D. (1982). A developmental analysis of the relation between peer acceptance and both interpersonal understanding and perceived social self-competence. *Child Development, 53,* 1485–1491.

Ladd, G. W. (1981). Effectiveness of a social learning method for enhancing children's social interaction and peer acceptance. *Child Development, 52,* 171–178.

Ladd, G. W. (1983). Social networks of popular, average, and rejected children in school settings. *Merrill-Palmer Quarterly, 29,* 283–307.

Ladd, G. W. (1990). Having friends, keeping friends, making friends, and being liked by peers in the classroom: Predictors of children's early school adjustment? *Child Development, 61,* 1081–1100.

Ladd, G. W., & Asher, S. R. (1985). Social skill training and children's peer relations. In L. L'Abate & M. A. Milan (Eds.), *Handbook of social skills training and research* (pp. 219–244). New York: Wiley.

Ladd, G. W., & Price, J. M. (1987). Predicting children's social and school adjustment following the transition from preschool to kindergarten. *Child Development, 58,* 1168–1189.

Ladd, G. W., Kochenderfer, B. J., & Coleman, C. C. (1996). Friendship quality as a predictor of young children's early school adjustment. *Child Development, 67,* 1103–1118.

La Gaipa, J. J. (1981). Children's friendship. In S. Duck & R. Gilmore (Eds.), *Personal relationships: Developing personal relationships* (Vol. 3, pp. 161–185). New York: Academic Press.

Lochman, J. E., Coie, J. D., Underwood, M. K., & Terry, R. (1993). Effectiveness of a social relations intervention program for aggressive and nonaggressive, rejected children. *Journal of Consulting and Clinical Psychology, 61,* 1053–1058.

Marcoen, A., & Brumagne, M. (1985). Loneliness among children and young adolescents. *Developmental Psychology, 21,* 1025–1031.

Newcomb, A. F., & Bukowski, W. M. (1983). Social impact and social preference as determinants of children's peer group status. *Developmental Psychology, 19,* 856–867.

Newcomb, A. F., & Bukowski, W. H. (1984). A longitudinal study of the utility of social preference and social impact sociometric classification schemes. *Child Development, 55,* 1434–1447.

Oden, S., & Asher, S. R. (1977). Coaching children in social skills for friendship making. *Child Development, 48,* 495–500.

Parker, J. G., & Asher, S. R. (1987). Peer relations and later personal adjustment: Are low-accepted children at risk? *Psychological Bulletin, 102,* 357–389.

Parker, J. G., & Asher, S. R. (1993a). Beyond group acceptance: Friendship adjustment and friendship quality as distinct dimensions of children's peer adjustment. In D. Perlman & W. H. Jones (Eds.), *Advances in personal relationships* (Vol. 4, pp. 261–294). London: Kingsley.

Parker, J. G., & Asher, S. R. (1993b). Friendship and friendship quality in middle childhood: Links with peer group acceptance and feelings of loneliness and social dissatisfaction. *Developmental Psychology, 29,* 611–621.

Parkhurst, J. T., & Asher, S. R. (1992). Peer rejection in middle school: Subgroup differences in behavior, loneliness, and interpersonal concerns. *Developmental Psychology, 28,* 231–241.

Patterson, C. J., Kupersmidt, J. B., & Griesler, P. C. (1990). Perceptions of self and of relationships with others as a function of sociometric status. *Child Development, 61,* 1335–1349.

Perry, D. G., Kusel, S. J., & Perry, L. C. (1988). Victims of peer rejection. *Developmental Psychology, 24,* 807–814.

Putallaz, M. (1983). Predicting children's sociometric status from their behavior. *Child Development, 54,* 1417–1426.

Putallaz, M., & Gottman, J. M. (1981). Social skills and group acceptance. In S. R. Asher & J. M. Gottman (Eds.), *The development of children's friendships* (pp. 116–149). New York: Cambridge University Press.

Putallaz, M., & Sheppard, B. H. (1990). Social status and children's orientations to limited resources. *Child Development, 61,* 2022–2027.

Putallaz, M., & Wasserman, A. (1989). Children's naturalistic entry behavior and sociometric status: A developmental perspective. *Developmental Psychology, 25,* 297–305.

Renshaw, P. D., & Asher, S. R. (1983). Children's goals and strategies for social interaction. *Merrill-Palmer Quarterly, 29,* 553–574.

Renshaw, P. D., & Brown, P. J. (1993). Loneliness in middle childhood: Concurrent and longitudinal predictors. *Child Development, 64,* 1271–1284.

Rockhill, C. M., & Asher, S. R. (1997). *The contribution of diverse behavioral characteristics to peer acceptance for boys and girls.* Manuscript submitted for publication.

Rose, A. J. (1995). *The relationship between children's social goals, social strategies, and friendship adjustment.* Unpublished master's thesis, University of Illinois, Urbana-Champaign.

Rose, A. J., & Asher, S. R. (1997). *Children's goals and strategies in response to conflicts within a friendship.* Manuscript submitted for publication.

Russell, D., Peplau, L. A., & Ferguson, M. L. (1978). Developing a measure of loneliness. *Journal of Personality Assessment, 42,* 290–294.

Rutter, M., Cox, A., Tupling, C., Berger, M., & Yule, W. (1975). Attainment and adjustment in two geographical areas: 1. The prevalence of psychiatric disorder. *British Journal of Psychiatry, 126,* 493–509.

Schwarz, J. C. (1972). Effects of peer familiarity on the behavior of preschoolers in a novel situation. *Journal of Personality and Social Psychology, 24,* 276–284.

Shantz, D. W. (1986). Conflict, aggression, and peer status: An observational study. *Child Development, 57,* 1322–1332.

Slaby, R. G., & Guerra, N. G. (1988). Cognitive mediators of aggression in adolescent offenders: 1. Assessment. *Developmental Psychology, 24,* 580–588.

Taylor, A. R., & Asher, S. R. (1984). Children's goals and social competence: Individual differences in a game-playing context. In T. Field, J. L. Roopnarine, & M. Segal (Eds.), *Friendships in normal and handicapped children* (pp. 53–78). Norwood, NJ: Ablex.

Taylor, A. R., & Trickett, P. K. (1989). Teacher preference and children's sociometric status in the classroom. *Merrill-Palmer Quarterly, 35,* 343–361.

Williams, G. A., & Asher, S. R. (1992). Assessment of loneliness at school among children with mild mental retardation. *American Journal of Mental Retardation, 96,* 373–385.

Wright, P. H. (1978). Toward a theory of friendship based on a conception of self. *Human Communication Research, 4,* 196–207.

1. Asher and Hymel (1986).
2. For reviews, see Asher and Coie (1990).
3. Coie and Dodge (1983); Newcomb and Bukowski (1984).
4. Dodge (1980); Hymel (1986).
5. Coie and Kupersmidt (1983).
6. Coie, Dodge, and Coppotelli (1982); Newcomb and Bukowski (1983); Parkhurst and Asher (1992); Kupersmidt and Patterson (1991).
7. Oden and Asher (1977); Asher, Singleton, Tinsley, and Hymel (1979); Ladd (1981); Hymel (1986); Putallaz and Sheppard (1990); Renshaw and Brown (1993).
8. See Coie, Dodge, and Kupersmidt (1990) for a review.
9. See Rockhill and Asher (1997) for evidence about the relative contributions of these characteristics.
10. Putallaz and Gottman (1981); Dodge, Schlundt, Schocken, and Delugach (1983); Putallaz (1983); Putallaz and Wasserman (1989).
11. Shantz (1986); Chung and Asher (1996).
12. Dodge (1980); Dodge and Frame (1982); Slaby and Guerra (1988); Erdley and Asher (1996).
13. Hopmeyer and Asher (in press).
14. For research on friendship, see Asher and Gottman (1981); Gottman and Parker (1986); Berndt and Ladd (1989); Bukowski, Newcomb, and Hartup (1996).
15. Parker and Asher (1993b).
16. From a secondary analysis of Rose (1995).
17. See Gottman and Parkhurst (1980) and Fine (1981) for examples.
18. For example, Bigelow and La Gaipa (1975); Furman and Bierman (1984).
19. For example, Asher (1978); Wright (1978); La Gaipa (1981); Duck (1983); Furman and Robbins (1985); Hartup and Sancilio (1986); Asher and Parker (1989).

20. Gottman and Parkhurst (1980, p. 245).
21. Parker and Asher (1993b).
22. Parker and Asher (1993a, pp. 270–271).
23. Parker and Asher (1993b).
24. Bukowski, Hoza, and Newcomb (1987).
25. For example, Berndt (1984); Berndt and Perry (1986).
26. Asher, Parker, and Walker (1996).
27. Rose and Asher (1997).
28. For example, Renshaw and Asher (1983); Chung and Asher (1996); Erdley and Asher (1996).
29. Dodge et al. (1983); Ladd (1983).
30. Perry, Kusel, and Perry (1988).
31. Asher and Gabriel (1993).
32. Manuscript in preparation by Asher, Gabriel, and Rose.
33. Kurdek and Krile (1982); Patterson, Kupersmidt, and Griesler (1990).
34. Franke and Hymel (1984).
35. Faust, Baum, and Forehand (1985); Cole and Carpentieri (1990); Kupersmidt and Patterson (1991); Boivan, Poulin, and Vitaro (1994).
36. Hayden, Tarulli, and Hymel (1988); Williams and Asher (1992).
37. Cassidy and Asher (1992).
38. Russell, Peplau, and Ferguson (1978); Asher, Hymel, and Renshaw (1984); Asher and Wheeler (1985); Heinlein and Spinner (1985); Marcoen and Brumagne (1985); Cassidy and Asher (1992); Parkhurst and Asher (1992); Crick and Ladd (1993).
39. Hymel, Freigang, Franke, Both, Bream, and Borys (1983); Renshaw and Brown (1993).
40. Parkhurst and Asher (1992).
41. Asher and Wheeler (1985); Crick and Ladd (1993).
42. Cassidy and Asher (1992).
43. Asher, Gabriel, and Hopmeyer (1993).
44. Parker and Asher (1993b); Renshaw and Brown (1993).
45. Parker and Asher (1993b).
46. Ladd (1990).
47. Ladd and Price (1987).
48. Ladd (1990).
49. Schwarz (1972); Ispa (1981).
50. Ladd (1990).
51. Ladd, Kochenderfer, and Coleman (1996).
52. Parker and Asher (1987); Kupersmidt, Coie, and Dodge (1990).
53. Parker and Asher (1987).
54. Asher and Parker (1989).
55. Kupersmidt (1983).
56. DeRosier, Kupersmidt, and Patterson (1994).
57. Taylor and Trickett (1989).
58. Asher, Zelis, Parker, and Bruene (1991); Asher (1993).
59. Asher et al. (1991).
60. Rutter, Cox, Tupling, Berger, and Yule (1975).
61. For reviews of this research see Ladd and Asher (1985); Coie and Koeppl (1990); and Asher, Parker, and Walker (1996).
62. Asher (1985).

63. Asher, Parker, and Walker (1996).
64. Oden and Asher (1977).
65. Ladd (1981).
66. Lochman, Coie, Underwood, and Terry (1993).
67. Taylor and Asher (1984).
68. Dodge, Asher, and Parkhurst (1989).

EDUCATOR'S COMMENTARY

ROBERT (CHIP) WOOD

JEANNETTE HAVILAND-JONES, Professor of Psychology, Rutgers University (see chapter 8), related the following account during an editorial gathering of the authors of this volume. I found it a fitting exemplar for the points I wish to make as I try to tie Asher and Rose's research to the reality of everyday life in today's public schools and to the challenges of institutional reform. (Thanks to Dr. Haviland-Jones for permission to share this account in her own words.)

HELPING TO FIX THE SUPERMARKET

"One of my students had been a grocery-store checkout person in the summer for her job and she was all adamant and embroiled with how nasty mothers are to their infant children in grocery stores—we've all seen this—the child reaches for something and the mother smacks it; the child cries and the mother smacks it. And you sit there as the person in the grocery store and you say, 'This is terrible, this shouldn't be happening, what should I do as a concerned citizen?' But mostly you're saying to yourself, 'This is a terrible mother!' You really are saying that; I find myself saying that—looking at this mother and saying, 'This is a terrible mother.' But why don't I say to myself, 'This is a terrible situation!' If I really think about this, if I stand back, I know this mother has been at work for 8 or 10 hours, I know she's been on the subway stuck somewhere, I know she's got home and discovered she now has to go to the grocery store with children who have been in day care who are miserable—she's miserable—but who's going to do her grocery shopping if she doesn't? Who's going to watch her children if she doesn't take them with her?

"If you really said to yourself, 'So all that I do in this world is that I own a grocery store and I don't like the fact that mothers smack their children in my grocery store. What will I do about it? Will I train mothers? No, I'll be much more innovative. I'll make a corner for mothers to sit with their children and pay an extra dollar for a runner to go out and get their stuff and bring it to her, or I'll set a television there and get a child-care person and let the mother have five minutes to wander through the store and grab her own attractive packages.' If you just said to yourself, 'Maybe we don't have to train the mothers, maybe they just need a break.' But we don't do that in schools. If you just looked at the kids who are really being bad and smacking somebody and, instead of saying, 'We don't like that, let's train them not to do this,' we said, 'Maybe the story is more like the mothers in the grocery store, and how come their school is like the grocery store? That's making it so tempting for them to act in a bad way and offering them so little support for their life situation. That makes this a very likely option for them—to smack somebody.' We really need to stand back."

Haviland-Jones points out that the children we seek to serve are often the messengers telling us what we need to do to "fix the supermarket" if only we will listen, watch, and pay attention, not just to the child but also to the way the environment we have created for the child impacts the child.

To continue the analogy, Asher and Rose, in their chapter, provide compelling evidence for the argument that peer relationships should be viewed as the "shopping cart" in the "supermarket." Children who have major difficulty in forming positive peer relationships will miss out on most of the shopping, even if we have made the store more user friendly. In school, these children will miss opportunities for inclusion, companionship and recreation, emotional support, and help and guidance. Asher and Rose's most compelling research (Rose, 1995) argues that to fill the shopping cart children need new strategies for handling problematic situations and that the ability to see and set goals for themselves that are prosocial and relationship enhancing, rather than retaliatory, may be the most important strategy of all. Asher and Rose commendably make the point that intervention can be productive for such children and argue for a strategy that involves the use of games and the acquisition of game-playing skills as a way to help provide the requisite social skills that can change the nature of friendship. In reviewing the literature in this field they point to even more ways that children's peer adjustment impacts on later school adjustment and lasting friendship formations. They also clarify different ways (such as sociometric scales) for identifying different peer relationships in the classroom. I found their ideas about the importance of "reliable alliances" for children and for children's development of differing friendship skills such as the "spirit of equality," managing disagreements, and coordinating multiple friendships important to practitioners attempting to understand how to help individual children in their classrooms. Their chapter is rich with examples of research that strikingly illustrate the impact of rejection experiences, social anxiety, and loneliness on the school experience of children as well as the positive results to be gained from having direct instruction in social skills for children at risk. In 10 out of 14 studies cited, "Social skills intervention led to increased peer acceptance" (p. 212). Asher and Rose clearly demonstrate that direct, intensive intervention will help the individual child who has undeveloped strategies for developing positive peer relationships. When children lack social skills, teachers and other school professionals such as counselors, social workers, and principals have the responsibility to help children learn how to be successful in individual encounters. This will require small-group instruction, one-on-one counseling, and intervention with parents and caretakers. Many helpers are needed in the supermarket.

At the same time we need to be helping to change the supermarket. Unfortunately, the environments of many of our schools militate against productive friendship development for all children because of a number of structural and functional values transmitted through curriculum, teaching methods, and assessment practices. Take, for instance, the value of competition. Being first, getting A's, running the fastest, being the prettiest, reading the best, testing the highest—all are values fostered regularly in school, excluding large numbers of children since there is so little room at the top. These values of "excellence" transmit to children a clear model for functioning in the world, including the world of friendship. Even while teachers are speaking words of kindness toward all, teachers themselves are feeling the pressure of competition from their adult peers and superiors to perform above the next class, the next school, the next test. To help fix the supermarket we must balance the amount of competitive activity of each day with an atmosphere of cooperative work and play. We must, as my colleague Ruth Charney has written, "teach children to care" by creating school structures and strategies that reinforce such behavior.[1]

At Northeast Foundation for Children, which I helped begin in 1981, we have developed an approach called The Responsive Classroom®, which is assisting public school teachers to establish ways to make friendship as important as winning, to make every individual in a class as important as every other.[2]

Clearly defined structures such as "Morning Meeting," where children routinely greet each other (and not just their best friends), share news, and engage in fun and meaningful activities at the beginning of each day, are helping to change the environment of schools.[3] Other programs referenced in this volume and through the Collaborative for the Advancement of Social and Emotional Learning (CASEL) are providing practitioners with avenues for both helping individual children and for helping teachers to adjust the academic and social environments in which children's friendships form.[4]

For a moment, let's examine the many ways research might be applied to helping to fix the supermarket, that is, addressing the daily environment of the classroom to make it more "user friendly"; or, in the context of Asher and Rose's interest, more "friendship friendly." We must balance the way we see intervention. Practitioners and researchers ought to do "environmental impact studies" of their classrooms and programs in addition to providing significant assistance to individual children. Asher and Rose help us to understand how useful the game context is for improving the social skills of individual children. Games are also important in the total classroom context for all children at all developmental levels. Yet they often disappear as a regular part of classroom life after third grade. In an often shortsighted way, too many schools wrongly argue that the individual's "time on task" is more important than cooperation and friendship. Asher and Rose make it clear that children without social skills and friendship will be the ones who drop out of school, never completing their tasks. Teachers must not only utilize games and cooperative activity in the classroom, they can and must teach recess and lunch for all their students with the same intentionality that they teach reading and math. This changes the values orientation of students. Competition, for instance, is then viewed in a more balanced way. There is room for relay races and soccer games. There is also room for noncompetitive recreation and "initiative" activities adapted from the field of outdoor education that build trust and a sense of the group working toward a common goal. Trying to get the whole class across a "poison peanut-butter pit" (boards raised on stumps, angled across the playground) changes the class's perception of itself as a group, in much the way Asher and Rose argue individual children need new understanding of their personal friendship goals.

Asher's 1991 and 1993 studies of children's desire for assistance with peer relationships found that children would like to talk with a "friendship expert" about their friendship issues. How important it is for schools to have trained counselors, social workers, principals, nurses, and other adults to be there for individual children who need such help. It is, in fact, criminal that many of these professionals are the first cut from payrolls in times of budget shortfalls. Children should be guaranteed the right to access these professionals during any schoolday, just as they are guaranteed a crisis intervention team at the occurrence of a shooting or other major trauma. It is true that individual children are in individual crisis each and every schoolday in a way that is beyond the scope of the individual classroom teacher. But as we begin to also help fix the supermarket, children can come to know and expect that their regular classroom teachers are also trained "friendship experts" with all the skills to help them resolve their issues, especially in the group context. Teachers can be given professional training in social skills development and intervention strategies as a requisite part of teacher education. They can be supervised on these issues as well as on their delivery of curriculum. In fact, friendship can become a part of the reading, math, social studies, and science curriculum; a part of the curriculum of lunch and the hallways and the buses; a part of the curriculum of the entire schoolday.

This is the effort we are engaged in through our work in The Responsive Classroom, as are other practitioners in other programs. In some of our research efforts, guided by the work of Stephen N. Elliott at the University of Wisconsin-Madison, we are beginning to understand the impact of social skills intervention in the classroom with a whole class of students.[5] This is one avenue Asher points to as an important next step in the research he has helped to pioneer. While continued research on children's individual strategies remains vital, this next step would truly bring the field of research in peer relations into a closer working relationship with regular classroom teachers using prosocial strategies as an integral part of daily classroom life. From this we might learn more about increasingly useful ways to help children care and learn. Asher and Rose helped me as a practitioner working with whole classes and school reform to remember and support the interventions they have helped to develop for individual children. They also validated for me the critical importance of continuing to help teachers to use whole group strategies to make the classroom environment more "friendship friendly"—to help fix the supermarket.

NOTES

References

Asher, S. R. (1993, March). Inviting children to self-refer. In C. Fisher (Chair), *Ethical issues in the reporting and referring of research participants*. Symposium conducted at the meeting of the Society for Research in Child Development, New Orleans, LA.

Asher, S. R., Zelis, K. M., Parker, J. G., & Bruene, C. M. (1991, April). Self-referral for peer relationship problems among aggressive and withdrawn low-accepted children. In J. T. Parkhurst & D. L. Rabiner (Chairs), *The behavioral characteristics and the subjective experiences of aggressive and withdrawn/submissive rejected children*. Symposium conducted at the meeting of the Society of Research in Child Development, Seattle, WA.

Rose, A. J. (1995). *The relationship between children's social goals, social strategies, and friendship adjustment*. Unpublished master's thesis, University of Illinois, Urbana-Champaign.

1. Ruth Charney, *Teaching children to care* (Northeast Foundation for Children, 1991).
2. For further information about The Responsive Classroom contact Northeast Foundation for Children, 71 Montague City Road, Greenfield, MA 01301.

3. CASEL, Department of Psychology, University of Illinois at Chicago, 1007 West Harrison Street, Chicago, IL 60607-7137.
4. As related by Steve Asher during an author's roundtable, Fetzer Institute, Kalamazoo, MI, January, 1996.
5. See Stephen N. Elliott, *Caring to learn: A report on the positive impact of a social curriculum* (Greenfield, MA: NEFC, 1993).

PART III

Applications

CHAPTER 8

The Questions of Development in Emotion

JEANNETTE HAVILAND-JONES, JANET L. GEBELT, AND JANICE C. STAPLEY

There is a child in my class of second-graders who cries all the time. If I mark something wrong on her math, she cries. If she is late, she cries. If one of the children makes a rude remark, she cries. I tell her to stop, I try to distract her, I give her quiet time, but still she cries. How do I stop this crying?

This crying problem is typical of questions that come our way as researchers on emotions.[1] If the question were not about crying, it probably would have been about hostility. At the same meeting someone else wanted guidance for a child who "kicked his desk" among other angry behaviors. Always we are asked about *stopping* behavior labeled "emotional." We have never been asked to *enhance* it.

One is seldom taught to think of emotion as an important ability, to say something like, "I have a child who seems to have an outstanding ability to be surprised and filled with wonder. How can I help him to realize his potential to explore?" It is even less likely that we teach the wisdom of asking about the crying child as if her crying heralded an unusual capacity for concentration, perhaps for empathy or for inward reflection. She might have the makings of a poet or a great philanthropist. On the side of the teacher's ability to analyze we do not teach people how to solve questions such as, "This child in my class cries all the time, but I am uncertain as to whether it is an anxious, fearful cry or a cry of sadness, or some combination. I think I should figure this out before I make any plans."

On the other hand, we seem to have some working knowledge of maturity in emotion. Most of us know that if the crying child is in the tenth grade rather than the second, then the crying carries ever more complex meaning. But what else might change between second grade and tenth grade? In what other ways are the emotions of adolescents more mature, complex, and meaningful than the emotions of second-graders? There is little formal teaching of these changes.

QUESTIONS OF EMOTION FOR RESEARCHERS

For us, as experts on emotion, we know that the way a question is asked reflects values, expectations, and knowledge. If one always asks about minimizing, regulating, or managing emotional influences—about getting rid of or reducing the crying or the anger—there is at the outset a narrow bias to the questions that one might ask. In the research domain our more positive bias largely reflects the spirit of recent trends emphasizing emotional "intelligence" or "literacy."[2,3] We are interested in people being more literate in emotion so that new and different frames of reference can be established.

In our research we usually ask about the uses of emotion in adaptive and self-organizing behavior and thought. To illustrate this in the present chapter we will cover (roughly) the Acquisition, Refinement, and Transformation (ART)[4] of children's emotion across the school-age years and into adolescence, a notably interesting period for emotional development. First, we will present a quick overview of early acquisition and refinement, including infant and child behaviors. Then, moving into the older years, we will include some work that we have done on children's subjective views of their emotional lives. We will also show how even psychopathology—depression—is transformed by age-related emotional changes during late childhood and adolescence.

Most of us are self- or home-taught emotion. Most people do not have the systematic second-order knowledge of emotion that comes with formal education, only the rudiments. We do not have a vocabulary for emotional processes or an assessment system. It is as if we had gone no further with language than to learn to speak the local "patois" at our mothers' knees. When one has a formal approach to emotion, one has many more and different questions to ask. Asking an emotion researcher about the crying child is like asking an artist or a pomologist if apples are red. The real color in red apples is not just red, and apples are only "red" in certain species and at certain times. Similarly with emotions. Saying something like "Smile and be happy" or "Crying is inappropriate" is just as useful as saying that "Apples are red." It is a shorthand convention and is not *untrue*, but knowledge allows the convention to be better understood and its limitations understood as well.

QUESTIONS OF EMOTION FOR EDUCATORS

Two questions concern education and emotion when they are considered together. One question is whether emotional knowledge is a domain of learning for some professionals, in particular, educators. To answer this question, we will present fairly new research about the emotional development of school-age children and adolescents, information that may be considered particularly useful to teachers and educational administrators. Because even this, completely covered, would fill several texts, we have chosen just a few pieces to illustrate the emotional development of children, and we have attempted to make a few interpretations that bring it more clearly into the realm of education.

Secondly, a larger issue is whether knowledge about emotion should be a general curricular matter for all public schools. Does it provide the basis for skills broadly needed by all voting citizens? To what extent is emotional literacy a skill to be added to the school curriculum? An informed educator could proceed to make decisions about this second issue much better than we as researchers could. Nevertheless, we will not restrain ourselves from making some illustrations of the larger issue— that knowledge of emotion may be reaching a point at which it is not a specialty but a generally needed skill. Teachers may need sophisticated training and skill, but perhaps everyone needs more knowledge and practice than is presently given.

PHASES OF EMOTIONAL DEVELOPMENT

Acquisition

First there is the *Acquisition* phase. Acquisition includes three aspects of emotional process that are usually separated in research.[5] It includes reflexive affect and temperament as well as acquisition of the labels for emotional categories. One not only acquires and practices different emotions but also demonstrates a style or temperament for them. Someone supersensitive to noise, for example, might be "fearful" on more occasions when the sound in the environment abruptly changes, but all children would have some occasion to be fearful or shy. The degree of fearfulness or shyness may be temperamental or genetically predisposed.[6]

Not only does everyone have some ability to demonstrate emotional reactions, but one learns to label emotion as well. One might ask whether a particular child knows when he experiences an emotion that is obvious to others. One can also ask when a child is influenced by and can label other people's emotions.

Research

An explosion of research in the last 20 years has focused on these questions of acquisition. We now know that infants either at birth or shortly after have a good range of emotional expressions whose intensity and specific elicitors vary by individual temperament. Infants do not "know" to express their emotions in the situations that will later be culturally normal for expression, but researchers have verified that infants cry in pain, express anger when their arms are confined, smile when well fed and dozing, look disgusted when ammonia is thrust in their face, and so forth. These are not learned behaviors but part of the human repertoire of responses, what we have called "reflexive" affects. People no more learn to express themselves emotionally at this level than they learn to visually track edges of dark and light or to detect the difference between soft and loud. However, as we know from cross-cultural research and even family research, basic expressions do not always translate into basic, matched labels for emotion.

Infants also can detect and even imitate facial expressions at such early ages that learning is limited here too. Shortly after birth infants can imitate some facial movements of a caretaker, and by 11 weeks at the latest, they can match their mothers' expressions of sadness, anger, fear, and happiness and join these expressions with behaviors that suggest the matching is meaningful.[7] Fearful expressions are accompanied by freezing the body, for example, and happy ones with interested attention, whereas angry expressions are accompanied by a significant amount of eye avoidance. This suggests that at a primitive sensorimotor level, even infants "know" the meaning of emotion. It implies that emotional expression carries meanings about children's internal states even when the child cannot label the feelings. Our crying child at the beginning is no doubt communicating something important with her crying, but can we decode it? If we only inhibit or minimize the message (the cry), what will the messenger (the child) do next?

Problems of Acquisition

Much of basic acquisition appears to occur in infancy and to be almost automatic among human beings, but it is not trivial, and inconsistencies abound. Many people, perhaps most, have weaknesses and biases in acquisition. People who say they are "never angry" or "never happy" (afraid, sad, etc.) are neglecting or misinterpreting their emotions. One pathological example is aggressively delinquent children. They do not usually detect distress in others or themselves, but confuse distress cues with the cues for anger. Dodge and others[8] have worked on programs to teach such children the normal cues. Another common bias occurs when women claim to be "more" emotional than men. It has proven extremely difficult to find gender differences in emotional experience or behavioral expression, but there are definitely gender differences in the reporting of emotions and in the skills for detecting them.[9] "More" is hardly an accurate way of describing these subtle skill differences. Given their nature it is also likely that most gender differences are specific to this time and culture.

Beyond the direct influence of stimulation on emotional responses, it is apparent that during infancy children begin to use information about emotion to make decisions for their own behavior. For example, they will look to other people's emotional expression to know whether they should approach a new toy or cross a dangerous area.[10] There is no research about how the teacher's emotional reaction to a math or a literature problem might tell her students whether it is worth their while to learn the subject, but it is likely that emotional information sets the scene for acquiring many intellectual behaviors. A classic example is the health class in which sexual reproduction is presented by an embarrassed teacher. His inability to present sexual knowledge with interest, humor, sadness, anger, and so forth but only with shame or embarrassment limits the students' abilities to focus or ask questions. Even the preparatory classes for parents that we have attended usually present the material with embarrassment. The teachers tend to pull their bodies tightly together, cover their mouths and glance away from the audience frequently. They blink frequently and rapidly. The message is clear: "Learn what I present, but make no inquiries and keep your distance from the material, do not try to 'own' it." But this same emotional orientation can be brought to bear on any material, with similar consequences for restricting interest and independent exploration.

Another example we observed was a teacher who was very distressed when her students had difficulty with their math. This communicated her hopelessness in the face of math problems to the class. Rather than see their teacher distressed, the class would change the subject to distract her. Few math problems will be followed to their conclusion under this circumstance. Such emotional problems in learning—gaps in the knowledge of students of otherwise good teachers—probably go undetected and seem mysterious.

Applications to Education

When applying research on the acquisition of emotions to an educational context, one can easily expect a certain amount of meaningful emotional expression and also emotional contagion. Within a group of children, emotions can be contagious from an adult to the children or from a child to a child. There is controversy about whether some aspects of an emotional signal (sound over vision or vice versa, for example) might carry more weight for children of particular ages, but there is little doubt that emotional signals are potent. If children in one school are usually more angry than in another school, it is worth looking for reasons in the general emotional information given by adults in the school or by certain target groups of children or by physical stimuli in the environment. Many adults, including teachers, are unaware of the signals to which young children may be very susceptible and they are unaware of the circumstances that elicit emotional responses from young children. Moderately high and constant levels of noise—for example, a nearby heating system or fan—stimulate anger. Continuing exposure to escalating and undigested information stimulates fear or anxiety whether the escalating information is contained in intellectual problems or crowded corridors. We have seen preschools in which 50 children are in the same large room with only waist-high dividers between groups. The children move from section to section and from adult to adult throughout the day, never settling into any part of the room that might become personal and never able to concentrate quietly, to stay with one friend or one beloved caretaker. The children have the appearance of group hyperactivity. Environments such as this would facilitate such a reaction. Although it is a topic beyond the scope of this chapter, one needs to attend to the emotional "climate" of a school, as well as to the emotional development of individuals.

Refinement

The second phase of emotional learning is *Refinement*. First, there is a modification of the signals from one type of signal, such as the vocal cry, to the spoken "ouch," or from the jumping glee of the youngster to the chuckle of the adult. Much of this learning relies on family and cultural modeling as well as direct training. Second, there is an association of emotional responses to new contexts and people. Both refinements of the acquired emotions allow for minimizing expressions, exaggerating them, and covering them with some other signals (deception). In other words, this includes both containment and enhancement strategies that bring emotions into line with social expectations. In the instance of behavior that falls under the refinement phase, we mean to include only simple, one-way changes or additions to the emotion repertoire. The basic meanings of emotions do not change here, only the manner and place of expression.

Infancy

The refinement of emotional expression and the meaningfulness of emotions is one of the first tasks of infancy. In face-to-face play mothers and infants modify and refine their expressions so that infants acquire "family" characteristics. For example, if the mother uses her eyebrows more than her cheeks to express herself, so will her child. Not only that, but the rate at which the expressions change is modified. A mother will usually only respond to about one in four of the baby's facial movements and will respond more often to expressions of interest and happiness than to ones of pain. An increasing amount of research speaks to aberrations in this pattern as well, so that we can begin to detect early emotional dysfunction. Infants of depressed mothers begin to imitate the depression, for example.[11] Whether this will have a strong or weak influence on later feelings is still a question.

There is little information but every reason to suspect that children will adopt features of their teacher's expression just as readily as they adopt her or his speech patterns or ways of solving problems and under many of the same learning circumstances. If there are differences in the emotion conventions between home and school, one can also anticipate problems in assessing emotional skills on both the child's and the teacher's parts.

Childhood

As toddlers and young children mature, there are ever more interesting refinements of the emotional display and decoding systems. Also, the application of emotions to particular social situations begins to approximate cultural demands as well as family demands. Children usually have a complete range of culturally appropriate emotional displays and labels by school age. Children have also learned to suppress undesirable emotional displays. For example, Malatesta and McFadden[12] report that North American children begin to press their lips together instead of displaying an angry mouth, and in many instances they begin to bite their lip instead of showing the round fear mouth. Saarni[13] finds that children are able to make appropriate deceptions during the elementary years, politely smiling when they are really disappointed, for example.

Although parents and teachers report that children display less emotion as they leave early childhood and enter middle childhood, research observation has not supported this report. For example, children display as much or more anger at school age as they did in late infancy in response to physical provocations. They will also use verbal anger in their voices and in their words, so they have become able to coordinate their emotional message across communication systems. It is more likely that children seem "less" emotional because they have refined their emotions to meet cultural expectations. When children do not meet cultural expectations for the timing, display pattern, and context of emotion, they are viewed as "temperamentally difficult" or emotionally immature. Again, how much of this is due to family versus cultural differences is unclear.

Our crying child is not meeting cultural expectations, but we do not know why this has happened. Perhaps she meets family expectations. It is also possible that the teacher is not reading the child's signals very well because her own cultural and familial background is not broad enough. Some people hear crying as annoying, others hear it as sad. Some hear whining, others fear. This is because the whole signal needs to be taken into account. A report of a "cry" does not give enough information to an expert, as the description of red in apples is not enough for an expert to classify apples. What are the pieces and context of this cry? How has it been refined? We have not heard about the occasions when the child does not cry. Perhaps those are significant as well. What does she do when she is not crying? Is she happy or angry, or is it not notable at all?

Limitations of Refinement in Childhood

There are particular limitations on children's understanding of the context of emotion, however, so there would be limitations on what our crying child would report. Just as elementary-age children have difficulty understanding intentions when outcomes are salient and have difficulty handling contradictory information in any domain, they have related problems with emotional knowledge. For example, elementary-age children watching a video of adults arguing often do not recognize when the argument has been resolved.[14] They remain fixed on their perception of the anger. Also, in this instance, if the anger displayed and the verbal content are not synchronous, the younger children tend to focus on the display, not on the content. Younger children have trouble with the concept of mixed emotions.[15] If told that someone is sad and happy, they will retell the story as if the sadness happened at one time and the happiness at a distant other time. Or the child might retell the story as if one part of the emotional feeling were real and the other were deceit.

Adolescence

During adolescence there is a refinement of many forms of emotion expression. One example of this occurs in the realm of gender differences. We find that some gender differences associated with emotion are first exaggerated and then performed more smoothly. The different communicative emotional postures of men and women seem to be used for the first time. In schools the exaggerated distancing of adolescent boys is often misinterpreted as hostile, when in reality it is largely a crude first approximation of male adults' distancing behavior or demand for "space" and privacy. Girls also adopt adult female behaviors, but this is muted.

New cognitive and social demands place adolescents in the position of refining certain emotional expressions such as contempt to mark their autonomy and independence or shame to mark their self-consciousness.[16] These emotional signals are used in communication to subtly indicate the adolescents' position in conversations. Of course, the early forms of these behaviors are often awkward. For example, a young adolescent girl was deeply interested in her father's revelation that he was afraid of flying. After he gave several compelling examples, he suddenly denied that he was ever afraid. The adolescent daughter, just as suddenly, looked shy, self-conscious, and shamed. This kind of reaction occurs when the young adolescent is aware of what other people are thinking. She realizes the deceit of her father and realizes that she has looked too closely into his real feelings, so she looks down and away and pulls her lips in—showing her own self-consciousness. Contempt is seen when adolescents begin to claim the right to have their own thoughts or arguments and to put them forward. Older adolescents rather crudely or amusingly shrug, lean away, sneer, flash their eyebrows, and so forth when explaining why the accepted belief (on the need to do homework or to attend religious services) is completely fallacious. The first uses of these markers are not subtle, but in our research, ordinary parents tend to respond in kind with more subtle forms or to ignore the crude displays. Nevertheless, they are an indication that adolescents are practicing adult forms of emotional and intellectual communication.

We have spoken to many teachers in middle schools who are not happy with young adolescents. These adults interpret the adolescents' emotional signals for distance, privacy, and sexual acknowledgment as hostile. It is unlikely that adolescents themselves are intending to signal hostility. It is the case, however, that when adults use such signals, they use them subtly, even diplomatically. Exaggerated, their meaning changes among adults. Just as subtly raised eyebrows indicate interest and an exaggeration in timing or height indicates skepticism in our culture, these refinements can get one into trouble when first practiced. Cross-cultural misuse of emotional signals often results in the novice within a culture appearing to be hostile, rude, or infantile. It might help to consider that adolescents are novices to the adult emotional culture. Some knowledge of likely paths of development, likely mistakes, and some humor can be very helpful when working with novices.

In early adolescence, children begin to plan to take care of themselves emotionally. That is, if they are going to be away from home, children will make plans to comfort themselves with a stuffed toy or with a plan to be busy. Before adolescence it is unusual for children to recognize emotional needs. While adolescents understand that they could be happy to be at camp and simultaneously sad to be away from their family, they will often deny the negative feeling or claim to "take care of it" themselves. Although the new planning skills and anticipation of emotional behavior are important adolescent skills, they will be rudimentary and often rigid. This is obviously important in social and romantic relationships.

Applications to Education

What might one glean from this sort of research that has an applied focus? One conclusion is that children will likely believe that you feel as you behave, and they will be likely to choose one part of the display to focus upon. Until adolescence children are unlikely to focus on explanations or to count intentions as more important than a behavioral outcome. They are also not likely to understand complex emotional situations but will resolve them in time and space or into true and false instances. Obviously they will be afraid of someone who looks frightening to them, regardless of explanations, angry at someone who restrains or pains them, and so forth, although they may learn to recover quickly and to inhibit the full infantile response.

The refinements of emotional behavior and skills take several forms in early childhood. Very early in life, the displays become familially and culturally appropriate in terms of muscle groups used, response frequency, and rapidity of display changes. Children learn to label emotion quite early, but it takes many years for them to integrate information from different sources. By school age, children can cover their emotional displays with smaller movements, with vocal expression, or with deceit, substituting one display for another, although they are somewhat awkward at first. Children tend to rely on behavioral displays of emotion when they contradict other sources of information such as explanations.

All during childhood and adolescence, the displays and the information about the appropriateness of the feelings are refined. During adolescence there is also a major change in the frequency with which specific emotions are displayed and their gender appropriateness. Once again, these changes are often awkward or crude when first seen. But these refinements are simple in comparison with the organization of emotion and social or intellectual systems. The transformation of emotions within systems will be the next topic.

Transformations

While Acquisition referred to the expression and perception of emotion and Refinement referred to the attaching and detaching of the expressions and feelings to particular contexts and behaviors, *Transformation* refers to changes in whole systems. The transformations that we have learned about from our current research include two different processes, but we realize we still have much to learn. First are the ways in which a particular emotional state transforms the processes of thinking, learning, or getting ready to act in that state. Different emotional states tend to elicit different information-processing modes. Second is how the emotional process itself is changed with experience and knowledge so that the context and meaning of emotion emerges as a personal construction. An emotion can remain simple, or it can be transformed to form a system of thoughts, behaviors, and processes. Fear can become subconscious phobia, for example. In this case, tiny bits of information that are traumatic and fearful can set a large system of thoughts and behaviors in motion. Fear does not usually operate in this subliminal fashion, but it can be changed so that it does.

Examples of Sadness and Depression

We develop scenes and expectations with emotional content that provide us with complex interpersonal roles and beliefs about our own values and personal goals. We do not have to be aware of these transformations. For example, sadness might be combined with guilt and fear and with the idea that one is worthless. In extreme forms this is a transformation of sadness to depression. Sad experiences then would lead such a person to depression. Someone else might combine sadness with interest and a sense of herself as empathic and caring for distressed people. Many people in the helping professions use sadness in this way to develop rapport with people needing help. They use the sadness to establish empathy, but the combination of sadness with their wonder at the complexity and depth of human lives leads them to be excellent teachers, therapists, or healers. Each network of emotions, thoughts, and behaviors transforms the experience of sadness into an aspect of personality and thereby changes the experience of the emotion itself.[17]

Crying in the classroom is emblematic of the transformation problem. In terms of crying and the information processing that accompanies it, crying is thought to be incompatible with many intellectual pursuits. Our crying girl is not participating in the established school tasks when she is crying. On the other hand, one might say that the context we supply for learning does not encourage the types of learning that accompany crying. In our research, sadness is related to thorough exploration of apparent dead ends. Sometimes this is called rumination when a person continues to reflect on seemingly hopeless situations. But rumination may be the source of insightful change when all the pieces finally fall into place after days or months of concentration. It may not always be successful, but it is related to very complex and sometimes slow modes of problem solving in adults. If it is generally true that sadness is related to complex thinking, then we may question why sadness or crying is not compatible with school learning. Why is doing a task in a timely or efficient manner always better than going slowly and following up some blind alleys? What are the bad as well as the good consequences of the rather strict schedules and multiple tasks that currently fit in our school-day? Perhaps there are learning situations that we can imagine in which staying with a problem, even in apparent despair, might be the best path or, at least, not a skill to be discarded. It is probable that each emotion brings with it particular information-processing strategies. How flexible they are and how they combine or interact in complex situations are not known yet.

On the other side of the transformation issue, we dread the possibility that the child's crying signals that she is depressed or seriously ill in some way. We attribute poor outcomes to her crying and we anticipate that the causes for her crying are deep and distressing. While we might not be wrong, there are several other possibilities to explore. How does the child herself interpret her crying? How does it fit into other contexts in her life? Does it mean the same thing to her as it does to the teacher? Has she transformed crying into something idiosyncratic? We know that there is not one answer to these questions, so exploration of the possibilities is needed.

Following the style of the sections on acquisition and refinement, we present brief views of some transformations as they commonly occur in childhood and adolescence. This is the newest area of research. Though it is a promising area and one that is growing, it is also the one in which we presently have the fewest answers.

Childhood

Although most transformations wait for the intellectual and social skills of adolescence, there are hints that younger children anticipate the complex functions of emotion. For example we have evidence that a link is established between aspects of language and aspects of emotion that might be considered a "transformation" of emotional experience. By nursery school age, children use different styles of narration for relating different emotional experiences. Angry stories are most likely to use the traditional plotted story with rising action, peak moments, clear problem statements, and resolutions. Fear stories focus their emotion on rising action; the best ones do not even resolve the rise. Happy stories are "moment-in-time" portraits with careful detail and quite often a poetic organization.[18]

Applications to Education

It is quite likely that educators already make use of the different information-processing functions of emotions. When teaching argumentative forms of thinking such as commonly used in scientific proofs, expert teachers may use a mild anger mood induction (debate, or other challenge) in the classroom. Argumentative forms of thought are ones used in geometry proofs or legalistic thinking. One asserts a hypothesis or idea, states the obstructions or objections, and then defends the hypothesis by defeating all opposition—with logic and demonstration.

When teaching poetic forms of writing or reading, teachers may use a mild happiness induction in the classroom (musical interludes or playful enactments). Isen's[19] work on positive moods and cognitive process has shown that more creative thought is used when children and adults are in a positive mood. She influences people's moods by showing humorous films or giving them a simple present. In tests of association, more remote, but useful, associations will be used. In diagnosing problems such as medical illness, more leads will be followed up. On creativity tests, people will get higher scores on fluency and unusual solutions when they are induced to be in a happier mood. If educators had more knowledge of emotion systems, they could plan more emotional enhancements of learning and teach emotional systems as well.

Adolescence

We have conducted a series of studies to help us understand the transformational development during adolescence. During adolescence emotions noticeably become the basis of identity and ideals. What adolescents care about is usually what they feel strongly about—not only feel intensely but also feel variably. Adolescents begin to form varied and intense attachments to ideals, people, and careers, just as their emotional life is transformed and as awareness of emotionality changes. Adolescents become aware of feeling everything, and this transforms their values and their understanding.[20]

Awareness of Emotion

One of our early studies[21] gathered information about fifth-, seventh-, and ninth-graders' awareness of their emotions. The students filled out emotion questionnaires every schoolday for two weeks. Although early adolescence has been called a time of unpredictable moodiness or "storm and stress" dating at least back to G. S. Hall,[22] there is little evidence from our research that young adolescents are themselves able to report mood swings. It is not until high school, well past the hormonal surges of puberty, that students are likely to report mood changes. Trying to abstract the meaning of moods and personality traits from concrete experience is difficult for adolescents. The public school students in New Jersey whom we interviewed have no "second-order" or formal instruction on these issues. What they know must be learned from personal experience and is limited by that.

The easiest emotions to accept and comprehend are the positive emotions (joy, surprise, and interest). These are reported by all of the students in all the grades to be much more changeable than other emotions. Students can report highs and lows with respect to happiness earlier than they can report highs and lows with respect to anger or sadness. Even college students prefer to think of themselves in terms of degrees of happiness rather than degrees of sadness, anger, or fear.[23]

Young adolescents have trouble acknowledging and tracking their negative emotions. For example, the younger ones report that negative passive emotions (sadness, guilt, shyness) occur at low and stable levels, but by ninth grade they report more changes. The negative active emotions (anger, contempt, and frustration) are still reported as low and stable even by ninth grade even though observational evidence suggests a high behavioral frequency.

Emotional refinement includes increasing awareness of mood changes, especially internally directed ones. It also includes changes in the perceived organization of social situations that elicit emotions. Emotional reactions, as well as the awareness of emotional reactions, show what adolescents care about. They transform the social and personal scenes of the child to those of the adolescent. Teachers may find that young adolescents are resistant to discussion of feelings and that this occurs just when adults believe that the adolescents' behavior is well connected to emotions. However, it is a common psychological reaction at all ages to deny that change occurs. It is only after the changes are partially assimilated that some awareness of them is gained. The emotions that will transform family life, commitment to careers and ideals, and particularly those that create romance are only slowly assimilated. The difficult aspects that are related to sadness, anger, or fear are especially slow.

Very few programs on sexual education use any basic emotional knowledge in their design. Although there is a folklore about adolescent emotionality, little knowledgeable work is being done to use or transform emotional development and apply the knowledge to significant adolescent problems. It is quite likely that adolescents have grave difficulty integrating sexual feelings with other emotions. A bias toward examining sexual issues in terms of happiness or excitement could be expected and could easily lead to risky conclusions. It might be helpful for students to know when they are becoming aware of integrating more complex emotions that they are not the only ones who are uncomfortable with their anger. Or that when they are "getting in touch" with their feelings of sadness early in high school, it does not mean that they are getting depressed. It could be reinterpreted for them as a sign that they are more mature.

Elicitors of Emotion

One of our studies also asked how thoughts about emotions are organized for adolescents. When they report emotions, do they associate emotional experiences with particular people or events? In other words, with whom and what do adolescents associate intense feelings? Analyses of the adolescents' responses suggested that there are systematic developmental differences for the social context of emotion. The patterns are consistent with general social development away from a family focus and toward a peer focus. Emotions are being attached to peer friends, especially romantic ones, and situations in which friends are the key participants. In contrast, for children the key people are members of the family and the situations are family scenes.

These changes in what we call the elicitors of the emotions we felt should be explored in more detail. Maybe to be emotionally mature is to be "on time" in terms of transforming emotional scenes. Two large-scale questionnaire studies of early and middle adolescence were conducted to address the question of developmental patterns in the contexts of emotion. Students were recruited from several urban and suburban public schools. In both studies they completed the EEQ (Elicitors of Emotion Questionnaire) to ask them about the people and situations they associated with their emotions.

Developmental patterns of change in terms of the people associated with emotions were found for joy, interest, anger, disgust, sadness, and surprise. The clearest changes can be seen in the reports of the people with whom emotions are experienced. There is a continuing increase in romantic attachment. Girls develop an elaborate emotional response to opposite-sex peers earlier than boys. Boys continue in middle adolescence to associate romance only with joy and excitement. The older the student, the less likely family members are to be mentioned, and this will be particularly obvious with respect to positive emotions. The only emotion that tended to "stay at home" during the early and mid-adolescent years was anger. This follows a national trend in that adults in the United States associate their anger experiences with their families. This trend is not usually seen in other nations. In the Eastern tradition, for example, thoughts of one's angry experiences are usually associated with strangers.[24]

As an example of adolescents' descriptions of their emotional contexts, consider disgust. The younger children mention bodily functions, such as burping, and other events that are very concrete and literal interpretations of disgust. The older students more often mention people's actions and interpersonal or romantic themes. They would be more likely to be disgusted if someone betrayed a confidence or pretended to like you, for example. Similar patterns occur for other emotions.

Applications to Education

What implications do these findings have for educators? First, it appears that there are systematic developmental transformations of students' experiences of emotion. When teachers recommend against moving a young but academically brilliant child into a program with older students because he is emotionally "immature," they intuitively may be referring to this aspect of development. Our research can be used to make more systematic the intuition that a student is emotionally immature. For example, a high school student who is angry when his pencil is knocked on the floor (a physical or object-oriented problem) acts young. Being angry at humiliation (an internal, or psychologically focused response) is far more likely among high school students than is being angry at a dropped pencil, although that would be very typical of elementary school children.

In addition to using knowledge of emotional development to help understand students who may be having social or interpersonal problems due to emotional immaturity, it is useful for educators to have a knowledge of basic patterns of emotional development in order to motivate students. However, the concerns of most educators seem to be on the problems. A brief look at how the subject of emotional development is handled in educational psychology texts shows that the focus is on pathology, not on development. But research on normal emotional development can even help shift the focus within the area of pathology. As an example, consider the transformation of depression as it reaches its adult gender configuration.

Transformations of Depression

To the layperson, depression is feelings of overwhelming sadness, and even the layperson knows that women and girls are more likely to be depressed than men and boys. However, gender differences in the assessment of depression go beyond differences in the sheer amount of depression claimed by each gender into differences in the organization of depression. In several studies[25] girls' reports of depression are related to mood items, but in only one case (irritability) are the boys' items so related. This suggests that depression and the awareness of emotion are clearly related for girls. But for boys depression, as it is currently measured, is somehow less related to any particular "feeling" or mood component, even though it is theoretically a "mood dysfunction." These studies suggest that the emotions that are frequent, lacking, or in conflict in the adolescent depression syndrome may be different for girls and boys—as are many emotion functions.

To further examine gender differences in the construction of adolescent depression, we administered the Children's Depression Inventory to adolescents. Then we factor-analyzed the results to see what items belong together. For girls, the items on the inventory are grouped by emotions. The highest rated items on the first group or factor (the one that accounts for most of the differences) are valuative: "I can never be as good as other kids" and "I hate myself." But this group also includes all the items relating to sadness, such as "I feel like crying every day" and "I am sad all the time." Given that only one emotion (sadness) showed up on this factor, we called it the "Sad Self" factor, although we might have called it the "Bad, Sad Self." The second girls' factor consists of all the items characteristic of anhedonia (anhedonia literally means "without joy"): "Nothing is fun at all" and "I never have fun at school." It also contains items about the absence of friendship. We call this the "Anhedonia Self" factor. One could think of it as "No Fun, No Friends." The third girls' depression factor contains the hostility items (e.g., "I get into fights all the time," "I am bad all the time," and "I never do what I am told") and is therefore called the "Hostile Self" factor.

The boys' depression factors appear to be quite different. Rather than deconstructing into a variety of moods (sad, not happy, hostile), as it does for girls, for boys the inventory deconstructs into a variety of good-bad evaluations. The highest items on the boys' first factor are "I am bad all the time" and "All bad things are my fault." This factor includes most of the emotion items of the scale, including hostility, guilt, and sad items. This is the "Negative Self" factor, but it should probably be called the "Bad Emotional Self." Being bad is associated with all the negative emotions on the measure, not just one. This also suggests that the negative emotions are not seen as very different from each other, but all are perceived as just "bad." The highest items on the boys' second factor are "I feel alone all the time" and "I do not have any friends." This factor is called the "Lonely Self," but it does not have any clear emotional focus. The third factor for boys consists mainly of items relating to failure and includes items like "I have to push myself to do my homework." This factor is called the "Failing Self." Even though the "fun at school" item shows up here, there is not a group of anhedonia items, so it does not have a solid emotional focus.

In our study, there were no gender differences in overall depression scores. However, there were differential mood factors for girls, but not for boys of the same age. For the boys, negative emotionality is implicitly a separable issue on the depression inventory. The boys appear to be grouping the affectively related items rather than relating discrete emotions to different issues. Even though the students in the depression study were all attending school and the mean depression scores were low to moderate, their experience parallels that of more dysfunctional adolescents. In general there is good overlap between the descriptors of dysfunctional and more normally developing adolescents. However since boys and girls differ in what "makes" them depressed, the depression scores may not predict similar degrees of dysfunction for boys and girls. It may be more difficult for boys to report that they are depressed. They may only be aware of being "bad," not of having emotional problems.

BROAD APPLICATIONS

Having considered what educators might need to know about emotion, let us return briefly to the question of educating the children. Everyone knows that public education of citizens has been important in the United States. Our founding parents determined that the citizens would vote and create government, and they had a conviction that education would be necessary for participation. As time has gone by a second goal of education for citizenship has emerged. To sustain the economy the citizens are educated for increasingly sophisticated work roles. There has been continuing revision of the definition of a voting "citizen" (originally not women, not men with no property, not people of color), but there has been little debate about the "basics" of public education needed by a citizen—government and work. With this sparse agenda, why should knowledge of emotion be in the curriculum? How does it contribute to the academic excellence that is sought after in most schools?

In terms of work, emotional skills are known to be related to ability to do well in any position that requires human interaction. Since more and more work requires service and communication, it is obvious that more skill is needed in emotional communication. In jobs that require intellectual flexibility and commitment, a versatile use of emotions will probably be important. Being able to systematically use one's own emotions, to create emotional climates that facilitate particular information processes or problem-solving strategies, may prove essential in moving in new directions or in thoroughly utilizing old ones. Knowing more about the diversity of emotional processes may help communication and planning with people from around the world. Thinking and feeling are part of the same system. Knowing the how, when, and where of either feeling or thinking is useful.

There was a theory at the turn of the last century that women who developed intellectual talents would dry up their wombs, so intellectually gifted girls were discouraged from expanding their knowledge. Smart women were considered to be about as useful as "two-headed gorillas," to quote one academic authority of the time. We seem to have come through the phase of considering reading, writing, and arithmetic to be dangerous pursuits. There still are intellectual disasters in terms of people who focus dangerously on intellectual skill—the scientist who was a child prodigy, who has no friends, and who comes close to destroying the world with a crazed invention is still a popular character—but we do not overgeneralize from this extreme case.

On the other hand, we have not recovered from considering emotions to be dangerous in and of themselves. When considering emotional people such as the crying girl described at the beginning of this chapter, we immediately think of the crying in terms of a dangerous affective disorder, in which the talent or skill for the emotion has run amok. From the extreme and singly focused cases we easily jump to the conclusion that any amount of an emotion may be dangerous to health or reason—probably a good deal less useful than a two-headed gorilla. With this fear of emotion as the focus, we usually think of learning how not to be emotional rather than whether or not the emotions are being refined and transformed to mature forms. Perhaps it is time for an educated look at emotional intelligence, emotional literacy, emotional work, and emotional process.

NOTES

References

Averill, J. R., & Nunley, E. P. (1992). *Voyages of the heart.* New York: The Free Press.

Brody, L. R., & Hall, J. A. (1993). Gender and emotion. In M. Lewis & J. M. Haviland (Eds.), *Handbook of emotions* (pp. 447–460). New York: Guilford.

Cummings, E. M., Vogel, D., Cummings, J. S., & El-Sheikh, M. (1989). Children's responses to different forms of expression of anger between adults. *Child Development, 60,* 1392–1404.

Dodge, K. A., & Coie, J. D. (1987). Social-information-processing factors in reactive and proactive aggression in children's peer groups. *Journal of Personality and Social Psychology, 53,* 1146–1158.

Dodge, K. A., Pettit, G. S., McClaskey, C. L., & Brown, N. M. (1986). Social competence in children. *Monographs of the Society for Research in Child Development, 51*(2), 1–85.

Fischer, K. W., & Ayoub, C. (1994). Affective splitting and dissociation in normal and maltreated children: Developmental pathways for self in relationships. In D. Cicchetti & S. L. Toth (Eds.), *Disorders and dysfunction of the self: Rochester symposium on developmental psychopathology* (Vol. 5). Rochester, NY: University of Rochester Press.

Gebelt, J. L. (1995). *Identity, emotion and memory in college students.* Unpublished doctoral dissertation, Rutgers—The State University of New Jersey, New Brunswick, NJ.

Goleman, D. (1995). *Emotional intelligence.* New York: Bantam Books.

Hall, G. S. (1904). *Adolescence: Its psychology and its relations to physiology, anthropology, sociology, sex, crime, religion, and education* (Vol. 2). New York: Appleton-Century-Crofts.

Haviland, J. M., & Kahlbaugh, P. E. (1993). Emotion and identity. In M. Lewis & J. M. Haviland (Eds.), *Handbook of emotion* (pp. 327–339). New York: Guilford.

Haviland, J. M., & Kramer, D. A. (1991). Affect-cognition relations in an adolescent diary: 1. The case of Anne Frank. *Human Development, 34,* 143–159.

Haviland, J. M., & Lelwica, M. (1987). The induced affect response: 10-week-old infants' responses to three emotion expressions. *Developmental Psychology, 23,* 97–104.

Haviland, J. M., & Walker-Andrews, A. (1992). An ecological approach to affect theory and social development. In V. B. Hasselt & M. Hersen (Eds.), *Handbook of social development: A lifespan perspective* (pp. 29–49). New York: Plenum.

Hornik, R., Risenhoover, N., & Gunnar, M. (1987). The effects of maternal positive, neutral, and negative affective communications on infant responses to new toys. *Child Development, 58,* 937–944.

Hudson, J. A., Gebelt, J., Haviland, J., & Bentivegna, C. (1992). Emotion and narrative structure in young children's personal accounts. *Journal of Narrative and Life History, 2,* 129–150.

Isen, A. M. (1984). Toward understanding the role of affect in cognition. In R. Wyer & T. Srull (Eds.), *Handbook of social cognition* (pp. 179–236). Hillsdale, NJ: Erlbaum.

Kagan, J., & Snidman, N. (1991). Temperamental factors in human development. *American Psychologist, 46,* 856–862.

Kahlbaugh, P. E., & Haviland, J. M. (1994). Nonverbal communication between parents and adolescents: A study of approach and avoidance behaviors. *Journal of Nonverbal Behavior, 18,* 91–133.

Kovacs, M., & Beck, A. (1977). An empirical clinical approach towards a definition of childhood depression. In J. G. Schulterbrandt & A. Raskins (Eds.), *Depression in children: Diagnosis, treatment and conceptual models* (pp. 1–25). New York: Raven Press.

Malatesta, C., & McFadden, S. H. (1995). *The role of emotions in social and personality development.* New York: Plenum.

Saarni, C. (1989). Children's understanding of strategic control of emotional expression in social transactions. In C. Saarni & P. L. Harris (Eds.), *Children's understanding of emotion* (pp. 181–208). Cambridge, England: Cambridge University Press.

Salovey, P., & Mayer, J. D. (1990). Emotional intelligence. *Imagination, Cognition and Personality, 3,* 185–211.

Scherer, K. R. (1988). *Facets of emotion: Recent research.* Hillsdale, NJ: Erlbaum.

Smucker, M. R., Craighead, W. E., Craighead, L. W., & Green, B. J. (1986). Normative and reliability data for the children's depression inventory. *Journal of Abnormal Child Psychology, 14,* 25–39.

Stapley, J. C., & Haviland, J. M. (1989). Beyond depression: Gender differences in normal adolescents' emotional experiences. *Sex Roles, 20,* 295–308.

Tronick, E. Z., & Gianino, A. F. (1986). The transmission of maternal disturbance to the infant. In E. Z. Tronick & T. Field (Eds.), *Maternal depression and infant disturbance: New directions for child development* (pp. 5–11). San Francisco: Jossey-Bass.

Webb, T. E., & VanDever, C. A. (1985). Sex differences in the expression of depression: A developmental interaction effect. *Sex Roles, 12,* 91–95.

1. We want to thank the teachers and administrators of Clinton Public School, Clinton, New Jersey, for their questions and insights during the preparation of this chapter.
2. For example, Goleman (1995).
3. Salovey and Mayer (1990).
4. This chapter is organized around an acronym provided by Averill and Nunley (1992) for three aspects of emotional learning: ART—Acquisition, Refinement, and Transformation. Our use of their terms is not identical to their original usage, but it follows them in substance.
5. For an overview of emotion see Haviland and Walker-Andrews (1992).
6. Kagan and Snidman (1991).
7. Haviland and Lelwica (1987).
8. Dodge and Coie (1987); Dodge, Pettit, McClaskey, and Brown (1986).
9. For a review of research, see Brody and Hall (1993).
10. Hornik, Risenhoover, and Gunnar (1987).
11. Tronick and Gianino (1986).
12. Malatesta and McFadden (1995). This reviews the history of research on emotions related to personality development.
13. Saarni (1989).
14. Cummings, Vogel, Cummings, and El-Sheikh (1989).
15. Fischer and Ayoub (1994).
16. Kahlbaugh and Haviland (1994).
17. If you have an interest in the history of science, Haviland and Kahlbaugh (1993) trace the relationship between cultural beliefs about emotion, scientific theories, and the techniques of research within the last century. One of the points is that even scientific theories and problem-solving strategies are limited or stretched by the emotional knowledge of the scientists' time period and training.
18. Hudson, Gebelt, Haviland, and Bentivegna (1992).
19. Isen (1984) has shown in many elegant studies that a positive mood influences information processing in several ways. If a teacher were looking for a demonstration experiment to use in the scientific study of emotion, using one of Isen's experiments would be quite possible and

interesting in a school setting. One could demonstrate the influence of mood on the categorization of information, for example, or on the decisions to contribute to good causes.

20. Haviland and Kramer (1991).
21. Although it is commonly known that men and women differ on measures of depression, our study looks at how this difference is embedded in general differences in emotional responses. See Stapley and Haviland (1989).
22. Hall (1904).
23. Gebelt (1995).
24. Scherer (1988).
25. Webb and VanDever (1985); Kovacs and Beck (1977); Smucker, Craighead, Craighead, and Green (1986).

EDUCATOR'S COMMENTARY

MARIANNE NOVAK HOUSTON

I FINISH THIS CHAPTER musing on so much good advice that I received as a child: "Crying will get you nowhere here"—this from a 4-year-old friend's mother many years ago. "Leave your feelings at home"—from a harried third-grade teacher attempting to cope with her 52 urchins in a parochial school classroom. "Don't wear your heart on your sleeve"—from a well-meaning father who was trying to teach me to toughen up and not be hurt by others' criticisms. Certainly a rather universal message was that emotions were our enemies and needed to be either conquered or hidden, or if they were useful at all it was a mystery just how. I'm not sure that there's more understanding today, 50 years later, of the importance or the role of emotions in personal development. And I leave the authors' discussion of the issue with several observations and questions from the perspective of a middle school teacher.

First, we need to know more about emotional systems in order to plan enhancements of learning. The cold, technical, factual approach to learning makes it less pleasurable and therefore less attractive to learners. The "turn-on" that learning can be seems too rare an experience, and this might be traced to our lack of knowledge about emotional systems: passion, joy, and fun make life—and learning—worthwhile. Connecting learning to living (to life), in fact, might be defined as wiring it to the emotional framework of the human being.

Second, we teachers have a critical role to play in facilitating the transformations mentioned. In order to do so, however, we need to "really get in there and mix it up" with our students. That is, we must come to know them more than just superficially. The value of one-on-one conversations cannot be overestimated in helping them tune in to what they may actually be experiencing. I call these conversations "reflecting together." Sometimes one needs to sneak up on them, take occasions when they come, dare to address an issue by gently opening the topic. On occasions where there has been a breakthrough and the student actually names the transformation, the next day it may seem as if the conversation never took place: There is a new level of student/teacher relationship, but one that either student or teacher may not feel comfortable acknowledging. This work requires love but great detachment. The rule I use is that of the Quaker "clearness committee": I only ask questions whose answers I could not possibly know, and I do not give advice. This enables students to find their own way, based on their own integrity.

Third, I believe that the knowledge of emotional development (through acquisition and refinement to transformation) is crucial to understanding and motivating students. It might also help us to shift our focus from interpreting behavior as a "problem" to the question, "Is this part of the normal transformation of emotions? What does this specific behavior mean in the larger context?"

Fourth, I look with some suspicion on the suggestion that the research community could contribute a more systematic method of determining emotional maturity. Such an effort may seem useful, but I fear that the same danger exists as with intelligence-measuring devices—that it would be subject to misuse. Because this particular child scores in x range on this particular day, using this particular instrument may yield a result that will be misinterpreted and work against the child's best interests. It's my feeling that measurement too quickly leads to labeling students: Labels are for jelly jars, not people!

Fifth, there is a potentially very useful suggestion in this article, one that every school community needs to take seriously: Look at the general emotional response of students or a group of students in a school, then look at the emotional information being given by the adults in the school, or by targeted groups of children, or by physical stimuli in the environment. Emotions do not exist in a vacuum, and even though home values or problems are important and can never be minimized, so are the "messages" being given by the school community. What is present in the broad school environment that may be eliciting the emotional behaviors? A responsive school staff needs to keep its ear to the group, to be aware of interstudent, or student group, interactions, as well as faculty behaviors. In addition, providing ready sources of sugars and caffeine (through dispensing machines now found in many schools) can also effect behaviors/emotions, and should be looked upon as stimuli, at least for some students. It may seem an unnecessary question, but are we, as adults, aware of the stimuli, circumstances, and signals that elicit strong emotional/behavioral responses from children?

Sixth, there are interesting comparisons between boys and girls and their unique emotional development patterns and problems. I am puzzled by the fact that frequently bright girls tend to "go underground" during adolescence. The result is that some of them fall behind (or don't progress as quickly as they could) in academic areas where they could excel, and they leave the road that might lead to scholarships and higher level participation. Is this behavior related to emotional development?

And if so, can we address the issues through a program that might encourage them to explore their own gifts and eventually more fully realize their potential?

Lastly, a sparse agenda, as is mentioned, is indeed set forth as the goal of education for all Americans, and a very good case is made for the need to educate our students emotionally for their lives as citizens and as workers. As important, however, is the need to understand the emotions as coadjutors with intelligence in the creation of a happy, adjusted human being, in any culture, at any time. This is the message of this chapter, for me.

CHAPTER 9

Linking Research and Educational Programming to Promote Social and Emotional Learning

JOSEPH E. ZINS,
LAWRENCE F. TRAVIS III, AND
PENNY A. FREPPON

EDUCATORS FACE A VARIETY of complex challenges every day, many of which are related to students' social and emotional needs. The degree of success these professionals have in addressing issues such as low academic achievement, drug abuse, teen pregnancy, and violence depends on how well they can identify the most salient aspects of the situation and the subsequent decisions they make based on these judgments. Teachers, principals, and special-services staff members must simultaneously reflect, make judgments, and act numerous times daily.

Most professionals support the notion that it is important to base practice on relevant theory. That is, their actions should be determined to a great extent from generalizations they deduce from research. These ideas should serve to steer and influence but not determine decisions they make.[1] Accordingly, educators need to develop a framework to guide daily decision making within the real world of the school that is based on reflection and inquiry. However, many practitioners are unable to describe the conceptual basis on which they act. Indeed, studies of educators' decision making frequently find it to be "more reactive than reflective . . . and more routinized than conscious."[2]

Researchers are often critical of practitioners for not making use of the findings from the studies they conduct, even suggesting that practitioners are not informed enough to provide the best services to their clients. Practitioners, on the other hand, frequently complain that researchers do not understand the complex realities and demands of daily fieldwork, and they view researchers as being unable to demonstrate the relevance of their studies. They are dismayed because scientists appear consumed by irrelevant questions and fail to appreciate the knowledge that arises from practice. Quite appropriately, Schön asked, "What is the kind of knowing in which competent practitioners engage? How is professional knowing like and unlike the kinds of knowledge presented in academic textbooks, scientific papers, and learned journals? In what sense, if any, is there intellectual rigor in professional practice?"[3]

Differences in practitioner and researcher perceptions are quite common. Beutler, Williams, Wakefield, and Entwistle observed that "in virtually every discipline . . . scientists have lamented that practitioners are inadequately trained, are insensitive to the value of scientific findings, and fail to read the right journals. Indeed . . . the science-practice duality is so pervasive that in some realms of study, separate disciplines have evolved, such as physics and engineering . . . and educational psychology and education."[4] For these reasons, it seems clear to us that if the highest quality, most effective services are to be provided, we need to decrease the tension that exists between the two groups and to identify better means of developing partnerships.

Our goals in this chapter are to discuss how research can be used to better advance practice, and how practice can inform research. A particular focus is on applications to social and emotional learning and the prevention of interpersonal violence. In undertaking this task, we have summarized relevant literature and reflected on our professional experiences from our respective disciplines, that is, school/community psychology (JEZ), criminal justice (LFT), and literacy (PAF). Readers may wonder why people from such diverse areas would work together on this topic. Rather than our differences being a hindrance, as they might appear initially, we have found that this diversity enables us to contribute unique but complementary perspectives, and as a result, our individual approaches are enriched.

We begin by examining the issue of linking science and practice and why accomplishing this goal is such a daunting task. Next, we provide a brief illustration of how practice can be guided by the research and theoretical literature through examination of a program designed to prevent interpersonal violence in schools. We conclude by offering suggestions about how to more effectively bridge the gap between these two seemingly dichotomous areas.

CHALLENGES OF LINKING RESEARCH AND PROFESSIONAL PRACTICE

When we began sharing ideas for this chapter, we were struck by the similarities of the concerns expressed within each of our disciplines regarding the challenge of linking research and professional practice. On one level, the issues and the solution seemed straightforward: All educators have to do is read the literature and apply it to what they do each day. However, as we examined the topic more deeply, we quickly found that the matter is much more complex. In this section we outline some of the most important issues.

Knowledge Acquisition

For years professionals have been lamenting the fact that it is increasingly difficult to keep abreast of new knowledge and skills and to avoid having their expertise become obsolete.[5] As the twenty-first century dawns, it is obvious that this professional responsibility will become even more challenging.[6] Since the beginning of the "information age" we have faced more than ever before the prospect of engaging in continuous on-the-job learning. If we do not keep current, we run the risk of basing decisions on outdated information. For instance, a colleague we know drew up a detailed proposal to teach a course on social and emotional learning but was told by the dean (a former teacher) that such affective education efforts had been tried in the 1970s and that "they didn't work then and certainly won't now."

If the reality of an exploding knowledge base is not overwhelming enough, consider how difficult it is to review information from related disciplines on topics of interest from different and potentially broadening perspectives. With respect to social and emotional learning, relevant new ideas can be found in a number of fields, including social and developmental psychology, remedial and special education, school counseling, and sociology. And, as we reflect on how overwhelmed we feel, we recognize that as university faculty we have far more administrative support to keep up-to-date than does the average practitioner in the schools.

For all of these reasons, a major barrier to integrating research and practice is acquiring knowledge. Preservice, university-based preparation programs are simply a starting point for practice, but professional growth is a career-long responsibility that carries with it time, effort, and financial costs.

Theory-Based Practice

As noted earlier, most of us would agree that it is important to base practice on a theoretical framework that helps to develop hypotheses and determine a course of action. In the field, theories of action can be based on professional experience and/or educational theory.[7] Sanders and McCutcheon made the case that professional knowledge gained from experience essentially is theoretical knowledge.[8] In contrast, North called this "accumulated body of traditions, practices, and beliefs . . . lore"[9] and discounted it as theory. Although resolution of this debate is beyond the scope of this chapter, the role that experience plays in guiding practice and research needs to be examined, and how educators theorize needs to be more thoroughly understood. What is clear is that we cannot rely on intuition alone or on cookbook techniques. Instead, we must engage in a "scientific problem-solving process" by thinking in a critical, analytical manner about what is taking place, what resources are available, what alternative actions are possible, what the consequences of each are, and so forth. Engaging in reflection about our practices improves the usefulness of the experiences gained through practice.[10] However, the value of engaging in this type of process must be instilled when professional training begins at the university, but too often these institutions react to student pressures to make the curriculum "meaningful" (i.e., focus only on information that can be directly applied to practice) by minimizing the emphasis on understanding the underlying theory and research that form the basis for practice.

Knowledge Application and Utilization

The preceding discussion addresses only part of the focus of this chapter. Also related is the application and use of knowledge in professional practice, as possession of it alone cannot effect change. We must not only acquire knowledge and develop a good conceptual understanding but also learn to apply it, as change enacted without adequate knowledge seldom accomplishes its intended goals.[11]

Similar to the acquisition issue, deterrents to applying knowledge include time, lack of administrative support, costs, motivation, and values. Researchers also contribute to this difficulty by failing to communicate explicitly the implications of their studies. Rather than being satisfied with answering questions of relevance to a specific policy problem, such as youth violence or the relationship between student retention and graduation rates, academics often seek a higher integration of data and theory.[12] A problem emerges, however, when translating the data from a specific study to a broader theoretical topic results in a "typical" research report. Such reports are often so divorced from the world of practice and policy, so littered with caveats and qualifications, that they are virtually incomprehensible and useless to most practitioners.[13] Further, researchers often do not clarify their vision of what they are trying to accomplish. We still have much to learn about how people learn to apply relevant knowledge to become scientists-practitioners.

Professional Isolation and Occupational Culture

Daily routines in schools typically do not encourage teaming, collaboration, brainstorming, sharing, and problem solving with colleagues. Little time is allocated formally to these activities, and to a large extent, once teachers close their doors they are on their own. An implied belief seems to be that competent practitioners are self-sufficient and have no unanswered questions, which creates an environment that is not conducive to inquiry.[14] An implicit and underlying assumption of many schools seems to be that learning experiences for educators are best accomplished in isolation. As a result, the advantages of group problem solving, of reflecting on one's efforts with peers, and of learning about new approaches are often lost. Teachers who wish to engage in these activities must do so on their own or give up the little available time they have at school that is not devoted to instructional duties (e.g., lunch). Staff development is often used as a vehicle to transmit technical skills and administrative knowledge rather than as a process for collaborative inquiry.[15] Such an overall perspective ignores, among other issues, the importance of not only learning new material but also of "letting go" of old patterns of behaving, a task found to be best accomplished in a group.[16]

Attitudinal/Motivational Considerations

Educational research has developed a negative reputation for many school personnel. Some feel distrustful of it because studies have been used against educators to demonstrate how poorly they are doing their jobs rather than to help them. As a result, individual educators may believe that they have been assigned the primary blame for failures that more appropriately belong to the entire educational and social system. Other educators see research as irrelevant, which further hampers their willingness to believe it may be useful.[17] And the fact is, much of it is not clearly relevant to daily practice. Additionally, new knowledge may implicitly or explicitly require change, and undertaking it entails a degree of risk, as there are no guarantees of outcomes. Thus, it is natural for all of us to avoid or resist change, to try to maintain the status quo. These and similar perceptions must be addressed to bridge the research-practice gap.

The next section provides an illustration of how research can be used to guide professional practice.

PREVENTING INTERPERSONAL VIOLENCE IN SCHOOLS: A PRESSING CHALLENGE FOR EDUCATORS

In this section we demonstrate how research on social and emotional learning can be applied to the prevention of interpersonal violence. We chose violence prevention because it flows from our current work and because preventing school violence is a task about which all schools are facing tremendous pressure to do something *now*. Further, school violence prevention is an appropriate topic because while there are a number of relevant programs from which to chose, little evaluation information is available about the various approaches.

At the outset we wish to note that in practice the process described is considerably more complicated than described and involves extensive collaboration among a variety of people. Our own work in this area includes educators (administrators, special-services staff, and teachers), health professionals, criminal justice personnel, and university researchers and faculty, as well as parents and community members.

The central question typically generated by practitioners is, "What should be done to combat interpersonal violence in schools?" This is, of course, a policy question. The related research question is, "What types of interventions have the greatest promise of reducing the incidence of interpersonal violence?" Success may be most likely when school personnel and researchers combine their efforts. School officials need to develop or adopt a program, while researchers focus on the impact of program components. These two perspectives are quite complementary.

Any planned intervention should be based on knowledge of the factors that contribute to or inhibit violent behavior. Thus, once the problem has been identified appropriately, the first step is to conduct an extensive review of the extant research literature on the correlates (or "causes") of school violence. Such a review for this topic reveals "risk and protective factors" that are logical targets for prevention programming.

A number of risk factors appear to be "consensus" choices. That is, they are repeatedly reported as being correlates of interpersonal violence and include poor/low school achievement, externalizing problem behaviors, interaction with antisocial peers, alienation from family and community, substance abuse, life transitions, poor parental child rearing, and exposure to violence.[18]

The presence of "protective factors" is associated with lower levels of interpersonal violence. Among those identified in the research literature are social interaction skills, conflict/anger management, interpersonal problem solving, communication, stress management, assertiveness, self-esteem, parental involvement, and the like.[19]

These risk and protective factors can be addressed in a number of ways, and the next task is to identify the most promising approaches to reducing or preventing them. Again, reliance on the knowledge base in the published research literature can provide direction. For maximum effectiveness, researchers have identified a number of characteristics that should be reflected in prevention programs.[20] These include targeting populations rather than individuals; inclusion of family, educational system, and community in intervention planning and implementation; and providing the intervention over multiple years. Further, the programs should be integral parts of the overall curriculum, based on relevant theory and research, and finally, focus on specific risk and protective factors.[21]

Armed with this background information about the necessary ingredients of a program with the greatest potential to be successful, we can next turn our attention to reviewing available prevention programs. Understandably, school officials who are faced with pressure to respond quickly to emerging problems frequently adopt intervention programs "off the shelf." Accordingly, this step is designed to assess readily available programs in terms of their fit with both identified risk and protective factors and the requirements of successful intervention programming.

A variety of school-based violence prevention programs should be reviewed to determine the extent to which they meet these general criteria. Several programs could be used as examples, but we selected Second Step: A Violence Prevention Curriculum, as it meets many of the requirements and purportedly is one of the most widely adopted programs.[22] Like many of the violence prevention programs, however, at this writing no published evaluation of the program is available.

Second Step is curriculum-based and designed to reduce aggressive and impulsive behavior and build social competence. The program teaches a variety of prosocial skills in a culturally sensitive manner. Versions are available for grades K–8, and additional grades are being prepared. Developed on the basis of a review of the literature that identified common skill deficits among violence prone youth, the skills taught target these behavioral deficits.[23]

Neither Second Step nor any other single program can address all of the risk factors and protective mechanisms identified in the literature as important. Therefore, it is necessary to determine those factors most amenable to change and to develop a continuum of services and interventions that would broadly target as many of the identified factors as possible. In addition to the Second Step Program, academic support, parent training in behavior management and communication skills, and involvement in a community project could be provided, as these elements have the potential of boosting Second Step's preventive power by targeting additional risk factors and fostering the development of more protective factors, thereby producing sustained change.[24] Table 9.1 provides a brief outline of the expanded Second Step Program we propose.

The design and implementation of any intervention involve a variety of people and use of the expertise each has to offer. Researchers are particularly well qualified to review and interpret the knowledge base, and practitioners know best what their needs are and the resources and constraints of their setting, while translating that knowledge into concrete intervention activities can best be accomplished through the cooperation of both groups. As a result, intervention activities that are solidly grounded in existing research and theory, yet also "doable" in the practice setting, can be identified.

TABLE 9.1

Examples of Risk and Protective Factors, Interventions, and Measures

Risk Factors	Primary Interventions	Measures
• poor school achievement	• peer tutoring, family literacy	• SSRS, GPA, school reports
• externalizing problem behaviors	• Second Step	• SSRS, school and parent reports
• interactions with antisocial peers	• Second Step, peer tutoring	• SSRS, school, self, parent reports
• alienation from family/community	• family literacy, school/community project	• self and school reports, SSCS
• alcohol and drug use	• Second Step	• self and parent reports
• life transitions	• peer tutoring, Second Step	• self, parent, school reports
• poor parental child-rearing	• parent training	• parent reports, attendance
• exposure to violence	• parent training, Second Step	• self and parent reports

Protective Mechanisms	Primary Intervention	Measures
• social interaction skills	• Second Step	• SSRS, school reports, skill checklist, SSCS
• conflict and anger management	• Second Step	• SSRS, self, school, parent reports, skills checklist
• interpersonal problem	• Second Step	• SSRS, self, school solving parent reports, skills checklist
• stress management	• Second Step	• SSRS, self-report, skills checklist
• resisting peer and media pressures	• Second Step, peer tutoring, community project	• self-report, skills checklist
• self-esteem enhancement	• Second Step, peer tutoring, school/community project	• SSCS, self-report, skills checklist
• assertiveness	• Second Step	• self, parent, and school reports
• parental involvement and support	• parent training, family literacy	• consumer satisfaction, parent and school reports
• bonding to family and school/community	• school/community project, family literacy	• school, self, and parent report

SSRS = Social Skills Rating System (Gresham & Elliott, 1990).
SSCS = Student Self-Concept Scale (Gresham, Elliott, & Evans-Fernandez, 1993).
Skills Checklist = Skills checklists in Second Step curriculum.

Another area of collaboration, and an essential component of a successful intervention program, is evaluation. Again, both researchers and practitioners have contributions to make and roles to play. Practitioners bring expertise for gauging program impact (success and failure), while researchers contribute knowledge about designing and analyzing measures to identify these program effects. Working together, practitioners and researchers can produce a comprehensive evaluation that not only identifies program effects but seeks to link differential effects to specific program components and implementation/administration issues. The combination of process and outcome evaluations generates a richer context in which to assess the overall program operation and provides detailed information for refining and revising the program. Thus, research (evaluation) data are used to inform and guide practice and ensure the effectiveness of the intervention, and attention is also devoted to the policy relevance of the evaluative efforts.

IMPROVING THE USE AND USEFULNESS OF RESEARCH IN PROFESSIONAL PRACTICE

The preceding discussion provided a brief illustration of how research can be used in developing a prevention program. Our primary intent was to show how research can guide practice, although we recognize that practice should also guide research.

Thus far we have suggested that a tension exists between researchers and practitioners because they bring different perspectives, concerns, and experiences to the table. In this section we propose some modest changes in the preparation and conduct of the roles of practitioners and researchers that, in our experience, can reduce the level of tension that exists and increase the use and usefulness of research.

Professional Preparation and Roles: Educators

A primary area to consider to achieve the goal of making research more useful is in the training educators receive and the roles in which they participate.

Technical and Conceptual Competence

First, all practitioners must be taught to be competent consumers of educational research. They do not necessarily have to be knowledgeable about the nuts and bolts of actually conducting it, but more attention needs to be placed on helping them develop the skills to evaluate and use the research of others. One of the most effective ways of avoiding jumping on the latest educational bandwagon and of learning what really works is to critically read the literature. As a result it is possible to learn whether the research demonstrates something of value that can be applied to practice.[25] Common problems in the literature such as over-statements or overgeneralizations of conclusions can be identified, research designs examined to ascertain that plausible alternative explanations have been ruled out, and the pertinence of findings (e.g., with respect to participant or setting characteristics) evaluated to determine their relevance.

Although new practices cannot be determined strictly through an analysis of research, direction can be provided. The literature review in the violence prevention illustration section demonstrated how identification of contributing factors involves research in a broad sense. It was an effort to identify what is already known about the issue. A critical appraisal can help avoid the tendency to rush into using research findings prematurely, even when faced with mounting pressures to address a pressing issue such as youth violence. This research-based knowledge can be used to confirm field experiences and to explain observations. Finally, no one is in a better position to generate new questions than those actually involved in providing day-to-day services.

Accountability for Professional Actions

Evaluation should become a component of daily practice, especially when new approaches are introduced. It needs to be thought of as an essential part of the program planning process and used on an ongoing basis to make decisions about how to conduct and change programs. As noted earlier, it is extremely difficult to determine the efficacy of our efforts without regular monitoring and assessment. Moreover, the public is demanding that we be more accountable. Sufficient motivation and confidence to examine and improve practice must be nurtured first at the university, and subsequently by knowledgeable administrators so that it is possible to truly be "reflective practitioners." Thus, "guarantees" of effectiveness for the procedures implemented will not be necessary, as some seem to believe, because progress will be evaluated systematically.

Clearly, the reflective practitioner is an evaluator. Part of what is reflected upon is what one has tried and how well it has worked. Too often issues are approached with the attitude that *the* answer can be found rather than from the perspective of dealing effectively with complex issues. In a related fashion, we tend to both expect and promise too much of our intervention efforts. The reality must be faced that too often there is no single answer to the problems of practice and that these problems themselves will change over time. Thus, the search for the most effective ways of engaging in professional practice, like the research endeavor, is a continuing process. Practitioners must monitor and observe, while researchers must attend to what their research findings mean for practice, and both must work together. Even the term "best practices," which recently has been used frequently, is troublesome, for it suggests that *the* answer exists, when in fact there often are a number of ways of practicing effectively and/or little empirical evidence on the superiority of one approach versus another.

Professional Preparation: Researchers

There are two major issues with regard to researchers. First, they need to be able to communicate with practitioners. One way is to share the results of their work in the right places, that is, in sources that practitioners read. The typical scientific journal is not a usual source of information; rather, newsletters, newspapers, and practice-oriented journals are more likely to be read by this audience. In addition, the relevance of the findings for practice should be explicit and not require significant interpolations and guesswork for readers. Second, more research should be a cooperative endeavor between investigators and practitioners. What is really needed is for researchers to perceive practitioners as essential partners so that they truly value and appreciate their input and experiences. Relevant research questions and methodologies can be generated through their joint efforts, so that it is far more likely that the information will be useful for practice.

Researchers will no doubt benefit from more extensive involvement in the real life of schools (ideally on an ongoing basis) so that they develop a firsthand understanding of the challenges practitioners experience every day, thereby avoiding the "ivory tower syndrome." Conducting brief workshops or occasionally consulting in schools are simply too superficial an involvement to obtain this important perspective.

Creating a Culture That Supports Reflection and Inquiry

A significant determinant of the value placed on reflection and inquiry is the school organization itself. An organizational structure that values these activities is far more likely to encourage practitioners to engage in reflection, empiricism, and evaluation. In such a setting a spirit of cooperation exists, collaboration occurs, curiosity is valued, mutual respect practiced, and support provided, which may lead to more of a willingness to try new ideas.

A key to such a culture is administrative support and sanction, especially when words are backed up with the building of opportunities for inquiry, such as making time available to reflect and solve problems. An ongoing commitment to growth, change, development, and improvement is essential. Likewise, trust among organizational members must be built so that sharing sensitive information, expressing doubts, raising questions, and engaging in self-revelation are encouraged. Under such conditions, a history of shared experiences can be built so that enduring groups and sustained interpersonal relationships exist.

Collegial Support

Establishing and maintaining satisfactory and productive working relationships is crucial in the provision of effective services,[26] and providing opportunities for educators to engage in discussions with colleagues is a key ingredient in the research and practice formula. As these professionals discuss, share, and solve problems, they can make significant strides in merging practice knowledge and research knowledge, and as stated earlier, begin to discard less effective old practices.[27]

One method of promoting interactions among colleagues is through peer support groups (PSGs), which have been found to be a widely adopted, effective means of facilitating the types of exchanges previously suggested.[28] PSGs are small groups with similar areas of interest that come together regularly to learn from one another, to solve individual problems, and to support one another in professional development activities. The relationship among group members is nonevaluative and egalitarian. Groups work to establish and maintain an atmosphere of trust and support to encourage sharing, growth, reflection, and risk taking. Consequently, PSGs provide members with practical help, emotional and moral support, new ideas, and assistance in dealing with stress, isolation, and burnout, all of which are important within a school culture that promotes inquiry and the translation of research into practice.

Participatory Action Research

As has been suggested several times, researchers and practitioners must collaborate more often to generate questions and develop relevant implications for research. The voices of practitioners must be heard and their input valued so that it becomes more likely that "real" problems are addressed (recognizing that there still is an important place for basic research!). Both must break out of the traditional mold whereby researchers are viewed as knowledge generators and practitioners as knowledge translators. Rather, it should be seen as a two-way street in which both have responsibilities to decrease the common complaints from both groups stated at the beginning of the chapter. Such joint efforts are being realized through projects such as that at the National Reading Center Consortium of the University of Georgia and the University of Maryland.[29] Their research is generated and sustained by the questions of classroom teachers and investigated by university and teacher research teams.

An initial step in developing reflective practitioners and practicing researchers should be a forum for interaction and exchange. To ensure that regular communication occurs between these groups, having an ongoing means of sharing may help change their routine habits of thinking and working so that the gap between research and practice is narrowed. In large measure, this gap is a communications gap. As the comments of

Petersilia summarized earlier indicate, researchers often fail to communicate their results to practitioners in a meaningful fashion.[30] Similarly, many practitioners do not engage in research-based practice and fail to communicate their questions to researchers. A change in university and school culture supportive of mutual understanding will help. Among other issues, there currently are different reward structures in the field and the university, making it difficult for both to be equally committed to traditional research or traditional practice, thereby hampering collaboration.

One of the ways mutual understanding between the practice and the research communities could be developed is by making practitioners responsible for conducting research and requiring them to be qualified researchers. At the same time, researchers could be made responsible for the implementation of programs (e.g., teaching in the schools) based on their research findings. Although such a suggestion is perhaps quite idealistic, it conveys the fact that long-term solutions rest in reform in both cultures.

It is also important to emphasize that all programs generally should include an evaluation component. Ongoing practice should be monitored and assessed, and substantial changes in current practices should be made based on evaluative data. Thus, if a school wished to revise its method of teaching social studies, sufficient funding for evaluation should be included along with the budget for new texts and other instructional resources. Then, as a matter of routine, practitioners would engage in defining the research goals and plans. Of course, researchers should also be involved.

Another helpful strategy for encouraging communication is for researchers to develop advisory boards that include practitioners, especially those who will be impacted by the project, when designing and implementing interventions. Furthermore, the benefits of involving parents are rarely acknowledged. Yet, as school and university cultures change, the inclusion of parents in research and evaluation can occur, resulting in even greater mutual understanding of the entire community.

The major point that we wish to make again is that at a minimum, affirmative steps can be taken to ensure that researchers and practitioners routinely confer with each other. Over time it would be expected that they would become more attuned to one another's concerns and language so communication is improved.

CONCLUDING COMMENTS

Simply providing educators with access to information will not lead to change. The school organizational climate must support these efforts to implement new practices. Likewise, constructive feedback or coaching from someone knowledgeable in the new technique is imperative. It is unrealistic to expect an innovation to be proficiently adopted without such support and guidance. Further, ongoing opportunities to discuss with colleagues new practices—their impact, problems encountered, modifications needed—in a supportive, collegial atmosphere are needed. As new programs are developed through research that has been influenced by practice, it is important that staff training include conceptual and procedural components to increase the probability of durable change.[31]

It is clear that there are no magical ways of linking research and practice. However, this chapter demonstrates that research and practice will both benefit when they mutually influence one another. While a key aspect of the usefulness of research is how directly it relates to beliefs, research can and should influence practice as it challenges the truth or falsity of beliefs, alters the nature of the beliefs, and provides new beliefs.[32] Similarly, much of our research would be improved if it were guided by what is learned from the field. To encourage the research-practice partnership, all educators must be adept at taking action and reflecting simultaneously. Using a problem-solving approach to meeting daily responsibilities and developing strategies to incorporate new techniques into their jobs may lead to more well-conceived, effective services. Similarly, researchers must become more in touch with the daily realities of the field and the needs of those working in it. The end result may be that researchers will learn to communicate clearly with practitioners. As a consequence, both groups may benefit from this partnership, and children and families may receive better services.

GLOSSARY

Inquiry—Systematic study, questioning, or investigation of an issue or situation.

Participatory Action Research—Collaborative inquiry involving the mutual efforts of educators, parents, and researchers.

Peer Support Groups—Small groups with similar interests who come together to problem-solve and grow professionally.

Prevention—Proactive activities designed to stop the emergence of a problem.

Protective Mechanism/Factor—Characteristics or behaviors that serve to buffer or protect an individual from developing a problem.

Reflection—The process of thinking about what one is doing, sometimes even as one is involved in the activity.

Risk Factor—Characteristics or behaviors that make an individual vulnerable or susceptible for developing a problem.

Scientist-Practitioner—A practitioner who assists people based on knowledge gained from his/her profession and who also contributes to the knowledge base.

NOTES

References

Argyris, C. (1982). *Reasoning, learning, and action: Individual and organizational.* San Francisco: Jossey-Bass.

Bastian, L. D., & Taylor, B. M. (1991). *School crime: A national crime victimization survey report.* Washington, DC: U.S. Department of Justice, Office of Justice Programs.

Baumann, J. F., Allen, J., & Shockley, B. (1994). Questions teachers ask: A report from the National Reading Research Center School Research Consortium. In C. K. Kinzer & D. J. Leo (Eds.), *Multidimensional aspects of literacy research, theory, and practice* (pp. 474–484). Chicago: National Reading Conference.

Beutler, L. E., Williams, R. E., Wakefield, P. J., & Entwistle, S. R. (1995). Bridging scientist and practitioner perspectives in clinical psychology. *American Psychologist, 50,* 984–994.

Brubacher, J. W., Case, C. W., & Reagan, T. G. (1994). *Becoming a reflective educator: How to build a culture of inquiry in the schools.* Newbury Park, CA: Corwin.

Buka, S., & Earls, F. (1993). Early determinants of delinquency and violence. *Health Affairs, 12,* 46–64.

Cochran-Smith, M., & Lytle, S. L. (1990). Research on teaching and teacher research: The issues that divide. *Educational Researcher, 1,* 2–11.

Cochran-Smith, M., & Lytle, S. L. (1992). Communities for teacher research: Fringe or forefront? *American Journal of Education, 100,* 298–324.

Coie, J. D., Dodge, K. A., & Kupersmidt, J. B. (1990). Peer group behavior and social status. In S. Asner & J. D. Coie (Eds.), *Peer rejection in childhood.* New York: Cambridge University Press.

Commission on Violence and Youth. (1993). *Violence and youth: Psychology's response.* Washington, DC: American Psychological Association.

Committee on Youth. (1995). *Second Step: A violence prevention curriculum.* Seattle: Committee on Youth.

Consortium on the School-Based Promotion of Social Competence. [Elias, M. J., Weissberg, R. P., Hawkins, J. D., Perry, C. L., Zins, J. E., Dodge, K. A.,

Kendall, P. C., Gottfredson, D. C., Rotheram-Borus, M. J., Jason, L. A., & Wilson-Brewer, R. J.]. (1994). The school-based promotion of social competence: Theory, research, practice, and policy. In R. J. Haggerty, L. Sherrod, N. Garmezy, & M. Rutter (Eds.), *Stress, risk, and resilience in children and adolescents: Processes, mechanisms, and interaction* (pp. 268–316). New York: Cambridge University Press.

Deal, T. E. (1990). Reframing reform. *Educational Leadership, 48,* 6–12.

Dryfoos, J. G. (1990). *Adolescents at risk.* New York: Cambridge University Press.

Ensminger, M. (1990). Sexual activity and problem behaviors among black, urban adolescents. *Child Development, 61,* 2031–2046.

Farrington, D., & Hawkins, J. D. (1991). Predicting participation, early onset, and later persistence in officially recorded offending. *Criminal Behavior and Mental Health, 1,* 1–33.

Fenstermacher, G. D. (1986). Philosophy of research on teaching: Three aspects. In M. C. Wittrock (Ed.), *Handbook of research on teaching* (pp. 37–49, 3rd ed.). New York: Macmillan.

Garmezy, N. (1987). Stress, competence, and development: Continuities in the study of schizophrenic adults, children vulnerable to psychopathology, and the search for stress resistant children. *American Journal of Orthopsychiatry, 57,* 159–179.

Gersten, R., & Brengelman, S. U. (1996). The quest to translate research into classroom practice: The emerging knowledge base. *Remedial and Special Education, 17,* 67–74.

Gresham, F. M., & Elliott, S. N. (1990). *Social Skills Rating System.* Circle Pines, MN: American Guidance.

Gresham, F. M., Elliott, S. N., & Evans-Fernandez, S. (1993). *Student Self-Concept Scale.* Circle Pines, MN: American Guidance.

Hawkins, J. D., & Catalano, R. (1992). *Communities that care: Action for drug abuse prevention.* San Francisco: Jossey-Bass.

Hawkins, J. D., Catalano, R., & Miller, J. Y. (1992). Risk and protective factors for alcohol and other drug problems in adolescence and early adulthood: Implications for substance abuse prevention. *Psychological Bulletin, 112,* 64–105.

Houle, C. O. (1980). *Continuing learning in the professions.* San Francisco: Jossey-Bass.

Howell, J. C., Krisberg, B., Hawkins, J. D., & Wilson, J. J. (Eds.). (1995). *A sourcebook: Serious violent and chronic juvenile offenders.* Thousand Oaks, CA: Sage.

Keith, T. Z. (1995). Best practices in applied research. In A. Thomas & J. Grimes (Eds.), *Best practices in school psychology-III* (pp. 135–144). Washington, DC: National Association of School Psychologists.

Kendall, P. C., & Braswell, L. (1993). *Cognitive-behavioral therapy with impulsive children* (2nd ed.). New York: Guilford.

Lambert, L. (1989). The end of an era of staff development. *Educational Leadership, 18,* 78–83.

Malouf, D. B., & Schiller, E. P. (1995). Practice and research in special education. *Exceptional Children, 61,* 414–424.

Myers, L. B., & Myers, L. J. (1994). Criminal justice computer literacy: Implications for the twenty-first century. *Journal of Criminal Justice Education, 6*, 281–297.

National Center for Injury Prevention and Control. (1993). *The prevention of youth violence: A framework for community action.* Atlanta, GA: Centers for Disease Control and Prevention.

North, S. (1987). *The making of knowledge in composition: Portrait of an emerging field.* Upper Montclair, NJ: Boynton/Cook.

Patterson, G. R., & Stouthamer-Loeber, M. (1984). The correlation of family management practices and delinquency. *Child Development, 55*, 1299–1307.

Petersilia, J. (1987). *The influence of criminal justice research.* Santa Monica, CA: Rand.

Sanders, D., & McCutcheon, G. (1986). The development of practical theories of teaching. *Journal of Curriculum and Supervision, 2*, 50–67.

Schön, D. A. (1983). *The reflective practitioner: How professionals think in action.* New York: Basic Books.

Showers, B., Joyce, B., & Bennett, B. (1987). Synthesis of research on staff development: A framework for future study and state-of-the-art analysis. *Educational Leadership, 45*, 77–87.

Shulman, L. S. (1986). Paradigms and research programs in the study of teaching: A contemporary perspective. In M. C. Wittrock (Ed.), *Handbook of research on teaching* (pp. 3–36, 3rd ed.). New York: Macmillan.

Tittle, C. (1991). On being labeled a criminologist. *The Criminologist, 16*(3), 1–4.

Webster, D. W. (1993). The unconvincing case for school-based conflict resolution programs for adolescents. *Health Affairs, 12*, 126–141.

Zins, J. E. (1985). Work relations management. In C. A. Maher (Ed.), *Professional self-management: Techniques for special services providers* (pp. 105–127). Baltimore, MD: Brookes.

Zins, J. E., Maher, C. A., Murphy, J. J., & Wess, B. P. (1988). The peer support group: A means of facilitating professional development. *School Psychology Review, 17*(1), 138–146.

Zins, J. E., Travis, L. F. III, Brown, M., & Knighton, A. (1994). Schools and the prevention of interpersonal violence: Mobilizing and coordinating community resources. *Special Services in the Schools, 8*, 1–20.

1. Shulman (1986).
2. Irwin (1987), quoted in Brubacher, Case, and Reagan (1994, p. 18).
3. Schön (1983, p. viii).
4. Beutler, Williams, Wakefield, and Entwistle (1995, p. 985).
5. Houle (1980).
6. Myers and Myers (1994).
7. Argyris (1982).
8. Sanders and McCutcheon (1986).
9. North (1987, p. 22).
10. Brubacher, Case, and Reagan (1994).
11. Gersten and Brengelman (1996).
12. Tittle (1991).

13. Petersilia (1987).
14. Cochran-Smith and Lytle (1992).
15. Lambert (1989).
16. Deal (1990).
17. Cochran-Smith and Lytle (1992).
18. A number of research projects have identified the same or similar risk factors. See Bastian and Taylor (1991); Buka and Earls (1993); Commission on Violence (1993); Ensminger (1990); Farrington and Hawkins (1991); Hawkins and Catalano (1992); Hawkins, Catalano, and Miller (1992); National Center for Injury Prevention and Control (1993); Patterson and Stouthamer-Loeber (1984); Zins, Travis, Brown, and Knighton (1994).
19. See generally Consortium (1994); Dryfoos (1990); Garmezy (1987); Hawkins and Catalano (1992); Jessor (1993).
20. For example, Consortium (1994); Dryfoos (1990); Hawkins and Catalano (1992); Howell, Krisberg, Hawkins, and Wilson (1995).
21. Dryfoos (1990); Garmezy (1987); Hawkins and Catalano (1992).
22. Committee on Youth (1995).
23. Coie, Dodge, and Kupersmidt (1990); Kendall and Braswell (1993).
24. Webster (1993).
25. Keith (1995).
26. Zins (1985).
27. Malouf and Schiller (1995).
28. Zins, Maher, Murphy, and Wess (1988).
29. Baumann, Allen, and Shockley (1994).
30. Petersilia (1987).
31. Showers, Joyce, and Bennett (1987).
32. Fenstermacher (1986).

EDUCATOR'S COMMENTARY

MICKEY KAVANAGH

I AGREE WHOLEHEARTEDLY with Zins, Travis, and Freppon that the importance and value of linking research with educational practice lies in the increased opportunity to reflect and act at the same time. Too much of the decision making in schools is simply a reaction to the latest crisis, and much too little time is spent planning and preventing crisis in the first place. One way educators can learn to shift the emphasis from reaction to prevention and planning is by following the work of researchers. Finding ways to improve the communication between researchers and teachers can only lead to better teaching, a more solid theoretical foundation for practice, and a more fluid process for delivering new knowledge directly to kids in the classroom. Furthermore, discoveries about how to improve the social and emotional learning of children can be better integrated into teachers' teaching styles in addition to their content-teaching skills.

This is not an easy goal to reach, for many reasons. In the first place, there is a serious need to change attitudes, as the authors note—teachers need to believe that there is value in research and that it has relevance to their jobs, and researchers need to value what teachers do. This is a critical initial step to improving two-way communication. All too often, we educators suspect researchers' requests to come into our schools as "one more thing 'they' want us to do," one more instance where "they" want to "use" us and our students for their own career advancement rather than as a collaboration that might help us and our students. It is not commonly acknowledged that we share the common goal of wanting to make things better for kids.

Teaching is a full-time, every-minute-of-every-day job. In a television special describing teachers' work on programs to improve education, Bill Moyers proclaimed, "These teachers work harder than you do, no matter what you do!" There is nobody I admire more than a good teacher. Most good teachers I know can only catch up on new research during the summer because their entire conscious and unconscious minds are so consumed by teaching every day of the school year. Applying any new research to what they do in the classroom can be a daunting task. As the authors accurately depict, teachers can be isolated and completely on their own once they close the door to their classrooms. They may, in fact, still be doing a terrific job with the children in that room, but they are not easily touched by the winds of change no matter how positive that change might be for both the teacher and the students.

Although it is a requirement for continued certification that all teachers update their training, we teachers don't read "the literature" much unless we're taking a course. So, I endorse the notion of finding ways to maintain ongoing exchanges between researchers and teachers.

Avenues do exist for teachers to keep abreast of change. Periodicals that summarize the current literature are available. Some examples include *Aids Alert*, which I receive monthly, and *The Prevention Researcher*. Many schools have or are developing library/media centers. These can be made user-friendly to teachers as well as students. Periodicals that meet the interests and needs of teachers and of the school system can be made accessible. One simple action is to arrange for the library-media specialist to make a brief report at every faculty meeting, either about the availability of ways to find out about new developments or about the content of recent education research. In addition, these specialists can be invaluable in escorting teachers into the computer age. When all is said and done, however, there is nothing as important as an ongoing relationship between researchers and educators to improve the effects and relevance of research to practice.

A second crucial point of this chapter with which I agree is the significance of establishing and maintaining an organizational culture that values reflection and inquiry. When crisis response is the driving force behind policy making and curriculum change, everybody gets burned out quickly. However, when you are living on the front lines, it is unusual to be able to see that there is another way. Practices I have observed that encourage reflection and inquiry almost always depend on enlightened principals and include the following examples: team collaboration and group problem solving during scheduled common planning periods; release time for teachers to work on planning teams during the schoolday; ongoing meetings with researchers that are planned for already established meeting times (e.g., staff meeting days); evaluation teams that make recommendations for program changes based on ongoing collaboration and reflection; team teaching and the inclusion of special education and bilingual students in mainstream classes, both of which necessitate continual collaboration and reflection between the regular education and special education teachers; school reorganization with an emphasis on pods or the school-within-a-school concept, where all the teachers in one pod (which is a subdivision of the student body) plan for and teach the whole group of students; peer evaluation—teachers coaching teachers by means of observation, feedback, support, and follow-up; and time-out rooms for disruptive students where they get time to reflect on their misbehavior and come up with a plan for reentry into the class. All of these examples place a value on reflection, planning, and collaboration.

We have had some success in New Haven both with linking research with practice and with establishing a culture that values reflection through the process of developing and implementing the Social Development Program. We have a comprehensive K–12 emotional and social learning curriculum in place, the product of active and ongoing collaboration between teachers and researchers and fully endorsed by the superintendent and the board of education. There were active Social Development committees at the elementary, middle, and high school levels for the first 4 or 5 years of the program. These committees operated in a climate that valued reflection and inquiry. Committee membership comprised educators (who could evaluate the effectiveness of particular curricula and report on the real life of schools) and researchers (who could identify effective programs, review them, and present research data and published curricula for committees to select for implementation). These groups met regularly, and their suggestions carried weight in the decision-making process. I cannot overemphasize how important it is that such a total commitment be made to keeping this process going. We are already finding that new programs are taking teachers' resources and attention away from maintaining the Social Development Program and that with less of an institutionalized connection between researchers and teachers the program's momentum has slowed down.

Real life for educators can be so much more complicated and chaotic than what is imagined or anticipated in research designs. Maintaining close links between research and practice is a goal that is worth pursuing. Educators and researchers must build and reinforce mutual trust. Researchers need to understand the forces pulling educators in so many different directions, which can most effectively be done by keeping in touch with the real life of schools. And educators need to find ways to stay in touch with research as well as time for reflecting on the way they do their work.

INDEX

Abuse, parental, 181

Academic achievement, and peer adjustment, 210–11

Accountability for education intervention programs, 266–67

Achievement: boys' emotional emphasis on, 248; definition of, 22; and peer adjustment, 210–11

Acquisition, Refinement, and Transformation (ART) model, 234

Acquisition phase of emotional development, 235–38

Activation control, 131

Adaptation, vs. intelligence, 27–28*n*4

Administration, school, responsibility for support of inquiry, 260, 267–70, 276–77

Adolescent development: brain development and, 95, 108; emotional competence curriculum for, 67–69; refinement of emotionality, 240–41; and self-concept, 42; transformation of emotionality in, 244–49

Adulthood, emotional intensity and regulation skills in, 144

Affect: and cognition, 4–5; definition of, 22; and motivation, 5, 30*n*43, 59. *See also* Emotion

Affective style, 109–10

Affordances, 42

Aggression: and emotion regulation, 135, 139; and gender differences, 134; as maladaptive coping strategy, 181; and misinterpretation of emotion, 236–37; persistence of, 140; and social skills training, 212, 214; and violence, 21, 136, 258, 261–65. *See also* Anger; Hostility

Ahadi, S. A., 143

Alliances, as element of friendship, 200–201

Altruism, 142

Altshuler, J. L., 172, 176

Amygdala, 98–99, 100–101, 110, 111, 123

Anger: aggression as consequence of, 139; and depression, 248; as educational mood induction, 244; and emotion regulation, 137–41, 147; family handling of, 177–78, 247; importance of expression, 149–50

Anhedonia, 248

Anxiety, 134

Arena, memory, 29*n*29

Aristotle, 39

Arousal, emotional: and information processing, 37, 242, 244; inhibition as response to, 132; intensity of, 131, 140. *See also* Emotionality

Asher, S. R.: dropout rates and peer rejection, 211; friendship quality measurement, 204–6; games as social competence tools, 212–13; peer rejection problems, 208, 209; social competence development, 199

Assessment of emotions, development of skill in, 12, 49, 236–37. *See also* Empathy; Sympathy